THE ECONOMIC LANDSCAPE

A Theoretical Introduction

J. Brady Foust
and
Anthony R. deSouza

University of Wisconsin—Eau Claire

Charles E. Merrill Publishing Company
A Bell & Howell Company

Columbus Toronto London Sydney

Published by
Charles E. Merrill Publishing Company
A Bell and Howell Company
Columbus, Ohio 43216

This book was set in Times Roman.
The cover was designed and prepared by Alice Thiede.

Library of Congress Catalog Card Number: 78-201

International Standard Book Number: 0-675-08432-6

Printed in the United States of America

1 2 3 4 5 6 7 8 9 10/85 84 83 82 81 80 79 78

Preface

This book introduces economic geography to students with no previous knowledge of the subject. It concentrates on location theory rather than on empirical studies of economic activities. Our objective is to demonstrate how a few locational principles provide an explanation of economic landscapes in market exchange economies—specifically the United States. We do not claim that a theoretical approach based on classical and neoclassical economics is the only or best explanation of economic spatial organization. However, we believe it contains essential knowledge for the beginning student.

Just as a neophyte in economics must be introduced to the ideas of the great classical and neoclassical economists, the beginning student in economic geography must be guided through the ideas of the great location theorists—Thünen, Christaller, Lösch, and Weber. One must constantly keep in mind, however, that their ideas and models were developed to analyze a particular time, place, and economic system. As an economic landscape evolves, their models must be modified. One measure of the power of a model is how well it lends itself to theoretical refinements. This criterion is certainly met by the great location models. One should also remember that the classical location theorists had a somewhat utopian view of the economic landscape. They were intent on developing a world that "could be." As Lösch said, our job is "not [only] to explain our sorry reality, but to improve it."

Many young geographers have rejected the classical locational models and have substituted a Marxist or ecological framework for the consideration of the economic landscape. They have not, however, rejected the classical models without a careful study of them. These ideas are essential, just as algebra is required for the calculus. We must also be careful not to substitute one insufficient view of the economic landscape for another. The existing economic landscape of the United States *has* evolved subject to the conditions specified by classical location theory and its neoclassical descendents. Any change, whether linear in the sense of preserving present trends or revolutionary in the context of a new order of social-economic justice, must begin with an understanding of the existing economic landscape.

Following an introductory chapter, the book is divided into two parts. Part 1 considers the classical location theories and builds and tests a highly simplified model of the space-economy. Part 2 adds a behavioral and dynamic dimension to the static landscape of classical location theory.

Throughout the text, we have refrained from introducing numerous real world examples of economic activities. We are content with providing one framework on which empirical facts can be hung. We, as teachers, have always found students to be more receptive to local and regional contemporary examples. Many of the abstract examples and graphics are nontraditional, but have been tested in our classes over the years. Most of the graphics are simple, to help the student make the conceptual leap from the simple to the complex. Each chapter contains a short list of suggested readings. Key words are included as a study aid for the student. Crucial definitions, techniques, supportative concepts, and biographical details are provided in boxes throughout each chapter. An extensive bibliography is included.

We are grateful to students and colleagues at various universities in the United States, Britain, and East Africa where we have taught over the last ten years who have helped with the ideas contained in this book. Our thanks go to Fred Haug, Dean of the School of Arts and Sciences at the University of Wisconsin-Eau Claire, who has strongly supported research among his faculty. We are also thankful for the support of a very few colleagues within our own department who maintain a vision of the university as a place for scholarly activities. Thanks go to Neal Lineback, David Jones, Karen Walby, and Terence Smith, who reviewed the entire manuscript. We are particularly indebted to Yvonne Plomedahl, who typed the manuscript with great skill and who put up with our after-the-fact revisions and constant antics. Special thanks go to Alice Thiede, Cartographer in the Department of Geography, for her efficiency and skill in drafting the illustrations. We are indebted to Greg Spatz and the production department at Charles E. Merrill for initiating and preparing this volume. Any undertaking succeeds or fails as a matter of timing. Ours was fortunate. Had the high coffee prices of 1977 come a year earlier, we might have failed.

Last, but not least, we thank our wives, Sarah and Nadia, for their understanding and patience-as-always while we devoted long hours to writing during an especially cold Wisconsin winter. We dedicate this book to them and to our sons, Graham, Matt, Jason, and Sam.

J. Brady Foust

Anthony R. de Souza

Contents

I Introduction

Economic geographers seek to understand patterns of economic activities. This understanding begins with the adoption of an approach for the selection and organization of facts. The purpose of this book is to introduce a *theoretical* approach to consider the complex economic patterns of the real world. A theoretical approach deals with the complexities of reality by developing idealized patterns under controlled conditions and comparing idealized patterns with reality. This approach provides a basis for understanding real-world patterns of economic activities.

A theoretical approach can be used to consider the patterns of any area or economic system, but this book is confined to a classical/neoclassical examination of the economic landscape of the United States. All approaches are "value-laden." A given approach presupposes a set of political, economic, social, cultural, and ethical values. The individual must decide whether a given approach is "good or bad" or "right or wrong." Marxist or "spaceship earth" approaches, for example, provide alternative explanations of economic landscapes.

Chapter Objectives

The purposes of this introductory chapter are to:

1. Give some examples of the kinds of patterns to be considered throughout the book;

2. Distinguish among the kinds of economic events which give rise to patterns;

3. Introduce some fundamental geographic concepts; and

4. Provide an introduction to general scientific methods with particular attention to the use of theoretical models.

Patterns

Geographers assume that patterns are the result of predictable forces and seek to discover and explain these forces. Figure 1.1 shows four patterns. Two contrasting agricultural regions separated by a distinct boundary are shown in figure 1.1A. How and why did this pattern develop? The location of settlements mapped according to size is given in figure 1.1B. What produced this regular pattern? The location of some manufacturing centers is shown in figure 1.1C. How can this pattern be explained? Another arrangement of cities is illustrated in figure 1.1D. What explains the differences between B and D? These are examples of the kinds of patterns and questions which concern economic geographers.

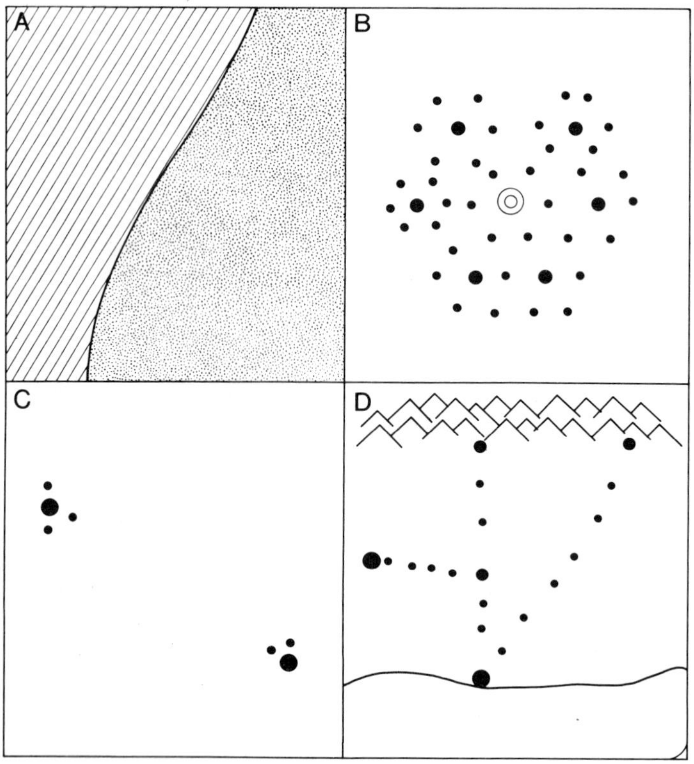

FIGURE 1.1 Selected economic landscape patterns.

Economic Events

Economic geography examines patterns of economic phenomena or "events." Specifically, it concerns itself with patterns of *production, exchange, and consumption*. Production, exchange, and consumption are the traditional concerns of economics, but economists rarely consider geographical arrangements produced by economic forces.

Three kinds of **production** can be distinguished. *Primary* production includes all activities involved in winning raw materials from the earth: agriculture, forestry, mining, and fishing. Agriculture is the only primary activity considered in this book.

Secondary production includes construction and manufacturing. It transforms primary raw materials into finished products. Changing the form of a raw material increases its economic value or utility. Steel, for example, is worth more than the iron ore, coal, and limestone from which it is made.

Tertiary production comprises service activities and includes wholesale and retail trade, transportation, the professions, and a variety of labor services.

Exchange involves changes in ownership (wholesale and retail trade). Most settlements, for example, are exchange points or centers of trade mediating the movements of goods between producers and consumers.

All items which have economic value are **consumed**. Some goods (e.g., food) are nondurable and are quickly consumed. Other goods, such as automobiles, tend to be much more durable. Some services (e.g., a taxi ride) last only minutes, while a college education can serve the consumer a lifetime.

Although economists and economic geographers consider production, exchange, and consumption, their emphases differ. Marshall, in his *Principles of Economics* (1920), summed up the emphasis of each with the statement that "the difficulties of the problem depend chiefly on variations in the area of space and the period of time over which the market in question extends; the influence of time being more important than space." For the economist, the key variable is time. The economic geographer, on the other hand, emphasizes the importance of space.

Fundamental Geographical Concepts

Geographers have a *spatial* point of view. In this section, the fundamental concepts essential for a spatial point of view are identified and defined. These fundamental concepts are grouped under three headings: (1) the properties of space; (2) spatial process and spatial structure; and (3) spatial interaction.

The Properties of Space

What kinds of space do geographers consider? What are the properties of space? Geographers sometimes consider three-dimensional space (a volume) when discussing weather and climate or landforms. Most of the time, however, they are concerned with two-dimensional patterns which can be represented on a plane. Maps in figure 1.1 are examples of two-dimensional space. Geographers also often consider one-dimensional space or, simply, the *line* distance between two points.

It is convenient to divide space into *abstract* and *concrete* space. Abstract space is a conceptualization of a one-, two-, or three-dimensional space independent of any point of reference on the surface of the earth. Abstract space is homogeneous in all respects and movement is equally easy in all directions. This abstract space is called an *isotropic surface* in the two-dimensional case and allows the development of idealized patterns. Concrete or ''environmental space'' is the actual surface of the earth with all the variety and differentiation of the real world.

A set of terms is required before we can discuss the properties of space. Only a small number of terms are required to describe, define, and measure space. We begin with a sheet of blank paper representing a two-dimensional abstract space. A featureless plane devoid of pattern is of no interest to the geographer. Once some phenomena is mapped onto the paper, however, the space is filled and a pattern develops. *Point, area,* and *line* are the most elementary terms that can be used to describe this pattern. Points may represent cities or manufacturing plants, lines can represent transportation arteries or boundaries between areas, and areas may represent agricultural or manufacturing regions.

How can relationships among areas, points, and lines be defined and measured? Suppose we place two points at random on our blank piece of paper (figure 1.2A). Point A can be discussed in terms of its *distance* from Point B and vice versa. If Point A is chosen as an arbitrary starting place, all other points can be defined in terms of their distance and *direction* from Point A. A line can be defined as a series of points or a given distance from a point in a specific direction (figure 1.2B). A series of defined lines describe a bounded area (figure 1.2C).

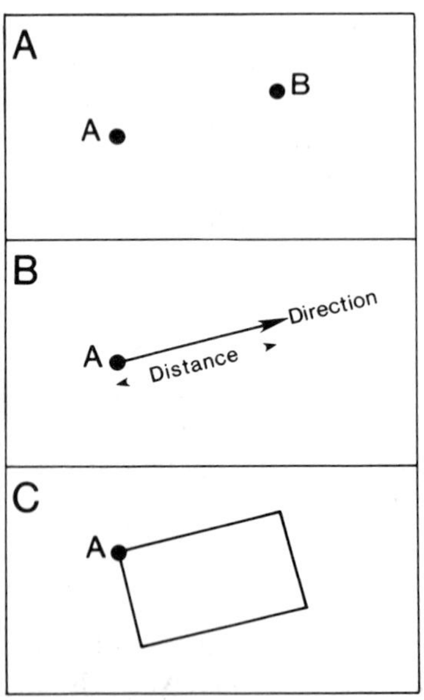

FIGURE 1.2 Abstract space: area, point, and line defined by distance and direction.

Another measure of space is *connectivity*. Consider figure 1.3 in which a series of points is given. Point A is connected to many other points by lines, whereas Point B is connected to only a few points. The points might represent cities and the lines scheduled air passenger flights. Point A has a higher degree of connectivity than Point B.

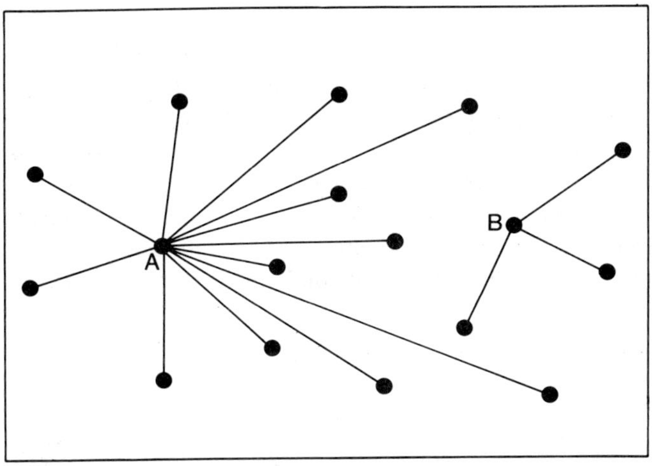

FIGURE 1.3 Abstract space: connectivity.

Other measures of space are extensions, compounds, or modifications of the concepts of distance, direction, and connectivity. An area can be defined by a series of distances and directions. Once defined, these terms can be used to describe and measure the *size* and *shape* of an area. A farm that is too large may not be conducive to efficient operation, but one that is too small may provide only a subsistence income. A large nation is more likely to have the resources needed for development, but largeness may inhibit effective control and organization. Figure 1.4 shows two hypothetical countries which have the same area, but quite different shapes. If we assume that connectivity within each country is the same, Country A must spend more on transportation than B. Chile is an example of a nation with a relatively inefficient shape.

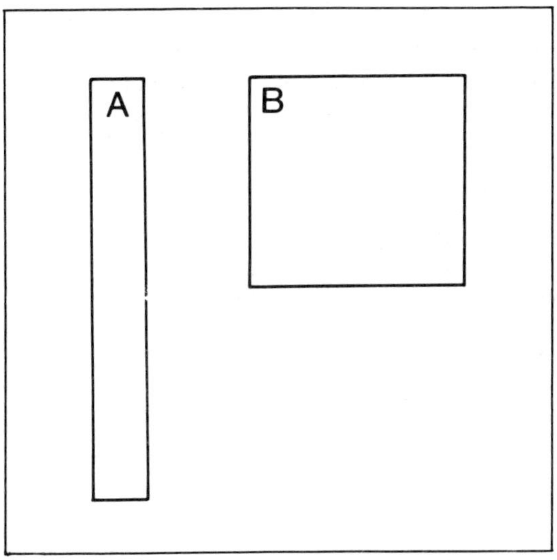

FIGURE 1.4 (A) Inefficient shape; (B) Efficient shape.

Other measures of space are similar extensions. A series of points is given in figure 1.5. Two definite clusters are shown. The points in Cluster A are closer together than those in Cluster B. Cluster A represents *agglomeration* or low *aggregate* distance. A shopping center, for example, reduces the distance consumers must travel to purchase goods by concentrating or clustering many stores at one point. A city itself is a clustering strategy reducing aggregate distance among residential, employment, retailing, recreational, and other functions. Similar or linked industries are often clustered. The concentration of auto subassembly plants in southern Michigan and aircraft manufacturing in southern California are examples.

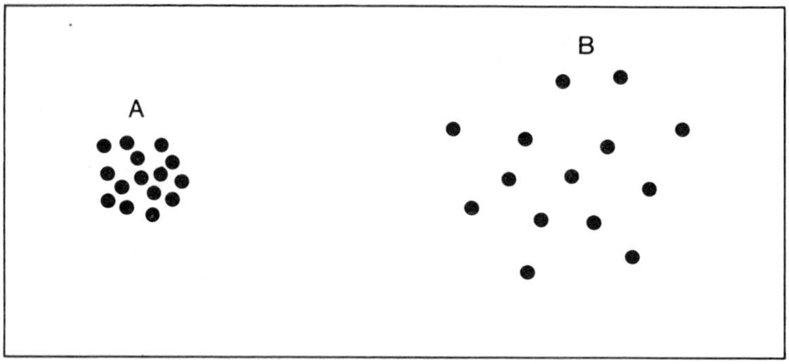

FIGURE 1.5 Abstract space: agglomeration.

Figure 1.6 illustrates another distance compound. Point X has a high degree of *accessibility*. Point Y, on the other hand, has a low degree of accessibility. Accessibility is another measure of aggregate nearness. Agglomeration refers to the total aggregate nearness among a number of points, while accessibility generally refers to the aggregate nearness of a given point to other points. Points with a high degree of accessibility have a tremendous advantage over inaccessible locations. The failure of a retailing operation is often correctly blamed on a "poor location." This implies that the location has a low degree of accessibility to potential customers.

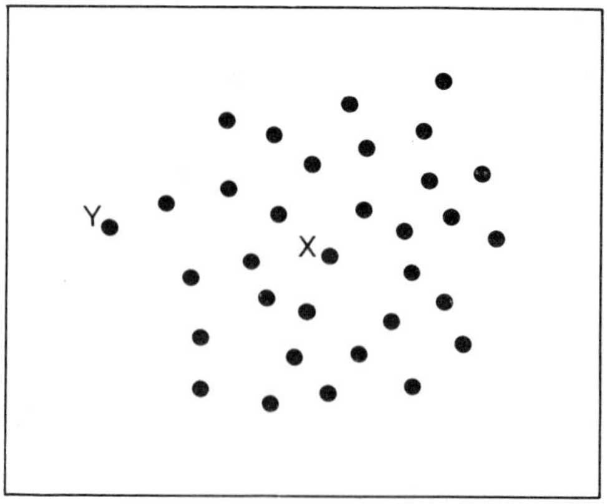

FIGURE 1.6 Abstract space: accessibility.

Distance, direction, and connectivity along with their compounds of size, shape, agglomeration, and accessibility are *absolute* concepts when applied to an abstract space such as an isotropic surface. Absolute distance, for example, is measured in standard units such as miles or kilometers. If the distance between City A and City B is ten kilometers and the distance between City B and City C is also ten kilometers, the distance between each pair is exactly the same. Another property of absolute distance is symmetry. If the distance between A and B is ten kilometers, then the distance between B and A is also ten kilometers. Because an isotropic surface is completely homogeneous in all respects, two areas of the same size will contain the same amount of resources.

Most of the idealized patterns developed in this book assume an abstract space. What are the advantages of using this abstract or isotropic approach? The main ones are simplicity and clarity. The concepts used to define, describe, and measure space in their absolute sense possess only the properties explicitly assigned to them. Variables, in the real world, are affected by many forces, but we are interested mainly in their spatially significant properties. The abstract or isotropic approach allows us to concentrate on the effects of space alone without the influence of other variables. The use of abstract space allows us to develop idealized patterns which are the result of the absolute measures of space. These can then be compared to the patterns of reality. The economic landscape is a *spatial expression* of many forces. The theoretical approach begins with an examination of the purely spatial aspects of the economic landscape.

The absolute concepts of distance, direction, and connectivity can also be applied to concrete or environmental space. Ten kilometers on the surface of the earth are the same as any other ten kilometers and an acre is always an acre, but the use of *relative* measures of distance, direction, and connectivity provides a much more meaningful view of concrete space.

Relative distance, for example, is measured in terms of cost, time, and/or effort. The property of distance symmetry which holds in abstract space is rarely true of concrete space. Figure 1.7 shows a point on the periphery of a city. A trip of ten kilometers from A on a rural highway may require much less cost, time, or effort than a ten kilometer trip from A to the center of the city. Start and stop traffic add to

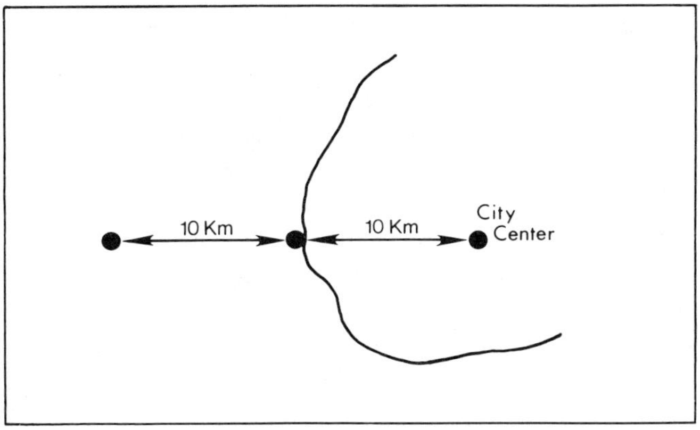

FIGURE 1.7 Relative versus absolute distance.

cost, congestion increases the time involved, and the effort (mental and physical) required for urban driving is high. The air distance between Points A and B in figure 1.8 is 100 kilometers, but there is a constant 50 knot wind prevailing from A to B at flying altitude. The cost and time of air travel is much greater from B to A than in the opposite direction.

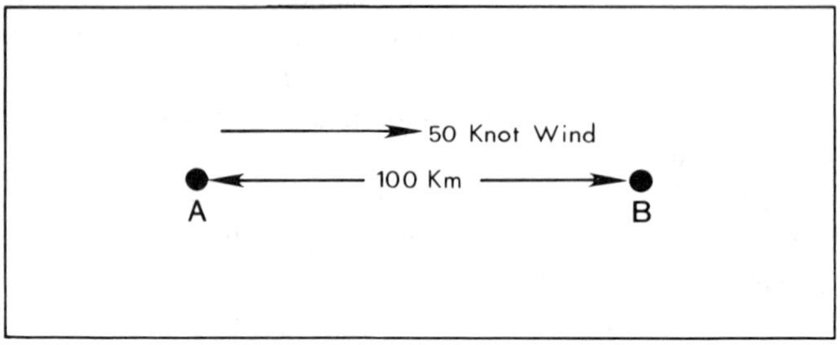

FIGURE 1.8 Lack of symmetry in concrete space.

Our view of real space can change dramatically when different kinds of relative distance are mapped. Figure 1.9A shows a hypothetical area mapped in absolute space. Figure 1.9B maps the same set of cities in relative space measured in terms of the cost of first-class mail from City A. In cost-space, all points are the same relative distance from A (13¢). Figure 1.9C shows the cities mapped in a cost-space of parcel-post rates. All cities in a given zone are the same relative distance from A. Figure 1.9D shows cost-space in terms of air passenger ticket prices. City Y is three times farther from A than City X in absolute space, but only twice as far away in air ticket cost-space. In terms of flying *time*, City Z is twice as far from A as City X (figure 1.9E), but in absolute space, both are the same distance from A. Notice the distortion of absolute space from A to Z and A to X. Relative distance is an important variable in economic geography because we are concerned with the *cost* of movement. All movement costs, therefore, economic landscapes represent strategies which attempt to minimize the cost of movement as much as possible. The cost, time, and effort of distance have been reduced by the invention of new transportation technologies and by repetition of the same activities in space.

The concrete qualities of space must be referenced to specific points or areas on the surface of the earth. Any *location,* for example, requires a fixed reference point. Geographers deal with two kinds of location. *Absolute* location (site) refers to a point's location in terms of some standard system such as latitude and longitude or street addresses. *Relative* location (situation) is a measure of connectivity and accessibility. We are not so much interested in the street address of a house (absolute location), for example, as we are in its location relative to work, schools, shopping opportunities, and recreational areas. The points in figure 1.10 represent cities. Suppose we are interested in building a single warehouse to serve all the cities on the map. City A has the best relative location to serve the entire region.

New York City provides another example of the importance of relative location. The absolute location of New York tells us nothing about the city if we are interested in understanding why it became one of the world's great cities and seaports. In 1820, there were four main ports on the northeastern seaboard compet-

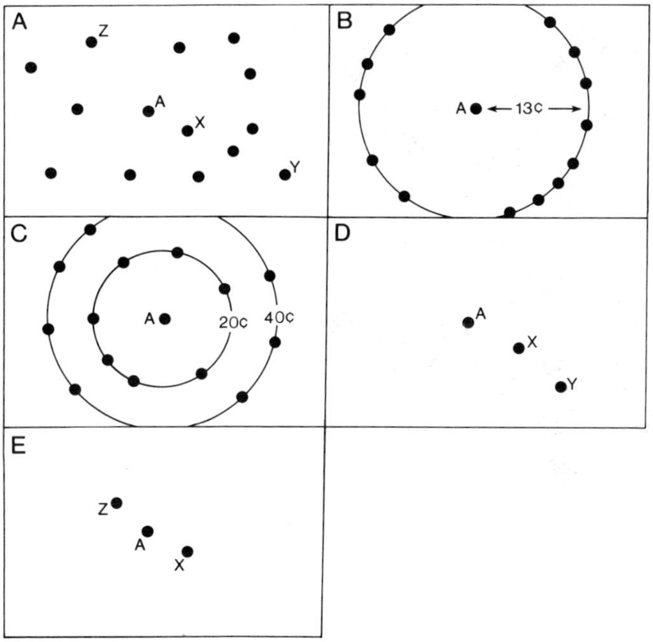

FIGURE 1.9 (A) Absolute space; (B) Relative space—first class mail cost from A; (C) Relative space—parcel post zones from A; (D) relative space—air passenger ticket prices from A; (E) Relative space—flying time from A.

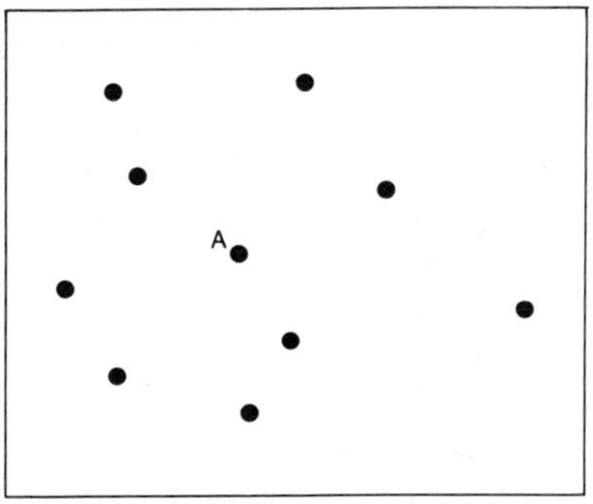

FIGURE 1.10 Relative location: central warehouse problem.

ing for trade between the United States and Europe: Boston, New York, Philadelphia, and Baltimore. New York quickly surpassed its rivals after 1825 and went on to become the principal city of the nation.

The answer to New York's success is found in a consideration of its relative location. The Appalachian Highlands represented a tremendous cost and time barrier between the resources of the American interior and the return flow of manufactured goods from Europe. Notice New York's location at the mouth of the Hudson River in figure 1.11. The Hudson is almost at sea level all the way to Albany. At Albany, the Hudson is joined by the Mohawk River which cuts a valley

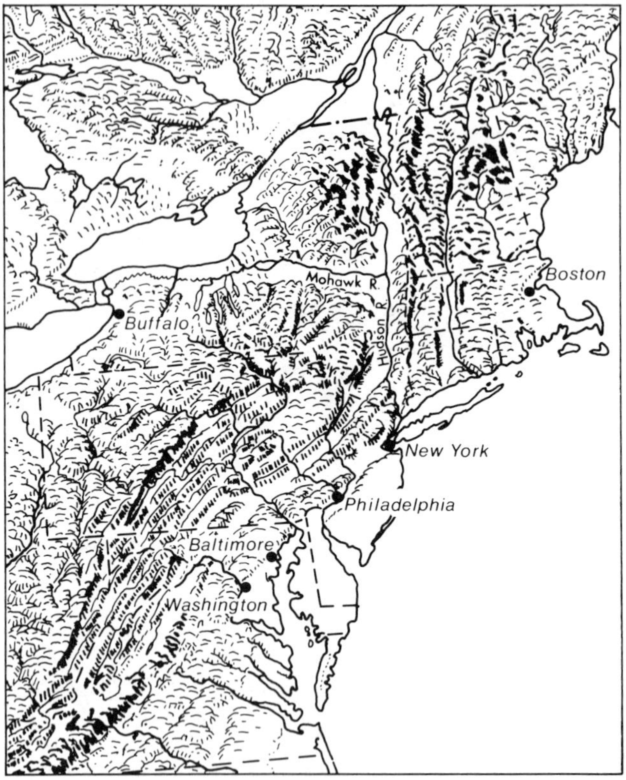

FIGURE 1.11 Hudson-Mohawk corridor and the relative location (situation) of New York City.

through the Appalachian Highlands. In 1825, the completion of the Erie Canal linked the Hudson-Mohawk corridor with Lake Erie. The water link between the Midwest and the Atlantic trade routes to Europe was complete and, of necessity, passed through New York. A location relative to a primary traffic artery provided the major impetus for New York's growth and prominence.

Resources are unevenly distributed over the earth's surface, giving some points a good relative location with respect to resources while others have poor accessibility. Some areas possess good agricultural land; other areas of similar size exist at the subsistence level. Some points are accessible to other areas because of the configuration of the physical environment—controlling a mountain pass, a major sea lane, or the center of an easily traversed plain. Other points may be inaccessible because of surrounding physical barriers.

The presence or absence of resources, the relative productivity of agricultural land, and the ease of transportation afforded by the physical environment all play roles in determining patterns of production, exchange, and consumption, but the initial focus of this book is on the abstract qualities of space. We shall concentrate on the ideal patterns which would evolve on an isotropic surface as the result of the abstract properties of space but the variations of concrete space which produce deviations from these ideal patterns are also considered.

Spatial Process and Spatial Structure

Spatial processes are movements or locational strategies. We are interested in movements such as the flow of raw materials to processing points, consumer travel to purchase goods, the distribution of a finished product from a manufacturing plant, and the trade in agricultural commodities. Locational strategies include growing the optimum crop in a specific area, arranging service settlements ideally, and selecting viable locations for a particular type of manufacturing.

Spatial structures limit, channel, or control spatial processes. The abstract properties of space and the conditions of environmental space constitute a powerful set of spatial structures. The influence of spatial structures is illustrated in figure 1.12 which shows a trade relationship between two cities without reference to environmental conditions (abstract space). What will structure this process? In abstract space, a straight line route will minimize the distance between the two cities (figure 1.12B). The effects of environmental space are shown in figure 1.12C. The route has been distorted by the presence of a physical barrier. The costs of cutting through the mountain barrier outweigh the costs of using the indirect route. Another effect of concrete space is shown in figure 1.12D. The ideal straight-line route between Cities C and D has been distorted to connect existing center A.

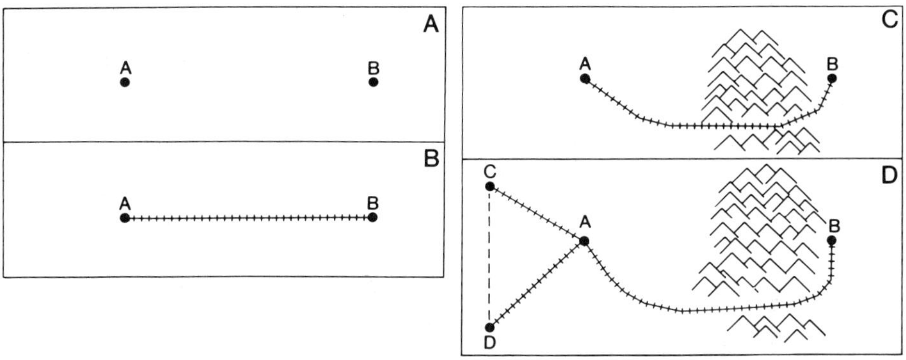

FIGURE 1.12 Spatial structures: (A) Abstract space; (B) Ideal trade route minimizing cost; (C) Distortion by physical barrier; (D) distortion of route between C and D to connect existing center A.

Natural routeways are very important, but often overemphasized. They are spatial structures and channel rather than generate movement. If either city in figure 1.12C is removed, trade through the pass will cease. If the pass did not exist, however, trade would still take place if the benefits of interaction outweighed the costs of movement. The natural environment generally only distorts the ideal patterns which the abstract qualities of space alone would produce.

Spatial Interaction

Flows of goods, people, and information are collectively termed spatial interaction. Much of spatial interaction is economic in origin: the flows of raw materials and finished products, the migration and commuting of labor pools, and the daily exchange of information necessary for production, exchange, and consumption. We have briefly discussed the forces that structure these flows, but what conditions are necessary to *generate* a flow between two cities?

Transferability All movement costs. The first requirement for interaction is that the value of the flow must outweigh the cost of movement. Some areas of the United States, for example, have a deficit of electrical power (East and Midwest) while others have a surplus of cheap power (Pacific Northwest and TVA). Beyond a given distance, however, there is no transfer because of the high cost of transmitting power more than 900–1000 kilometers. The hydropower of the Pacific Northwest is produced at a much lower rate than in the Northeastern United States. A supply/demand relationship exists, but electricity transmitted from Grand Coulee dam to New York would have to be sold at a higher rate than locally produced power to pay the cost of transportation. In other words, electrical power is not *transferable* beyond a certain distance. Transferability is illustrated in figure 1.13. The cost of local production is shown for three different locations (A, B, and C). Transfer costs are given from A. The product is transferable between A and B, but not A and C.

Complementarity A flow of goods, people, or information from A to B requires a supply of some item in A and a demand for that item in B. Without a supply in one place and a demand in another, no interaction will take place even if the condition of transferability is met. This explains the lack of trade in snowmobiles between Minnesota and Florida and the low volume of air passenger traffic between New York and Tierra del Fuego. There is no trade in crude oil from Wisconsin to eastern refineries and Norway does not export citrus fruits.

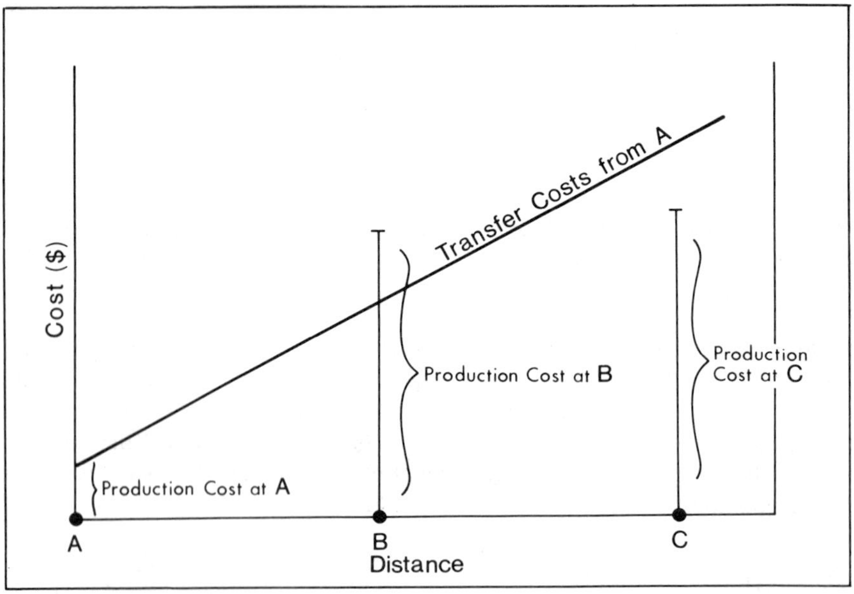

FIGURE 1.13 Transferability.

Intervening Opportunities For interaction to take place between A and B, there must be a lack of intervening opportunities. Figure 1.14A shows the location of three cities. A major department store is located in City A. The conditions of transferability and complementarity hold. Consumers from B and C travel to City A to shop. A second store is opened in City B (figure 1.14B) and the flow stops. City B represents an intervening opportunity for both B and C.

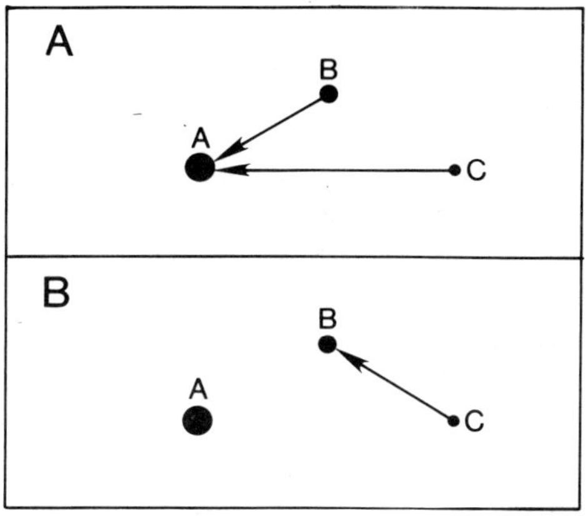

FIGURE 1.14 Intervening opportunities: (A) Shopping patterns before intervening opportunities introduced at B; (B) Shopping patterns after intervening opportunities introduced at B.

Scientific Inquiry

Progress toward the solution of problems of interest to the economic geographer very often comes through the use of a scientific methodology. A scientific method manipulates our experiences of events and consists of three steps: (1) the selection of a set of variables and relationships which are assumed to be important forces controlling or structuring an event; (2) the development of hypotheses about the selected variables and relationships that can be tested by observable facts; and (3) the testing of the hypotheses with empirical data.

Empirical testing of observable facts is called validation (figure 1.15). The diagram suggests that the validation process is never ending. In a sense this is so, but if our hypotheses are supported continuously by evidence from observations and require no modifications, they become *laws*. Interrelated sets of laws which represent observed regularities become *theories*.

Research in economic geography is rarely as elegant as the application of a scientific method suggests. Research may begin with a hunch, which is later refined, or may be spurred by good fortune. A scholar may be lucky enough to find something interesting which was not anticipated. It is also impossible to subject conclusions and predictions to the kind of testing used in the physical sciences. Physical scientists construct controlled laboratory conditions to test their conclusions. The events considered by social scientists usually cannot be subjected to controlled conditions.

Economic geography is not an exact science, but there are many patterns of human behavior that are stable enough to allow us to make sound predictions.

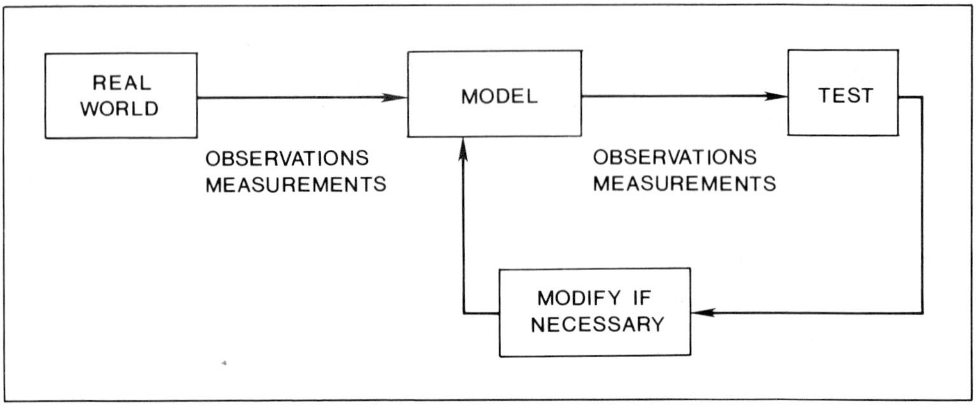

FIGURE 1.15 The model validation process.

Successful prediction is based on the "rule of large numbers." The behavior of large groups is more predictable than the behavior of individuals. We may predict quite accurately, for example, that the average person buys three loaves of bread per week, but to predict that a given individual will buy three loaves is much more risky. There are always exceptions to the average consumer. The exceptions, however, tend to cancel one another. Thus we end up with a fairly stable pattern of behavior for a group and can make predictions about group behavior. This is the kind of prediction used by a life insurance company. They can predict the average life span for a large group well enough to set premium prices based on age, but cannot accurately predict the life span of a given individual.

Facts and Theory

> "Now, what I want is Facts. Teach these boys and girls nothing but Facts. Facts alone are wanted in life. Plant nothing else, and root out everything else. You can only form the minds of reasoning animals upon Facts: nothing else will ever be of service to them. This is the principle on which I bring up my own children, and this is the principle on which I bring up these children. Stick to the Facts, Sir!" The speaker, the schoolmaster, and the third grown person present, all backed a little, and swept with their eyes the inclined planes of little vessels then and there arranged in order, to have empirical gallons of facts poured into them until they were full to the brim. (Dickens, *Hard Times*)

This is how many people feel. They want facts, not fuzzy theory. However, there is no conflict between facts and theory. They support one another, each making the other more meaningful. Facts without theory and theory without facts do not mean very much. Analysis in economic geography must have a footing in facts, but also needs theory to make the facts intelligible and to order them into meaningful relationships. "Theory is the matrix of all science, and the science with an underdeveloped theoretical arm is very much like a ship without a rudder; it drifts rather aimlessly and gets nowhere except by sheer good fortune" (Abler, Adams, and Gould, 1971).

Models

The development of theories and laws is a trial and error process which involves the testing of initial hypotheses. These initial or rough hypotheses are called *models*. Validated models become laws and theories. We build models of *events*. Every occurrence is an event. The movement of consumers to purchase goods is an event. The process of finding a location for a manufacturing plant is an event. The pattern of agricultural production is an event. These events are the result of complex forces. The modeling process is an attempt to discover *key* variables controlling the event. For example, the formula $A = \pi r^2$ is a model of the area of a circle. It has been validated so many times that we now accept it as a law, but it is a good illustration of the concept of a model. Pi and the radius are the key variables determining area. Figure 1.16 shows a generalized graph of population density with increasing distance from the center of a city. We are interested in predicting a regular change in Y (density) given a particular X (distance). The formula of the curve is a model of this event. A model, therefore, can be defined as a hypothesis about the key variables which we think control or allow the prediction of an event. A model connects key variables with event outcomes in an orderly way.

Models have four distinct characteristics:

1. *Abstraction*. A model is an abstraction from reality. It is not a scale reproduction of an event, but rather a selection of a few variables and relationships. A model never conveys the whole truth because the real world is too complex and dynamic.

2. *Structure*. Each model has a specific structure. We are interested not only in the key variables controlling an event, but also in the relationships between the variables. The key variable in the model of a circle is the radius, but we must specify the structure of the relationship among the radius, area, and the constant (pi). It is not enough to say that population density is a function of distance from the center of a city. We must determine the nature of the functional relationship between density and distance.

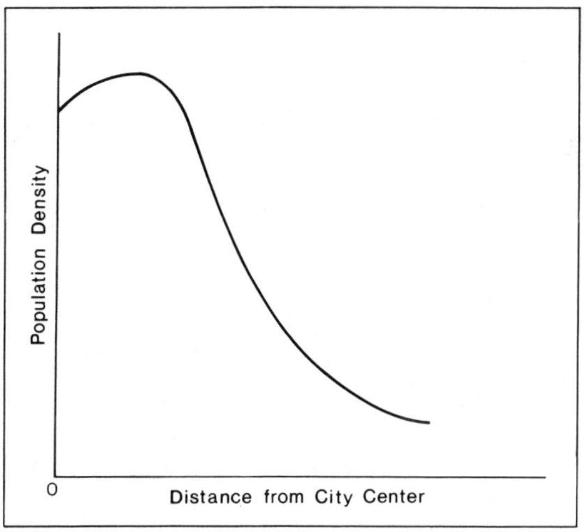

FIGURE 1.16 Change in population density with distance from a city center.

3. *Domain*. Every model has a domain—a specific set of conditions or constraints under which the model holds. Most economic models are constrained with the Latin phrase *ceterius paribus,* all other things being equal. In other words, many variables not under consideration are being held constant so we can concentrate on the effects of a few selected variables. Perhaps the most common constraint used in theoretical economic geography is the isotropic surface. This domain makes absolute and relative distance equal and removes the distorting effects of environmental space. Models based on imaginary constraints are called *normative* models; those based on existing conditions are called *descriptive* models.

Normative models are often criticized because of the unrealistic assumptions of the domain. The domain is not important if the model works satisfactorily. Most of the assumptions of the economist's model of perfect competition, for example, are not true of the real world, but the model has proved to be an accurate predictor of real-world economic conditions.

This point can be amplified with another example. We know from Newtonian physics that the distance a freely-falling body travels is a precise function of time: $D = \frac{1}{2}g\ T^2$; where, D = distance, T = time, and g = a gravitational constant. Suppose we have a very accurate stopwatch and time the fall of a shot-put from the top of a building to the ground. We will be able to measure the height of the building quite precisely with this method, yet the set of conditions (domain) under which this model is meant to hold is not present. The model assumes that the body is falling in a vacuum. The atmosphere will have some effect on the shot-put (distort the results), but not enough to significantly affect the prediction of the height of the building.

4. *Analogy*. A model is an analogy of an event. We translate the properties of the real event into properties that can be manipulated. It is too expensive, for example, to construct 100 full-size aircraft wings to test variations in design, but we can build scale model wings and test them in a wind tunnel. The scale models are analogs of the real events.

A thermometer is an analog of temperature. It is a column of mercury in a glass tube, not the temperature. The real event (temperature) has been translated into something else (mercury in a tube). The mercury is calibrated at the boiling and freezing points of water and rises or falls in a predictable way with respect to these fixed points as the temperature changes.

Throughout this book, we use two kinds of models: (1) *Graphical* models are generalized charts, maps, or diagrams. We redraw patterns to give them an idealized form. By abstracting the distortions of the real world, we hope to gain a better understanding of the forces underlying these patterns. (2) *Mathematical* models involve the use of symbols (e.g., A, B, X) and mathematical operations (e.g., addition, division, powers). The interaction model symbolized on the next page, for example, is used to predict the flow of goods, people, or information between two cities. The symbols (I_{ij}, P_i, P_j, D_{ij}) stand for variables and the mathematical operations (multiplication and division) stand for relationships among variables. The model states that the interaction between two cities is *directly* proportional (multiplication) to the populations of the cities and *inversely* proportional (division) to the distance between them.

$$I_{ij} = \frac{P_i P_j}{D_{ij}}$$

where

I_{ij} = interaction between City i and City j,
P_i = the population of City i,
P_j = the population of City j, and
D_{ij} = the distance between City i and City j.

Model Construction The stages of model construction are diagrammed in figure 1.17. Models are developed to increase our understanding of some real event. From the real world event, we proceed through a series of stages.

Model building is illustrated by the following example. The summer tourist industry is very important in the economy of Wisconsin. What variables control the flow of summer tourists to the state? There are hundreds of variables that influence recreational travel, but we want to select the most significant. From the real event, we produce an abstract version of the event. In this stage, we designate the variables we think may be important in attracting visitors to Wisconsin.

What do summer recreational visitors to the state do? What kinds of activities interest them? Swimming and camping are important activities, but many people also own summer cottages in the state. The first variables chosen for our model are: (1) the number of swimming opportunities per county; (2) the number of camp sites

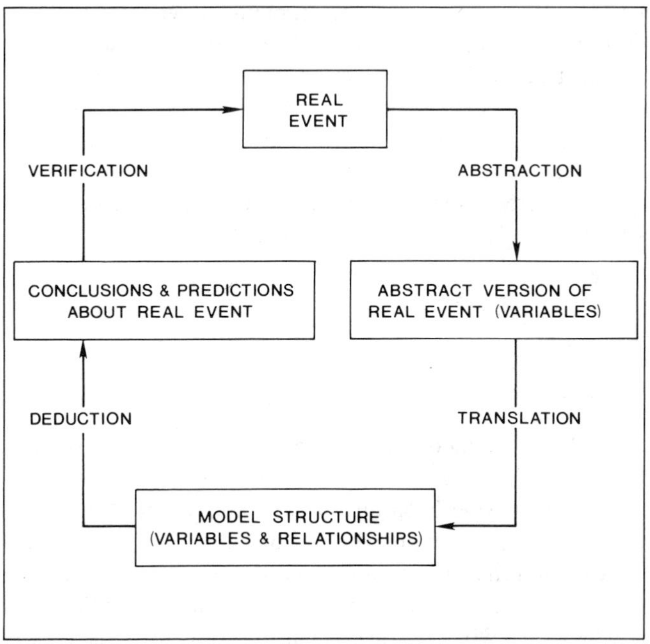

FIGURE 1.17 Stages in model building (After Chorley, 1964).

per county, and (3) the number of seasonal residences per county. We may also consider factors which could limit or inhibit recreational travel from out-of-state. Driving time is such a limiting factor. Driving time from home to each county in Wisconsin becomes the fourth variable. Our abstract version of the real world event now consists of a set of symbols:

$$V_i = f\,(SO_i,\ CS_i,\ SR_i,\ DT_i)$$

where

V_i = the number of recreational visitors to each county i in Wisconsin,
SO_i = the number of swimming opportunities in county i,
CS_i = the number of campsites in county i,
SR_i = the number of seasonal residences in county i,
DT_i = driving time from the home town of the visitor to county i, and
f = means that V_i is *a function of* the four variables.

It is not enough, however, to state that recreational travel is a function of these four variables. How do these variables interrelate? Which is the most important? This leads to the next stage of model construction in which the *relationships* among the variables (structure) are specified. Mathematical operations are used as analogies of real event relationships so that:

$$V_i = SO_i + CS_i + SR_i - DT_i$$

The model hypothesizes that as the number of swimming opportunities, camp sites, and/or seasonal residences increases, the number of recreational visitors will increase, but as driving time increases, the number of visitors will decrease.

The next stage of model construction is the prediction of real events which leads us back to reality by comparing the results of the model with the real events. Prediction and verification require the use of statistical methods. We may want to go through this process several times, adding new variables and deleting old ones to see if we can improve the accuracy of prediction, but this elementary example indicates the way in which models of real world events are constructed.

Summary and Plan

This chapter has emphasized that the theoretical approach is one way to visualize an economic landscape in a world of "free enterprise." Categories of events of interest to the economic geographer have been enumerated and attention given to key words and concepts expressing a geographical point of view. The chapter also included a brief discussion of scientific methodology and the use of models.

The material that follows concentrates on the aspects of economic activities. Part 1 consists of four chapters which deal with a static economic landscape. Chapter 2 is addressed to the question of agricultural land-use patterns. It begins with a brief discussion of production functions and then introduces simple assumptions about human behavior in space. After we gain insight into abstract patterns of an agricultural landscape, we relax our initial constraints and introduce some of the complexities of the real world. The chapter begins with an abstract geographical system and proceeds to more factual descriptions of agricultural patterns. Chapters 3 and 4 study the geography of retailing and services and the location of manufacturing. Their organization resembles chapter 2. Chapter 5 analyzes transport costs. The economic landscape developed in Part 1 is assumed to be static. Little attention is given to the effects of past growth and change on present patterns and to the fallibility of human decisions. Part 1 concludes with an overview of the models of a static economic landscape and provides a transition to the second part of the book.

Part 2 drops the assumptions of optimal human behavior and of a timeless economic landscape. Instead of considering how people could or should make locational decisions in an "ideal world," it deals with the complexities of reality. Spatial decision making is considered in chapter 6. It contains a discussion of the value of descriptive models and illustrates some of the ways in which decision makers engaged in agricultural, manufacturing, and service activities might make sub-optimal locational choices. We assume people are satisficers; they make sub-optimal decisions because they have imperfect knowledge about present and future events. Among the themes treated are a behavioral matrix, game theory, diffusion theory, and catastrophe theory. From the discussion, a complex economic landscape emerges produced by myriad objective considerations and subjective opinions and preferences. Chapter 7 examines economic growth and change. Economic and location models are explored. The consequences of different types of growth are discussed and the debate on the limits to growth is summarized. As with the first part of the book, Part 2 ends with an overview of these more dynamic economic landscape models.

Numerous illustrations will aid the reader in studying the materials in this book. Definitions and other technical information have been placed in boxes. At the beginning of each chapter is a set of objectives, and at the end a list of key terms. It is always a good idea to look at the works cited in the text and invaluable to follow up the suggestions for further reading.

KEY WORDS

abstract space
accessibility
agglomeration
concrete space
connectivity
consumption
complementarity
descriptive model
direction
distance (relative and absolute)
domain (of a model)
exchange

isotropic surface
intervening opportunities
location (relative and absolute)
normative model
primary production
production
secondary production
spatial process
spatial structure
tertiary production
theoretical approach
transferability

SUGGESTED READINGS

Fundamental Geographic Concepts

Nystuen, J. D. (1963), "Identification of Some Fundamental Concepts," *Papers of the Michigan Academy of Science, Arts, and Letters,* **48,** 373–84.

Abler, R., J. Adams, and P. Gould (1971), *Spatial Organization,* Englewood Cliffs, N.J.: Prentice-Hall.

Bunge, W. (1966), *Theoretical Geography,* Lund Studies in Geography, Ser. C, No. 1, The Royal University of Lund, Sweden.

Models

Chorley, R. J. and P. Haggett (1967), *Models in Geography,* London: Methuen.

Alternate Approaches

King, L. G. (1976), "Alternatives to a Positive Economic Geography," *Annals* of the Association of American Geographers, **66,** 293–308.

part 1

Static Models of Optimum Locational Patterns

2 Agriculture

Introduction

Agriculture is the basis for civilization. Throughout most of our history as a species, we were hunters and gatherers subsisting on what nature chanced to provide, supporting only a very limited number of people. Agriculture made possible a nonnomadic existence, the rise of cities, and the development of new technologies. Until the last century, agriculture produced very little food per worker so that almost everyone was engaged in food production. The small surplus released few people for other pursuits. An agricultural revolution occurred in the last 200 years, however, and made possible the large-scale employment in secondary and tertiary activities which characterizes the developed areas of the world. Only four percent of the total population of the United States lived on productive farms in 1970. The proportion of farmers in the total labor force was roughly the same, but, of course, we are all *ultimately* dependent upon the food produced by the agricultural sector.

Chapter Objectives

Primary: Examine the major forces which control patterns of agricultural production.

Secondary:

1. Introduce the economic principles underlying agricultural input combinations.

2. Discuss in detail the Thünen and Ricardian models which form a basis for the analysis of agricultural patterns.
3. Present an elementary synthesis of the above two models.

Economic Principles

Agricultural Input Combinations

All production requires three inputs: land, labor, and capital. *Land* is the most obvious input in agriculture, but economists define land as all "natural resources," including rainfall and other climatic variables as well as soils and mineral resources. Humans supply labor. *Capital* takes the form of tools, machinery, seed, fertilizers, and other materials which must be purchased. What combination of these inputs—land, labor, and capital—are required to produce a given crop?

Assume that capital is held constant so that we can consider only various combinations of land and labor. One worker cannot produce much wheat on a square meter of land. Conversely, one worker attempting to farm a million hectares would produce very little wheat in a year if we assume that he must spread his year's labor over the entire amount of land. The farmer would start plowing the million hectares in the spring and by harvest time would still be plowing! The *optimum* amount of land for one unit of labor must lie somewhere between these extremes.

The total amount of wheat produced on a *fixed amount* of land by a steadily increasing labor input is given in table 2.1. With land and capital held constant, total output is a function of labor. Economists call this type of relationship a *production function*. The same data are graphed in figure 2.1 yielding a *total product* curve. The total output for each plot of land divided by the number of labor units gives the *average product* per worker (figure 2.2). The *marginal product* of labor is the addition to total output resulting from each unit increase in labor. Total product increases by thirteen units (Tract 1 to Tract 2) with a unit increase in labor (table 2.2), hence the marginal product is thirteen.

All three products are graphed in figure 2.3; labor is increased while land is held constant. The graph illustrates the relationships among total, average, and marginal

TABLE 2.1 Wheat output per tract of land (each tract = 10 hectares)

Tract No.	No. of Workers	Output in Bushels
1	1	10
2	2	23
3	3	38
4	4	52
5	5	60
6	6	63
7	7	64
8	8	63
9	9	60
10	10	50

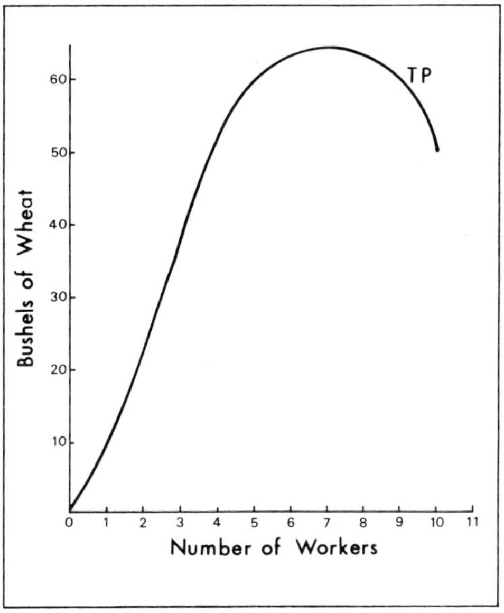

FIGURE 2.1 Total product curve (data from table 2.1).

TABLE 2.2 Average product, marginal product, and input ratio for hectare tracts

Tract No.	No. of Workers	Land/Labor Ratio	Total Product	Average Product of Labor	Marginal Product of Labor
1	1	10.00	10	10.00	—
2	2	5.00	23	11.50	13
3	3	3.33	38	12.66	15
4	4	2.50	52	13.00	14
5	5	2.00	60	12.00	12
6	6	1.67	63	10.50	3
7	7	1.43	64	9.14	1
8	8	1.25	63	7.87	−1
9	9	1.11	60	6.66	−3
10	10	1.00	50	5.00	−10

average product: total product divided by the amount of the input used to produce the output.
marginal product: the additional total output which results from the addition of one unit of the variable input.
''Law of Diminishing Returns'': continuous increases in one input factor, while holding the other inputs constant, will lead to a decrease in the per unit output of the variable factor. Diminishing returns are easily illustrated by agriculture, but all forms of production are subject to the law.

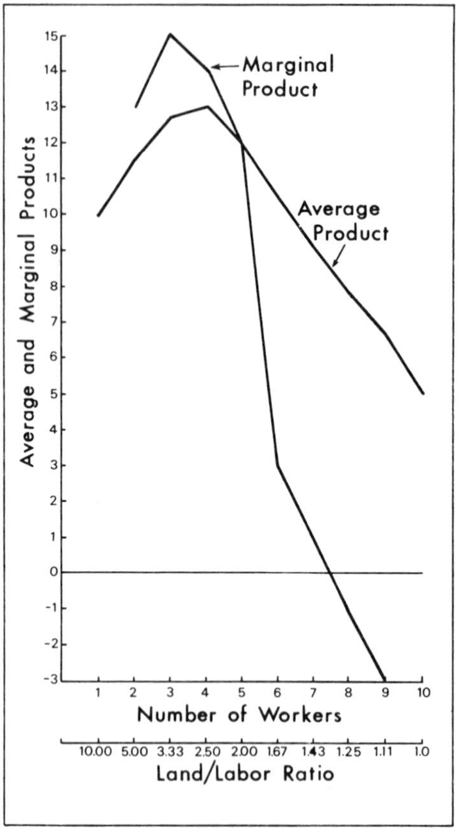

FIGURE 2.2 Average and marginal product curves (data from table 2.2).

products. Economists have divided this production function into three stages. Average product (AP) rises throughout all of Stage I, but the fixed input (land) is present in an uneconomically large proportion compared to the variable input (labor). In other words, the *scale* (land/labor ratio) is too large in Stage I. Farm size (fixed input) would be adjusted downward if the total demand for wheat approximated Stage I conditions.

Stage III is also an uneconomic condition. Adding units of labor *decreases* total production (TP). Stage III can be illustrated by imagining a field so crowded with workers that they trample more of the crop than they harvest. No rational producer would operate in Stage III even if the variable input were free. Assume, for a moment, that the fixed input is land and the variable input is irrigation water which is "free." All other inputs are held constant. With no water, total product is zero, but as more and more water is added to the fields, the total product begins to rise. We will reach an optimum amount of water (maximizing TP), but beyond that point (into Stage III) additional water will diminish the total crop.

The marginal product (MP) is zero at the boundary between Stage II and Stage III. This is called the *intensive margin* because land is cultivated too intensively (too

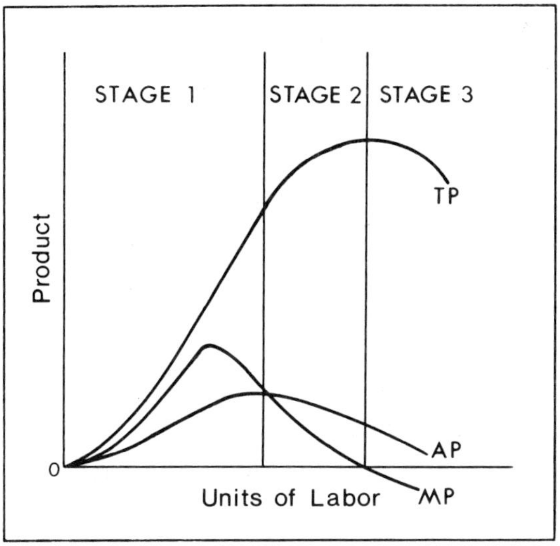

FIGURE 2.3 The stages of production.

much labor, water, or other inputs) in Stage III. Conversely, at the boundary between Stage I and Stage II, average product (AP) is maximized and marks the *extensive margin* of production. In Stage I, the land is not cultivated intensively enough (or too extensively). Rational producers will operate only in Stage II.

The quantity of the fixed input (in this case, land) must be adjusted if the crop is to be produced in quantities not covered in Stage II. Changing the fixed input would shift all the curves to the left or right which can be seen through an examination of tables 2.3 and 2.4. A single worker cultivating one hectare of land (table 2.4) is the same as three workers cultivating three hectares (table 2.3). These hypothetical data are plotted in figure 2.4. The horizontal axis represents the *land-labor ratio* which *declines* to the right. The origin of the graph is at 3,0 rather than the customary 0,0. The scales of the horizontal axis require some additional explanation. The unit distance used is the denominator of a fraction whose numerator remains constant.

TABLE 2.3 Total, average, and marginal products for labor (3-hectare tracts)

Tract No.	Hectares	No. of Workers	Land/ Labor Ratio	Total Product (Labor)	Average Product (Labor)	Marginal Product (Labor)
1	3	1	3/1	10	10.0	—
2	3	2	3/2	24	12.0	14
3	3	3	3/3	39	13.0	15
4	3	4	3/4	52	13.0	13
5	3	5	3/5	61	12.2	9
6	3	6	3/6	66	11.0	5
7	3	7	3/7	66	9.4	0
8	3	8	3/8	64	8.0	−2

TABLE 2.4 Total, average, and marginal products for different sized tracts cultivated by one worker

Tract No.	Hectares	No. of Workers	Land/ Labor Ratio	Total Product (Land)	Average Product per hectare of land	Marginal Product per hectare of land
1	3/8	1	3/8	8.0	21.3	—
2	3/7	1	3/7	9.4	21.9	26.1
3	3/6	1	3/6	11.0	22.0	22.4
4	3/5	1	3/5	12.2	20.8	12.0
5	3/4	1	3/4	13.0	17.3	5.3
6	3/3	1	3/3	13.0	13.3	0.0
7	3/2	1	3/2	12.0	8.0	−2.0
8	3/1	1	3/1	10.0	3.3	−1.3

The distance between 3/1 and 3/2 is the same as the distance between 3/7 and 3/8. The total, average, and marginal product curves (solid lines) for labor are exactly the same as those of figure 2.3. Stage I for labor ends where the average product is maximized and Stage III begins where the marginal product of labor is zero.

Examine the average and marginal products of *land* (dashed lines). Stage I for land ends where the average product of land is maximized and Stage III of land begins where the marginal product of land is zero. The average and marginal product curves of land are "mirror images" of the average and marginal product curves of labor. At Stage I for labor, too little labor is used or too much land is provided (Stage III for land). Conversely, at Stage III for land, too much land or too little labor is used (Stage I for labor).

If only land and labor were required to produce wheat and the average product of labor *continued to rise* (no diminishing marginal product), then all the world's wheat could be grown in a flowerpot! There is a particular combination of inputs (land, labor, and capital) at which production is economic. A production function is a good example of an economic principle which has definite *spatial implications*—a set of constraints controlling patterns on the landscape. American agriculture, for example, has traditionally used the single-family farm for food production with the farmer and his family forming the basic unit of labor (fixed input). The upper and lower limits of the variable input (land) are determined by this fixed amount of labor. The amount of land farmed must be at least large enough to bring the family above the subsistence level (lower limit), but must be small enough to be operated economically with the amount of labor available (upper limit). For some crops (such as vegetables), the scale may be quite small, for others (such as wheat), large-scale operations are required. The settlement pattern of agricultural areas in the United States is one of fairly consistent farm sizes within the regions that specialize in a particular crop. Economic forces inherent in the production function (given a fixed input of labor) are responsible for this rather uniform pattern. Average farm sizes have consistently risen with fewer and fewer farmers producing on larger amounts of land. How is this possible if the farm family has remained the basic unit of labor?

Production has shifted from the intensive margin of Stage II to the extensive margin, and farmers have substituted capital (tractors, combines, improved varieties of crops, fertilizers) for labor in order to farm larger acreages.

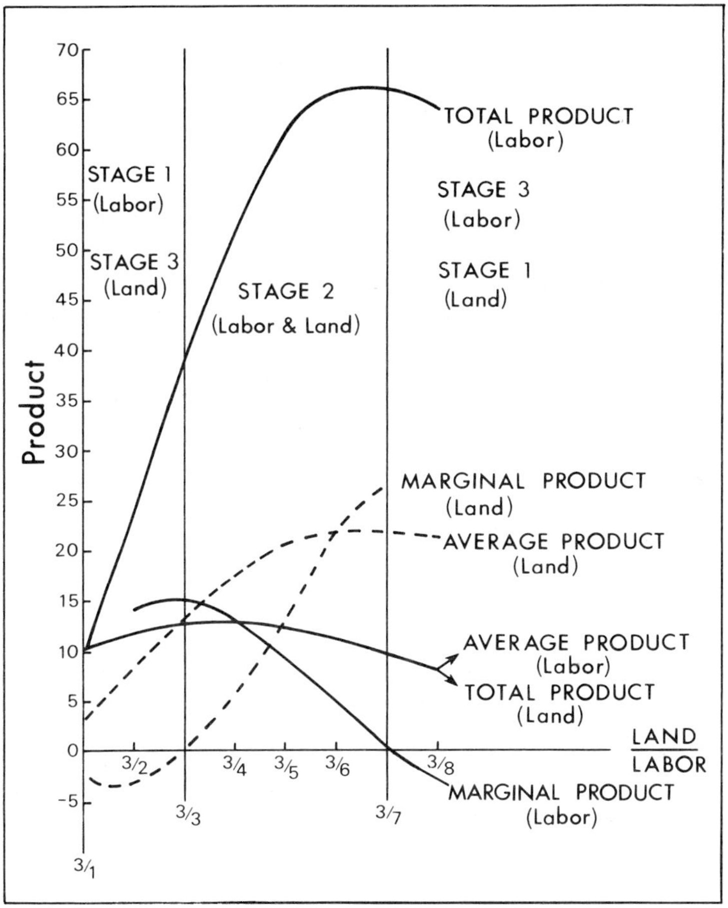

FIGURE 2.4 Product curves for land and labor (common land/labor ratios).

The Intensity Limits of Agriculture

Agriculture, by nature, requires a much greater amount of space per unit of output than the secondary and tertiary sectors of the economy. Assume that ten hectares are required to feed five people. The unit of output is the food required for one person and the land/output ratio is 2:1. Ten hectares devoted to an automobile plant, on the other hand, may produce enough cars for 1,000,000 people with a land/output ratio of 1:100,000. The time/space ratio of agriculture must also be considered. The two hectares used to feed a single person will be devoted to that person for an entire growing season, whereas an automobile plant occupying ten hectares may produce a finished car every few minutes. Because automobiles are durable, it may be five years before an individual requires another car, but food will be required constantly.

Our technology has not yet produced farms that are as efficient in their use of space as factories. We can increase the amount of food produced per unit of land by adding more labor (such as the intensive cultivation practiced in much of Asia) or by adding capital (more fertilizer, herbicides, better seeds, irrigation water), but as long as land remains relatively less expensive than labor or capital, we tend to operate near the extensive margin of land in the United States.

The Thünen Model of Agricultural Production

Our primary goal in this chapter is to understand agricultural patterns. These patterns cannot be explained solely by agricultural input combinations, but economic production functions form an integral part of the classic model which geographers have used to analyze agricultural patterns. The *Thünen model* was first proposed in 1826. This section introduces a modified version of the model.

Johann Heinrich von Thünen (1783–1850) was born on the North Sea coast in East Friesland in northwest Germany. He studied agriculture in Holstein and at the University of Göttingen. Most of his life was spent on his 1146 acre estate, Tellow, which he purchased in 1810. His life was devoted to improving agricultural production in Mecklenburg through the application of some English agricultural principles, mathematical analysis, and experimentation. The basic framework for his classic book, *Der Isolierte Staat* (The Isolated State), came from intensive investigations in the management of Tellow. The first draft was written in 1818–19 and *The Isolated State* was published in 1826.

Much of Thünen's later work centered on his attempt to determine a "natural wage." Geographers have paid much more attention to his work than economists, but Blaug (1968) has called him the "founder of marginal analysis" and the "first truly modern economist" because of his emphasis on marginal productivity.

We must first establish the conditions under which the simple model is meant to hold (the *domain* of the model). The domain consists of an imaginary landscape over which certain specified conditions prevail (constraints). We then determine the agricultural patterns which result. Real patterns of agricultural production are extremely complex and reflect a variety of economic, climatic, and cultural conditions. A very simple and specific domain allows us to concentrate our attention on a few controlled variables.

Constraints

1. The landscape is an *isotropic* surface; an unbounded, "mathematically flat" plain which is homogeneous in all respects. Movement is equally easy in all directions which means that absolute and relative distance are the same. An unbounded surface eliminates the need to consider boundaries.

2. Transportation costs are a simple linear function of distance. Costs are the same per kilometer regardless of the distance travelled. Initially, only one form of transportation is assumed.

3. The physical environment of our imaginary landscape is completely homogeneous. All land is of equal fertility. Every hectare produces exactly the same output with a given amount of labor and capital.

4. A single city or marketplace exists at the center of the isotropic surface. Farmers sell all their output at this market and the city produces manufactured goods to be exchanged for agricultural products.

5. Prices are stable and fixed at the marketplace. A farmer delivering a load of wheat at the city must take the price offered. Farmers cannot alter the price of crops through individual or collective action.

6. Government intervention is excluded. No price supports or other controls are allowed. Agricultural production is solely a reaction to economic conditions.

7. All inhabitants are *optimizers*. They have perfect knowledge of all possible outcomes of a given action and act solely to maximize profits. Real landscapes are the result of a trial-and-error process and never reach that optimal condition because of constantly changing circumstances. Our imaginary optimizers, however, reach equilibrium conditions instantly without going through a series of evolutionary, suboptimal solutions.

With these constraints, the only variables affecting the pattern of agricultural production are transportation costs, input combination possibilities, and market prices. What agricultural patterns will develop under these constraints?

The Single-Crop Case

Figure 2.5 shows the conditions faced by growers of a single crop. The condition of even fertility means that we can always deal with *hectares* of wheat rather than some yield measure such as dekaliters because each hectare yields the same output of wheat. A hectare of wheat delivered to grain elevators in the central marketplace will bring a gross payment of $45, but the farmer must pay the *cost of transporting* the wheat to market. This might include gasoline, time, insurance, and other costs. In Thünen's day it meant wear and tear on the oxcart, grease for the axles, and shoes for the oxen. At Point D_1, the transportation cost to the market is $10 so that the *net* income a farmer receives is $35 (market price per hectare of $45 − $10 transportation costs per hectare = $35).

Transportation costs rise until we reach a distance at which they equal the market price for wheat (Point D_3 in figure 2.5). Beyond this point no wheat will be grown. That point is called the *spatial margin of production* and is part of the key concept of the Thünen model—economic rent (see box on p. 33).

Study the definition of economic rent carefully. This is *not* contract rent, the amount we agree to pay a landlord for a given period of time. Economic rent is a *relative* measure of the advantage one parcel of land has over another. This relative measure can be illustrated in several ways. Examine the net income curve for wheat once more (figure 2.5). Economic rent can be thought of as the difference in income between D_1 (or any point) and the margin of production. We can also compute

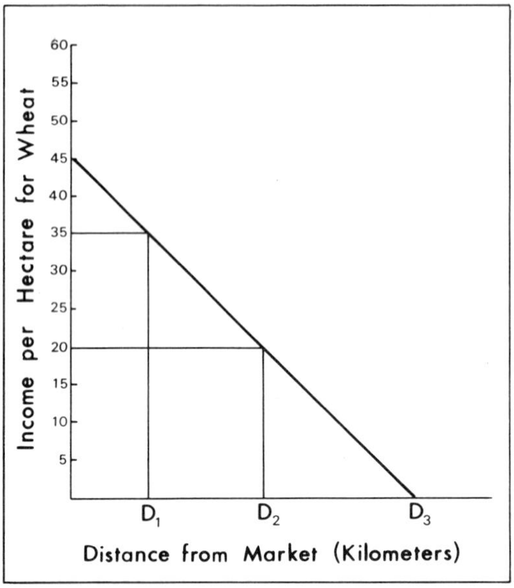

FIGURE 2.5 Single crop case.

economic rent by taking the difference in net income between D_1 and D_2 and say that the economic rent of D_1 compared to D_2 is $15. For a third example, let us assume that wheat brings $5 per dekaliter and that production costs are $25 per hectare. A hectare that produces 5.1 dekaliters of wheat will be a *marginal hectare*. The income from that parcel of land barely pays for production costs (net income = $.50). Suppose another hectare yields 100 dekaliters of wheat. The economic rent of this second unit of land is $74.50 when compared to the marginal unit ($75 − $.50 = $74.50).

Economic rent in the Thünen model is solely a *function of distance* because distance determines total transportation costs and therefore net income. This assumes that the market price is a constant. Transportation cost then becomes the variable determining economic rent. What happens if there is a change in either the market price or the transportation rate? If the market price of wheat (p_w) increases while the transportation rate remains the same, the economic rent of a given unit of land will increase and the margin of production will shift outward (figure 2.6). The economic rent of a given parcel of land will decline and the margin of production will shift inward if the transportation rate increases while the market price remains constant (figure 2.7). Notice however, that at zero distance (marketplace), the change in economic rent is also zero.

The curve which graphs net income (or economic rent) as a function of distance is called a *bid-rent curve* (see box on p. 34) because it determines the maximum amount a potential producer can bid for the use of a unit of land at a given location. A simple example of the concept is provided by imagining that all the land is owned by a single landlord. In Thünen's time, he might be the "lord of the manor" living in the castle in the center of the market town. Each year the serfs in the countryside (to continue our feudal example) submit sealed bids to the landlord stating the rent each

Economic rent is the *difference* in returns obtained from the use of a unit of land compared to that obtained at the *margin of production*. It is sometimes defined as the relative difference in potential income between a given unit of land and a "marginal unit." Returns from a marginal unit are just barely enough to pay for the cost of bringing it into production. In our discussion of a production function, the marginal plot has a marginal product of zero. A real-world example of economic rent is shown in the accompanying figure. Two plots of land are for sale (A and B) and each is the same size. Plot A is easily accessible from an Interstate highway which carries 30,000 vehicles per day. Plot B is several kilometers away on a sparsely traveled county road (20 vehicles per day). Assume a large oil company is interested in buying land for a new filling station. They are willing to pay $200,000 for Plot A. How much will they pay for Plot B? Plot B is absolutely worthless as a filling station site, so the economic rent of A is $200,000. The rent is then a measure of the advantage of the location of A over B.

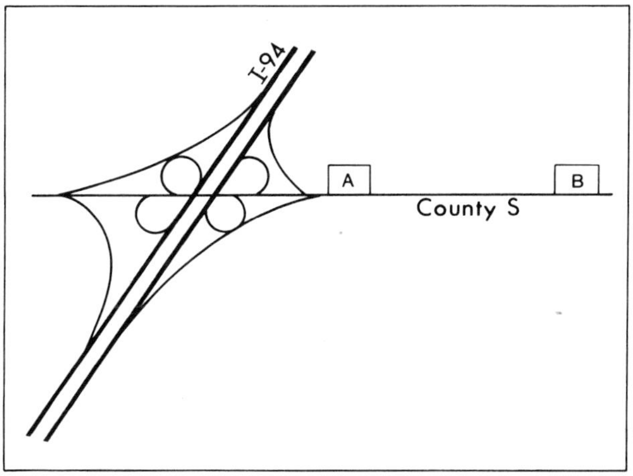

will pay for a particular unit of land. Bids are opened and each hectare is assigned to the highest bidder for the coming growing season. The maximum amount a serf can bid for a given hectare is determined by the bid-rent curve. At D_1 in figure 2.5, for example, the maximum amount is $35. If a potential user of the land at D_1 bids more, his net income will be negative.

Intensity Implications of the Single-Crop Case We must refer back to our discussion of the three stages of a production function to consider the intensity implications of the single-crop case. Remember that optimizers will only operate within Stage II; that is, between the intensive and extensive margins of land. The intensity of land use will diminish as the distance from the market increases if we hold the amount of labor constant (the farm family). Net income *per hectare* declines with increasing distance and each production unit (farmer) must cultivate more and more acreage to maintain a subsistence income (see box p. 36). With labor held constant, this implies diminishing intensity. Farmers near the marketplace will

A bid-rent curve is a linear equation which takes the form

$Y = a - bX$

where

Y = the market price,
X = the distance to the market, and
a and b = *parameters* of the equation.

The parameter a is called the "Y-intercept" or "origin" because it determines where the line will intercept the Y-axis. At this point, $X = 0$ so that $Y = a$. The b parameter is called the "slope" and measures the change in Y with each unit change in X. The accompanying figure graphs the equations $Y = 10 - 1X$ and $Y = 10 - 3X$. Both equations have the same Y-intercept (a), but different slopes (b's). Y declines by 1 unit (per unit change in X) in the first equation and by 3 units in the second.

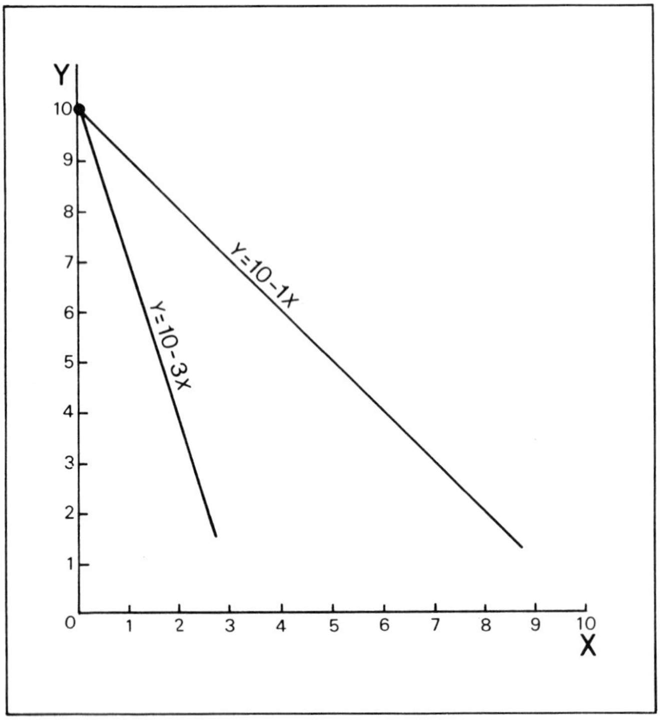

operate near the intensive margin of land whereas farmers more removed from the market will operate near the extensive margin of land. This condition implies diminishing population density (larger farms) with increasing distance from the market.

These intensity implications are illustrated in figure 2.8. Let the net subsistence income per year for a farm family be \$3500. A producer at D_1 requires only 100 hectares to meet this subsistence wage while a producer at D_2 must cultivate 175

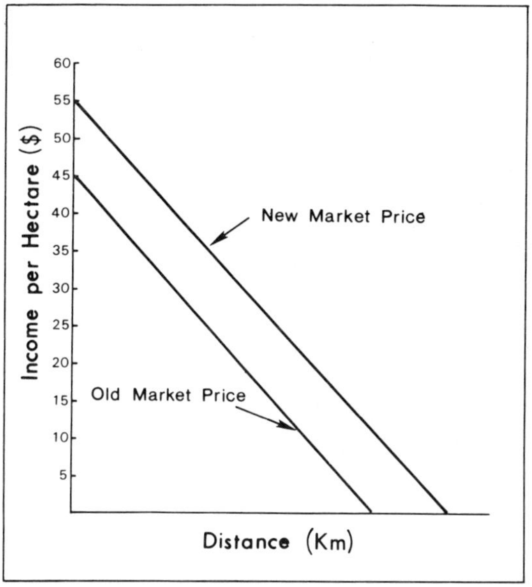

FIGURE 2.6 Effects of a change in market price (transport cost held constant).

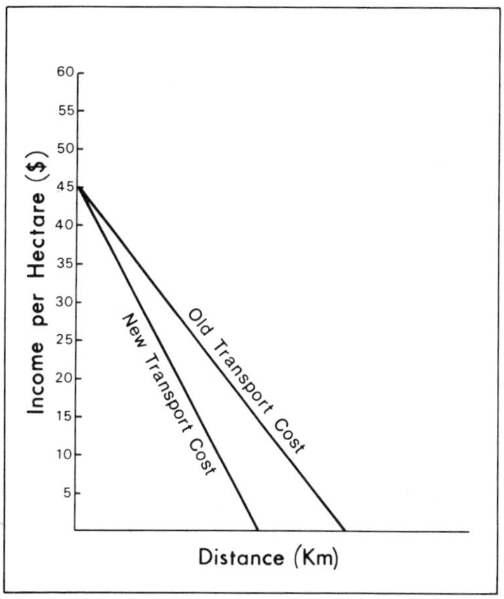

FIGURE 2.7 Effects of a change in transport cost (market price held constant).

hectares. A producer at the margin of production (D_0) will theoretically require an infinite amount of land to meet the subsistence wage. Intensity decreases because the amount of land must increase with labor held constant. The margin of production, therefore, is somewhat closer to the market than the graph indicates. Production will cease at the extensive margin of land if that point is reached before zero economic rent.

Many variables have been held constant or assumed away in order to keep this initial model simple. Agriculture, for example, certainly requires capital, but we have assumed that each unit of land in the Thünen model requires the same amount of capital and can thus be ignored as a *variable*. Land, labor, and transportation costs are then the key components of the model. We are also assuming that the basic cost of labor is what economists call a "subsistence wage." A constant subsistence wage has been "built in" to all values given in the model as a constant cost of production. Income above the subsistence wage we might call "profit" in a very strict economic sense. Suppose a farmer at D_1 in figure 2.5 pays a rent of $35 per hectare for the use of the land. His net income is *not* zero because we have assumed that he must earn at least a subsistence wage or he will not farm at all. His books will show a profit (the subsistence wage), but only in an accounting sense. You should consult any introductory microeconomics text for a further explanation of the difference between accounting and economic profits.

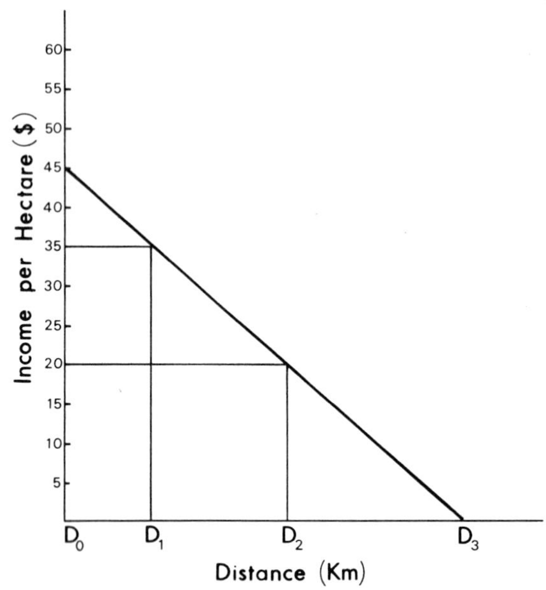

To obtain net of $3500:
at D_1 100 hectares (100 · $35 = $3500)
at D_2 175 hectares (175 · $20 = $3500)
at D_3 ≈ ∞ hectares

FIGURE 2.8 Intensity implications.

A Multi-Crop Model

The basic Thünen model can be extended to consider the patterns produced by economic rent when several crops are involved. Assume three crops: vegetables, potatoes, and wheat. Each crop brings a different market price per hectare (P_m) such that the market price for vegetables (P_v) is greater than the market price for potatoes (P_p) which in turn is greater than the market price for wheat (P_w):

$$P_v > P_p > P_w$$

The market price inequalities may be a function of demand (people are willing to pay a higher price for vegetables), or the intensity of production (a hectare of vegetables yields more than a hectare of wheat), or both.

Assume also that the transportation rate *(T)* for each crop is different so that:

$$T_v > T_p > T_w$$

Vegetables are more perishable, fragile, and bulky than wheat. Tomatoes dropped into a boxcar by conveyor will not bring a high market price. Wheat will keep for a long time under proper conditions and can be easily loaded for transporting. Potatoes are intermediate; they are less perishable and fragile than vegetables, but more so than wheat.

The results of these assumptions are graphed in figure 2.9. The *origin* of each bid-rent curve is the market price of the commodity and the *slope* is the transportation rate (see box on bid-rent curve). The steeper the curve, the greater the transportation *rate* per kilometer. Vegetables are the most profitable crop from 0 to D_1 because throughout this distance net income exceeds the net income from potatoes and wheat. At D_1, however, the net income from vegetables equals the net income from

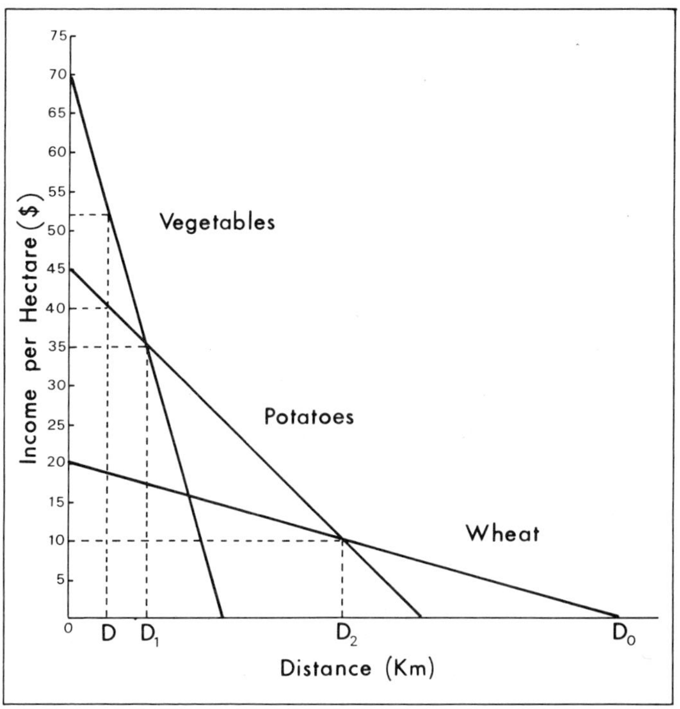

FIGURE 2.9 Three-crop case.

potatoes and beyond D_1 (to D_2) potatoes become the most profitable crop. From D_2 to the margin of production (D_0), wheat is the most profitable crop. Farmers at a given location have one option within the limits of the model. They must grow the most profitable crop. They either perceive this as their best option (which any optimizer would do) or are forced to by the competitive bidding of others. A farmer at D who wants to grow potatoes can bid only $35 per hectare. A potential grower of vegetables can easily exceed that bid for each hectare of land at D. Suburban housing, for example, can always encroach on farmland at the periphery of a city if the distance involved remains economic for commuters. Suburban housing can bid a much higher price per unit of land than even the most profitable forms of agriculture.

There is no necessity for the intensity (labor investment per hectare) to rise with nearness to the market when several crops are produced. Farmers near the market may produce crops which need small amounts of land and labor yet yield a large output per hectare. Crops grown near the market, however, must pay the high rents found at those locations which usually implies intensive cultivation. The scale change (measured in average farm size) with increasing distance for the multi-crop case will not be a smooth curve. There will be a "kink" in the curve at the boundary of each crop as the optimum land/labor ratio is adjusted for each kind of production.

The linear Thünen model can be translated into a two-dimensional case by rotating the bid-rent curves around the net-income axis. This rotation produces the patterns shown in figure 2.10 which are commonly called *Thünen rings*.

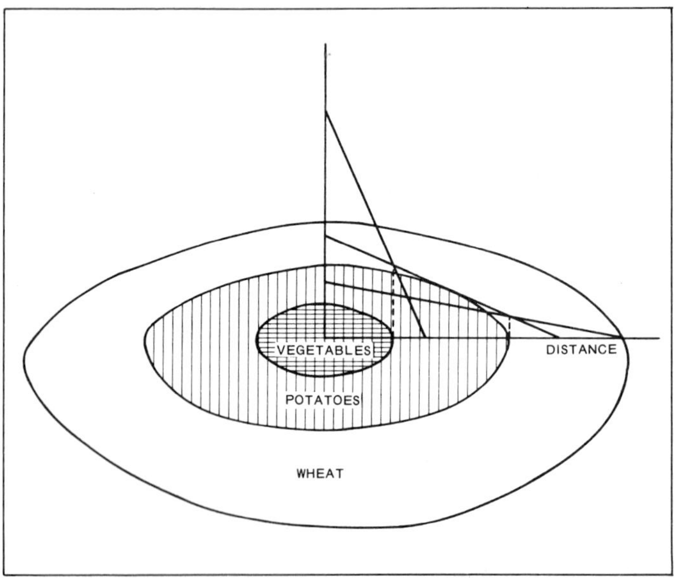

FIGURE 2.10 The Thünen model translated to a plane.

Further Modifications of the Thünen Model

Transportation Structures The addition of transportation structures alters the symmetry of the rings. Consider the effects of water transportation shown in figure

2.11. Transportation costs are lowered for those areas nearest the river. Agricultural commodities can be transported over land by the shortest route to the river and then moved by less expensive water transportation to the marketplace. Each zone of production is distorted along the axis of the river. The innermost zone changes least because water transportation is no faster than land and speed is most important for perishables. The zones of distant commodities are more distorted. Figure 2.11 indicates that the river flows from right to left. Zones are more distorted upstream because river transportation is cheaper downstream.

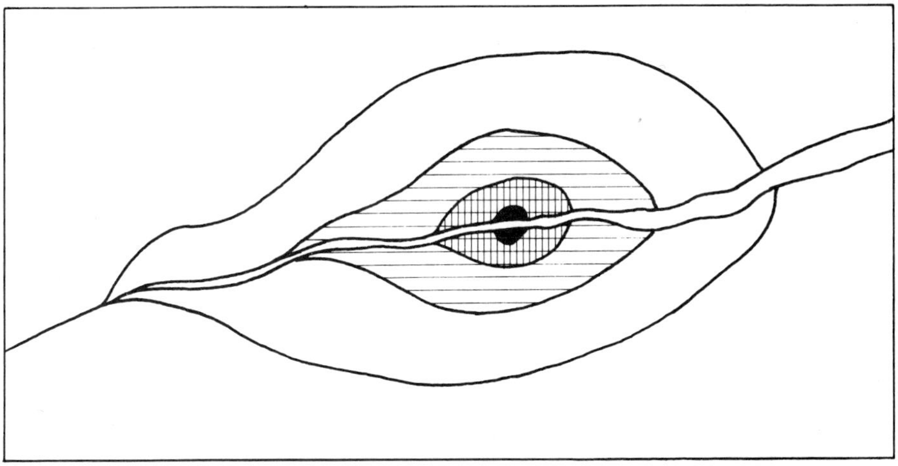

FIGURE 2.11 Transportation effects.

The Influence of a Subsidiary Market The effects of an additional (smaller) market town are shown in figure 2.12. Each secondary town develops its own

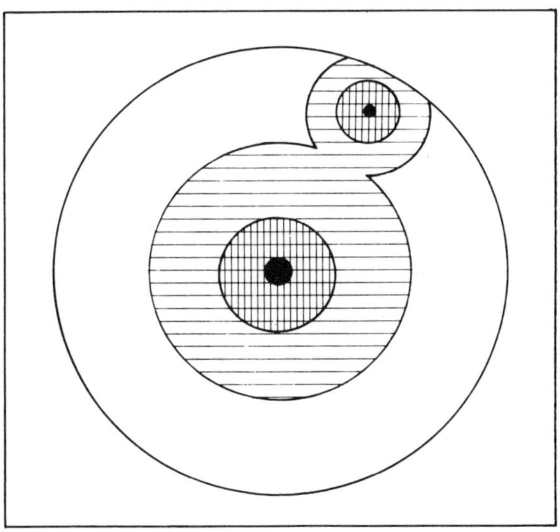

FIGURE 2.12 Effects of a subsidiary market.

microzonal system, although some microzones may be absent as the result of competition from nearby larger zones oriented toward the central city.

Local Fertility Differences The effect of a "fertile" area (fertility* greater than the general level of the isotropic surface) is shown in figure 2.13. With agriculture dependent upon rainfall, the normal Thünen rings for the three-crop case prevail. The rent of Crop C decreases from $15 at the market to zero at the margin of production. Under "normal" (isotropic) conditions, Crop C will not be produced until D_2 is reached. But suppose that around D_1 unusual fertility conditions prevail, such as an artesian source of irrigation water. The yield per hectare for Crop C rises around D_1 in such a way as to form rent isopleths (see box) which are higher than the rents for Crops A and B (which do not change as D_1 is approached). Crop C is substituted for A and B where the net return for C exceeds that of the surrounding crops.

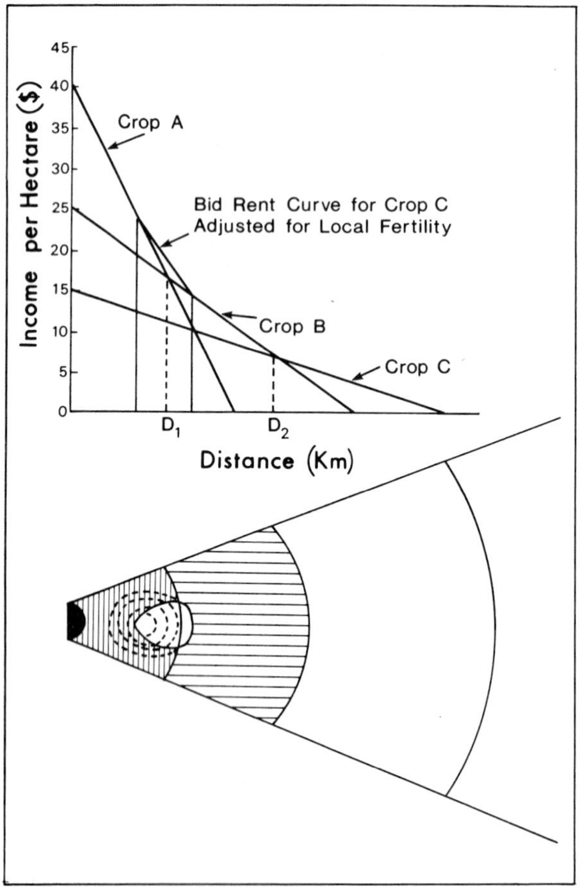

FIGURE 2.13 Local fertility differences.

*Fertility is used throughout this book to refer to all environmental conditions which affect agricultural yields, including rainfall, temperature, and soil quality.

An isopleth is a *line connecting points of equal value* and is a very important cartographic tool employed by geographers. ''Isopleth'' is a generic term, but there are many specially named isopleths. A contour line, for example is a line connecting points of equal elevation. The *isobars* on a weather map connect points of equal barometric pressure. The isopleths in figure 2.13 connect points of equal rent. We usually make a specific term by combining the prefix ''iso'' (''equal'') with another descriptive word. ''Iso-cost'' and ''iso-rent'' are examples. This concept will play an important role in this book, so you should consider its definition carefully. There are two important properties of isopleths which you should also keep in mind: (1) isopleths of different values can *never cross,* and (2) the distance between isopleths indicates the rate of change across space in the variable being mapped. When isopleths are close together, the rate of change is rapid, and *vice versa.* The accompanying figure is a map of iso-rent lines. Rent ($) falls very rapidly (per kilometer) to the right, but very slowly to the left.

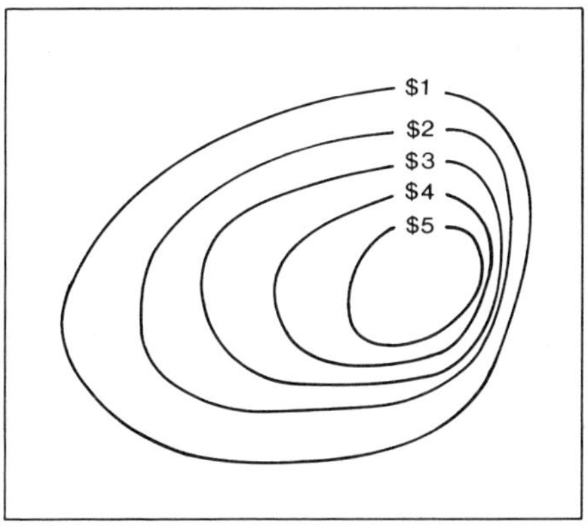

Evaluation of Thünen's Model

Thünen presented a normative model of agricultural land use. Among the conclusions to be derived from his model are the following: (1) there is an inverse relationship between location rent and transport costs; (2) there is a limit to commercial farming on a homogeneous plain with an isolated market town at its center; (3) land values and intensity of land use increase toward the market; and (4) crop types compete with one another, and are ordered according to the principle of highest economic rent.

Thünen's most important contribution to studies of spatial organization was the use of the principle of ''highest and best use'' and the concept of location rent. These two notions identify three major aspects of land use patterns: (1) circular bands or circles of land use around points of greatest accessibility; (2) axes of land use development along major transport arteries; and (3) multiple nuclei with the emergence of additional satellite centers.

Some limitations of Thünen's model have been noted:

1. His model does not succeed in describing the spatial structure of an economic system. It oversimplifies the relationship between town and country. Although he introduced multiple markets, his analysis concentrated on various types of agricul-

ture within a single market area having a large town at its center. He ignored the fact that agriculture tends to stimulate the growth of small weight-losing processing centers (e.g., sugar mills and distilleries), and that these industrial centers are connected to other larger centers.

2. His model assumes that differences in land rents have their origin solely in differences in costs of production.

3. His model is static and deterministic. It represents a land use system at one point in time and therefore cannot predict changing patterns of rural land use. Furthermore, it assumes that any change in technology, demand, or transport cost brings instantaneous adjustments in land use patterns.

4. His model assumes constant transport costs, but this was an appropriate assumption under transport conditions in nineteenth century Germany.

5. His model assumes that a farmer is an optimizer who has perfect information and uses it with complete rationality to maximize profits. Clearly it is unrealistic to assume that farmers are optimizers; they are satisficers, they make sub-optimal decisions because they have less than perfect information, and they are subject to considerable uncertainty about weather and economic conditions.

Despite these and other limitations, Thünen's model remains a valuable construct for teaching and research. It provides many insights into patterns of rural land use. The chief virtue of his model is that it can be used as a norm against which actual land use patterns can be compared.

The Thünen Model: Empirical Evidence

The Thünen model is a set of morphological (structure) laws which can explain the pattern of Thünen rings. Suppose a future deep-space probe relays back to earth pictures of a very regular pattern on the surface of some distant planet. We would immediately be concerned with finding an explanation for those patterns. Thünen rings are not evident around cities in the United States in either satellite or conventional aerial photography. If they were, there would be a general public understanding of the Thünen model. Other factors must be involved. The rings may not be visible because of the scale or because their boundaries are transitional and therefore blurred. The primary reason for the lack of Thünen rings around large cities in the United States, however, is a lack of landscape homogeneity.

The real utility of the Thünen model is the fact that it forms a conceptual basis for more complicated systems. We have to have a sound grasp of elementary concepts before moving to more rigorous applications. An examination of the empirical evidence for the Thünen model will help to clarify its utility as a conceptual tool.

We should first recognize that Thünen was writing in the early part of the nineteenth century when a feudal agricultural system prevailed in northern Germany. There is ample evidence that rudimentary rings existed around major market centers in Thünen's time as Johnson (1970) noted in both Thünen's native Mecklenburg and Tudor England. These areas did not approximate an isotropic surface and producers did not have the perfect knowledge available to our imaginary optimizers, so the rings were not as regular as our precisely drawn diagrams. Chisholm (1962) noted the same patterns around London in 1811, and the empirical aspects of the fertility implications of the single-crop case were explored in Harvey's (1963) study of the Kentish hop industry. Many of the conditions which prevailed in Thünen's Mecklenburg in the 1820s are approximated today in some underdeveloped countries (Chisholm 1962; Horvath 1969) producing rudimentary rings.

The Thünen principle has also been applied in a limited context to the contemporary United States. Gottman (1961) emphasized the intensity of production and the fresh-market orientation of agriculture around the coalescing urban clusters (Megalopolis) of the northeastern seaboard. Gottman emphasized that a farm with good soil is more valuable than one with poor soil *only* if their locations are equal. "The rockiest pasture ten miles from Boston is more valuable than the finest black loam in central Illinois" (Gottman 1961, p. 263).

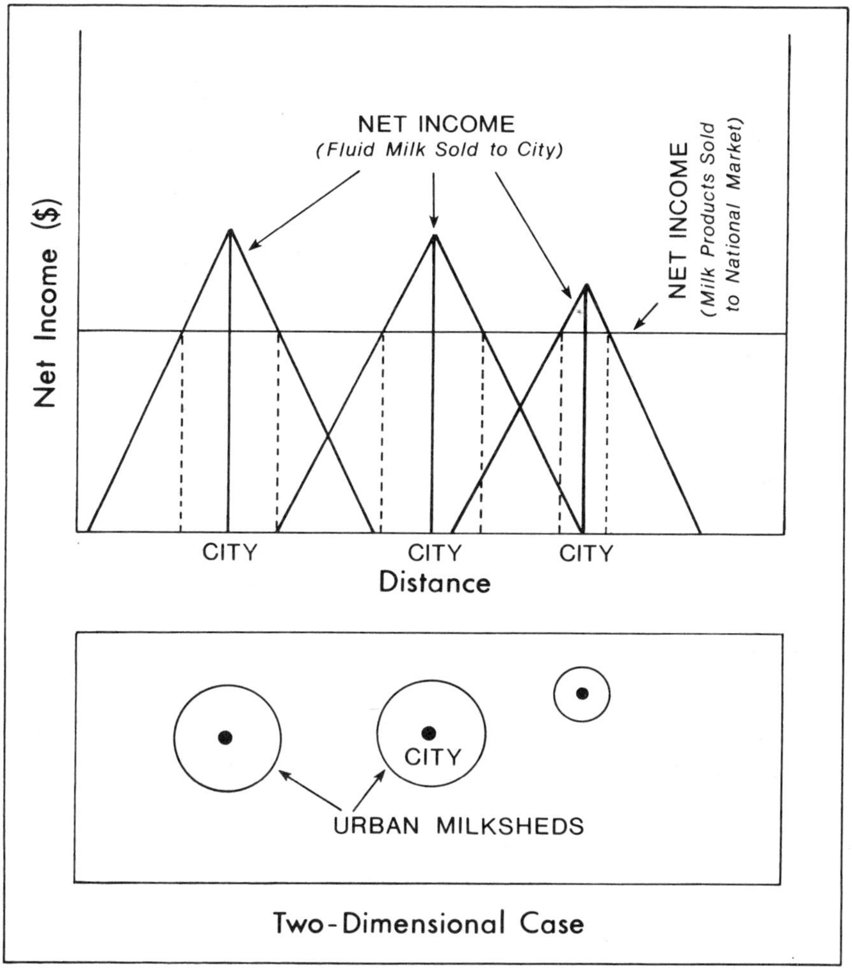

FIGURE 2.14 Urban markets for fluid milk.

Durand (1964) implied the same conditions in his study of the major milksheds of the United States. Durand's conclusions are diagramed in figure 2.14. Dairy farming is the prevailing form of agriculture across much of the northern half of the northeastern United States. The belt stretches from Maine to Minnesota. Dairying developed in response to environmental and cultural conditions and concentrates mainly on milk products (butter, cheese, powdered milk) for the national market. Near major cities, however, transportation costs favor the production of fluid (fresh) milk for local urban markets and pockets (or milksheds) of fluid milk production surrounded by other types of dairying are evident. The same analogy can be applied to the pockets of truck farming and other forms of intensive agriculture which form interrupted rings around most American cities.

Macro-Thünen Analysis

The classic Thünen model is micro (urban hinterland) in scale, but it can also be applied at the macro (national or international) level. The immense concentration of demand for agricultural products focused on the English Channel (Great Britain and northwestern Europe) can be thought of as a single market center. A number of studies have shown that crop yields decline rather regularly with increasing distance from this large demand core (Van Valkenberg and Held 1962; Chisholm 1962). Peet (1969), in particular, explored the historical development of this pattern in a Thünen context.

Muller (1973) used this type of analysis for the United States with the Eastern Megalopolis forming the single "national market." Muller concentrated his attention on the intensity implications of the Thünen model by considering only the effects that distance from the national market has on net farm income. His analysis produced a series of roughly concentric isopleths of net income focused on Megalopolis. The results of Muller's analysis are generalized in graphic form in figure 2.15. Net income per hectare declines with distance from the national market (Megalopolis).

A Ricardian View of Agricultural Land Rent

An alternative view of agricultural land rent was provided by Thünen's contemporary, the English economist David Ricardo. The Ricardian view has dominated the thinking of geographers about real-world agricultural patterns basically because they have tended to think in physical (environmental) rather than economic terms. Ricardo defined rent as a payment for "the use of the original and indestructible powers of the soil." Land, for Ricardo, is an inexhaustible and nonreproducible agent, unalterably fixed in supply, and homogeneous in quality except for differences in fertility and location. Ricardo focused his attention on fertility. If land is homogeneous, the limitations of supply create scarcity rents. When land differs in quality, the scarcity of hectares of a particular fertility gives rise to differential rents. Geographers, in their considerations of real-world agricultural patterns, have paid the most attention to fertility differences.

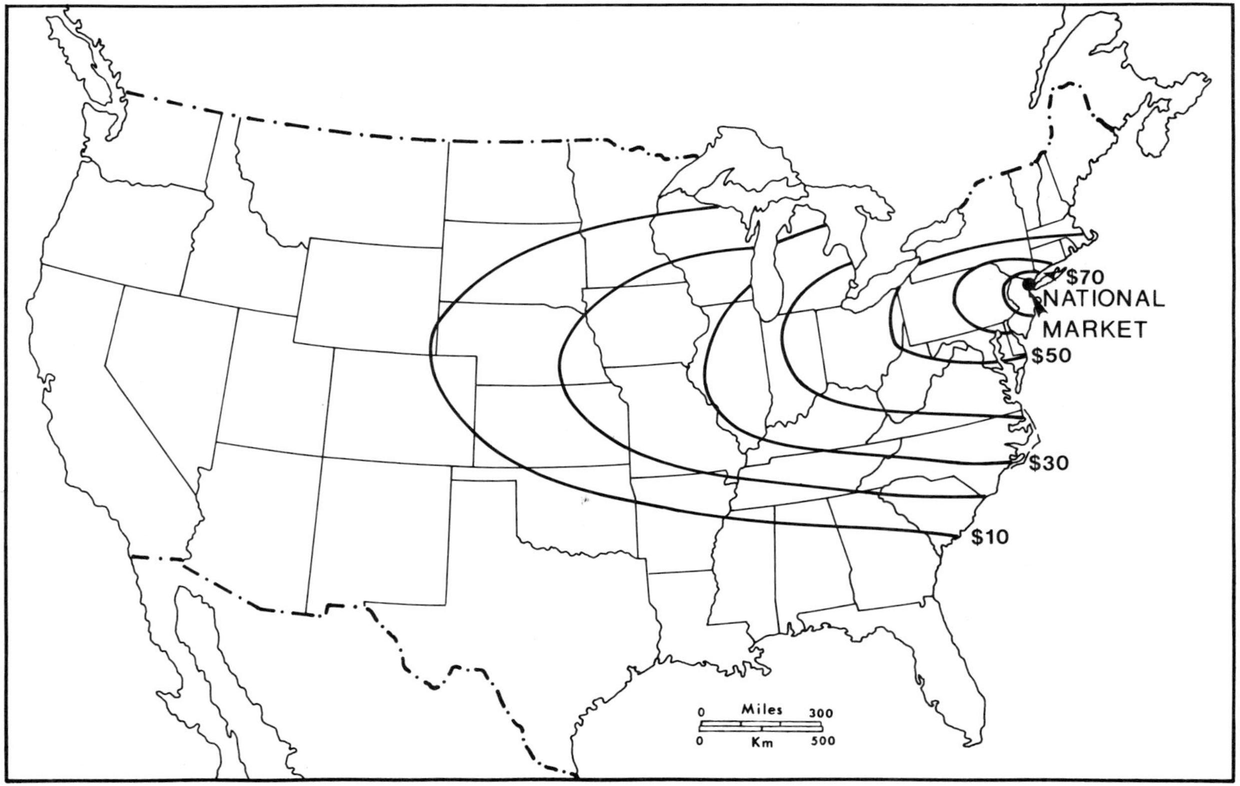

FIGURE 2.15 Generalized net income contours (After Muller, 1973).

Agriculture *is* a land-based activity. We often assume that the quality of land plays the major role in determining patterns of agriculture. A map of agricultural production in the United States certainly shows patterns. Large sections of the country concentrate on the production of specific agricultural specialties. The Ricardian view assumes that the quality (fertility) of the land is the major determinant of these patterns; the morphological laws underlying these patterns consist of a set of qualitative differences. Fertility does play a role, of course, but is land quality the primary cause of these patterns?

Land quality is a combination of three variables: (a) climate, which can be subdivided into temperature and precipitation; (b) soil quality; and (c) terrain or slope conditions. Together, these elements determine total "fertility." Each type of agriculture requires a set of *minimum fertility conditions* which are unevenly distributed across the surface of the earth. The Ricardian model assumes that agricultural patterns are structured by these minimum fertility limits.

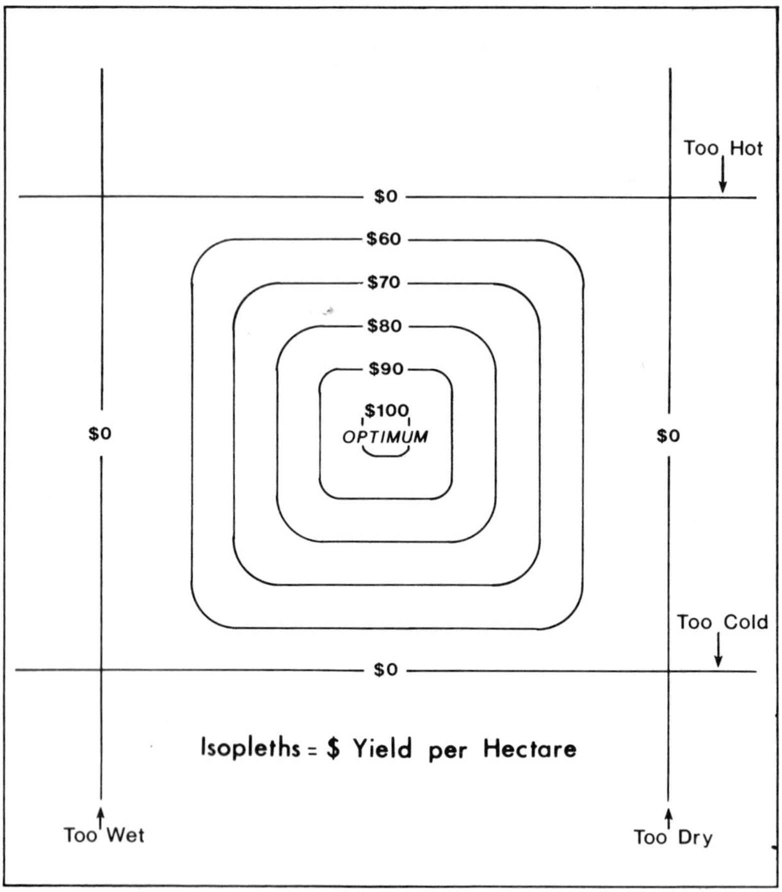

FIGURE 2.16 Optimal and marginal fertility ranges [Source: H. McCarty and J. Lindberg, © 1966, *A Preface to Economic Geography*, p. 61, Englewood Cliffs: Prentice Hall, Inc. Reproduced by permission of the publisher].

Assume that only two elements of fertility, temperature and rainfall, are critical for a particular kind of agriculture. The range of the crop is given in figure 2.16. Increasing rainfall is plotted on the horizontal axis and increasing temperatures on the vertical. Absolute physical limits of the crop are too wet, too dry, too cold, and too hot. These absolute limits may delimit a very small area for some crops. Bananas and certain wine grapes are examples. For other crops, such as wheat, the absolute limits are quite large. A series of isopleths (connecting points of equal dollar yield per hectare) have been drawn inside the absolute limits. The highest yields per hectare mark *optimum* conditions. The Ricardian model assumes a direct relationship between the values of these isopleths and land rent. The higher the fertility (yield), the higher is the economic rent.

Ricardo and Thünen: A Synthesis

Is fertility the prime determinant of agricultural patterns? Consider an extreme example. We have the technology to grow oranges at the South Pole using greenhouses and artificial lighting and heat sources. Oranges are not grown under polar conditions because no one is willing to pay the required market price. Suppose, however, we discovered that oranges grown at the South Pole cure cancer. The price those oranges would command would more than offset the high production costs of Antarctic citrus farming.

The isopleths in figure 2.17 are based on *cost,* not yield per hectare. Costs rise as we move away from the crop's optimum physical conditions. A cross-section has been drawn along the line A-A′ (bottom of figure 2.17). The cross-section is a *space-cost curve* and graphs the change in cost across distance. Let the market price of this particular crop be $80. The limits of production are determined by the intersection of the market price line and the space cost curve. The locus of these points mapped on a plane give the *spatial margins to profitability* for the crop (figure 2.18). If the market price rises, the spatial margins to profitability (SMP) will shift outward and, if the market price falls, they will shift inward. This can be seen by considering market prices MP_2 and MP_3 in figure 2.17. The concept of spatial margins to profitability place environmental conditions in an *economic* context.

We ignored the effects of transportation costs in our discussion of the Ricardian model. How will the spatial margins to profitability be altered if transportation costs play a role? Figure 2.19 shows a space-cost curve based on environmental (fertility) conditions. The spatial margins to profitability are X_1 and X_2 with a market price of MP_1 and zero transportation costs. Now assume that the market for the crop is at O and the market price is MP_1. Transportation costs are shown by the line $MP_1 - D$. The spatial margins to profitability shift to Y_1 and Y_2.

The Effects of Technology

Changes in the cost of production can also alter the spatial margins to profitability. Production costs can rise for such reasons as changing wage rates for agricultural labor, increased fertilizer prices, and more expensive machinery. Fertilizers

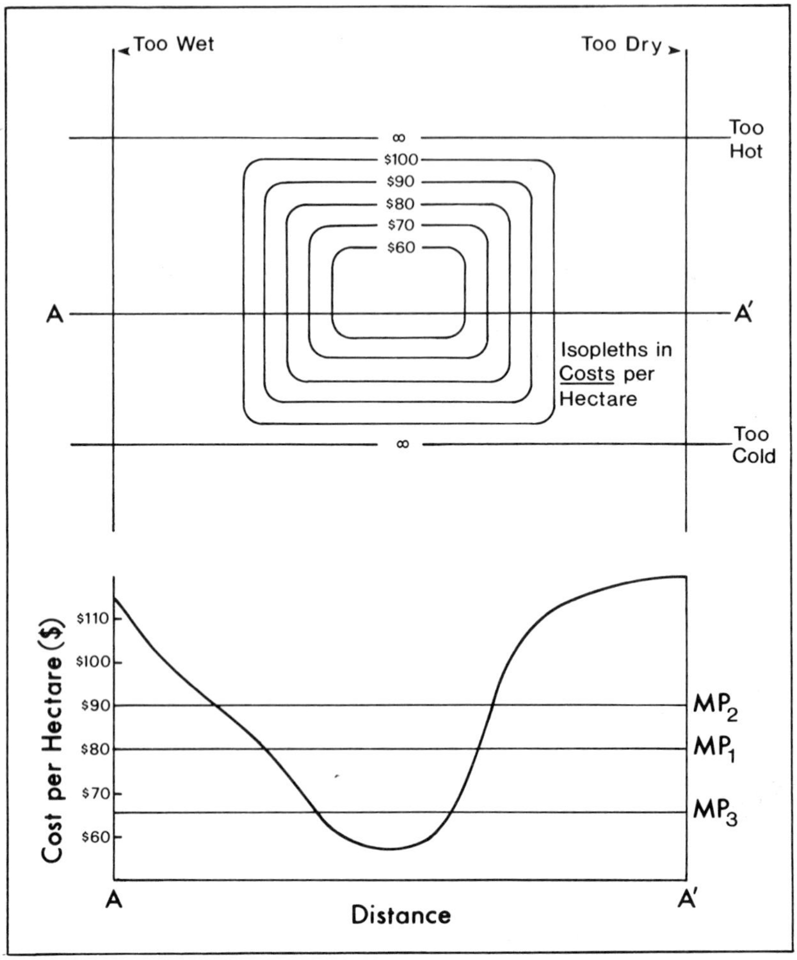

FIGURE 2.17 Optimal and marginal limits: the space-cost curve.

can improve soil fertility and irrigation and drainage systems alter moisture supplies. Steep slopes can be terraced. Pesticides and herbicides improve yields and scientific breeding produces superior strains of plants and animals. Drought resistant crops push the margins of agriculture into the dry areas of the earth and rapidly maturing crops extend the boundaries poleward. The northern limit of corn harvested for grain, for example, shifted northward in the United States as hybrids with shorter growing seasons were introduced.

The major point is this: "marginal land" is an economic term, not simply a reference to environmental conditions. Changing technology can shift the margins if the increased yields justify the cost of improvements. The increased demand for food with rising populations has historically been able to pay the cost of technological improvements. Many types of agriculture have shifted into once marginal land with increasing demand and improved technology.

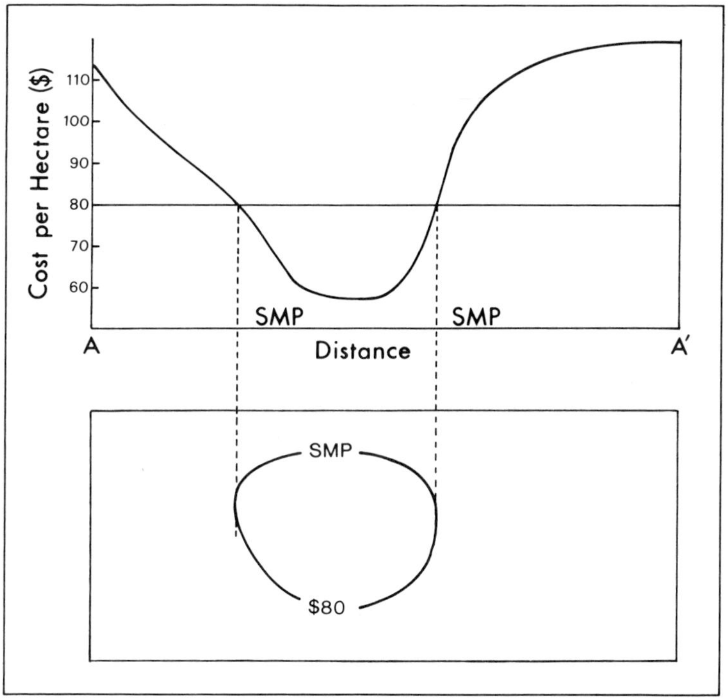

FIGURE 2.18 Spatial margins to profitability.

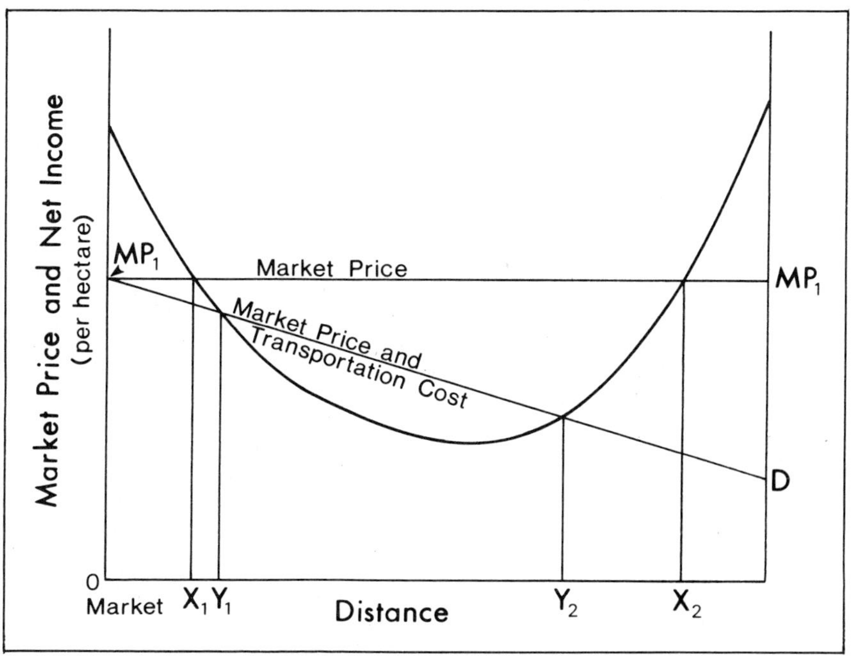

FIGURE 2.19 Fertility spatial margins to profitability versus transportation costs.

Outer climatic/economic limits of agriculture may be altered in the future. Large portions of the earth's surface are too cold for agriculture (short growing season); other areas are too dry for cultivation. Roughly ten percent of the earth's land surface is tropical rainforest which presently produces very little of our food supply. Low productivity is often the result of poor tropical soils and plant and animal diseases. There are probably technological solutions to the disease problems of the tropics, and hydroponic farming has demonstrated that plants can be grown without soil if certain nutrients are added artificially. The humid tropics have the main requirement for hydroponic farming—abundant water. Suppose one-quarter of the tropics (2.5 percent of the earth's land surface) could be utilized for hydroponic farming and, because of the year-long growing season, five crops per year could be produced. This future technological possibility would be the equivalent of single-cropping 12.5 percent of the earth's land surface. Today, only roughly 20 percent is cultivated. Tropical hydroponic farming would shift the macro-spatial margins to profitability, but this can only be dictated by economic (demand) conditions.

The general goal of commercial agriculture is to maximize profits by producing the *optimum* crop (or livestock/crop combinations). The optimum is always a function of *both* economic and environmental conditions. Economic (demand) conditions also reflect cultural variations. Some societies have taboos against the use of milk (some ethnic groups of West Africa) or pork (Islam and Judaism). There are crops that could be grown in the United States which would produce many more calories per hectare than those currently grown; soybeans are an example. But most Americans prefer other foods to soybeans. Large sections of the country (such as the Corn Belt) are used to produce beef and pork. These areas would produce many more calories per unit of land if we ate the crops directly rather than feeding them to animals. On the other hand, animals make marginal land useable. The early settlers of Wisconsin, for example, found the land would only grow hay. They faced two options: (a) learn to eat hay, or (b) use animals (dairy cattle) to convert hay into something more edible and commanding a higher market price.

Government Intervention

There is a great deal of government control over agriculture even in capitalist countries such as the United States. Much of this control is an attempt to regulate the supply of agricultural products, thereby influencing demand and price. Examples of supply control include Soil Bank programs which paid farmers not to grow crops and the acreage controls which limit production. Embargoes on some types of foreign production limit the available supply of the crop in the United States supporting higher domestic prices.

Government controls sometimes have little effect on total production. Acreage controls on tobacco, for example, were established in 1939; an attempt at supply control. Each farmer was given a fixed acreage allotment, but each soon adopted a strategy of intensive cultivation on the fixed land input. The land/labor ratio was increased and yields were improved through greater applications of fertilizers and pest control (inputs of capital). Montgomery County, Tennessee is an example. The average yield per acre in the county rose from 150kg per hectare in 1938 (before acreage controls) to over 331 kg per hectare in 1964. Government intervention, in this particular case, had little effect on the total supply of the crop.

The Effect of Demand

Market prices are a function of supply and demand. Much of the preceding section concentrated on factors that change the supply of agricultural commodities. A rise in demand, relative to supply, should raise the market price of a crop and shift the spatial margins to profitability outward. Demand is a function of many variables, but increasing population has been the major force involved in food production. The demand for specific products also changes as incomes rise. People in the United States, for example, tend to increase the proportion of meat in their diet as their incomes rise.

There are vast differences in the *price elasticities* (see box on p. 52) of agricultural commodities. Price elasticity is a relative measure of the change in demand which occurs when the price of a commodity changes. Coffee, for example, is *price inelastic;* the change in the quantity demanded is proportionally less than the change in price. If coffee prices rise by ten percent, the demand for coffee will decline by less than ten percent. This is also true for some other food products. Farmers in the United States have attempted to raise the price of inelastic products by reducing the supply. Dumping fresh milk and slaughtering feeder pigs are cases in point. The Brazilian government has, on occasions, burned large amounts of harvested coffee to reduce the supply and raise the price. The results of supply reductions in coffee are shown in figure 2.20. The demand curve for coffee is the line P–Q. When the price of

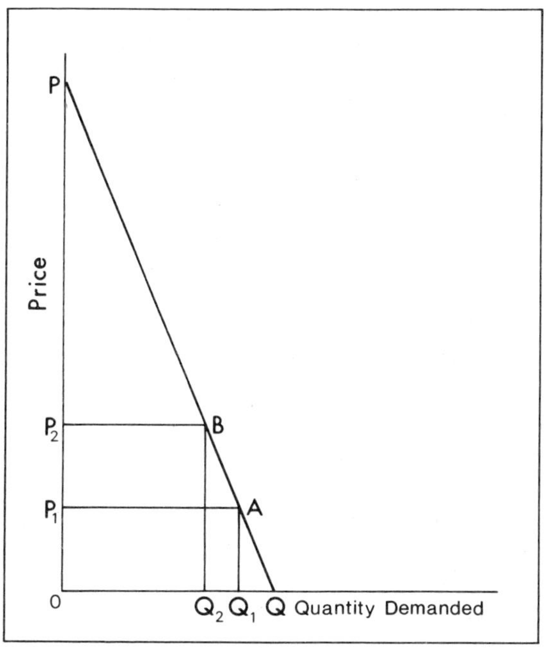

FIGURE 2.20 Supply, demand, and total income for a price inelastic product.

coffee is P_1, the total demand for coffee (quantity) is Q_1, and total income is the area OP_1AQ_1. Reducing the supply of coffee drives the price up to P_2, but the total income is increased to the area OP_2BQ_2. This is only possible for price inelastic commodities, but does illustrate the relationships among supply, demand, price, and total income.

The price elasticity of a good is the relative change in the quantity demanded in response to a change in price or, in other words, the percentage change in quantity resulting from a one percent change in price. For most goods the relationship is *inverse*—a price increase causes a decrease in the quantity demanded and vice versa. Economists usually designate the coefficient of price elasticity by the lowercase Greek eta (η) and have identified three classes of price elasticity:

1. *unitary elasticity:* a one percent change in price brings about a one percent change in quantity demanded ($\eta = 1$);
2. *price elastic:* a one percent change in price results in a *greater than* one percent change in quantity demanded ($\eta > 1$);
3. *price inelastic:* a one percent change in price results in a change in quantity demanded *less than* one percent ($\eta < 1$).

Distance/Fertility Tension

We have seen that *both* distance from the market and fertility are variables which affect agricultural patterns. Which has the *greater* effect? They may be mutually opposing forces when areas of high fertility are somewhat distant from major markets. Figure 2.21 illustrates this situation. Fertility increases along the vertical axis and transportation costs rise along the horizontal. Transportation costs are a measure of the relative distance to the markèt. All crops would be grown in their optimum fertility areas (within the limits imposed by demand) if transportation were instantaneous and free. The curve plotted in figure 2.21 is the trade-off between distance and fertility and is a line of *equal income* per unit of land. If transportation costs are high (T_2), the crop will be grown in areas of less than optimum fertility (F_1). As transportation costs fall, production shifts to more fertile areas (T_1, F_2). Commercial wheat farming is an example of this trade-off. Transportation costs have fallen (relatively) throughout most of American history. With this decline, the center of wheat production has moved steadily westward. New York was once the leading wheat state, then Ohio, then Illinois, until it became stabilized in Kansas. Part of this shift resulted from the westward migration in the United States. Most wheat, however, is consumed along the Eastern Seaboard and lowered transportation costs have also been responsible for this westward shift in production. Areas near the market have been, in turn, devoted to crops with higher transportation rates.

Macro-Fertility Patterns and the Thünen Principle

The Thünen concept of economic rent can be applied to the Ricardian view of fertility. The two crops shown in figure 2.22 have different optimum (environmen-

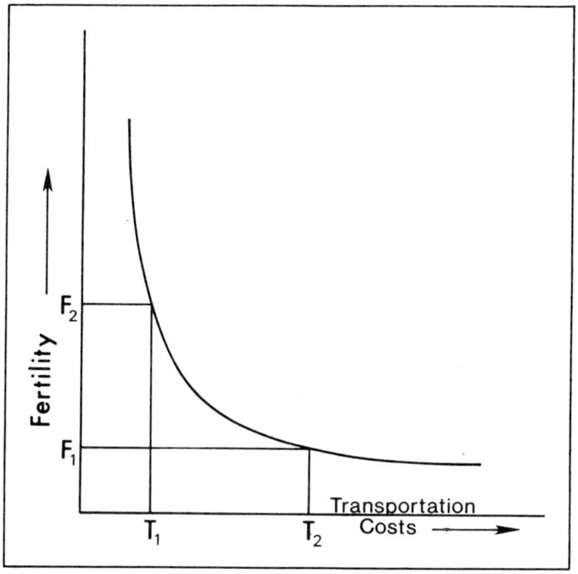

FIGURE 2.21 Transport costs and fertility as opposing forces.

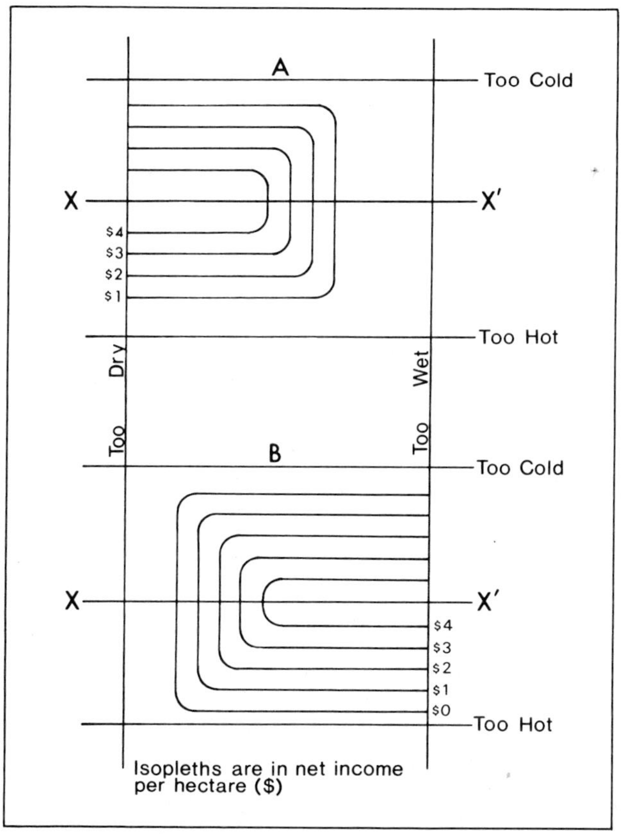

FIGURE 2.22 Optimum ranges of two crops

tal) ranges. Both parts of the figure show the same part of the earth's surface. Crop A tolerates much drier conditions than B, but there is an overlap in their optimum ranges. Isopleths shown in this figure are in *income-per-hectare*. Figure 2.23 results when both crops are graphed along the line X-X′. The boundary between the two is at D_1, if we hold all other conditions constant.

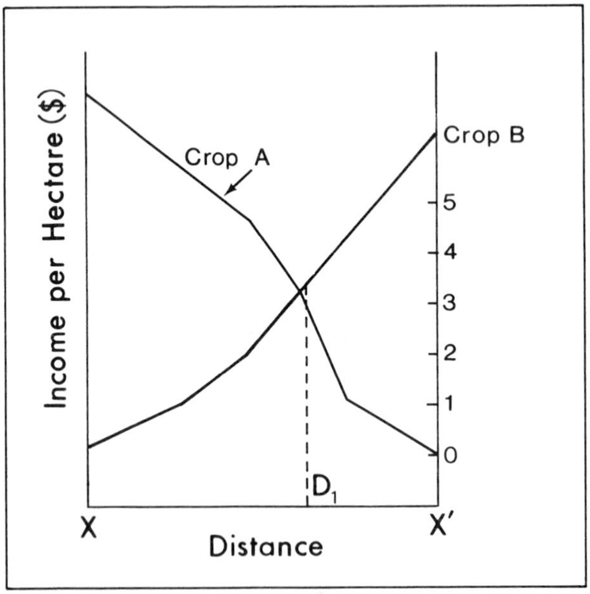

FIGURE 2.23 Fertility bid-rents for two crops.

An Empirical Example Rainfall exhibits much greater change than temperature as we move west across the United States (from X′ to X in figure 2.22). Temperature exhibits the greater change if we travel from north to south (length of the growing season increases). Two major types of agriculture along the line plotted in figure 2.24 are mixed farming (Corn Belt agriculture) and commercial wheat farming. Mixed farming is based on corn and other cultivated feeds which do not tolerate dryness as well as wheat. Figure 2.25 shows the income per acre for both types of agriculture in each county along the east-west traverse. The horizontal axis begins in Iowa and terminates in New Mexico, and both distance and rainfall are shown. A regression line (see box on p. 56) has been fitted through the data for mixed farming (income per acre versus rainfall) and a second line has been fitted for wheat income per acre. Income is highest at the origin of the graph for both crops (more rainfall) and declines with distance (decreasing rainfall). The decline in income per acre for mixed farming is steeper than the decline for wheat. Each type of farming has a different *rate* of response to changes in fertility just at each crop in the classic Thünen model has a different transportation rate. The boundary between the two crops should be where the bid-rent curves cross. They intersect at an average rainfall of 20 inches (50.8 centimeters) which is the rainfall line commonly proposed by geographers as the eastern boundary of commercial wheat farming.

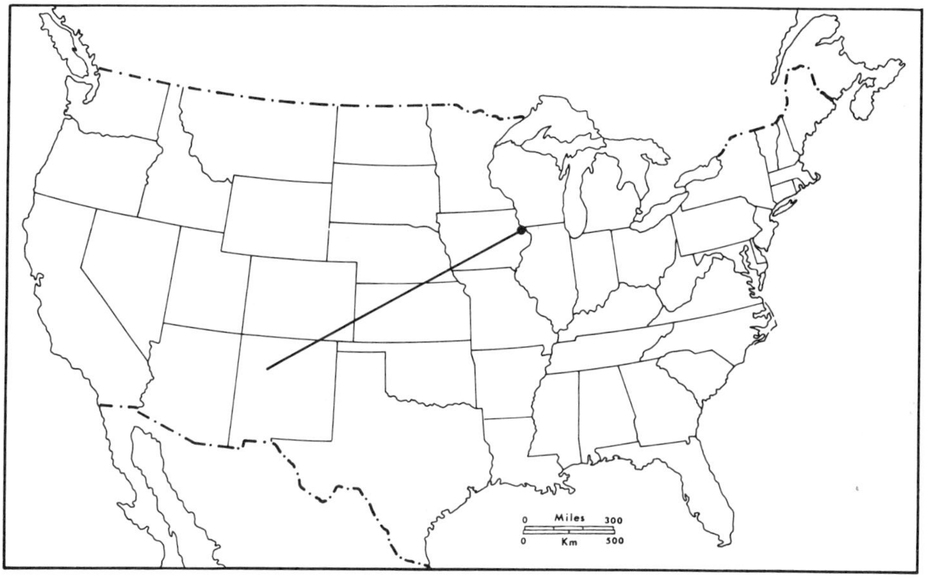

FIGURE 2.24 Traverse line for two types of agriculture.

Wheat farming intrudes east of the 20 inch rainfall line and mixed farming spills over the line to the west, but neither is the *prevailing* form of agriculture beyond the bid-rent intersection. Figure 2.25 illustrates the economic principle determining agricultural patterns. The average yield per acre for wheat in Iowa in 1969 was 33.09 bushels, while the average for Kansas in the same year was only 28.76 bushels per acre, so the area west of the 20 inch line does not represent optimum (fertility) conditions for wheat. An Iowa farmer could earn a higher income from wheat than his Kansas counterpart (assuming comparable operating costs and market prices). Mixed farming in Iowa, however, represents a higher potential income than wheat. Wheat is relegated to drier areas not because they are better suited (climatically) to its production, but because wheat represents the most profitable alternative. Other forms of agriculture (e.g., livestock ranching) become the more profitable alternatives as we move along the traverse (figure 2.26).

The key question remains: which is more important, fertility (Ricardo) or distance to the major market (Thünen)? The answer is difficult to determine because distance-to-market and fertility are not mutually opposing forces in the United States, but rather are complementary. The major market is the eastern megalopolis; therefore, transportation costs increase to the west. Rainfall is a prime factor in agricultural fertility in the country, but it also declines to the west. The correlation between distance and rainfall along the traverse of figure 2.24 is .93 (plotted in figure 2.27). Each (rainfall and distance) could be used as a surrogate for the other. The correlation between net income per hectare and distance from the market (see previous discussion of Muller's work) would not be significantly different from a

Regression is a statistical method used to determine a "best-fit" line through a scatter of data points. Each dot in the accompanying figure (p. 56) represents a state. The exact location of the dot on the graph is determined by (a) the percentage of the state's population which is college educated; and (b) median family income in the state. This type of figure is called a *scatter diagram*. There is obviously some relationship between the two variables; as X (college education) increases, Y (median family income) increases. Regression is a means of estimating the "average" relationship between the two variables. We might also say that regression gives the average change in Y, given a one unit change in X. The regression line plotted in the figure takes the form $Y = 4253.85 + 465.44X$ (refer to discussion of linear equations on p. 34). Suppose we measure the vertical distance from each dot to the regression line and sum these distances (to obtain an aggregate distance). No other line can be drawn among the dots which will yield a lower aggregate distance! We are often interested in relationships between variables. One way to measure such a relationship is the statistical index known as the *coefficient of correlation* (r). The correlation coefficient can range from -1 to $+1$. When $r = \pm 1$, the correlation between the two variables is perfect. When r is near 0, the relationship is poor. The sign of r indicates whether the relationship is positive (*direct*) or negative (*inverse*). The coefficient of correlation for our example is $r = +0.67$ (as X increases, Y increases, and there is a strong relationship between the two).

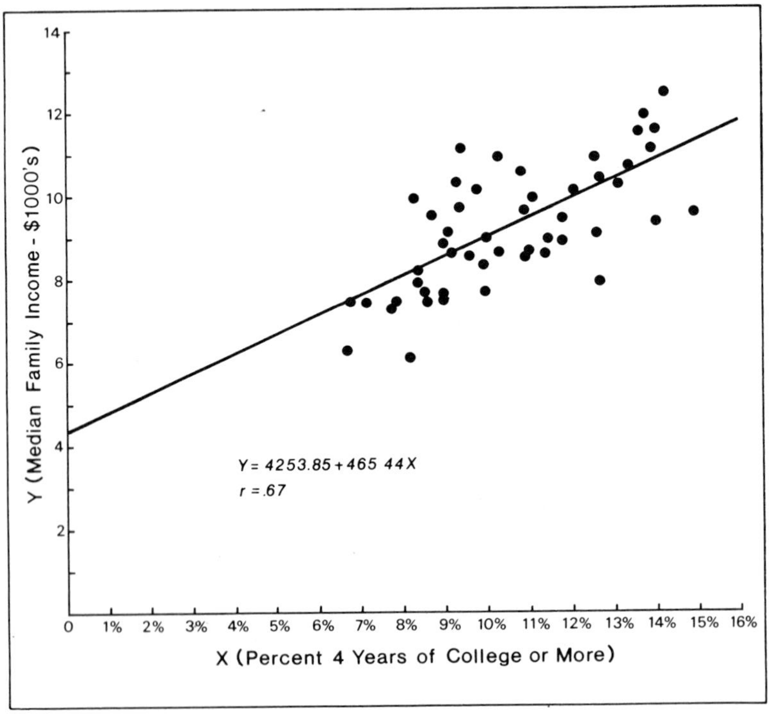

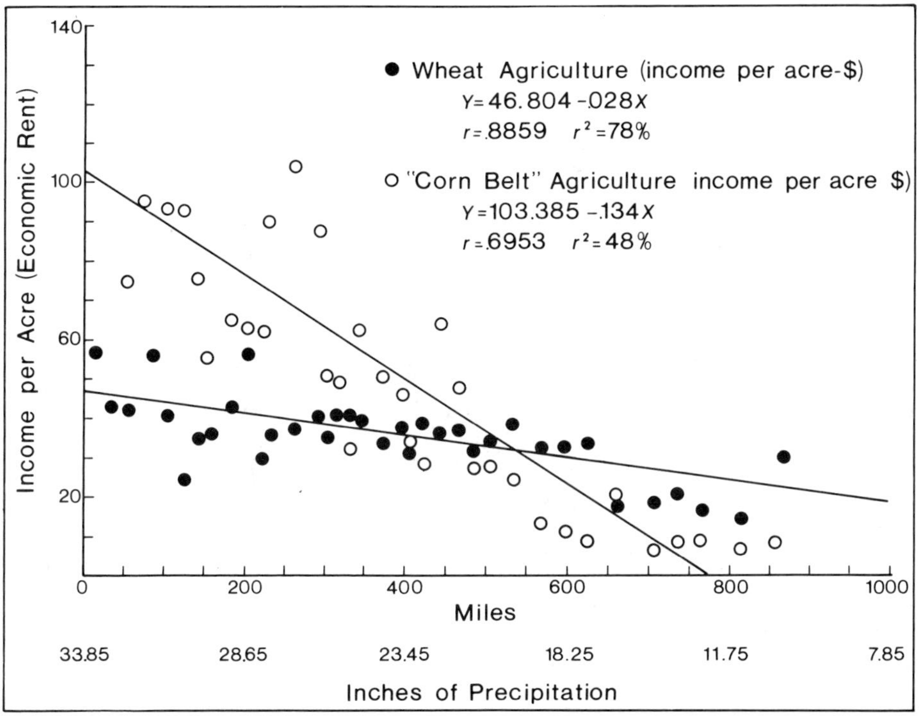

FIGURE 2.25 Regression lines for "Corn Belt" and wheat agriculture (income per acre and rainfall).

correlation based on rainfall and net income. If the major market for agricultural production in the United States were centered on Los Angeles and the eastern one-half of the country were sparsely populated, the fertility and distance axes would be opposed. Would agricultural patterns be different under those conditions than existing patterns?

Summary

We have considered the basic Thünen model that has been used by geographers to explain some agricultural land use patterns and have extended the model to deal with alternate explanations of the key variables controlling patterns of agriculture. The key concept of the chapter was *economic rent*. As long as we keep that concept in mind, an understanding of the agricultural space economy is possible, regardless of the particular model employed. We have not considered in detail the cultural and political forces that influence agricultural patterns. A complete understanding of agricultural patterns comes through a *total* consideration of economic, cultural, physical, and spatial factors.

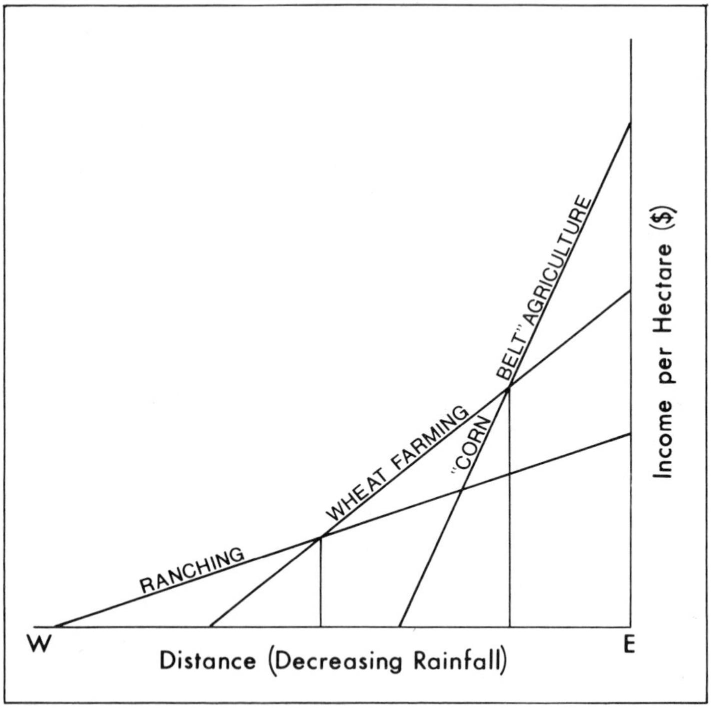

FIGURE 2.26 Three-crop fertility model for the United States (hypothetical).

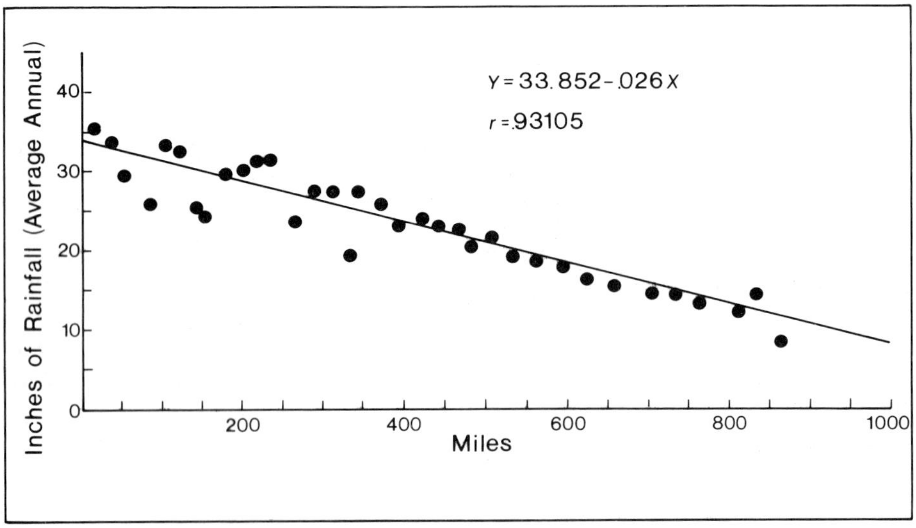

FIGURE 2.27 Regression line for distance and average annual rainfall.

KEY WORDS

average product
bid-rent curve
economic rent
extensive margin
isopleth
isotropic surface
intensive margin
marginal hectare
marginal product
optimizer
price elasticity
production function
slope
space-cost curve
spatial margin of production
stages of production
subsistence wage
Thünen rings
total product
Y-intercept

SUGGESTED READINGS

Basic Sources

Chisholm, M. (1962), *Rural Settlement and Land Use*. London: Hutchinson.

Dunn, E. S. (1954), *The Location of Agricultural Production,* Gainesville: University of Florida Press.

Found, W. C. (1971), *A Theoretical Approach to Rural Land Use Patterns,* Toronto: Macmillan.

Hall, P., ed. (1966), *Von Thünen's Isolated State,* London: Pergamon Press.

McCarty, H., and J. Lindberg (1966), *A Preface to Economic Geography,* Englewood Cliffs: Prentice-Hall.

Ricardo and Thünen

Blaug, M. (1968), *Economic Theory in Retrospect,* Homewood, Ill.: Richard D. Irwin.

Empirical Examples and Macro-Thünen Analysis

Harvey, D. (1963), "Locational Changes in the Kentish Hop Industry and the Analysis of Land Use Patterns," *Transactions* of the Institute of British Geographers **33**, 123–44.

Horvath, R. (1969), "Von Thünen and the Area Around Addis Ababa, Ethiopia," *Annals* of the Association of American Geographers **59**, 308–23.

Muller, P. (1973), "Trend Surface of American Agricultural Patterns: A Macro-Thünen Analysis," *Economic Geography* **45**, 228–42.

Peet, R. (1969), "The Spatial Expansion of Commercial Agriculture in the Nineteenth Century," *Economic Geography* **45**, 283–301.

Government Intervention

Abler, R., J. Adams, and P. Gould (1971), *Spatial Organization,* Englewood Cliffs: Prentice-Hall, pp. 351–52.

Applications of Thünen to Urban Land Use

Sinclair, R. (1967), "Von Thünen and Urban Sprawl," *Annals* of the Association of American Geographers **57**, 72–87.

3 Retailing and Services

Introduction

Agriculture requires large amounts of space and a dispersed pattern of population. Agriculture is an *areal* activity. The provision of goods and services, on the other hand, must take place at points to be efficient and requires distinct clusters of population (settlements). Retailing and services are *punctiform* activities. A large number of goods and services offered at a single point reduces the aggregate distance a consumer must travel to satisfy needs and wants. A number of goals can be accomplished in a single trip.

The Thünen model dealt with dispersed farmers who sold their agricultural output in a settlement (market). The isolated city, in turn, provided the surrounding agricultural hinterland with manufactured goods, services, and other commodities not locally produced. The city became a distribution point for retailing and services. Farmers traveled to the market, not only to sell their agricultural output, but also to purchase needed goods and services.

What is the optimum pattern of these distribution points? What arrangement of settlements will minimize the distance consumers must travel for goods and services? Is there evidence of an efficient settlement pattern in reality? The body of knowledge that considers these questions is called *central place theory*. First proposed by Walter Christaller in 1933, it has been extensively added to by subsequent theorists such as Lösch (1954) and a number of American geographers (especially Berry and Garrison).

The settlement in the Thünen model was supported solely by trade with the surrounding agricultural hinterland. A central place is, in a strictly technical sense, a settlement supported only by this kind of trade, but this definition will be relaxed to include any settlement that trades with the surrounding area. The population of a true central place is then dependent upon the size of the trade area it can capture. The greater the size of the trade area, the greater the sales of the town and the more people who can find employment in retailing and services.

Settlements exist by trading with their hinterland and other areas. Sales totally within the hinterland we shall call *settlement-forming* trade. A true central place is based exclusively on these functions and can never support a population that transcends its hinterland. The number of jobs and, therefore, population is a direct function of the demand generated in the hinterland. Most settlements have other functions that are not dependent upon hinterland size. A manufacturing plant that sells to a national market, a town that has a major state university or is a county seat, or a resort settlement that attracts people from the entire nation provide examples of jobs that are not directly dependent upon the local retail and service hinterland. Such activity is called *settlement-building* trade. Each settlement also does some business with itself—goods and services sold to the residents of the center. This is usually called *settlement-serving* trade.

Central place theory deals with settlement-forming trade, the ideal arrangement of central places, and the patterns and sizes of trade hinterlands. The goods and services that make up this settlement-forming trade are collectively called *central functions*.

Chapter Objectives

Primary: Examine in detail classic central place theory as a model of the forces controlling the pattern of retailing and services.

Secondary:

1. Introduce the economic and locational principles necessary for understanding central place theory and its extensions.
2. Consider the relationships between central places and their hinterlands.
3. Develop ideal sizes and shapes of hinterlands.
4. Show the hierarchical patterns produced by the interlocking of hinterlands.
5. Discuss in detail the Christaller model and its modifications.
6. Present some empirical evidence of an organized central place hierarchy in the United States.

A Simple Model

The discussion of central place theory begins with a very simple normative model. As always, we must establish a set of conditions under which the model is meant to hold (domain). This set of conditions is almost identical to those of the Thünen model.

Constraints

1. An isotropic surface.
2. Transportation equally easy in all directions.
3. A uniform distribution of demand and population.
4. Settlements supported solely by trade with their hinterlands.
5. Producers and consumers with perfect knowledge who act with economic rationality; in short, they are optimizers.

For our initial model, we will also assume a *linear market* in which consumers are evenly distributed along a line. Imagine a road running across an isolated plain as in figure 3.1. All settlements (distribution points) are on the highway.

Given the above assumptions, how many settlements are required to serve the population? What size will their trade areas be? What is the ideal spacing of the distribution points? These are questions which we will investigate below.

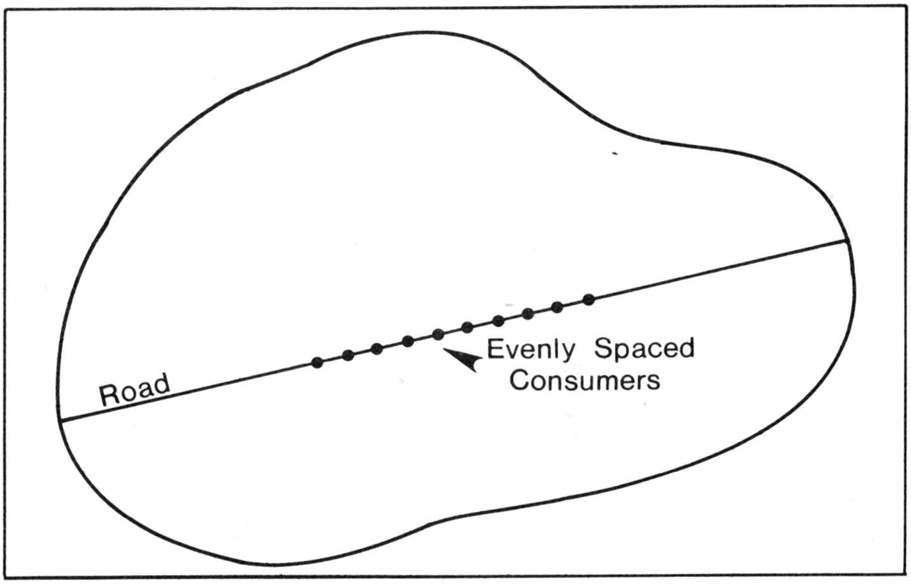

FIGURE 3.1 A linear market.

Thresholds

Suppose we want to offer a good (central function) at a point along the road. What will determine the success or failure of this attempt? We must sell enough of the good or service to meet operating costs and our "subsistence wage" (see chapter 2). This minimum amount of sales is called the *threshold* of a good and is one of the key concepts of central place theory. In the definition, the phrase "minimum level of demand'' is used, but given our constraint of evenly distributed population and demand, we can speak of a ''minimum number of *people*'' required to support a central function.

> *Threshold:* the minimum level of demand required to support a given central function.

The Range of a Good

The second key idea in central place theory is the *range of a good*. We sell our imaginary central function at a given price (P_1 in figure 3.2A). A consumer who

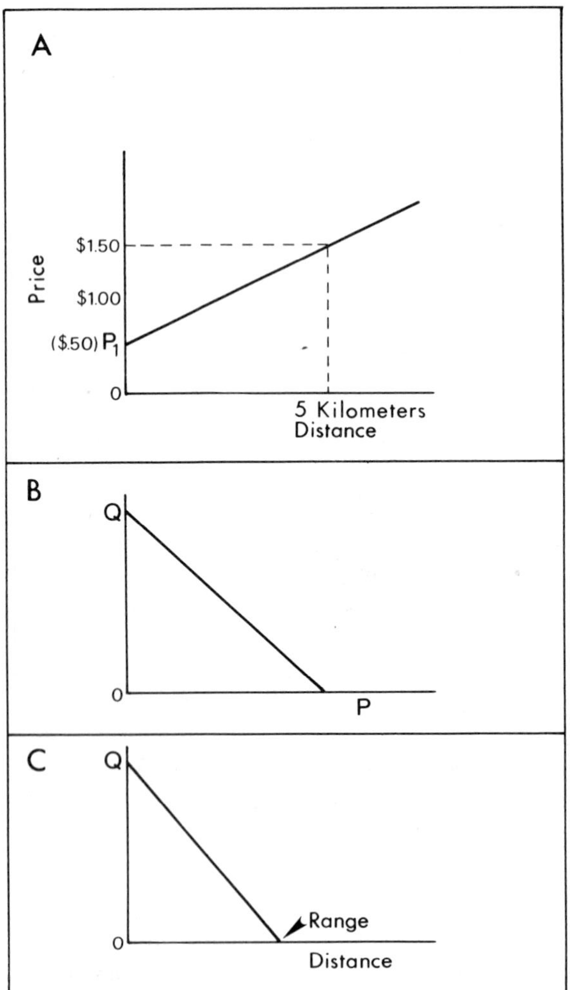

FIGURE 3.2 Price, demand and the range of a good.

lives next door to the store pays the store price. A consumer who lives at some distance from the marketplace must pay the store price *plus* the cost of travel to the settlement. If bread is 20¢ a loaf and travel costs are 10¢ per kilometer, a consumer who lives five kilometers from the store and makes a trip to buy a single loaf of bread pays $1.50 (figure 3.2A). The price a consumer pays is a direct function of distance as shown in figure 3.2A. In chapter 2, we introduced the idea of a demand curve; as the price of a good increases, the quantity demanded declines (figure 3.2B). Price increases with distance from a central place (settlement or distribution point) and demand declines with price; therefore, demand should decline with distance. We can find a distance (price) from the central place at which demand is zero. That point is the range of a good (figure 3.2C). The range of the good is the distance *R* in both directions from a distribution point on our linear market (figure 3.3A).

The threshold of a good can also be conceptualized as a distance (*T*) from a production point (figure 3.3B). The distance must be great enough to capture the customers required to meet the threshold. The most general statement that we can make about the goods and services offered on the landscape is that for each central function, $R \geq T$. This simple inequality is a necessary condition.

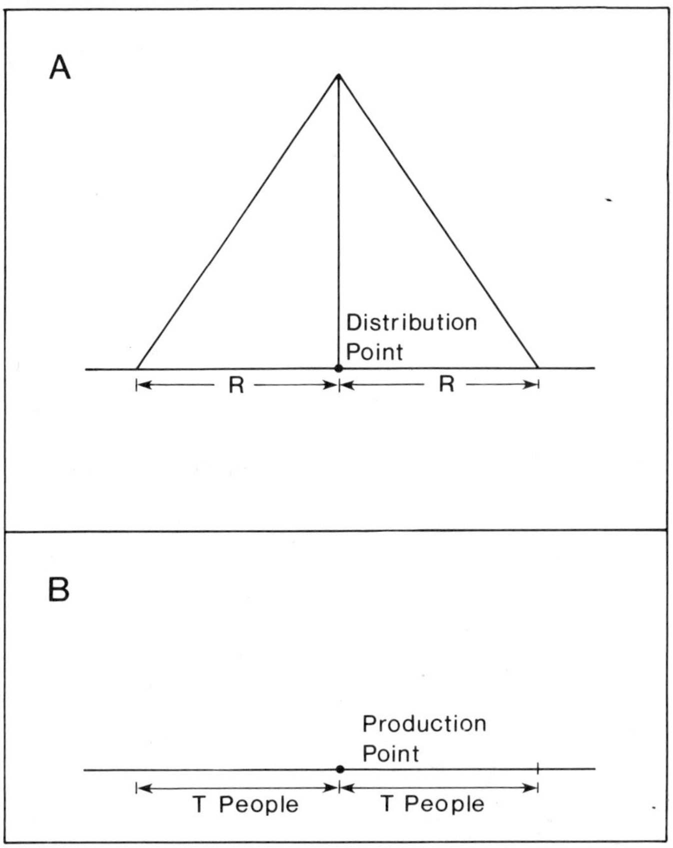

FIGURE 3.3 Range and threshold as distance.

The Order of a Good

Different goods can have different thresholds. Goods that are low in price, purchased frequently, and are short-run necessities (bread, beer, baby food, and toilet paper) will have low thresholds. Costly goods that are purchased infrequently will have higher thresholds (clothing, furniture). Goods with low thresholds are called *low-order* goods and *high-order* goods have high thresholds. We can order central functions on the basis of their threshold size. The highest order good has the largest threshold and the lowest order good has the smallest threshold. The goods in table 3.1 are ordered in this manner. The highest order good has a threshold of 1,000 and the lowest order good has a threshold of 1. We are assuming that 1,000 goods are represented in the table, each with a distinct threshold.

TABLE 3.1 Goods (threshold size)

1000, 999, 998, 997, . . ., 14, 13, 12, 11, 10, 9, 8, 7, 6, 5, 4, 3, 2, 1

The Order of a Center

Just as we can order goods (central functions), we can also speak of the *order of a center*. The order of a center is determined by the highest order good offered by the center. Low-order centers offer only low-order goods; high-order centers offer high-order goods, but they also offer lower-order goods. In table 3.1, a center that offers good 1,000 will offer all lower-order goods. If a center has a hinterland of 1,000 people (threshold of good 1,000), then it certainly meets the threshold of goods 999,998, . . ., 2, 1. A center whose highest order good has a threshold of 25 can offer only goods with a threshold of 25 or lower.

The Emergence of a Central Place Hierarchy

Given the above assumptions and definitions, how will the arrangement of central places be ordered? Assume that the highest order places—A-level (see table 3.2)—offer all goods from 1,000 to 1. The market area of each A-level place must contain at least 1,000 people (threshold of the highest order good). If there are 10,000 rural consumers along our imaginary linear market, ten A-level centers can be established. Two A-level centers and their market areas are shown in figure 3.4. We have

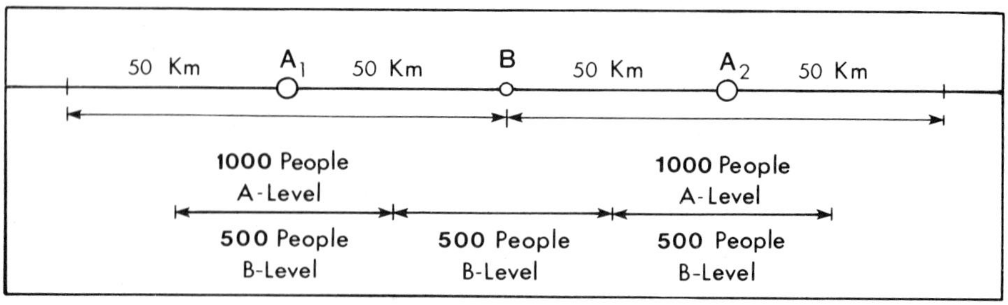

FIGURE 3.4 A $k = 2$ hierarchy.

assumed a population density of ten people per kilometer so that the minimum market area of each A-level center is 100 kilometers (50 kilometers on either side of each A-level center). We assume that competition forces market areas to be as small as possible (100 kilometers = 1,000 consumers). This minimizes the travel cost the most distant (from any A-level center) consumer must pay. A consumer on the dividing line between two A-level centers is indifferent. He will divide his purchases equally between the two centers. Settlements providing central functions are concentrated at a few points. Jobs in each settlement are directly dependent upon trade with the hinterland.

TABLE 3.2 Goods (threshold size)

centers	1000,	999,	998,	. . .	,502,	501,	500,	. . .	,252,	251,	250,	. . .	, 3,	2,	1
A	X	X	X	X	X	X	X	X	X	X	X	X	X	X	X
B							X	X	X	X	X	X	X	X	X
C											X	X	X	X	X

Consider table 3.2 again. The good that defines the A-level of the hierarchy has a threshold of 1,000, but we can find a good with a threshold of A/2 or 500. The threshold market area for that good is 50 kilometers in length (25 on each side of a distribution point). A market area of 500 centered on A_1 and A_2 allows an additional 500-person market area centered on the midpoint between the two A-level centers. A central place locating there can offer all goods with a threshold of 500 or less. This is the *B-level* and the good that defines the B-level has a threshold of 500 and is called a *hierarchical marginal good.*

> *Hierarchical marginal good:* the highest order good offered by a given level of the central place hierarchy. This good defines a level of the hierarchy and determines the total number of goods offered by centers of that level.

A consumer at P_1 (figure 3.5) will purchase B-level goods at B and A-level goods at A_1. Centers of a given level offer all the goods and services of lower levels plus a set of goods and services which defines the higher level. In our model, A-level centers offer all the goods found in B-level centers plus goods with thresholds from 501 to 1,000. It is this set of functions that defines the A-level.

What threshold size will define the C-level? The threshold value will be B/2 (250) and C-level centers squeeze in midway between higher-order centers (B and A_1, B and A_2). A-level centers are 100 kilometers apart. Suppose gas stations are D-level functions. There will be a settlement with a gas station every 12.5 kilometers along our imaginary road. The threshold that defines the D-level is C/2 or 125 people. This linear hierarchy follows the ''rule of 2's'' in that each successive level is defined by a function with a threshold one-half the size of the next highest hierarchical marginal good. The rule of 2's also applies to market area sizes and the spacing of centers. In central place theory, this type of hierarchy is known as a $k = 2$ hierarchy (k stands for the German word Konstant) in that 2 is the constant parameter of the system.

We have used the concepts of threshold and range logically to construct a hierarchy of central places given a very simple set of assumptions. The number of required centers is minimized, the number of consumers served is maximized, and the aggregate distance consumers must travel for a given set of functions is also minimized.

Higher order centers have larger populations than lower order centers because they can offer more functions and, therefore, employment. Higher order centers are also more widely spaced on the landscape, have larger market areas, and occur less frequently. We are now ready to consider the more complex hierarchies (two-dimensional) developed by Christaller and others.

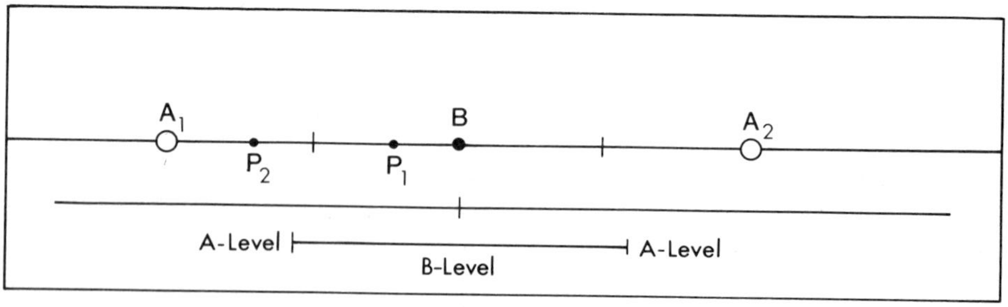

FIGURE 3.5 Shopping patterns.

The Christaller Central Place Model

Introduction

The foundations of central place theory were established in 1933 by Walter Christaller. Christaller attempted to construct a deductive theory to explain the size, number, and distribution of clusters of urban trades and institutions. The inspiration for his ideas was the work of economic location theorists such as Thünen, Alfred Weber, and German settlement geographer Robert Gradmann.

The Nature of Central Places

Christaller began his analysis by considering the nature of central places. The following summary abstracts the main points.

1. *Centralization as a Principle of Order* (Christaller 1966, pp. 14–16): "The crystallization of mass around a nucleus is 'an elementary form of order.' The same centralistic principle is found in some forms of human community life" (p. 14).

2. *Central Places* (pp. 16–17): Centralistic principles apply to towns as centers of regional communities and mediators of local commerce; they function as central settlements. Towns, like the regions surrounding them, may be of many sizes, shapes, and forms.

The best term to describe central settlements is central place. The word "place"

Walter Christaller, German geographer (1893–1969), said that his favorite "toy" as a child was an atlas, but it was not until his late thirties that he studied geography formally. He did much of his work at the University of Erlanger, where he studied under Robert Gradmann. In the early 1930s he wrote his doctoral dissertation and classic work, *The Central Places of Southern Germany*.

Christaller was regarded as a radical, and his ideas on the spatial structure of an economic system were accepted slowly in Western Europe and North America. In his later years he was awarded the gold medal from the King of Sweden, the highest geographical award that country can bestow, and the Association of American Geographers gave him their outstanding award *in absentia*. The United States government refused to give this outstanding geographer an entry visa because he was at one time a member of the Communist party.

is neutral, neither implying settlement units, nor political communities, nor economic units. "Thus *place* includes as far into the surrounding settlements as the inhabitants of those settlements exercise . . . central professions. The place may be larger or smaller than the settlement unit or community" (p. 17). Places with central functions extending over large regions are called higher order places. A large number of central places have only local significance for the immediate vicinity. They are called lower order central places.

3. *Importance and Centrality* (pp. 17–18): Population size and the importance of central places are not necessarily synonymous. This does not mean that there is a lack of correlation between the importance of a central place and the size of the region dominated by a center. The population of the hinterland indicates the relative importance of a central place. The "*centrality* of a place" means "the relative importance of a place with regard to the region surrounding it, to the degree to which the town exercises central functions" (p. 18). Thus, central places may have higher, lower, increasing, or decreasing centrality.

4. *Central Goods and Services* (pp. 19–21): The centrality of a place means that certain functions are performed, that certain goods are produced or offered for sale (central goods), and that certain services are rendered (central services). Central goods and services are produced and sold at a few points, but consumed at many scattered points. The importance of central places consists not so much in the production of goods as in the offering of goods and services. Least-cost locations of industries may not be found even in the larger central places.

5. *The Complementary Region* (pp. 21–22): The trading function of a place indicates its economic centrality, and the trading function ties a central place to its complementary region. The term "complementary region" carries with it the idea of the mutual dependence of a central place on its supporting region and the surrounding region on its center.

6. *The Economic Distance and the Range of a Good* (pp. 22–23): The size of a complementary region is fairly constant because its radius is a function of economic distance, a dimension ". . . determined by the costs of freight, insurance, and storage; time and loss of weight or space in transit; and as regards passenger travel,

the cost of transportation; the time required, and the discomfort of travel'' (p. 22). Economic distance determines the range of a good; that is, the maximum distance a dispersed population is willing to go in order to purchase a good offered at a central place.

Christaller argued that the attraction of a central place for a surrounding population does not depend completely on distance. It also depends on the variety, quality, and price of goods and services. But the range and variety of goods depends upon receipts business people expect to obtain from sales. If effective demand for a particular good is too small to guarantee a satisfactory income, the good will not be offered for sale. For Christaller the density of population is critical in determining the variety of central place functions. Effective demand for a good or a service depends on consumer incomes and tastes. These factors led Christaller to conclude that ''. . . consumption of central goods is decisive in the development of central places'' (p. 35).

Assumptions

Christaller argued that it was unnecessary to begin his analysis of hierarchies of central places with a description of reality. He controlled complexities of the real world with simplifying assumptions which we have introduced. Unlike our initial model, the landscape considered by Christaller is two-dimensional.

Hierarchical Interrelations

To demonstrate hierarchical interrelations between central places in an economic landscape, Christaller constructed three geometric models. Central places are arranged according to marketing, transport, and administrative principles. According to Christaller, the three principles establish, each according to their own laws, the most favorable systems of central places.

The Marketing Principle

The marketing principle assumes the largest provision of central-place goods and services from the minimum number of central places. This form of spatial organization can be seen in figure 3.6 which shows a two-level hierarchy of central places and their complementary regions. In figure 3.6 each B-level center is located midway between three neighboring centers of the next highest order. Midway points are corners of hexagonal complementary regions of the next highest order. Each higher order place is surrounded by six places of the next lowest order.

Figure 3.7 illustrates the progression of central places and market areas for a three-level hierarchy. The market area of each A-level center passes through six lower order centers (B-level). A-level market areas are *three* times larger than B-level market areas. In figure 3.7 each A-level market area includes all of the B-level market area centered on an A-level center plus one-third of the six surrounding B-level market areas (⅓ of 6 = 2 + 1 = 3). Distances separating places at the same level of the hierarchy are the same. If lower order central places are located 1

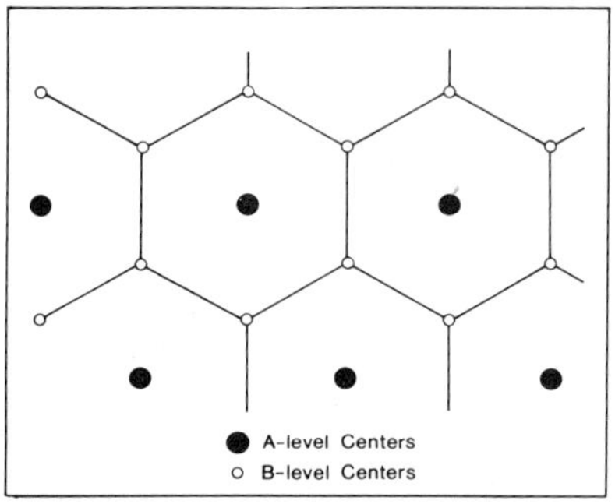

FIGURE 3.6 Location of centers: $k = 3$ hierarchy.

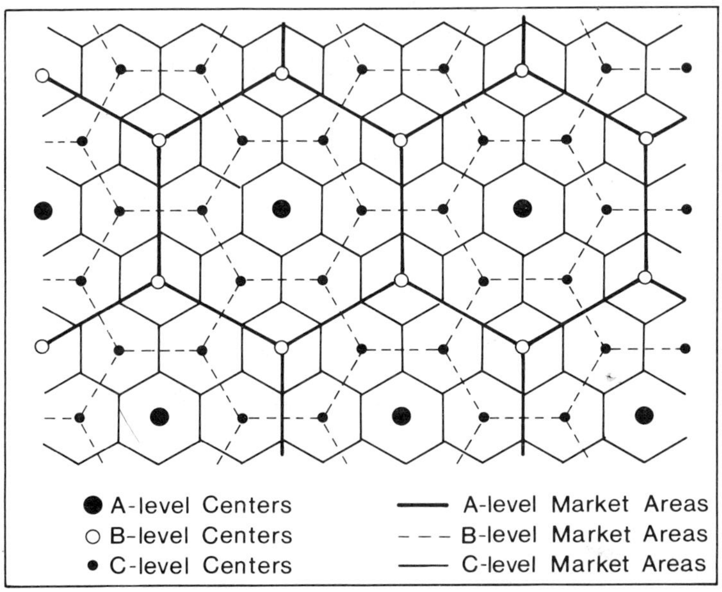

FIGURE 3.7 Market areas: $k = 3$ hierarchy.

unit apart, then rival higher order central places, serving three times the area and three times the population, are located $\sqrt{3.1}$ units apart or 1.732 units apart. This kind of arrangement of central places is a $k = 3$ network. The number of complementary regions at successively less specialized levels of the $k = 3$ hierarchy progresses by the rule of 3's; that is, market areas increase geometrically: 1, 3, 9, 27.

Christaller argued that the system of central places developed on the basis of the range of a good is rational and efficient from an economic point of view. Yet he noted that the $k = 3$ model is imperfect because of distortions. Deviations under actual conditions include those caused by historical circumstance, economic characteristics such as income, and geographical conditions such as variations in topography.

The best geometry of market areas on an isotropic surface is a regular hexagon. Circular market areas either leave some consumers unserved or they overlap. Hexagons "tile" space more efficiently than any other geometric form. The size of a given market-area hexagon in the normative case is just large enough to capture the threshold population for that particular level in the hierarchy.

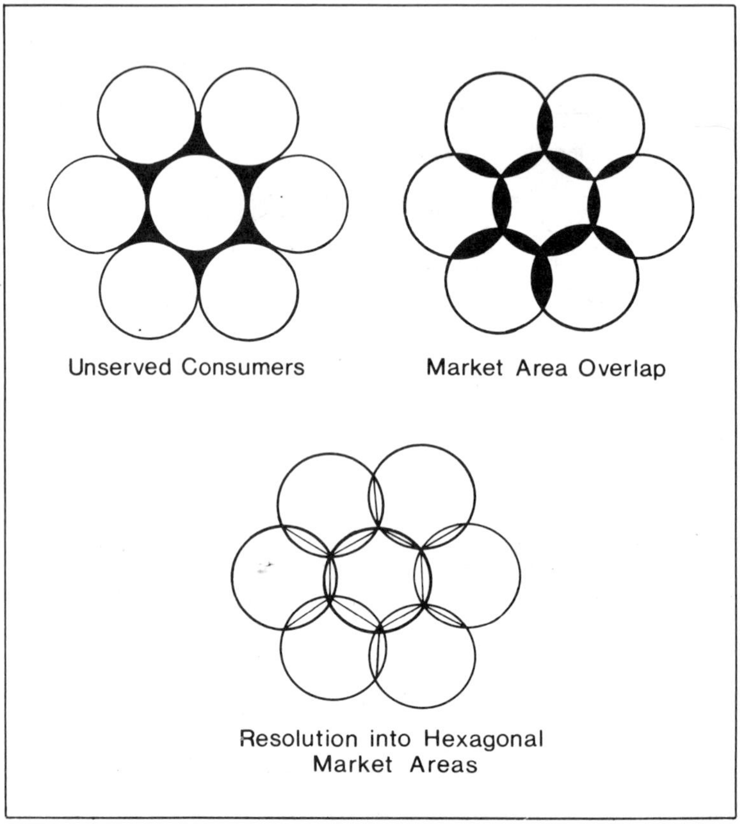

The Traffic Principle

Figure 3.8 shows a $k = 3$ (marketing) hierarchy on which an optimum road network has been drawn. One of our original constraints assumed equally easy transportation in all directions, but a road network produces a linear structure of transportation and amplifies the development of the hierarchy in certain directions. We assume that optimizers will build optimum transportation networks. Straight-line roads are possible on an isotropic surface and minimize the length of road to be constructed between any two points. We also assume that the highest order centers will be the first priority of connection producing the triangular lattice of figure 3.8. Notice, however, that the B-level centers do not lie on the A-level road network. More miles of road must be constructed if the B-level centers are to be connected. How can connectivity be *maximized* and network length *minimized?*

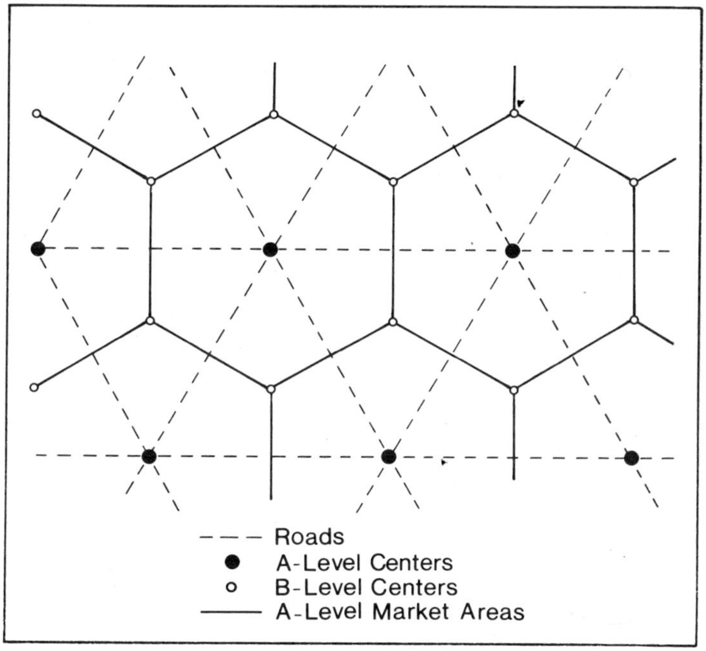

FIGURE 3.8 Optimum transportation net: maximum connectivity for A-level centers ($k = 3$).

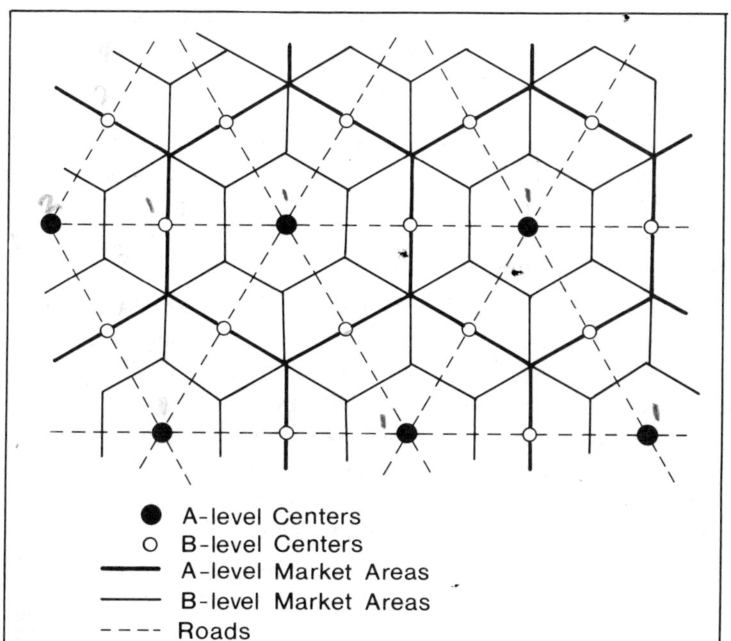

FIGURE 3.9 A $k = 4$ hierarchy.

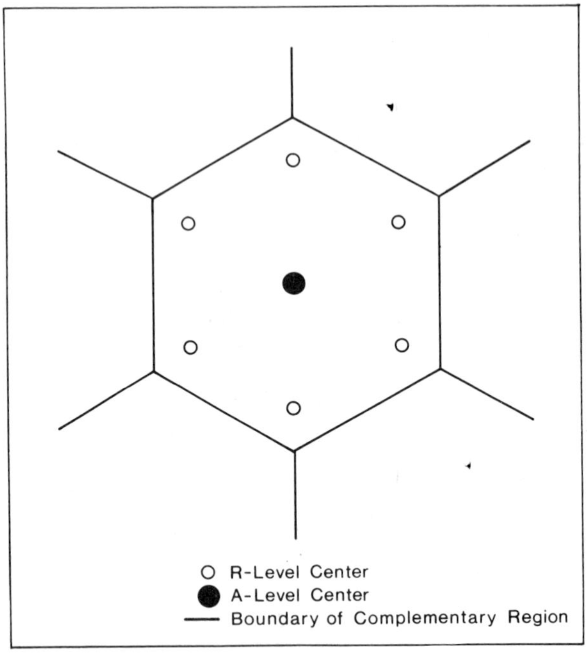

FIGURE 3.10 Two-level hierarchy of central places under the administrative principle.

The B-level centers have been shifted to a point *midway* between each pair of A-level centers in figure 3.9. This arrangement maximizes connectivity (all lower order centers are also on the net) and minimizes network length. The constant value of the hierarchy, however, must be changed with the new pattern of centers. A $k = 4$ hierarchy results when we attempt to maximize a transportation system. The B-level market areas in figure 3.9 are *one-fourth* the size of the A-level market areas. Each A-level market area serves all of the B-level area centered on it plus *one-half* of the surrounding six (three) for a total of four.

The Administrative Principle

The administration principle is based on political rather than economic consideration. It assumes a clear-cut separation of complementary regions and is achieved when each central place controls six dependent centers (figure 3.10). Complementary regions nest according to a rule of 7's ($k = 7$). In the $k = 7$ hierarchy the progression of complementary regions is 1, 7, 49, 343. Complementary regions in the $k = 7$ hierarchy are larger than in either $k = 3$ or $k = 4$ systems, which means that consumers must travel farther to reach a center of a given level in the system. Assume that B-level complementary regions are low level political units (townships) and the A-level complementary region is a higher order political unit (county). For administration, the *entire area* of each low order unit must be included within the area of the higher order unit.

Southern Germany

Christaller tested his central place model in Southern Germany. An important question for Christaller was how to determine the centrality of a place. A list of functions, grouped according to grade, does not give an adequate measure of centrality. Christaller sought to quantify the importance of central places precisely. Telephone connections provided Christaller with the best readily available measure of relationships between places.

> If we say that importance equals the number of telephone connections, then we might say: In a region of 4,000 inhabitants there are 100 telephone connections . . . ; in the central place of a region with 2,000 inhabitants, there should, therefore, be 50 telephone connections for satisfying the local demand of the central population. But if there are 80 connections in the central place, the surplus importance of the central place will be: 80 − 50 = 30 connections. The importance of the dispersed places of the region (with 2000 inhabitants living dispersedly) should be 50 telephone connections.

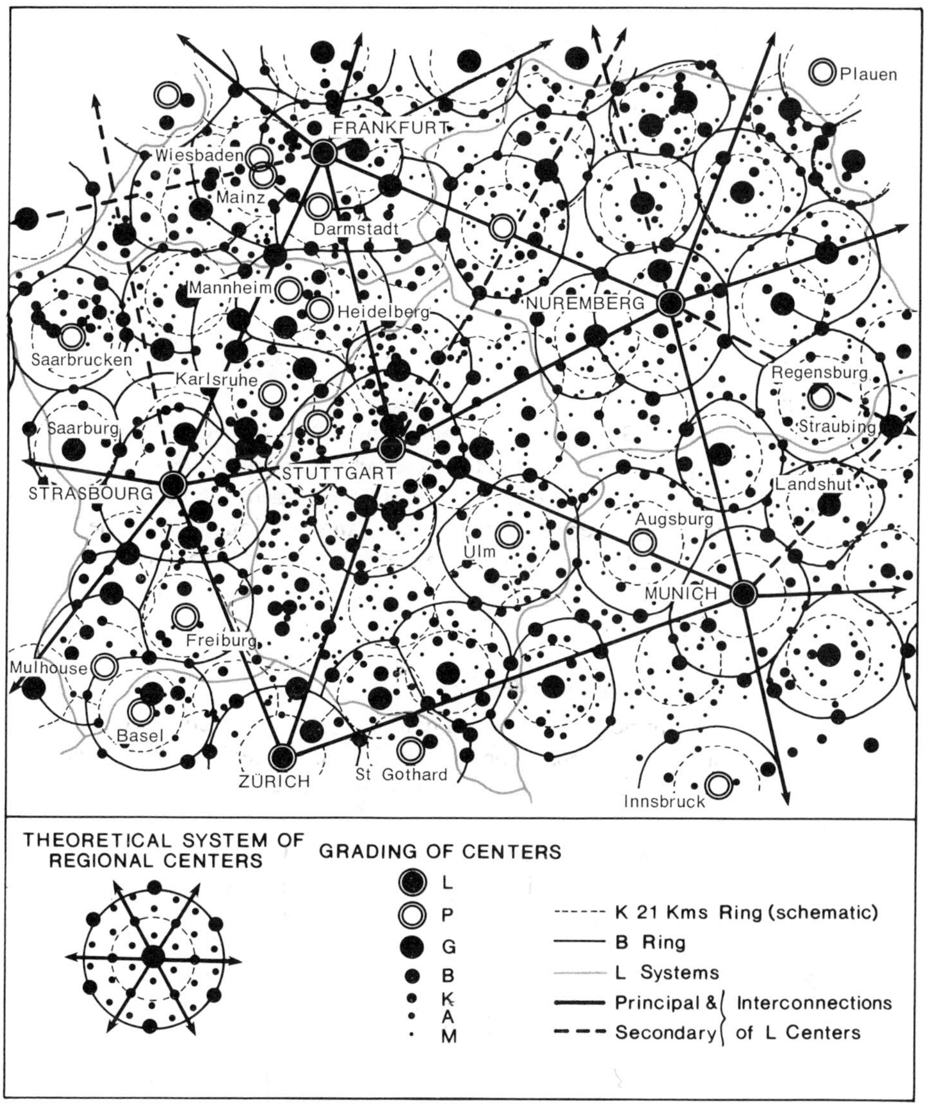

FIGURE 3.11 The distribution of central places in South Germany.[From R. E. Dickinson (1964) *City and Region,* London: Routledge and Kegan Paul, p. 75, fig. 3.]

> But if there are only 20 connections in the dispersed places, the importance deficit will be 30. Hence the importance deficit of the dispersed places is balanced by the importance surplus of the central place. (p. 147)

Christaller's formula for the centrality of a place (that is, the goods provided above local needs of its inhabitants) is:

$$Zz = Tz - Ez\left(\frac{Tg}{Eg}\right)$$

where

Tz = the number of telephone connections at the central place,
Ez = the number of inhabitants of the central place,
and Tg and Eg = the number of telephones and inhabitants of the region respectively.

The expression Ez (Tg/Eg) is what the importance of the center is expected to be in proportion to its population, and Tz is the actual importance. The difference between the expected and the actual importance of a central place is what Christaller termed the "importance-surplus" or the centrality. Thus, Tg/Eg is the telephone density of the entire region.

From this assessment emerged a ranking of central places. The theoretical distribution for central places according to the marketing principle is summarized in table 3.3. Christaller claimed that figures computed for Southern Germany were also typical for most of Germany and western Europe. The hierarchy of central places has seven levels ranging from market hamlet (Markort) to regional capital city (Landeshaupstadt). Sizes of complementary regions and distances separating central places increase at successively higher levels of the hierarchy. Centers at each level of the hierarchy serve three times the area (column 4) and three times the population (column 5). The distance between similar centers increases by $\sqrt{3}$ over the preceding smaller category (column 2). In the table, the smallest centers are located about seven kilometers apart, because four to five kilometers, roughly a one hour walking distance, corresponded to the complementary area for the smallest centers. Centers of the next order of specialization, township centers, are located 12 kilometers apart or $\sqrt{3.7}$.

The actual distribution of cities, towns, and villages in South Germany is shown in figure 3.11. Networks of central places nest within the complementary regions of Landeshaupstadts. The Landeshaupstadts consist of Munich, Frankfurt, Stuttgart, and Nuremburg, together with the border cities of Strasbourg, France and Zürich, Switzerland.

Christaller found that the expected pattern was approached best in poor, thinly settled farm districts that were virtually self-contained. Deviations from the rational pattern were not common in many parts of South Germany. Discrepancies were noted in other parts of Germany, however. The theoretical ideal, for example, was not found in the highly industrialized Rhine-Ruhr.

TABLE 3.3 The urban hierarchy in South Germany

Central Place (1)	Towns: Distance Apart (2)	Towns: Population (3)	Tributary Areas: Size (Sq. km) (4)	Tributary Areas: Population (5)
Market hamlet (Markort)	7	800	45	2,700
Township center (Amtsort)	12	1,500	135	8,100
County seat (Kreistadt)	21	3,500	400	24,000
District city (Bezirksstadt)	36	9,000	1,200	75,000
Small state capital (Gaustadt)	62	27,000	3,600	225,000
Provincial head city (Provinzhaupstadt)	108	90,000	10,800	675,000
Regional capital city (Landeshaupstadt)	186	300,000	32,400	2,025,000

Source: E. L. Ullman (1941), *American Journal of Sociology* **46**, 857.

Extensions of the Christaller Model

Lösch's Economic Landscape

Following Christaller's original model there have been several attempts to modify and elaborate his ideas, one of the most interesting being the scheme proposed by a

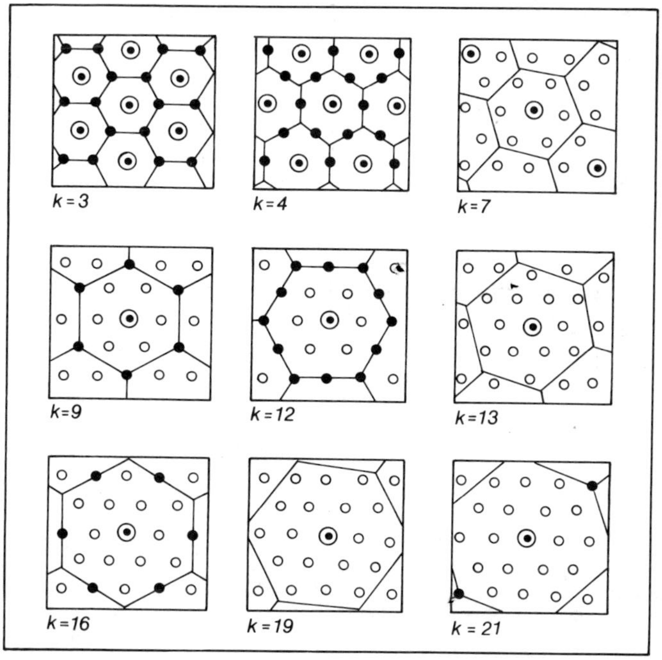

FIGURE 3.12 Nine smallest market areas in a Löschian landscape. [From Peter Haggett (1965) *Locational Analysis in Human Geography*, London: Edward Arnold, p. 119, fig. 5.4.]

fellow German, August Lösch (1906–45), in *The Economics of Location*. His work on the nature of economic regions was based on classical economic theory. He also concluded that the hexagon is the most economical shape for economic areas. Lösch's main contribution, however, was to extend Christaller's fixed assumptions of the marketing, traffic, and administrative principles which he regarded as interesting, but special limited cases.

Lösch produced a more comprehensive and flexible system of central places by changing the orientation and size of his hexagonal economic areas. Figure 3.12 shows the nine smallest hexagonal territories in a Löschian landscape. They have k-values of 3, 4, 7, 9, 12, 13, 16, 19, and 21. In this diagram, central places with specialized production sites are shown by double circles, dependent places are shown by open circles if they lie within the field of a central place, and by closed circles if they lie on the edge of a hexagonal field.

Although both Christaller and Lösch used hexagonal fields as basic units in their economic landscapes, there is a difference between them in the way they combined market areas. Christaller built his hierarchies from top to bottom: market areas descend in size from a large region dominated by a metropolitan center that can

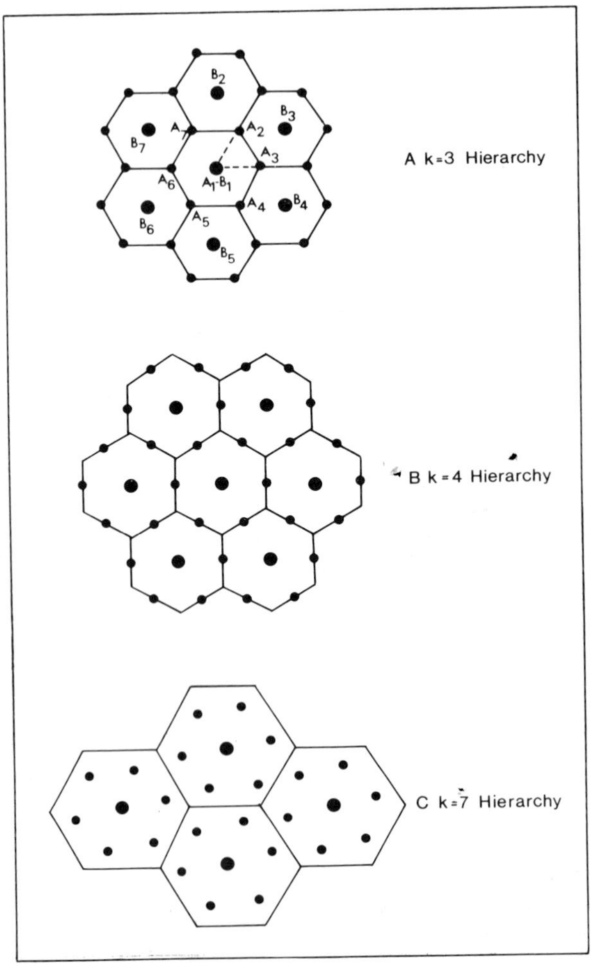

FIGURE 3.13 Lösch's basic market areas.

support the most "national commodity" (highest threshold) to an area so small in size and population that it can just support the most "local commodity" (lowest threshold). Lösch developed his central place hierarchy from the opposite point of view. He considered first the good with the smallest market area, and then added other goods with successively larger market areas.

Basic Market Areas Lösch started his analysis with the ideal region. He said: "The ideal region is both the only way to learn about the *essential*, and the first step towards investigating the *actual* structure of any real economic region" (1938, p. 107). Lösch developed his model under assumptions of an isotropic surface and the supposition of a uniform product.

Lösch assumed an economic landscape of local self-sufficient farmsteads, and then developed the three smallest market areas. The smallest of these hexagonal areas is shown in figure 3.13. Let us suppose, Lösch said, that a farmer at A_1 produces a commodity beyond his needs and sells the surplus at either farmstead A_2 or A_3. The result is a triangular market area. If A_1, helped by economies of large-scale production, increases output it may become a central place (B_1), and the farmer sells the output in a hexagon consisting of six triangles. The market area of B_1 could be expanded by invading the market areas of neighboring centers B_2 through B_7, either by rotating the hexagon around B_1 (figure 3.13B) or by rotating and enlarging the hexagon so that it runs through open countryside without touching any settlement (figure 3.13C).

The nest of the three smallest market area sizes all centered on the highest order central place is shown in figure 3.14. These market area sizes correspond to $k = 3$, 4, and 7 nets. Lösch suggested that these market areas are only the smallest in an infinite series. By rotating and enlarging hexagons again and again, successive market area sizes with k values of 9,12,13,16,19,21, and 25 can be derived. Figure

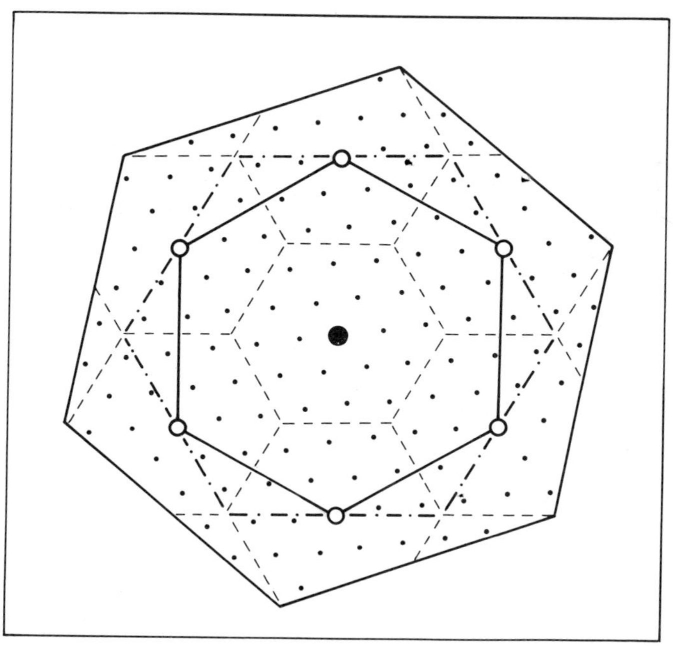

FIGURE 3.14 The nest of Lösch's three smallest market areas.

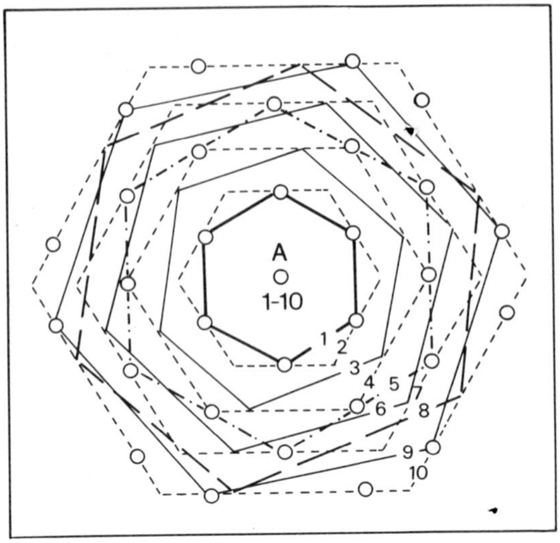

FIGURE 3.15 Network of ten common-centered market areas.

3.15 illustrates the arrangement of all ten hexagonal nets rotated around the metropolis (A). Lösch argued that not all ten market area sizes are possible. Solutions that do not share markets, such as $k = 7,13$, and 19, are very efficient. They are more likely to occur in practice than others, such as $k = 12$. Thus, in a Löschian landscape there is a discontinuous series of central place solutions, because of variations in the efficiencies of these solutions.

Lösch paid special attention to states of conditional equilibrium. By "conditions of location equilibrium" Lösch meant the forces that account for the location of economic activity. He explained that "nature works according to laws, but man acts according to his *idea* of laws. In other words, nature *must*, man *may*, act correctly. In order to do so, he must have some conception of how he shall act. As to economic equilibrium this means that *in order to guide his* activities he needs insight into the conditions of equilibrium" (1954, p. 93). There is an equilibrium of central place locations for independent producers and consumers when five conditions are met:

1. locations for trading establishments must be as advantageous as possible;
2. locations for trading establishments must be so numerous that the entire space is filled (establishes the shape of market areas—hexagons);
3. excess profits for trading establishments must disappear;
4. areas of supply, production, and sales must be as small as possible (establishes the *size* of market areas);
5. at the boundary of market areas it does not matter to which of two neighboring areas a producer or consumer belongs.

Since the size of a market area required for a trading establishment to survive differs from one good to another, the result is a complex nest of common-centered hexagonal market areas (figure 3.15).

City-Rich and City-Poor Sectors By rotating all the possible hexagonal nets around the metropolis, Lösch obtained the maximum coincidence or agglomeration of production locations, the maximization of the amount of purchases made locally,

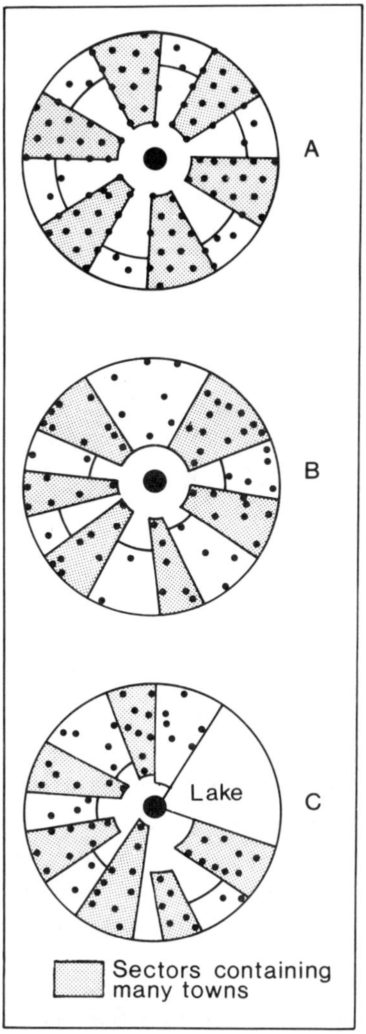

FIGURE 3.16 Lösch's economic landscapes. [From August Lösch (1954) *The Economics of Location,* Stuttgart: Gustav Fischer Verlag, p. 125.]

and the minimization of total distance between production points. The result is shown in figure 3.16A. The pattern consists of 12 alternating city-rich (or production rich) and city-poor (or production poor) sections. The arrangement of linear clusters of central places conformed with what Lösch regarded as a major characteristic of human spatial organization: the principle of least effort. Lösch provided some evidence that sectors are approximated in the real world for the environs of Indianapolis and Toledo (figure 3.16 B and C).

Figure 3.17 represents the location and functions of central places in one 60° sector radiating from the metropolis (A). Only the metropolis produces all goods. The goods provided by the metropolis in ascending order of specialization are 1,2,3,4, ... 15, and they require market areas 1,3,4,9,12,13,16,19,21, and 25 times the size of the smallest hexagon. Every lowest order central place provides the lowest order good, designated by the number 1, but there is considerable variation

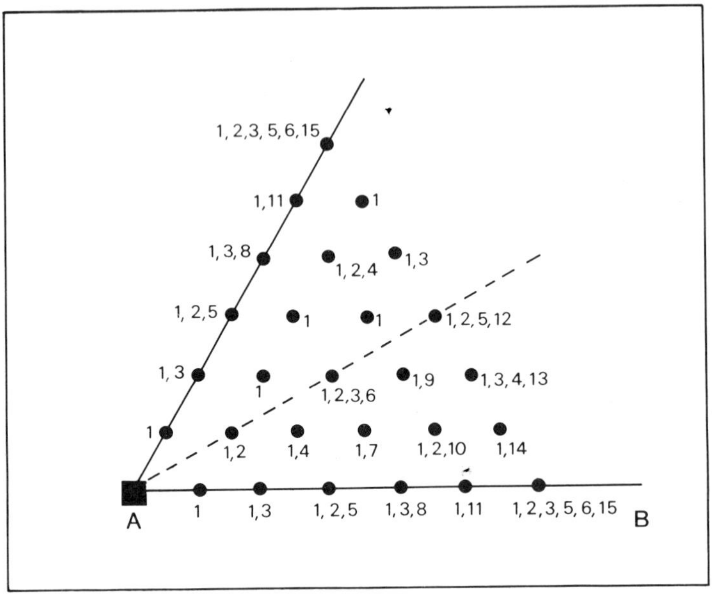

FIGURE 3.17 Size, spacing, and functional structure of central places in one 60° sector of a Löschian economic landscape.

in the incidence of functions provided by higher order centers. Reading along the transect from A to B, goods provided by central places beyond the metropolis are: 1; 1,3; 1,2,5; 1,3,8; 1,11; 1,2,3,5,6,15. This transect shows that as distance from the metropolis increases, the importance of larger centers increases.

Economic Regions in Reality Lösch considered limitations of theory when analyzing the actual economic landscape. In the theoretical model, he postulated three types of economic regions: market areas, regional networks, and regional systems. These three regional types are increasingly complicated, self-sufficient, and, most important, increasingly rare in the real world.

Lösch noted that when the assumption of an isotropic plain is relaxed and the supposition of a uniform product is dropped, single product market areas overlap and are irregular in size and shape. Regional networks of markets are likely to occur in belts or zones. Lösch argued that regional systems differ most of all from the theoretical model. Discrepancies between theory and reality exist because economic landscapes are the product of a historical process. Disturbed patterns of central places are sometimes the result of concentration and resource irregularities. In the real world one can expect neither an economically self-sufficient landscape, nor a metropolis which produces and supplies everything. The largest center in an economic region may not possess all the functions that the complementary region demands. Consequently, many goods are exchanged between economic regions. Within an economic region, several eccentrically located major cities may exist, especially in highly industrialized areas.

Lösch concluded that the economic landscape is anything but simple; it may even appear chaotic. An "economic landscape is a system of different markets; an organism, not merely an organ" (1954, p. 219).

Christaller and Lösch Compared

Christaller and Lösch agreed that the triangular pattern of settlement distribution and hexagonal-shaped market areas represent the optimal spatial organization for a single good under the constraint of uniform population densities on an unbounded plain. They agreed on three major concepts of central place theory: range, threshold, and hierarchy.

Yet Christaller and Lösch part company when they developed their central place systems. As we have seen, they developed their economic landscapes from different starting points. Christaller built his hierarchy from the highest order good downwards, and Lösch built his from the ubiquitous good upwards. It appears that Christaller's procedure for deriving his system provides a framework for the analysis of an economic landscape founded in an area of sparse settlement, and that Lösch's method provides a better framework for the analysis of a landscape in a region of dense, long-established settlement undergoing change. Furthermore, Christaller's system sheds light on the distribution of retailing and service activities especially for agricultural regions, and Lösch's system appears more relevant to an understanding of the distribution of market-oriented manufacturing activities.

The Löschian hierarchy of central places is quite different from that developed by Christaller. Christaller's formulation consists of a number of tiers in which all places at the same level of the hierarchy are the same size and have the same kinds of functions, and all places on a given hierarchical level contain all the goods of smaller central places. Lösch's formulation is less rigid. It consists of a more continuous distribution of central places. Cities of the same size do not necessarily perform the same functions, and larger cities, as in reality, do not take on all those found in smaller cities.

A major purpose of Christaller's analysis was to show that there are economic ways of developing rational arrangements of central places and that there are wasteful ways. He had a strong desire to put his theory to work. More than one-third of his publications were devoted to ways in which settlement patterns could be made to fit the requirements of his model.

Lösch was not bent on trying to persuade planners to adopt his ideas. His main object was to explain the complexities of economic regions. He attempted to show the ideal relations between central places and their complementary regions. He did this by superimposing all possible hexagonal solutions in a regional system, which is a formulation quite different from Christaller's three separate, conflicting hierarchical principles. Lösch stated, but did not elaborate, the conditions of location equilibrium, and thus stipulated the conditions under which a network of hexagons and a spatial structure would develop.

To summarize the discussion of Christaller and Lösch, researchers have claimed that their models are essentially descriptive, static, and not necessarily a mirror of reality. They view Lösch's system as more comprehensive than Christaller's, but difficult to verify by reference to empirical fact. Certainly the rather simple, more elegant Christaller model has been more susceptible to empirical analysis.

Some geographers assert that classical central place theory is a deductive base from which to understand the location of tertiary economic activity, and, more generally, of settlement location as an economic process. Others disagree, and note certain inadequacies. Formulations of Christaller and Lösch, for example, developed on the basis of classical economic theory, ignore nonoptimal consumer behavior. Christaller and Lösch did not explain the historical process of developing capitalism as the framework within which settlements become centers of dominance. Furthermore, it is said that their models deal essentially with closed, local economic systems. Thus, central place theory can deal only with relationships between retailers and consumers within a region. It cannot deal with settlement patterns that have grown out of long-distance trading connections between regions. Nonetheless, their models provide many insights into the relationship between settlement formation and economic growth. The inadequacies cited do not invalidate discussions of classical central place theory, which is concerned primarily with the location of retailers and service centers in a closed geographical system.

Isard's Modifications

Walter Isard (*Location and Space Economy*) criticized the equal-area pattern of hexagons used by Christaller and Lösch. Regular hexagons, he said, are unlikely to occur in practice because of urbanization economies or economies of urban concentration. These are savings in production costs obtained when activities agglomerate or cluster around a point. They include access to a larger market, the concentration of commercial, banking, and financial facilities, the development of urban labor markets, and communication savings such as opportunities for face-to-face contact with specialist services.

Isard rejected Lösch's method of depicting the impact of urbanization economies. He objected to Lösch's system of nets of market areas: it assumes a uniform distribution of consuming population, and yet it permits different sizes of concentration of secondary and tertiary activities in six city-poor and six city-rich sectors, and along main transport lines. Isard argued that it was necessary to modify Lösch's hexagonal network to conform to the underlying population pattern. As a consequence of the relatively high density of population at the central core or metropolis implied in the Löschian system, the size of hexagons needed to meet the threshold for a commodity is likely to be smaller at the core and larger toward the periphery.

Isard produced a diagram (figure 3.18) which retains as many of Lösch's assumptions as possible, and illustrates a distorted hexagonal network of market areas decreasing in size toward the main core. The diagram also depicts a secondary core at which business activities and population are concentrated. Isard pointed out that it was extremely difficult to work with hexagonal forms and, as figure 3.18 shows, "the hexagon loses much of its significance as a spatial form once agglomeration forces are admitted, and . . . inequalities in population distribution recognized" (1956, p. 274). The hexagon is a pure concept for geographers much as perfect competition is a pure concept for economists. A framework free of hexagonal geometry provides a more realistic basis for understanding the forces that affect locations of production sites and retail stores.

Locations of main traffic arteries are quite different from those in Lösch's system. Isard located major transport routes through the center of sectors, not along their boundaries. Isard's arrangement of transport lines is logical. It illustrates the importance of urbanization economies and the effects of modern modes of transportation. In order to avoid complications, he did not locate a hierarchical array of satellite centers along transport lines. For examples of patterns of secondary and

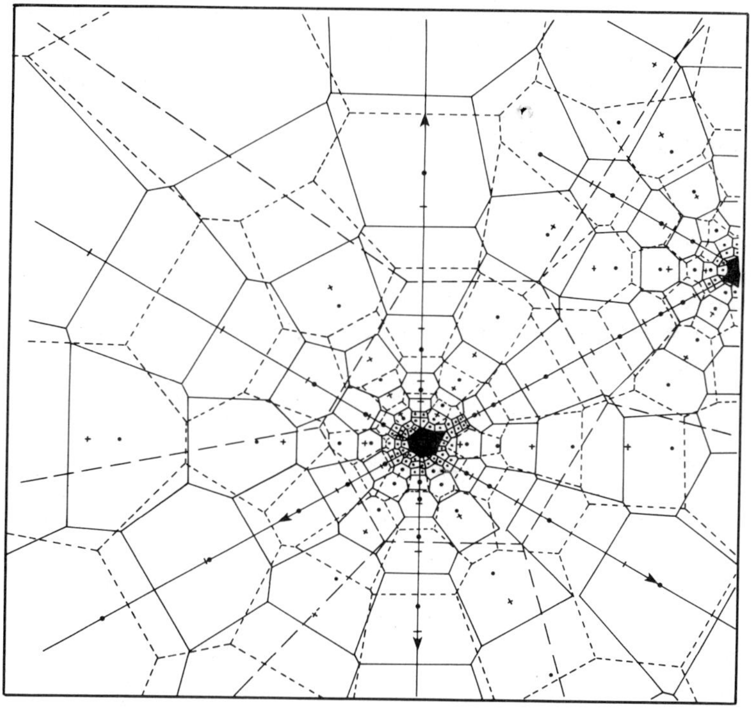

FIGURE 3.18 Isard's landscape modification. [From W. Isard (1956) *Location and Space Economy*, Cambridge, Mass.: M.I.T. Press, p. 272, fig. 52. Reprinted by permission of The M.I.T. Press, Cambridge, Mass.]

satellite centers, he referred readers to population and land use maps around major metropolitan areas.

Wholesaling and the Mercantile Model of Settlement

The argument that central place theory is a "special case" is presented by Vance (1970). He said, if parochialism is the rule, central place theory suffices as an explanation for the trading-settlement structure of an area. Central place theory deals with relationships between customers and sellers of goods and services *within* regions. It does not account for wholesale trade that links regions. Wholesaling which involves the sale of goods from one entrepreneur to another is conducted primarily between higher order centers (then filters down to lower order centers), and their locational patterns are influenced by *external* trade linkages. In addition, local settlement hierarchies are affected by the need for long-distance external ties.

Internal/External Change

According to Vance, classical central place theory focuses on internal change. He said local self-sufficiency is essential to the classical model. Expansion of a trading-settlement system in the central place model grows out of the gravitation of customers to sellers of goods and services.

What happens if local self-sufficiency never existed or if it ceases to exist? Vance said in this case there will be external trade. Consider, for example, groups of people in different areas who produce surpluses of locally demanded goods. An ability to produce surpluses carries with it a desire to expand trade beyond the confines of a local area. Expansion occurs if outside consumers are informed about areas of abundance, and if producers are aware of areas of scarcity. It is the task of wholesalers to provide information and forge links between areas of abundance and areas of scarcity. They provide producers with markets and assure consumers access to products.

Wholesalers subject regions to external change and stimulate growth of wholesaling centers. The wholesaling center, for Vance, is the ''unravelling point'' in the geography of trade. Wholesaling centers link production areas, mediate trade flows, and determine the metropolitan centers from which central place patterns develop to meet demands of consumers.

The Mercantile Model

Vance's study tried to show that trading-settlement patterns do not grow entirely within the classical central place model. He doubted whether any region in North America was economically isolated enough to have begun in a closed local system. He preferred to view the history of settlement patterns in terms of local trading patterns (central place model) and long-distance trading connections (mercantile model). According to Vance, broad scale settlement of North America must be seen in the context of distant trade. Settlement and economic growth were introduced from the outside. Cities such as Boston, Philadelphia, and Charleston were created before their hinterlands expanded.

Vance described the development of distant trade between Europe and North America and the subsequent evolution of the American urban hierarchy. Study of figure 3.19 reveals the main contrasts between urban evolution in the mercantile model and central place model. Prior to settlement, Europeans sought knowledge to evaluate the economic potential of an area. After being successfully tested for economic potential, mercantile centers were established to link European countries and their sources of raw materials. Mercantile centers grew as the size of the trading system increased, and eventually the central place model began to characterize settlement. Subsequently settlements grew in accordance with both central place and mercantile models.

Evidence from Reality

The theory of central places has been subjected to criticism. Researchers have often noted that theoretical networks of central places do not resemble real economic landscapes. But in the real world it is unreasonable to expect ''ideal'' hexagonal patterns of towns and cities. Central place theory is incomplete: many functions support cities. About one-half the support of American cities comes from nontertiary activities, especially manufacturing. Central place theory should not be dismissed out of hand because pleasing hexagonal forms are not apparent in the real world. Morrill (1970) asserted that the usefulness of central place theory depends on the way it answers the following questions:

1. Does the spatial organization of retailing and services reflect the level and distribution of purchasing power?

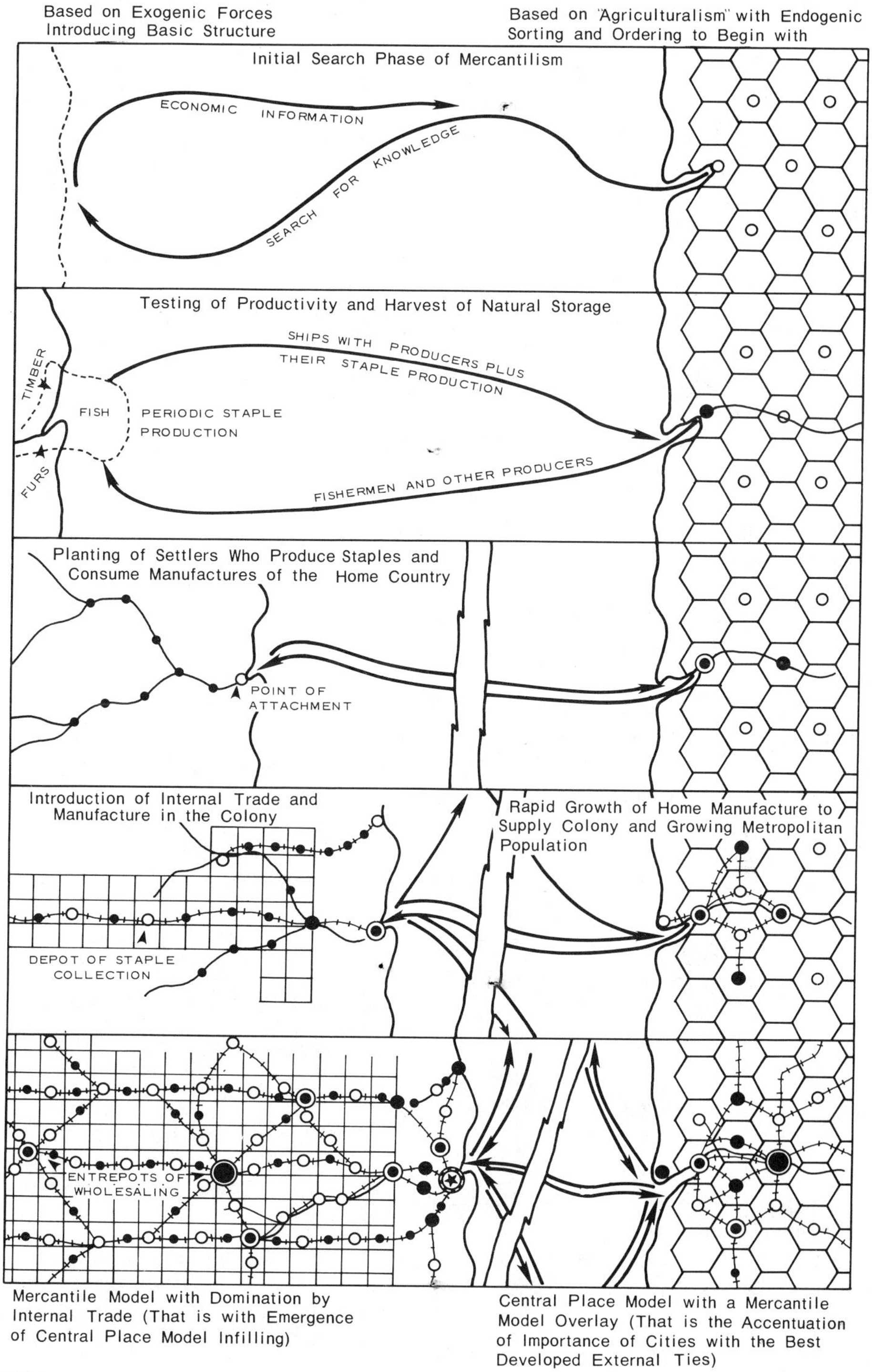

FIGURE 3.19 Urban evolution in the mercantile and central place models. (Copyright J. E. Vance, Jr., from *The Merchant's World: The Geography of Wholesaling*, Prentice-Hall, 1970, p. 151, fig. 18.)

2. Do central place activities tend to be regularly spaced in areas with similar physical, cultural, and economic environments?

3. Do consumers try to reduce distances travelled to purchase goods and services?

4. Do consumers shop at a hierarchy of centers for different types of goods and services?

Many studies have dealt with these questions that apply to tertiary activities within cities and to systems of cities. The object of this section is to explore evidence in support of the basic tenets of central place theory. We cannot hope to describe all the empirical studies carried out in this context, but limit the discussion to a few examples located in North America.

Thresholds

We all make intuitive estimates of thresholds as a matter of practical action. Suppose you are driving a 1962 Volvo in an area of the country you know nothing about. The car is having some minor mechanical trouble. A road sign comes into view (figure 3.20A). Will Smalltown have a Volvo dealership? Almost certainly not, but you can probably make a fairly precise list of the functions offered by the settlement (groceries, gas station, tavern). The next road sign is shown in figure 3.20B. The probability of Largetown having a Volvo dealership is good, and you can also make fairly accurate guesses as to the other functions offered in a city of 60,000.

When we cannot obtain a particular good (service) locally, we always consider the probability of it being available at the closest center of the *next highest order* although we do not use those particular terms. We intuitively realize that the good will rarely be offered at lower order centers.

Entrepreneurs are interested in whether or not a given type of business will succeed in a particular location. Small businessmen, unable to afford extensive marketing surveys and store location studies, must often make intuitive, "seat-of-the-pants" decisions. If an individual decided to start a diaper service in a city of 50,000 in the Upper Midwest his business is probably doomed to failure since the city is not large enough to profitably support this type of business. The estimated threshold for diaper services in the Upper Midwest is over 100,000. Let us look at a method of threshold estimation that is a useful technique for small business planning.

Calculation of Thresholds Researchers have used regression analysis to calculate threshold estimates. In a study of Southern Ontario, Yeates (1966) found the best fitting relationship took the form:

$$N = a\ (P)^b$$

where

N = the number of establishments of a particular type of business in a town,
P = the population of the town, and
a and b = the parameters to be fitted by regression.

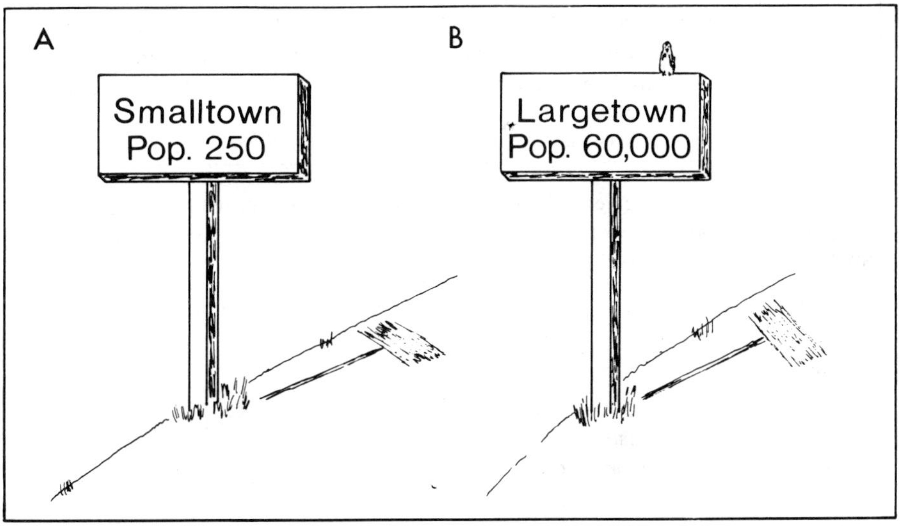

FIGURE 3.20 Threshold estimation.

Setting N equal to 1 (establishment) and solving for P gives the threshold population estimate for the particular type of business.

Such a method for estimating thresholds rests on two assumptions. First, it is assumed that the population of a town or city is a reliable surrogate for the entire market area of the settlement. A considerable amount of a firm's sales may come from the complementary region, but estimates of market area populations are tedious and difficult to make. Central place theory allows us to assume the following relationship:

$$P_c = k\ (P_c + P_m)$$

where

P_c = the population of the center,
P_m = the population of the rural trade area, and
k = a constant (which is usually called the *urban multiplier*) measuring the proportional relationship between town population (P_c) and the population of the entire trade area ($P_c + P_m$).

The urban multiplier (k) is regarded as fairly constant throughout a region with similar socioeconomic characteristics, and thus, town populations form consistently proportional estimates of total market area populations. This assumption permits the use of readily available city population data for estimating threshold populations.

The second assumption is that regression analysis is an acceptable method of estimating the "average" or expected values for data that are subject to error. Consider the example of filling stations. There will be considerable variance in the data but, in general, the larger the town the greater the number of filling stations. Regression analysis calculates the average rate at which filling stations are added with increasing population. If we find the average population that corresponds to one filling station, we can follow this average relationship upward to find the number of people required to support two, three, four, . . . , filling stations.

The urban multiplier gives the constant proportion between a center's population and the population of its market area (exclusive of the center). The multiplier is often written:

$$Pc = \frac{k}{1\text{-}k} Pm$$

where

Pc = center population,
Pm = market area population,
k = a constant of proportionality,

if $k = 0.5$, $Pc = Pm$,
if $k > 0.5$, $Pc > Pm$,
if $k < 0.5$, $Pc < Pm$.

The concept of the urban multiplier is derived directly from central place theory and assumes that there is a direct relationship between center population and market area population.

In regression analysis the best fitting curve $N = a\ (P)^b$ is expressed as:

$$\log N = a + b \log P$$

where

N = the number of establishments in a type of business in a town,
P = the population of the town, and
a and b = the parameters to be fitted by statistical analysis.

The best fitting curve is exponential, which means that establishments of a given business type are added at a decreasing rate as the population of a town increases. In a 1975 study of threshold estimates for Wisconsin we calculated that 186 people are required for one filling station, but 1,135 people are needed for four (table 3.4). Data given in the table may be plotted on double logarithmic graph paper (figure 3.21). Variable Y (population) is plotted on the vertical axis, and variable X (number of establishments) is plotted on the horizontal axis. Dashed lines indicate the number of people necessary to support one, two, three, and four filling stations.

It is important to remember that threshold values are relevant only for that area at that time. Threshold values change from region to region and from time to time as a result of differences in population density, transportation systems, and consumer tastes. Table 3.5 gives some examples of these differences in threshold values.

Threshold Values of Business Types Threshold values for a variety of business types have been calculated in different parts of the United States (Berry and Garrison 1958; Yeates and Lloyd 1970). We estimated threshold values in 1975 for 57 central place activities using population census and establishment data collected for 100 Wisconsin towns. Retail and service functions maintaining a statistically significant relationship between population and number of establishments are shown in table 3.6 in order of increasing threshold size.

Threshold Estimates and Small Business Planning Threshold estimation can be used for small business planning, but only with caution and in conjunction with other data and methods. If opening a particular type of business activity in a

TABLE 3.4 Populations required to support additional establishments of selected functions in Wisconsin

Function	Number of Establishments			
	1	2	3	4
Taverns	77	244	478	711
Fuel oil dealers	164	685	1,577	2,850
Filling stations	186	459	799	1,135
Beauticians	268	851	1,673	2,702
Insurance agencies	293	666	1,077	1,514
Farm implements	309	3,426	14,004	38,025
Restaurants	316	754	1,253	1,797
Hardware stores	372	1,925	5,032	9,949
Auto repair shops	375	1,148	2,209	3,517
Motels	384	2,072	5,557	11,189
Real estate agencies	418	1,226	2,301	3,597
Auto dealers	420	1,307	2,937	4,063
Plumbers	468	2,717	7,604	15,780
Physicians	493	1,352	2,436	3,702
Lawyers	497	1,169	1,927	2,748
Radio-TV sales	521	1,815	3,765	6,316
Dentists	563	1,744	3,379	5,402
Supermarkets	587	2,968	7,610	14,881
Appliance stores	607	3,709	10,691	22,659
Liquor stores	613	4,738	15,669	36,509
Furniture stores	637	4,833	15,819	36,686
Drugstores	638	4,285	13,053	28,771
Auto parts dealers	642	5,496	19,284	46,991
Laundromats	649	5,665	20,114	49,264
Women's clothing stores	678	5,471	18,544	44,133
Department stores	691	5,408	18,012	42,295
Dry cleaners	692	4,131	11,746	24,655

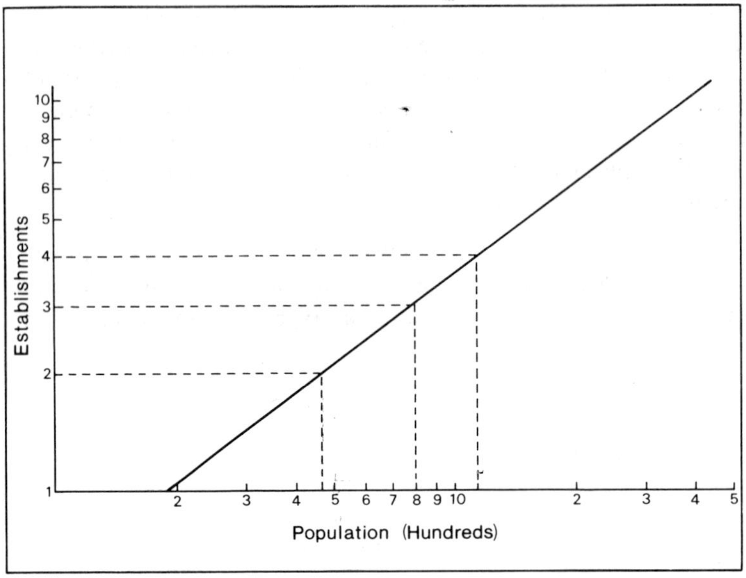

FIGURE 3.21 Populations necessary to support multiple filling stations in Wisconsin, 1975.

TABLE 3.5 Thresholds for selected functions (Washington State, Canterbury, New Zealand, and Wisconsin)

Function	Threshold Size		
	Washington	New Zealand	Wisconsin
Taverns	282	—	77
Gas stations	196	261	186
Physicians	380	491	493
Barber shop	386	668	632
Dentists	426	1019	563
Hardware store	431	414	372
Auto repair	435	293	375
Lawyers	582	830	497
Apparel stores	590	388	678
Banks	610	759	643
Farm implements	650	431	309
Florist	729	1280	726
Dry cleaner	754	781	692
Jewelry stores	827	926	722
Undertakers	1214	1137	—

Sources: Washington (Berry and Garrison 1958A). New Zealand (King 1961). Wisconsin (Calculated by authors, 1975).

TABLE 3.6 Threshold populations for fifty-two functions in Wisconsin, 1975

Function	Threshold	Function	Threshold
Taverns	77	Dentists	563
Food stores	92	Supermarkets	587
Fuel oil dealers	164	Hotels	603
Filling stations	186	Appliance stores	607
Feed stores	247	Liquor stores	613
Beauticians	268	Electric repair shops	631
Insurance agencies	293	Barber shops	632
Farm implements	309	Furniture stores	637
Restaurants	316	Drugstores	638
Hardware stores	372	Auto parts dealers	642
Auto repair shops	375	Banks	643
Lumberyards	380	Laundromats	649
Motels	384	Women's clothing stores	678
Shoe repair shops	387	Bakeries	687
Real estate agencies	418	Dry cleaners	692
Auto dealers	420	Shoe stores	712
Building materials	444	Movie theaters	716
Plumbers	468	Jewelry stores	722
Variety stores	475	Optometrists	726
Hospital and clinics	490	Florists	726
Physicians	493	Billiard halls	742
Veterinarians	494	Sheet metal works	747
Lawyers	497	Men's clothing	752
Radio-TV sales	521	Public accountants	757
Freight lines and storage	535	Photographers	794
Drive-in eating places	537	Frozen food lockers	1,000

town is contemplated, the existing number of establishments in the town can be compared with the expected number predicted by the regression model. If the actual number is less than predicted, the market area *may* be able to support an additional establishment. If the existing number of establishments exceeds the predicted, there is a high probability of saturation.

Suppose an entrepreneur is trying to decide which of two towns would best support a hardware store franchise which he intends to open. Town A has a population of 8,750 and three hardware stores. Threshold population required to support four hardware stores in Wisconsin was 9,949 in 1975 (table 3.4). Thus, Town A probably represents a saturated market for this type of business. Town B has a population of 4,800 and two hardware stores. The market for hardware stores does not appear to be saturated. Town B may be able to support an additional store. Other factors should also be considered before a locational decision is made: scale of existing establishments, potential competition, population trends, and local purchasing power. Threshold estimation has provided, in this hypothetical example, a technique for *initial* analysis: Town A has been eliminated, and attention can be focused solely on Town B.

The Central Place Hierarchy

We have seen in previous sections that there are cumulative increments of business types; higher order centers have more business types than lower order centers. In general, they also contain more people and are more widely spaced. These ideas are supported by the findings of John Borchert, who studied the trade center hierarchy in the Upper Midwest of the United States.

The Upper Midwest: Population Distribution

The region coincides with the Ninth Federal Reserve District, which extends some 2,500 km. along the Canadian border from Montana in the west to the Upper Peninsula of Michigan in the east. It includes the states of Montana, North Dakota, South Dakota, and Minnesota, 26 counties of northwestern Wisconsin, and fifteen counties of Michigan's Upper Peninsula. One might expect to find in this rather homogeneous region the regular (equal-area) pattern of hexagonal market areas suggested by Christaller. But the underlying density of farm population varies considerably throughout the Upper Midwest (figure 3.22). Rural population concentration is greatest in eastern Minnesota, and declines toward the west, and in northeastern Minnesota, northern Wisconsin, and the Upper Peninsula of Michigan. Areas of sparse population are agriculturally poor areas with short or dry growing seasons. A hexagonal lattice that conforms to the distribution of farm population in the Upper Midwest is shown in figure 3.23. The size of cells is smaller in areas of high population, and larger in areas of sparse settlement, but the population of each cell is constant.

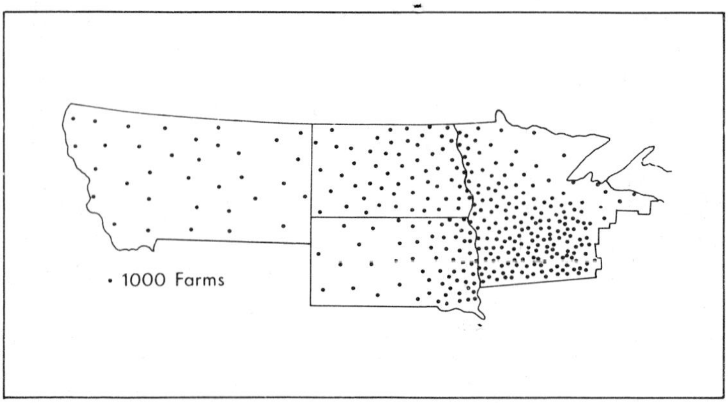

FIGURE 3.22 Distribution of farms in the Upper Midwest. [From John F. Kolars and John D. Nystuen (1974) *Human Geography: Spatial Design in World Society,* New York: McGraw Hill, p. 100, figs. 5-10.]

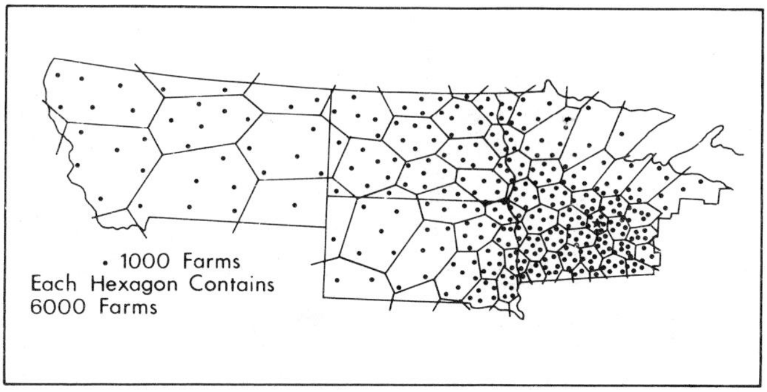

FIGURE 3.23 Hexagonal lattice conforming to the underlying rural population pattern in the Upper Midwest. [From John F. Kolars and John D. Nystuen (1974) *Human Geography: Spatial Design in World Society,* New York: McGraw Hill, p. 101, figs. 5-11.]

The Upper Midwest: Hierarchy of Business Types

Borchert (1963) demonstrated that a well-developed hierarchy of central place functions exists in the Upper Midwest. He selected 46 functions and determined those functions typical of various orders in the hierarchy of business types. Figure 3.24 shows these functions grouped into convenience, specialty, and wholesale categories. The diagram also shows eight types of central places. The bundle of central place goods and services characteristic of each type of trade center is as follows:

1. *Hamlets,* lowest order central places, have only gasoline service stations, and eating and drinking establishments.
2. *Minimum convenience* and *full convenience* centers provide everyday necessities. Minimum convenience centers have hamlet-level functions plus a bank, hardware store, drugstore, grocery, and two other convenience goods. Full convenience centers have all ten convenience and hamlet-level functions plus specialty stores concerned with laundry or dry cleaning, clothing, jewelry, appliances or furniture, and up to three other specialty functions.
3. *Partial shopping and complete shopping* centers offer specialty goods and services. Partial shopping centers have four to eight specialty functions and complete shopping centers have nine or more specialty functions, plus all those business functions of lower-order places.
4. *Secondary wholesale-retail, primary wholesale-retail,* and *metropolitan wholesale-retail* centers are the highest order places. Wholesale centers have all the specialty, convenience, and hamlet-level functions. Secondary wholesale-retail centers have 10 to 13 wholesale functions and over 50 wholesale establishments, primary wholesale-retail centers have all 14 wholesale activities and over 100 wholesale establishments, and metropolitan wholesale-retail centers have the complete range of wholesale functions and more than 500 wholesale establishments.

The frequency of trade center types in the Upper Midwest is shown in table 3.7. As the hierarchical level increases, the number of trade centers decreases. The table also indicates a strong relationship between trade center class and population size classes.

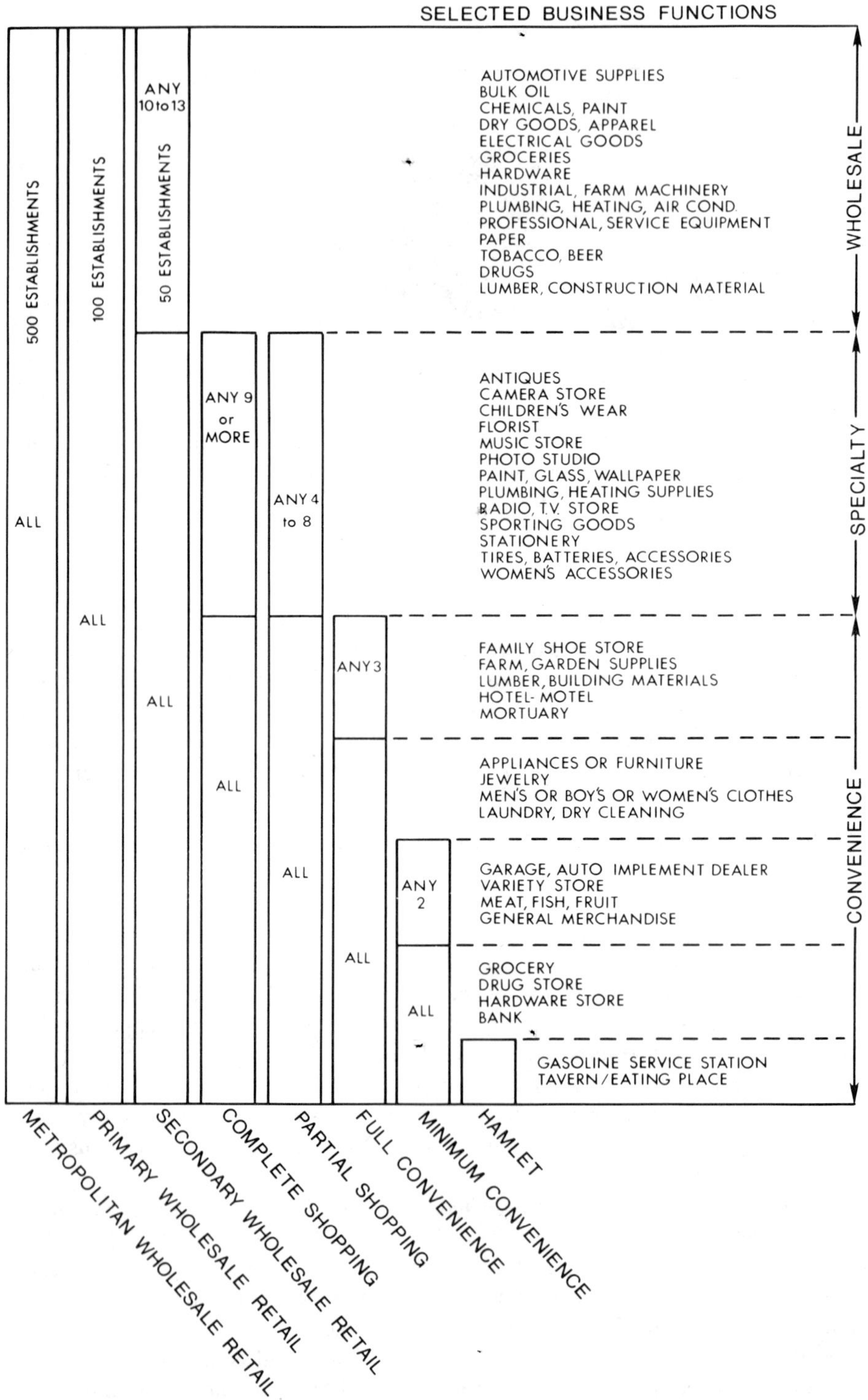

FIGURE 3.24 Trade center types in the Upper Midwest. [From John R. Borchert (1963) "The Urbanization of the Upper Midwest 1930-1960," *Upper Midwest Economic Study*, Urban Report No. 2, University of Minnesota, Minneapolis, Minn., p. 12, fig. 4.]

Minneapolis-St. Paul is the largest trade center, and constitutes the only metropolitan wholesale-retail center in the region. Besides business functions listed in figure 3.24, the Twin Cities area provides other services for its massive trade area, such as regional head offices of insurance companies, specialized medical, educational, and administrative facilities. People living up to 1,600 km away may never visit the Twin Cities. They obtain goods and services from lower-order trade centers. The highest level centers that many people living beyond the Twin Cities need to reach are primary and secondary wholesale-retail centers such as Eau Claire, Duluth, St. Cloud, Fargo-Moorhead, and Billings. Nonetheless, the Twin Cities form the controlling center of the economy of the Upper Midwest. Trade area residents feel the influence of the metropolis through communications, banking, agricultural marketing, and retail-wholesale relationships.

The Upper Midwest: Central Place Pattern

The geographical distribution of trade centers in the Upper Midwest is mapped in figure 3.25. The pattern conforms roughly to central place theory. Wholesale-retail centers are widely spaced and low-order centers are the most numerous. Greater spacing of trade centers of all classes to the north and west is a striking feature of the map.

Kolars and Nystuen (1974) examined the correspondence between a five level $k = 4$ hierarchy and the actual sequence of settlements along U.S. Highway 10 from Minneapolis-St. Paul to Spokane. They divided the highway from east to west into three parts: Humid Midwest (roughly Minneapolis-St. Paul to Fargo), Great Plains (Fargo to Billings), and Rocky Mountains (Billings to Spokane). They found that the $k = 4$ model underestimates the number of settlements along U.S. 10, especially across the Great Plains (table 3.8).

TABLE 3.7 Frequency and median size of trade center types in the Upper Midwest

Type of Center	Number of Centers	Median Population (Thousands)
Wholesale-Retail Centers		
Metropolitan	1	1440.0
Primary	7	55.4
Secondary	10	32.2
Shopping Centers		
Complete	78	9.5
Partial	127	2.5
Convenience Centers		
Full	111	1.5
Minimum	379	0.8
Hamlets	1539	0.2

Source: John R. Borchert (1963), "The Urbanization of the Upper Midwest, 1930-1960," *Upper Midwest Economic Study*, Urban Report, No. 2, University of Minnesota, Minneapolis, Minn., p. 11, table 2.

There may well be too many trade centers in the Upper Midwest. The pattern of trade centers is a legacy of the pioneers. Most of the 2,500 cities and villages dotting the map of the Upper Midwest were established under conditions quite different from those that prevail today. After railroads opened up the region in the late nineteenth century, immigrants established small farms, and low order central places developed to meet the needs of farm families. They were closely spaced in response to slow, difficult travel. In recent decades, two radical changes have produced stress within the original framework of settlements: migration and transportation.

Migration has had the greatest influence on the structure of trade centers. In the past half-century farm population declined sharply as farms increased in size and farmland was abandoned. Farm population declined by 300,000 between 1960 and 1970, the region experienced net out-migration during the same period. In the Upper Midwest people are shifting from farms and small trade centers into larger urban areas and from central cities into suburbs and countryside. Improvements in transportation after 1914, such as the widespread use of automobiles and paved roads, enabled consumers to bypass smaller centers and patronize larger centers. Because of loss of farm population and changes in consumer mobility, small trade centers cannot compete with larger towns that offer a greater variety and quantity of service. Table 3.9 shows the main changes in the trade center hierarchy between 1930 and 1960: the decline or stagnation of the majority of small trade centers and the concentration of growth in a relatively small number of larger trade centers.

TABLE 3.8 Number of expected and observed trade centers along U. S. 10 (U. S. Interstates 94 and 90)

Region	Expected	Recorded	% More Recorded Than Expected
Humid Midwest	8	13	162
Great Plains	9	23	255
Rocky Mountains	14	19	136

Source: John F. Kolars and John D. Nystuen (1974), *Human Geography: Spatial Design in World Society*. New York: McGraw-Hill, p. 105, table 5.3.

United States: High Order Central Places

Minneapolis-St. Paul is one of 24 high order central places in the United States. Borchert (1967) divided these important trade centers into three orders based on their size and functional complexity. The first-order center is New York City, which is the national metropolis providing the widest range of specialized activities. In addition to New York City, there are six second-order centers or regional metropoli: Boston, Philadelphia, Detroit, Chicago, San Francisco, and Los Angeles. Added to

TABLE 3.9 Proportion of trade centers of the Upper Midwest in 1930-1960 growth rate classes

Trade Center Class	Number of Centers	Percent of Trade Centers in 1930-1960 Growth Rate Classes			
		Fast	Moderate	Slow	Decline
Wholesale-Retail					
Metropolitan	1	100	0	0	0
Primary	7	72	14	14	0
Secondary	10	80	10	0	10
Shopping					
Complete	79	62	26	4	8
Partial	126	54	26	9	11
Convenience					
Full	112	43	36	15	6
Minimum	379	28	30	23	19
Hamlet	1,539	12	11	41	37

Source: John R. Borchert (1963), "The Urbanization of the Upper Midwest, 1930-1960," *Upper Midwest Economic Study,* Urban Report, No. 2. University of Minnesota, Minneapolis, Minn., p. 19, table 3.

the seven second-order centers are 17 metropolitan centers to make a total of 24 centers.

The first-, second-, and third-order central places and their trade areas are mapped in figure 3.26. The map shows great distortion in the distribution of high order trade centers when they are mapped into absolute space. Most of the important centers are located in the industrial Northeast, and five of them are clustered along the east cost. The spacing of centers fails to confirm central place expectations. However, when the cities are mapped in population space a much more regular pattern results (figure 3.27). The cartogram demonstrates an important point: the size and location of central places is adjusted to the distribution of people and purchasing power.

Rank-Size Rule

The hierarchical structure of trade centers is reflected not only in their functional complexity, but also in their relative size. An urban size hierarchy is obtained when urban centers are ranked by population size. The most well-known attempt to represent this hierarchy is the rank-size rule popularized by Zipf (1949). In its simplest form, this rule states that if all urban settlements in an area are ranked in descending order of population size, the population of the rth city is $1/r$ the size of the largest city's population. Symbolically, the rank-size rule may be expressed as:

$$P_r = \frac{P_1}{R}$$

where

P_r = the population of the rth city,
P_1 = the population of the largest city,
R = the size rank of the rth city in the set.

When plotted on double logarithmic graph paper, this relationship produces a straight, downward-sloping line with a gradient of 45° (figure 3.28). The hypothetical rank-size distribution describes an urban system containing a few large metropoli, a larger number of medium-size cities, and a still larger number of smaller towns.

Figure 3.29 shows the application of the rank-size rule to the United States. The size distribution conforms closely to the rank-size rule. When the rule is applied to individual cities, we expect Los Angeles (the second-ranking city) to have one-half of the population of the first-ranking city, New York. In 1970, Los Angeles had a population of 8.35 million instead of 8.10 million as predicted by the rank-size rule (table 3.10). Chicago, the third-ranking city, had a population of 6.71 million against an expected 5.40 million. Philadelphia, the fourth-ranking city, had a population of 4.02 million as against 4.05 million, and Minneapolis-St. Paul, the twelfth-ranking city, had a population of 1.70 million as against 1.35 million. Despite deviations for individual cities, the differences tend to cancel to produce a very regular rank-size distribution. Figure 3.30 illustrates that rank-size relationships have been rather stable over a period of 150 years for the United States.

TABLE 3.10 Recorded and expected size of the top twelve urbanized areas in the United States, 1970

Urbanized Area	Recorded (millions)	Expected (millions)
New York-Northeastern N. J.	16.20	16.20
Los Angeles-Long Beach	8.35	8.10
Chicago-Northwestern Ind.	6.71	5.40
Philadelphia	4.02	4.05
Detroit	3.97	3.24
San Francisco-Oakland	2.98	2.36
Boston	2.65	2.31
Washington, D. C.	2.48	2.02
Cleveland	1.95	1.80
St. Louis	1.88	1.62
Pittsburgh	1.84	1.47
Minneapolis-St. Paul	1.70	1.35

Source: County and City Data Book, 1972, U. S. Bureau of Census.

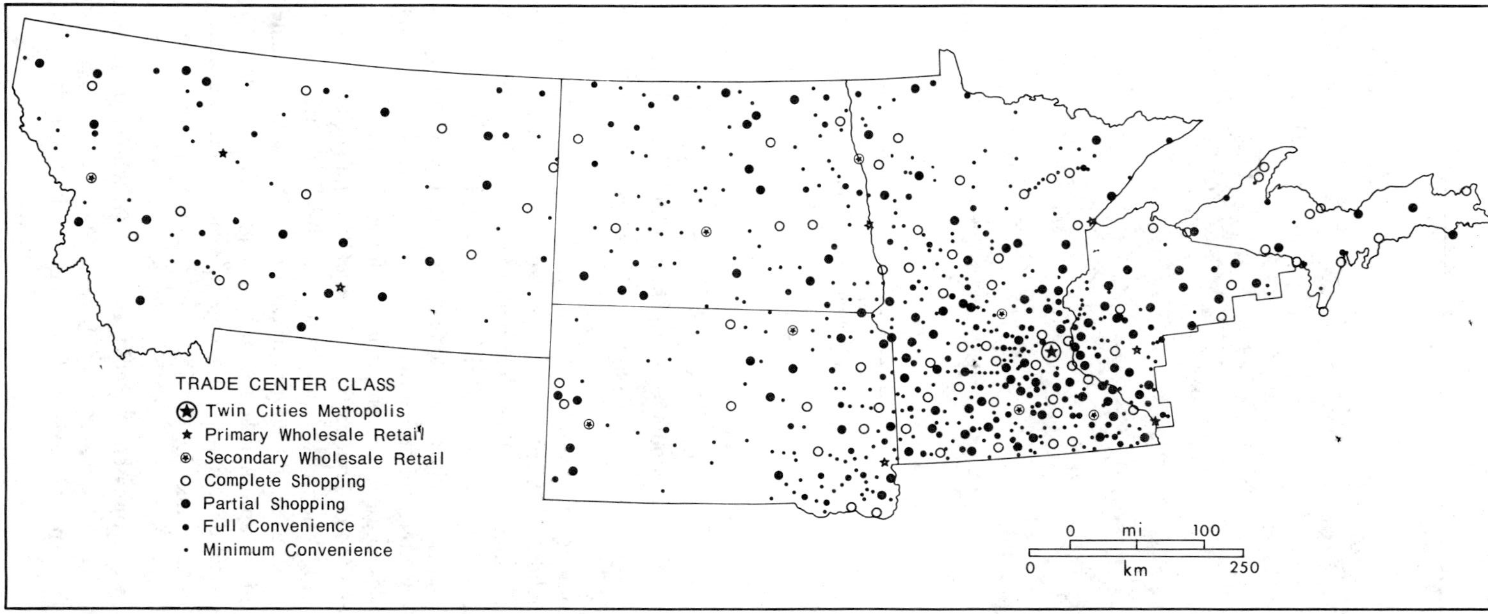

FIGURE 3.25 Distribution of trade centers in the Upper Midwest. [From John R. Borchert (1963) "The Urbanization of the Upper Midwest 1930-1960," Upper Midwest Economic Study, Urban Report No. 2, University of Minnesota, Minneapolis, Minn., pp. 13-14, fig. 5.]

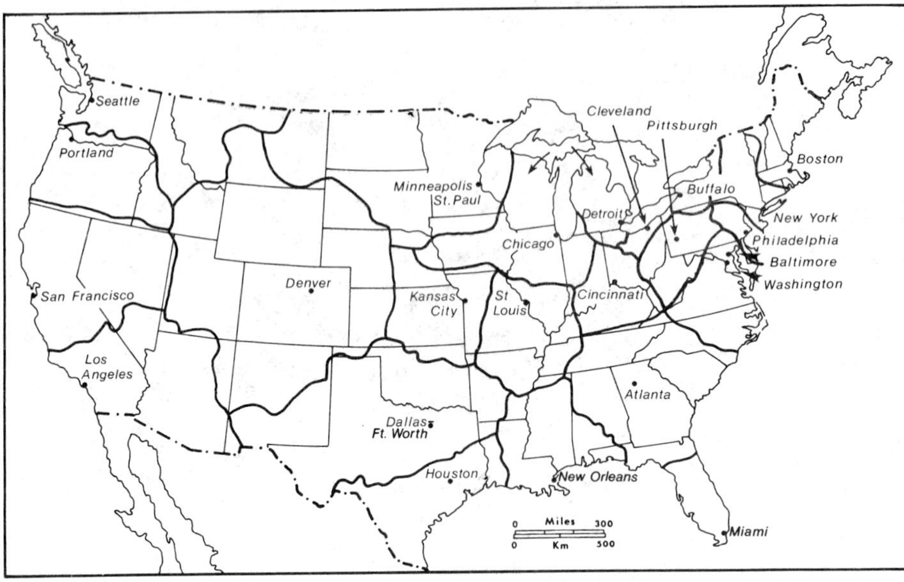

FIGURE 3.26 Higher-order trade centers and trade areas in the United States.

Zipf argued that a rank-size distribution indicates a ''balanced'' system of cities. Yet there are situations where the population of the first or largest city is greater than would be expected from the rank-size distribution, and a condition of *primacy* exists (figure 3.31).

Berry (1961) tried to interpret city-size distributions through a comparative study of 37 countries. He found that 13 countries had rank-size distributions, 15 had primate distributions, and nine had intermediate distributions (table 3.11). He suggested there is no simple explanation for these different types of city-size distributions. Numerous forces that act randomly over a long period of time produce rank-size distributions, and a few powerful forces such as the impact of imperialism on underdeveloped countries cause variations from the rank-size model. Berry concluded that as countries become politically, economically, and socially more complex, they tend to develop ''normal'' (straight line) rank-size distributions (figure 3.32). His conclusion was based on the work of Simon (1955), who postulated that a rank-size distribution is a limiting case for stochastic growth processes. Thus, in the early phases of national development a simple primate pattern prevails, and is gradually transformed into a rank-size distribution that is the equilibrium or steady state of an urban growth process.

A similar viewpoint was expressed by Beckmann (1958), who said the rank-size distribution can be understood by drawing an analogy with biologic growth. Biologists can predict for a species the size of the whole individual if the size of one

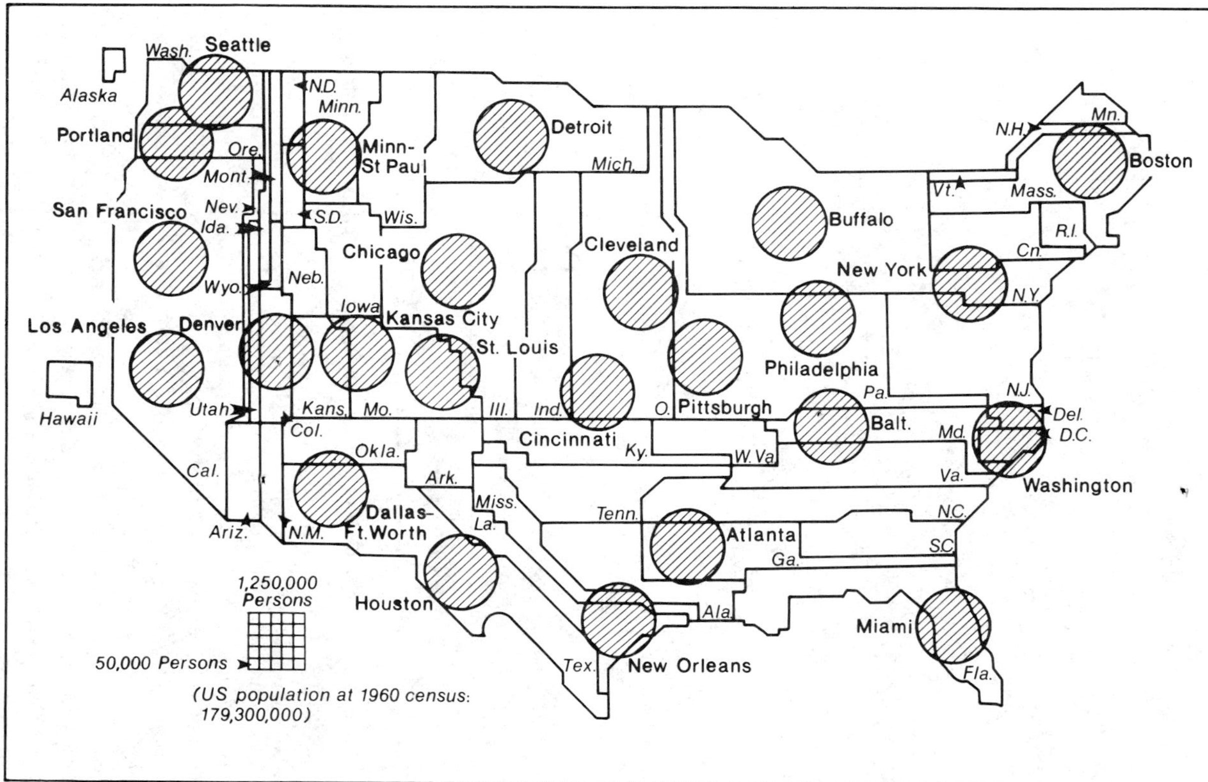

FIGURE 3.27 Higher-order trade centers in the United States mapped in population space. (From Abler, Adams, Gould, *Spatial Organization: The Geographer's View of the World*, © 1971. Reprinted by permission of Prentice-Hall, Inc., Englewood Cliffs, New Jersey.)

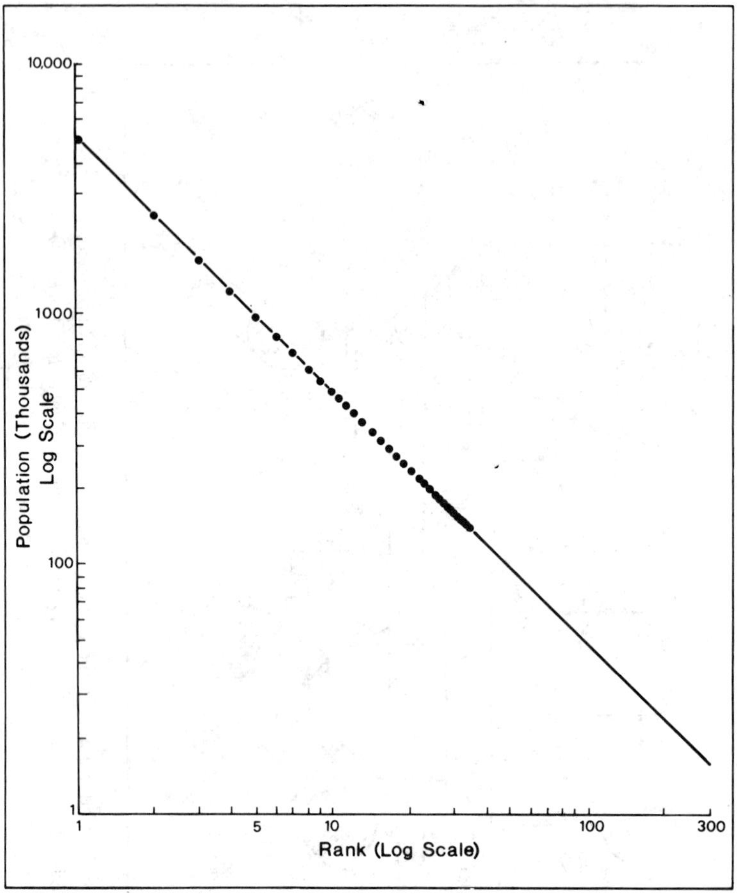

FIGURE 3.28 Rank size rule: hypothetical size of the population of cities in relation to their ranking.

part is known. This is called the "law of allometric growth." Beckmann defined the rule formally as follows: "The rate of relative growth of an organ is a constant fraction of the rate of relative growth of the total organism (1958, p. 247)." The law of allometric growth leads to the conclusion that a normal rank-size curve will result when the relative growth of cities at any level of the hierarchy is, on average, a constant fraction of the rate of growth of the entire hierarchy of cities in a system. Rank-size refers to the stability of a *whole system* of cities. Individual cities in a system, however, may vary in importance over time. Between 1870 and 1950 New York City maintained its lead position, Los Angeles gained dramatically, and cities such as New Haven and Savannah slipped in rank. Regular growth of the United States' urban system has been accompanied by variations in the relative growth of individual cities.

To what extent is there a correspondence between central place theory and the rank-size concept? Some writers have argued they are incompatible (Vining 1955 and Stewart 1958). The central place hierarchy is based on the *functional size* of

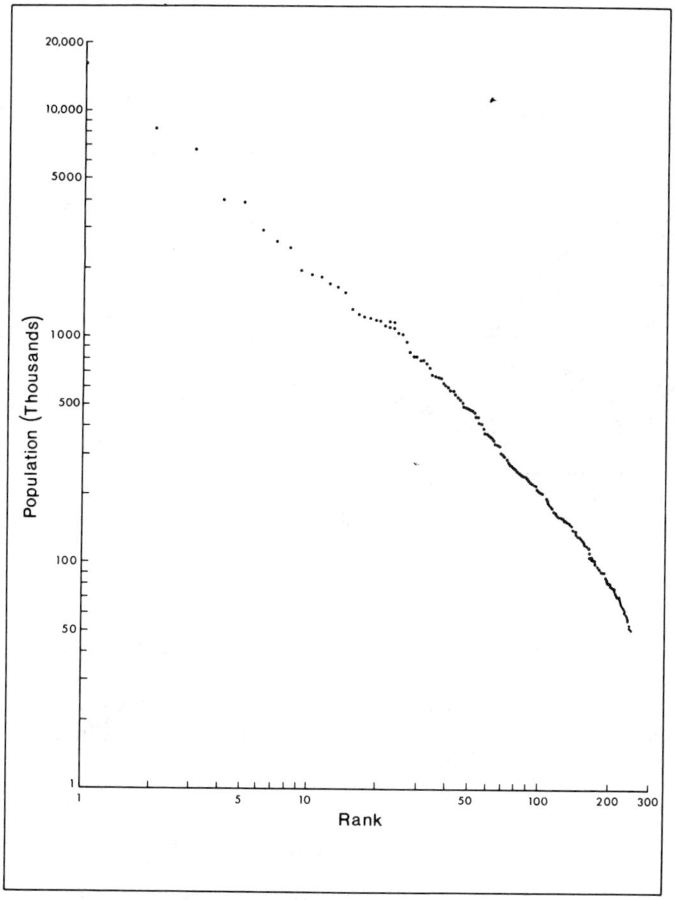

FIGURE 3.29 Rank size distribution of urbanized areas in the United States, 1970. [Source: *County and City Data Book,* 1972, U. S. Bureau of Census.]

centers. Functional size is determined by the number and order of central functions offered by a place. Functional size is essentially tied to the role of settlement-forming functions in the center's economy. The total population of a place is a function of *both* settlement-forming and settlement-building functions. Two centers may belong to the same level of the hierarchy (functional size) yet be somewhat different in population. The rank-size rule is based on the population of centers, *not* functional size. Population size produces a smooth rank-size curve; functional size produces a stepped hierarchy.

Both a stepped hierarchy and a smooth rank-size curve are shown in figure 3.33. Centers X and Y belong to the B-level of the central place hierarchy; they are the same functional size. The population of X, however, is considerably larger than that of Y.

Let us assume that Center X has no settlement-building functions, while Center Y has a large manufacturing plant, a state-supported junior college, and is a county seat. These settlement-building functions allow Center Y to support a population

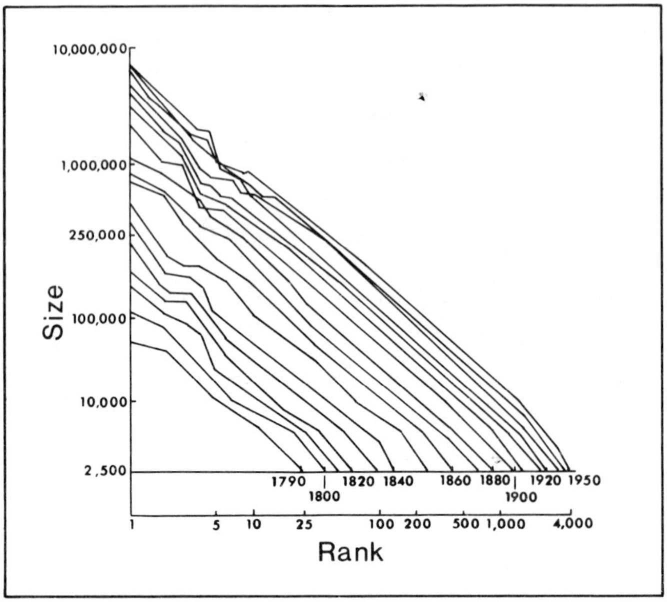

FIGURE 3.30 Rank size distribution of United States urban population, 1790-1950. [Source: C. H. Madden (1956) "Some Indicators of Stability in the Growth of Cities in the U. S.," *Economic Development and Cultural Change* **4** 239, fig. 1. Copyright 1956 by the University of Chicago Press.]

greater than it could employ if it had to depend solely upon its central place role. Each settlement should have a slightly different set of settlement-building functions giving rise to population differentials among centers of the same functional size and producing a smooth rank-size curve in terms of population.

The discrepancy between the stepped and continuous curves may also be a function of scale. Rank-size distributions apply to large, fairly self-sufficient economic areas (U.S. or European Common Market) and the central place model applies to their smaller subsystems (upper Midwest).

Structural Elements of the Central Place Hierarchy

In this section we cite some of the empirical research which has focused on structural elements of the central place hierarchy. Our knowledge of structural elements of the central place hierarchy has been greatly extended by the work of Berry (1967). His work is based on controlled field studies and the application of statistical techniques.

Population Size and Functional Units Figure 3.34 shows the relationship between population and functional units in southwest Iowa. Most centers fall very

TABLE 3.11 City-size distributions in thirty-seven countries

Countries with Rank-Size Pattern	Countries with Primate Pattern	Countries with Intermediate Patterns
Belgium	Austria	Australia
Brazil	Ceylon	Canada
China	Denmark	Ecuador
El Salvador	Dominican Republic	England and Wales
Finland	Greece	Malaya
India	Guatemala	New Zealand
Italy	Japan	Nicaragua
Korea	Mexico	Norway
Poland	Netherlands	Pakistan
South Africa	Peru	
Switzerland	Portugal	
United States	Spain	
West Germany	Sweden	
	Thailand	
	Uruguay	

Source: Brian J. L. Berry (1961), "City Size Distributions and Economic Development," *Economic Development and Cultural Change* **9** 573-88.

Central place theory is *structured;* all the elements of the theory are tied together in a logical and proportional way. Central place theory assumes, for example, that the population of a center is a function of the number of central functions it can support or the size of a center's trade area is directly related to its functional size. We are interested in determining how accurately central place theory describes the structure of settlements (as retail and service centers) in reality. To do this, we must determine whether or not empirical evidence supports the structural elements of central place theory.

close to the regression line. Two centers, however, have a larger population than we would expect statistically given the number of functional units in each (predicted from the regression line). Berry (1962) found logical explanations for these two anomalies. Each town had relatively large settlement-building functions. Glenwood was the site of a state mental institution and Red Oak had a manufacturing plant. When the population of each town supported by these noncentral functions (inmates in Glenwood; employees and dependents in Red Oak) is subtracted from their total populations, the number of people supported by settlement-forming functions can be estimated. These estimates fit the regression equation in figure 3.34 quite well.

We have defined a central function as a good or service offered by a central place. Suppose a center has a gasoline station. The addition of a second gas station will not increase the number of central functions in the center. The cross-road hamlet in the figure has two general stores each of which is also a gas station. One store is a Post Office and the other has liquor sales. The number of central functions is four (general store, gas, post office, liquor). Each central function, once offered, is counted only once, but there are two other measures of retail and service activity commonly used in central place theory:

1. *Establishment:* This term refers to ownership and control. In our example, there are two establishments.
2. *Functional unit:* Each *separate* time a central function is offered, it is counted as a functional unit. Our imaginary hamlet has six functional units.

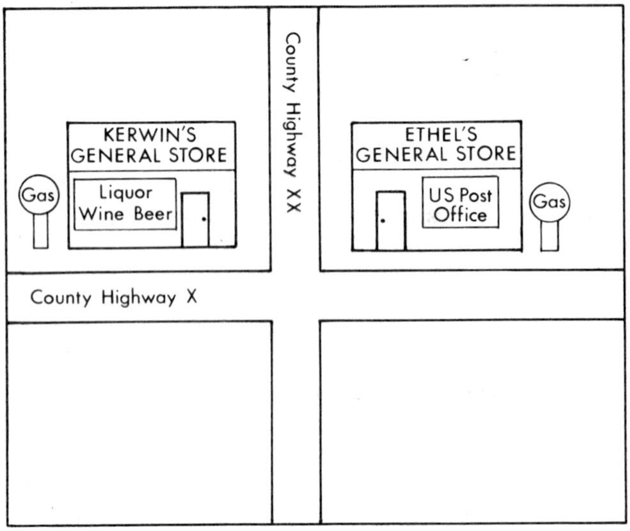

Population Size and Central Functions Several studies have shown a curvilinear or log-linear relationship between the population size and the number of central functions performed by centers. This relationship indicates that the population of a central place is a function of the total number of business types offered and is generalized by the best-fit line in figure 3.35. There are deviations from the average or expected relationship. Some settlements have more central functions than expected (X-centers in figure 3.35); they are usually tourist centers whose excess central functions are supported by a transient population. Las Vegas, Nevada is a good example. Other settlements (0-centers in figure 3.35) fall above the best-fit line. They have larger populations than we might expect given their functional size. This usually indicates the presence of settlement-building functions and is also typical of suburbs which may have a large population, but small functional size because of the shopping opportunities offered in the central city.

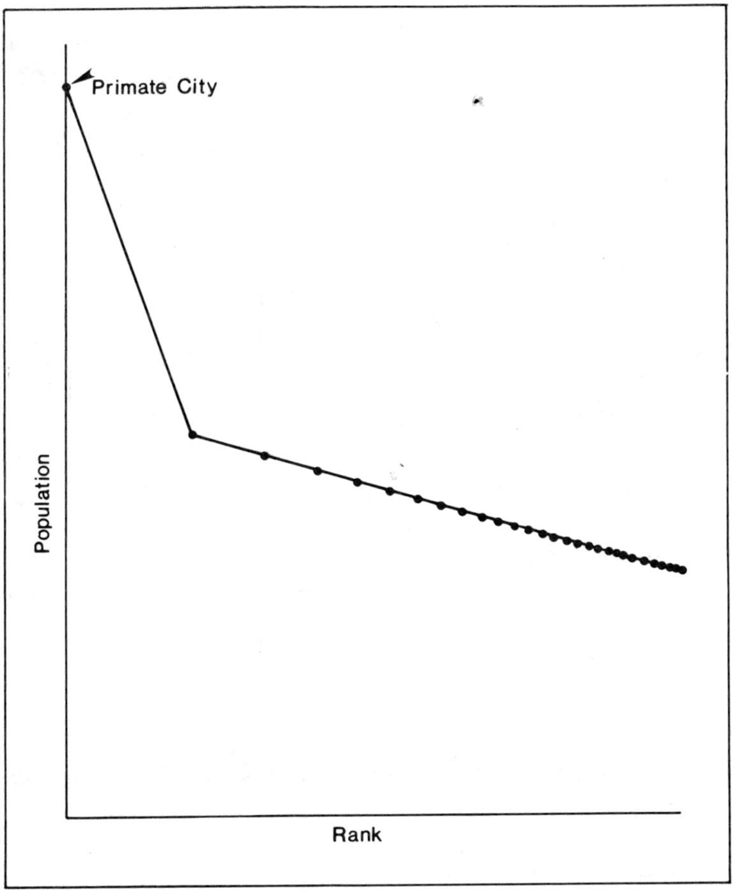

FIGURE 3.31 Primate distribution of city populations.

Establishments and Population Size This relationship is shown in figure 3.36. Increases in the number of establishments are proportional to increases in center sizes. The population/central function and the population/functional unit relationships are *not* proportional. This raises the question of how centers meet increases in demand brought about by population changes. Existing establishments may expand; new establishments of the same functional type may be added; or some combination of the two may be used. The strategy chosen depends upon a number of factors, but empirical evidence (including figure 3.36) indicates that increasing the number of establishments tends to happen more frequently. This is especially true of lower order functions and centers.

Trade Area Size and Population Density The size of a center's trade area determines the total population served by the center. The trade area must be large enough to meet the threshold of the highest order good offered by the center. Trade

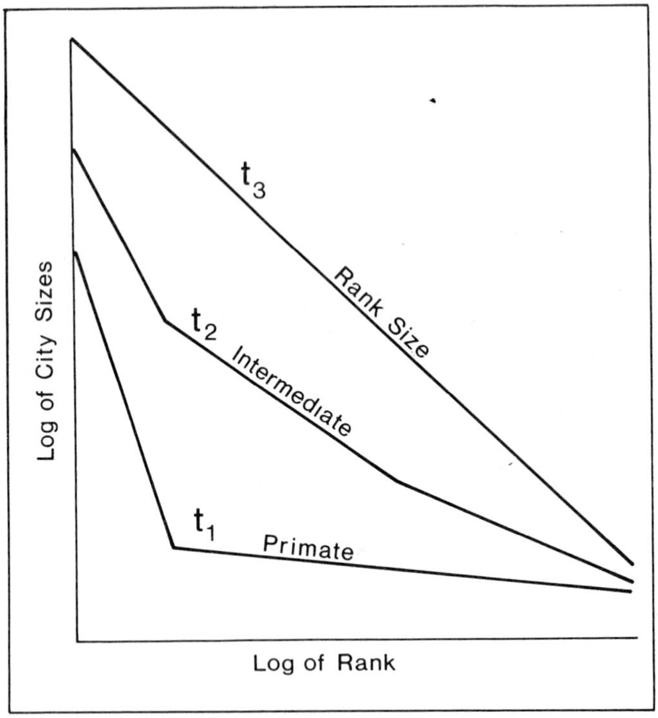

FIGURE 3.32 Idealized evolution of city size: distributions under increasing population size through three time periods.

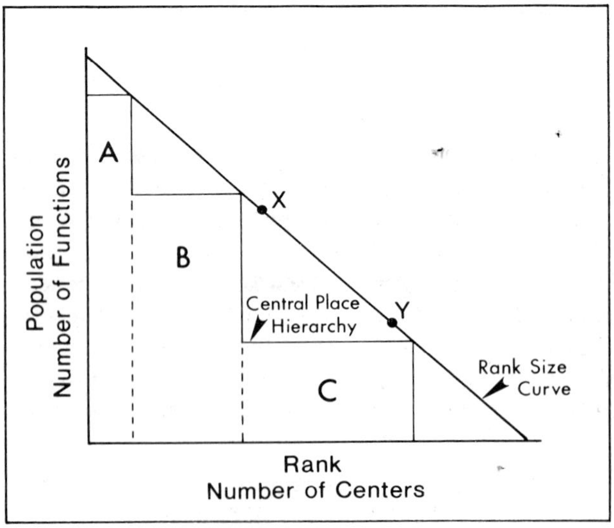

FIGURE 3.33 Combined rank-size/central place hierarchy curves.

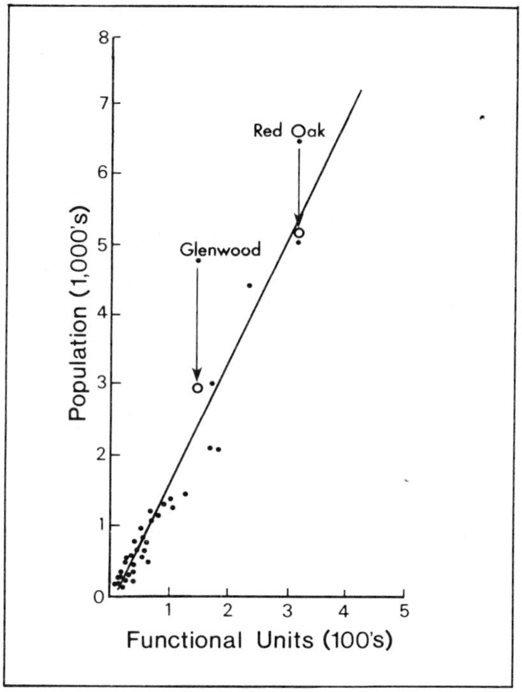

FIGURE 3.34 Population/functional units relationship (Southwest Iowa). [From Brian J. L. Berry and Harold M. Mayer (1962) *Comparative Studies of Central Place Systems*, Final Report NONR 2121-18 and NR 389-126, Geography Branch, U. S. Office of Naval Research.]

area size must be adjusted to meet changes in population density. The size of a trade area must increase as population density falls to maintain a constant total population served. If the concept of a threshold has any validity, empirical evidence should show a tendency toward adjustment to variations in population density.

A perfect theoretical adjustment is shown in figure 3.37. Each center of a given level serves exactly the same population (threshold for the level), but there is considerable range in trade area size. Center 1_a serves a much smaller trade area than center 1_b, indicating a higher population density around 1_a. We do not expect a perfect relationship in reality, but the data collected by Berry (1962) indicates a strong tendency toward this type of adjustment (figure 3.38).

The 45° line in the figure is a line of *constant population density*. Each level of center (for example, villages) is arrayed along a line with a slope *greater* than 45°. The variation in trade area size, therefore, is greater than the variation in total population served, suggesting density adjustment.

If the central place hierarchy is sensitive to small local variations in population density (figure 3.38), adjustments to larger, regional variations in density should also occur. Figure 3.39 illustrates the relation of trade area sizes to total population served by the central places in five contrasting regions in the United States. These regions range from sparsely settled areas served by rural central places (Iowa and North Dakota) to urban Chicago which has a population larger than most states.

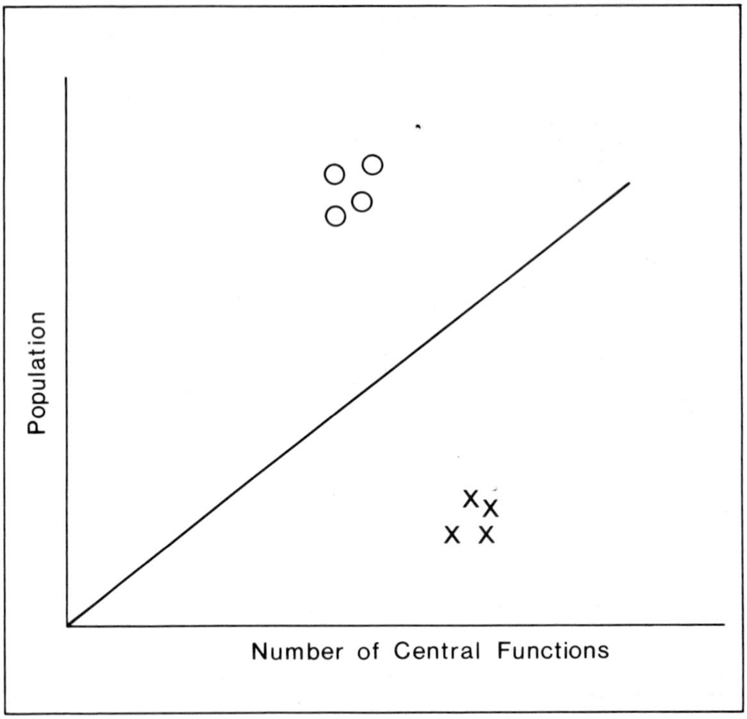

FIGURE 3.35 Anomalies and the relationship between central functions and population.

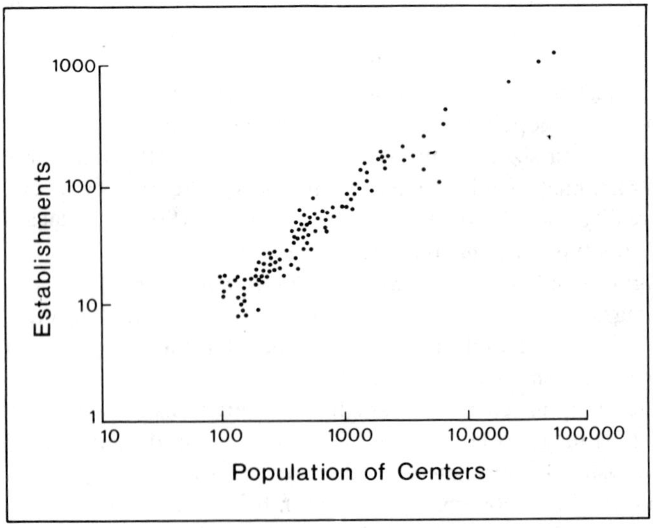

FIGURE 3.36 Relationship between establishments and population size.

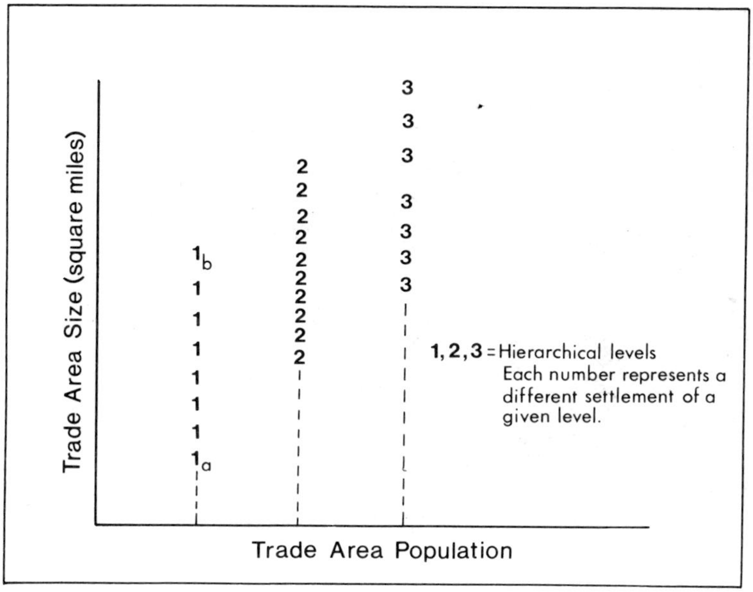

FIGURE 3.37 Perfect density adjustment.

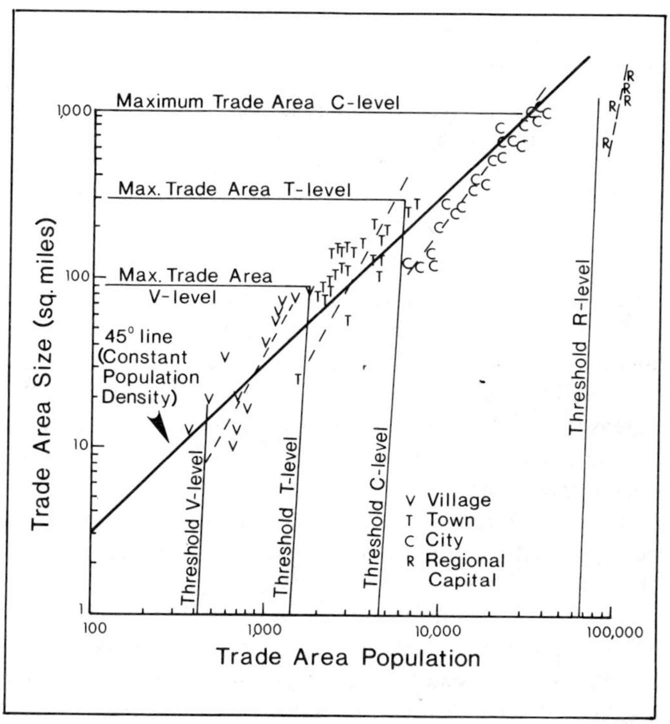

FIGURE 3.38 Density adjustment (Southwest Iowa). [From Brian J. L. Berry and Harold M. Mayer (1962) *Comparative Studies of Central Place Systems*, Final Report NONR 2121-18 and NR 389-126, Geography Branch, U.S. Office of Naval Research.]

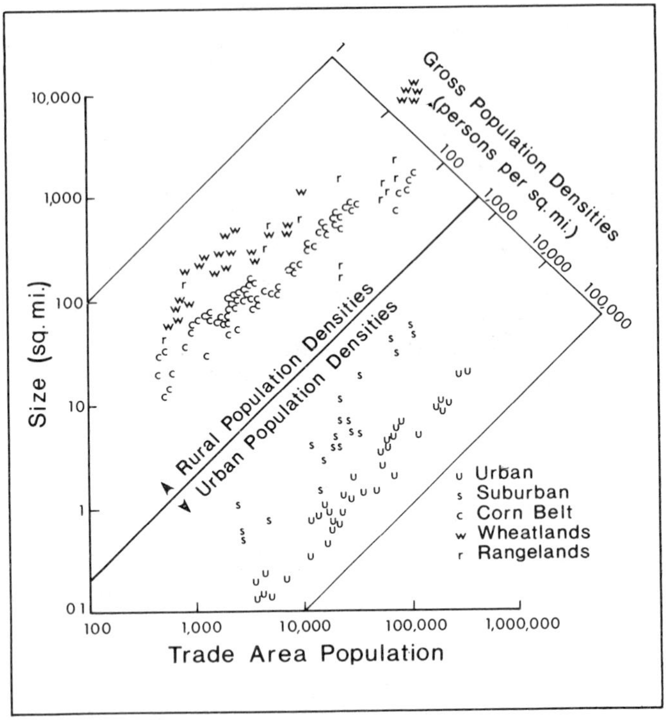

FIGURE 3.39 Density adjustment: large regional variations in population density. [From Brian J. L. Berry and Harold M. Mayer (1962) *Comparative Studies of Central Place Systems*, Final Report NONR 2121-18 and NR 389-126, Geography Branch, U.S. Office of Naval Research.]

This population is served by a hierarchy of shopping centers ranging from corner grocery stores to the metropolitan central business district. The forces controlling the structure and pattern of urban shopping centers are the same as those inherent in the rural central place hierarchy. It is simply a matter of differences in scale and population density. In low density areas (wheatlands or corn belt in figure 3.39) centers must serve large areas (square kilometers) to capture a threshold population. Centers in densely populated areas (urban and suburban Chicago) meet threshold conditions with much smaller market areas.

Berry (1967) noted that different levels of the hierarchy in each of the rural areas and the level of business centers within cities are so consistent that straight lines may be drawn linking the upper limits of each level (figure 3.40). Notice, however, that the lines separating each level are not vertical (remember figure 3.37), indicating that the adjustment to variations in density is not perfect. It is evident from figure 3.40 that level-1 centers in high density areas serve larger populations than level-1 centers in low density areas. Some goods whose thresholds are met in level-1 centers in high density areas may not be offered until level-2 is reached in low density areas.

Berry (1967, p. 33) noted that "functions with the greatest threshold requirements at any level of the hierarchy move up to the next level." This indicates that there may be an adjustment of the entire functional structure (hierarchical margins)

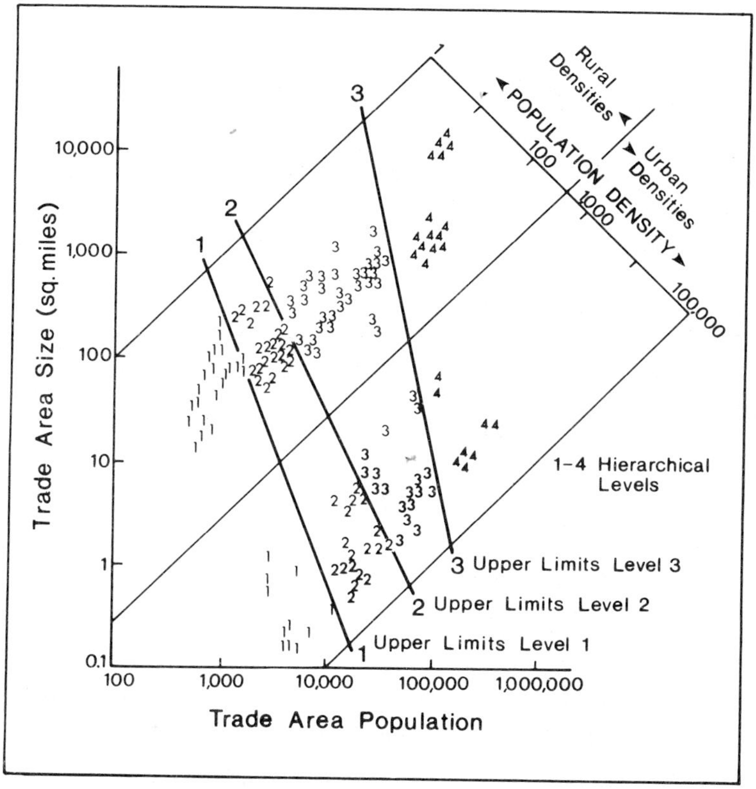

FIGURE 3.40 Hierarchical limits of settlements. [From Brian J. L. Berry and Harold M. Mayer (1962) *Comparative Studies of Central Place Systems*, Final Report NONR 2121-18 and NR 389-126, Geography Branch, U.S. Office of Naval Research.]

when large population density changes occur. There is some empirical evidence for this adjustment, but we should also note that the threshold of a given good may change with density. Building, land, and labor costs are lower in sparsely populated areas; a given function may meet its threshold with a smaller total population.

Remember also that a threshold represents the *minimum* market population, not the maximum a function can serve. A given function in a rural area may serve just a threshold population, while the same function in a densely populated region may serve many times the threshold population. There is some empirical evidence for this also. Long waiting lines at gasoline stations were characteristic in large cities during the fuel crisis of 1974. Such lines were not found in small and medium-sized centers. This may indicate a smaller total population served by gas stations in more sparsely settled areas.

Spacing of Urban Centers King (1962) analyzed the distribution of urban places in a comparative study of 20 sample areas in the United States to determine the regularity in the spacing of urban centers. He applied the technique of *nearest-neighbor analysis,* which was first developed by plant ecologists, to measure the difference between actual and expected settlement arrangements. The nearest-neighbor index of spacing is obtained by comparing the observed pattern with a theoretical random distribution; that is,

$$R = \frac{Dobs}{Dexp}$$

where

R = the nearest-neighbor index of spacing,
$Dobs$ = average observed distances between each urban center and its nearest neighbor,
$Dexp$ = expected average difference between each urban center and its nearest neighbor.

The expected average distance is given by:

$$Dexp = \frac{1}{2\sqrt{A}}$$

where

A = density of urban centers.

The nearest-neighbor index of spacing ranges from a theoretical low of zero, when the settlement pattern is clustered, to a maximum value of 2.15 when the pattern is uniform. A value of 1.0 results when the distribution is random.

King's results ranged from 0.70 in the case of the Utah sample area to 1.38 in Missouri. Most of the sample areas had R-values between 0.5 and 1.5. King concluded that the United States settlement pattern is not uniform, but approximates a random pattern. Deviations from a uniform pattern are the result of environmental, economic, cultural, and historical factors.

Several researchers have claimed that a characteristic distance separates centers which function predominantly as central places. Higher order centers are spaced more widely apart than lower order centers. Lösch (1954), for example, found a close correspondence in Iowa, a state with a relatively uniform environment, between observed and theoretical distances in a $k = 4$ system (table 3.12). Brush (1953) examined the spacing of hamlets, villages, and towns in an area of southwestern Wisconsin and noted a negligible difference between actual and theoretical settlement spacing (table 3.13). By contrast, Dacey (1962), who selected the same area studied by Brush, conducted a nearest-neighbor analysis and concluded that the overall settlement pattern was more random than regular. We cannot, however, expect the distribution of central places to be regularly arranged in absolute space. Figure 3.27 revealed, for example, that regularities anticipated by central place theory are more apparent when we use a transformation of distance based on population density.

Bogue (1949) provided an empirical confirmation of the tendency of population to agglomerate around metropolitan centers by population density gradients from the center of 67 United States cities. Generalized cross-sections showed: (1) that population density declines with distance from the metropolis; (2) that density and

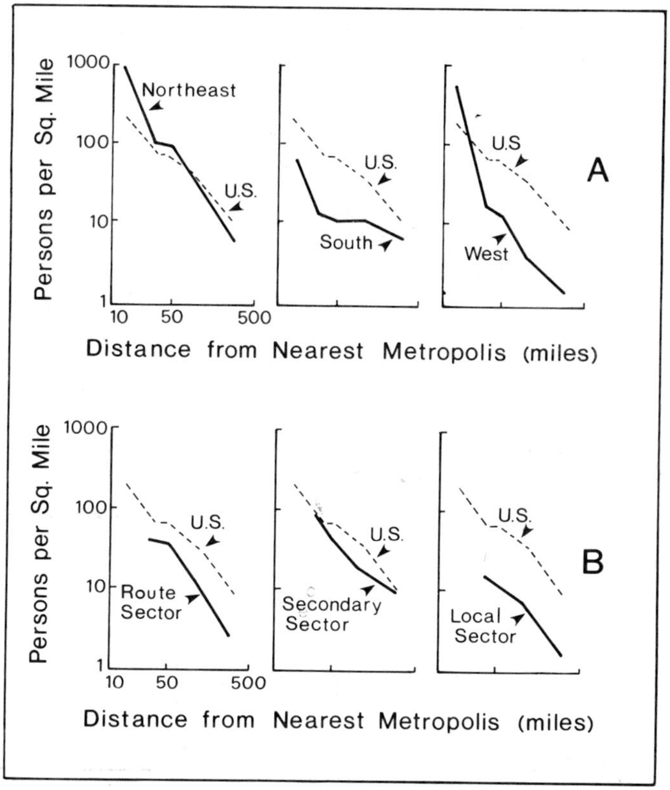

FIGURE 3.41 Intercity density-distance relationships by region (A) and by Sector (B) in the United States. [From Donald Joseph Bogue. *The Structure of the Metropolitan Community: A Study of Dominance and Subdominance*. (1950) New York: Russell & Russell, 1971.]

the rate of decline vary with the size of the metropolitan community; (3) that density and rate of decline vary with the region of the United States (figure 3.41A); and (4) that density and rate of decline vary with the direction from the metropolis (figure 3.41B). Bogue recognized three types of sectors: (1) a route sector that has a major highway leading from the city to other major metropolitan areas; (2) a secondary sector that has at least one city of 25,000 or more people; and (3) a local sector that has neither a major highway nor major urban center. Density trends for the three sectors (figure 3.41B) indicate that densities are greatest in the secondary sector. Densities along route sectors are lower than might be expected from Lösch's model of city-rich and city-poor sectors. Nonetheless, Bogue's empirical study does lend support to Lösch's hypothesis concerning the arrangement of urban centers around the metropolis.

TABLE 3.12 Regional systems in Iowa: theory and reality correspondence with theoretical system for $K = 4$

Size Class of Regions	Centers: Number		Centers: Distance Apart (Miles)	
	Theory[1]	Reality	Theory[1]	Reality
1	615		5.6	
2	154	153	11.2	10.3
3	39	39	22.4	23.6
4	10	9	44.8	49.6
5	2-3	3	89.6	94.0
6	0-1		179.2	

Source: August Lösch (1967), *The Economics of Location,* Stuttgart: Gustav Fischer Verlag, p. 435.

[1] The values actually obtained for class 1 were the starting point for the calculation of all theoretical values.

TABLE 3.13 Spacing of central places in southwestern Wisconsin

Between-Center Distances	142 Hamlets	73 Villages	19 Towns
Theoretical Distance	5.8 miles	10.4 miles	20.5 miles
Mean Measured Distance	5.5 miles	9.9 miles	21.2 miles
Range of Variation	1.0-12.0 miles	3.5-18.5 miles	7.0-38.0 miles

Source: J. E. Brush (1953), "The Hierarchy of Central Places in Southwestern Wisconsin," *Geographical Review* **43**, p. 393, table 2.

Consumer Travel as a Mirror of the Hierarchy

We have concentrated on the functional structure and arrangement of central places. A central place system can *only* result from consistent aggregate consumer behavior. Christaller's theory of central places states that consumers behave, on the average, predictably. They obtain goods and services from the nearest possible center. We will examine a few examples of low and high order goods and see whether theory matches reality.

Figures 3.42 through 3.45 show the shopping preferences of both rural and urban consumers for selected central functions. A line is drawn from the residence of a rural consumer to the central place where the good in question is purchased *most frequently*. A circle is drawn around each place in the maps for urban consumers. If the individual purchases the good most frequently in his own settlement, a ray is drawn from the circle to the settlement; if purchases are made more frequently in another town, an arrow is drawn from the residence settlement circle to the preferred central place's circle.

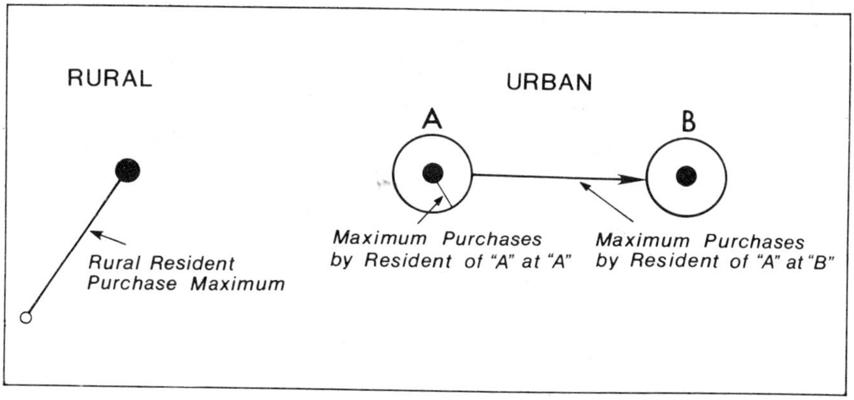

Figures 3.42 through 3.45 show the primary purchase movements (see box above) of consumers for four different goods in southwestern Iowa. Clothing is the highest level good (city-level) followed by furniture and dry cleaning (town-level). Groceries are the lowest level function (village-level). Consumers must consider the order of a good because it limits the number of possible purchase points. Within the framework of where goods are actually offered, however, consumers have some options about where the function is purchased. The distinction is primarily made between *convenience* and *shopping* goods (see box p. 124). Consumers will generally travel to the closest possible place for convenience goods, but will often travel to higher level centers for shopping goods even if they can be obtained locally.

Clothing is a city-level shopping good (figure 3.42). Three city-level places are present in the figure: Atlantic, Red Oak, and Omaha-Council Bluffs (the latter is a regional-level center and also offers city-level functions). Consumers generally go to the closest place that offers clothing, forming a rather clear trade area boundary between Atlantic and Red Oak in both the rural and urban preference maps. Notice, however, that Omaha-Council Bluffs is able to attract consumers over much greater distances than are the two city-level centers. The few purchases made in Griswold, Oakland, and Elliot consist of work clothing which is a lower-order good than general clothing.

Figure 3.43 shows consumer travel patterns for furniture (town-level shopping good). The most important feature of the figure is the emergence of Griswold as a

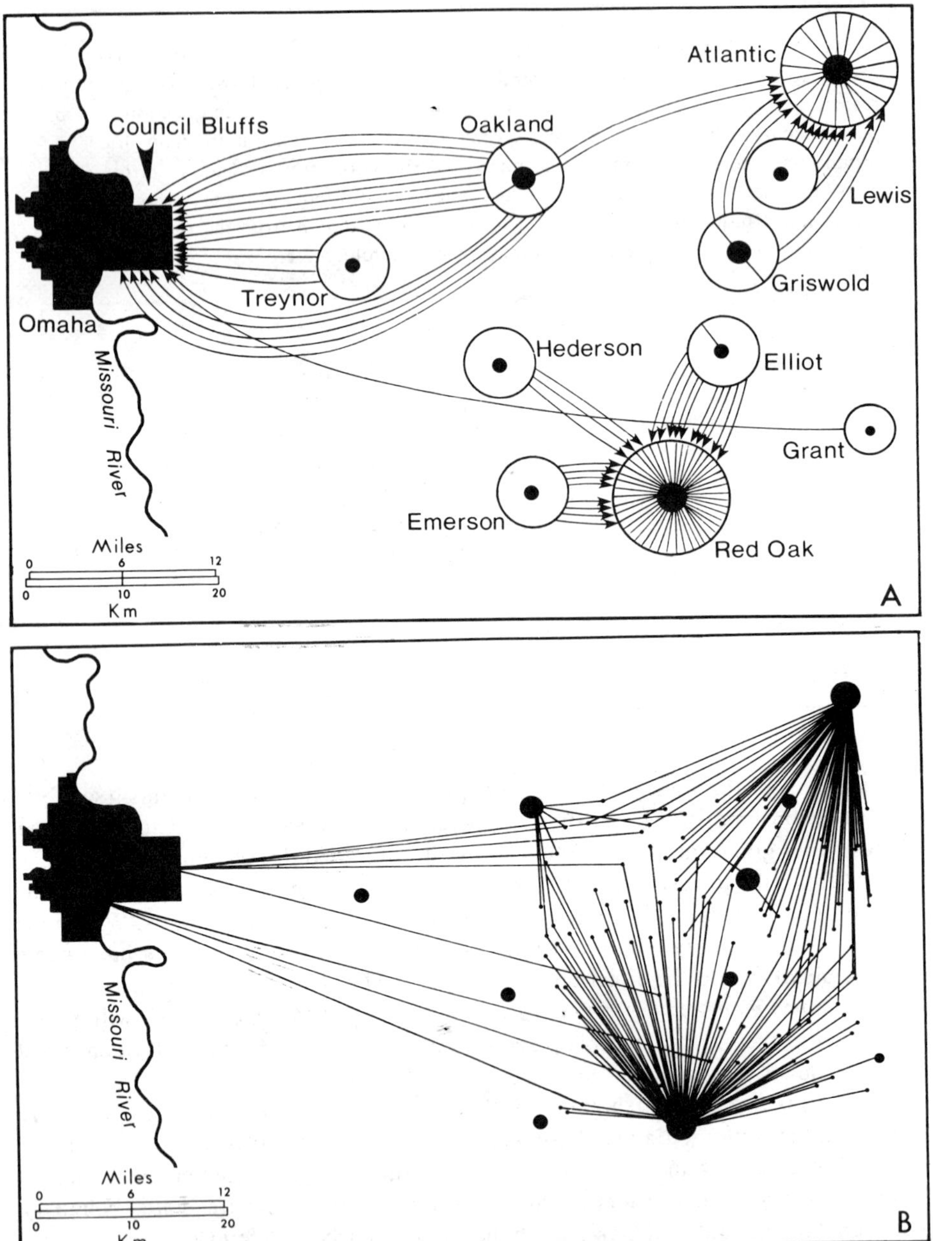

FIGURE 3.42 Purchase movements of urban (A) and rural (B) consumers for clothing in southwestern Iowa, 1960. [From Brian J. L. Berry and Harold M. Mayer (1962) *Comparative Studies of Central Place Systems,* Final Report NONR 2121-18 and NR 389-126, Geography Branch, U.S. Office of Naval Research.]

central place at this level. This is especially evident when the rural preference map Griswold has ''squeezed in'' between Atlantic and Red Oak. Once again, however, consumers are willing to travel much greater distances to Omaha-Council Bluffs to shop for furniture than to the lower order centers where selection is limited and prices may be higher.

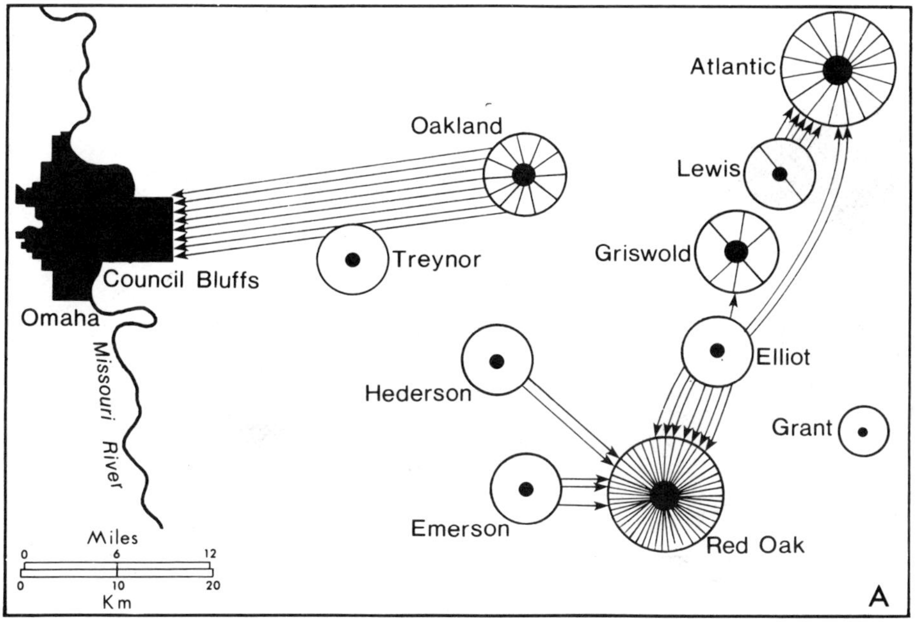

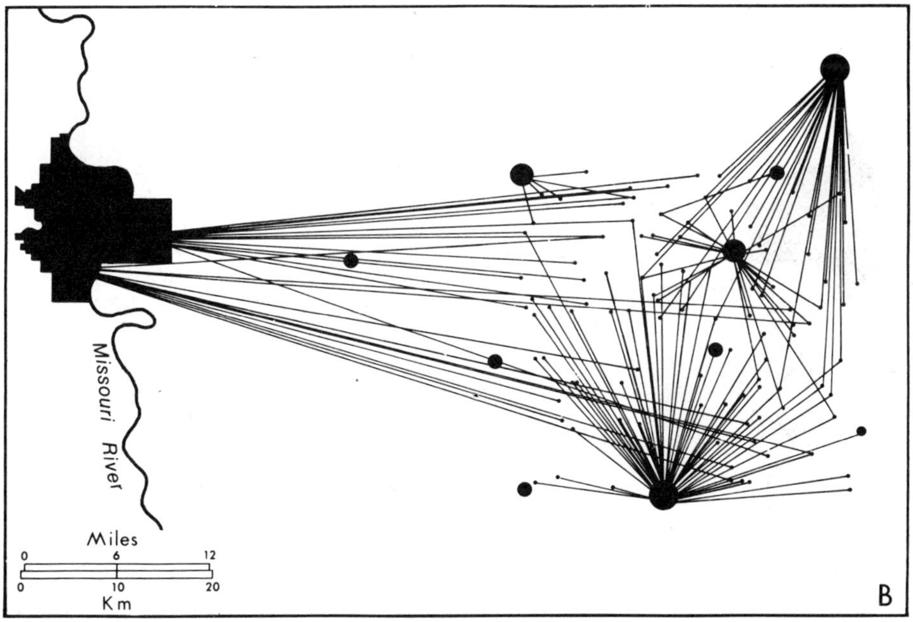

FIGURE 3.43 Purchase movements of urban (A) and rural (B) consumers for furniture in southwestern Iowa, 1960. [From Brian J. L. Berry and Harold M. Mayer (1962) *Comparative Studies of Central Place Systems*, Final Report NONR 2121-18 and NR 389-126, Geography Branch, U.S. Office of Naval Research.]

Dry cleaning is also a town-level good, but it is a convenience good (figure 3.44). One dry cleaner is much like any other and this service is utilized rather frequently. Consumers in figure 3.44 go to the closest possible center for dry cleaning. Oakland is a good example. For furniture, many residents interviewed in Oakland traveled to

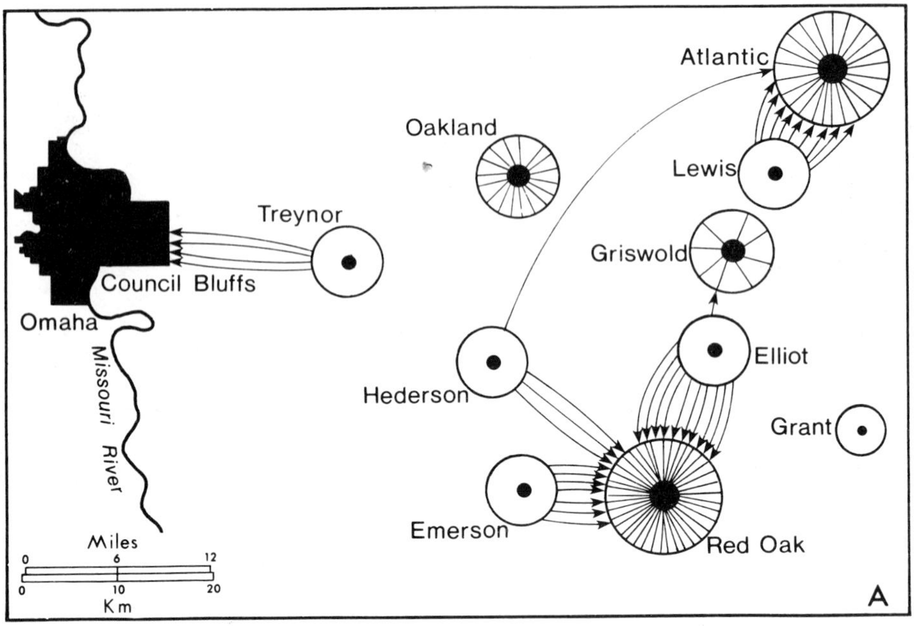

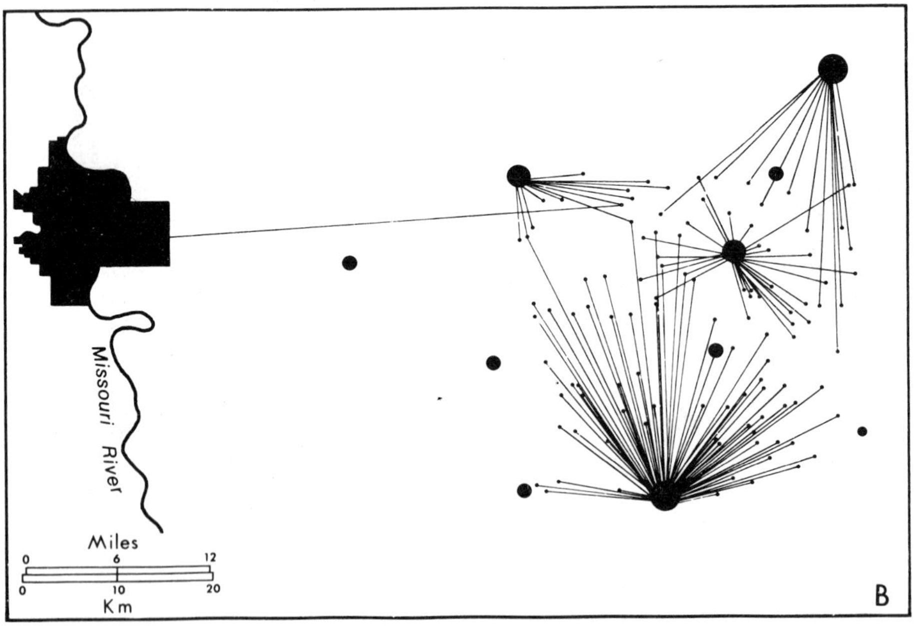

FIGURE 3.44 Purchase movements of urban (A) and rural (B) consumers for dry cleaning in southwestern Iowa, 1960. [From Brian J. L. Berry and Harold M. Mayer (1962) *Comparative Studies of Central Place Systems*, Final Report NONR 2121-18 and NR 389-126, Geography Branch, U.S. Office of Naval Research.]

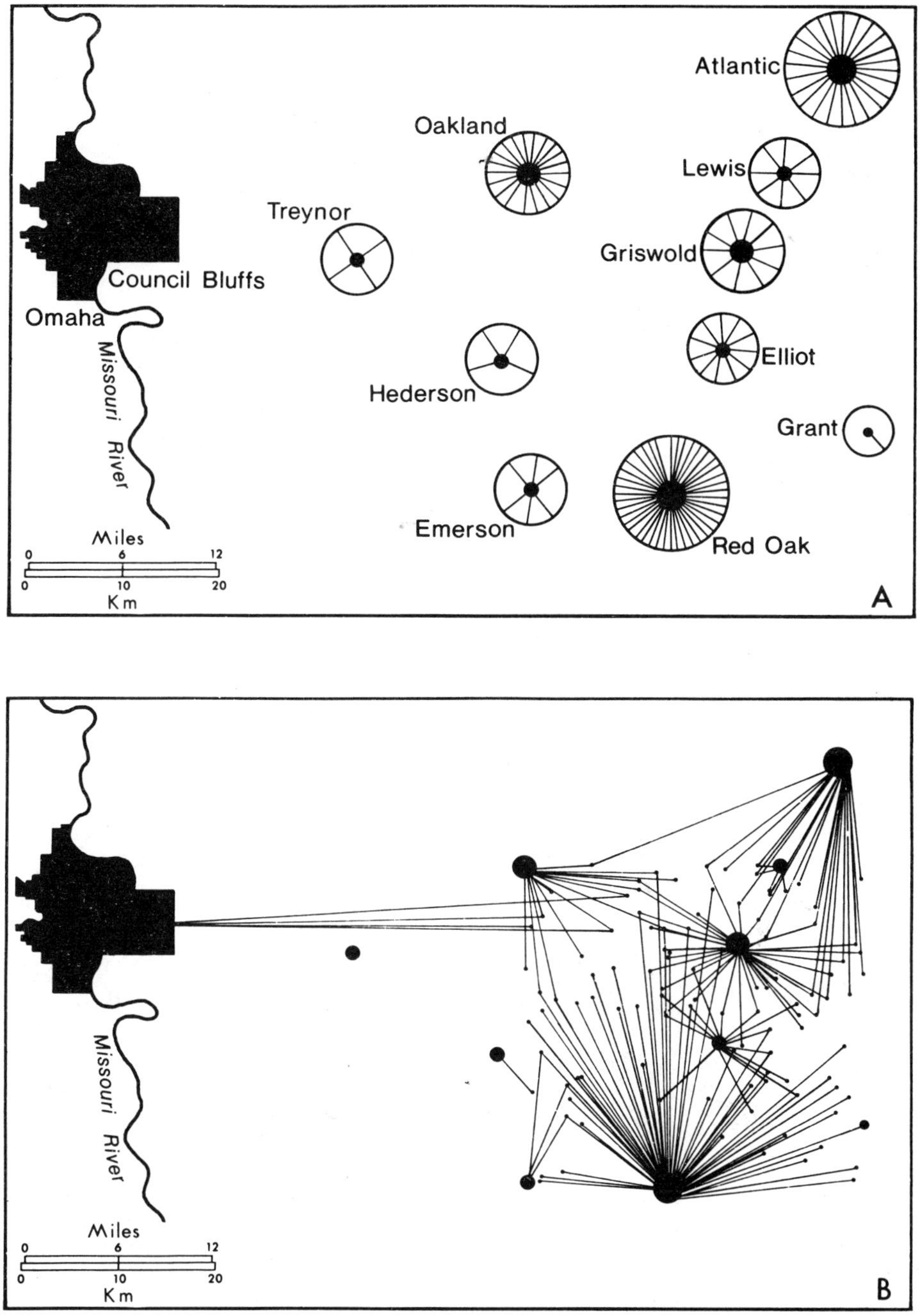

FIGURE 3.45 Purchase movements of urban (A) and rural (B) consumers for foodstuffs in southwestern Iowa, 1960. [From Brian J. L. Berry and Harold M. Mayer (1962) *Comparative Studies of Central Place Systems*, Final Report NONR 2121-18 and NR 389-126, Geography Branch, U.S. Office of Naval Research.]

Convenience goods are low in price, uniform in quality and style, and are purchased frequently. They are often termed "short-run necessities" and include the goods and services we need on a day-to-day basis such as groceries, gasoline, and drugstore items.

Shopping goods tend to be higher in price, vary considerably in quality and style, and are purchased infrequently. They are goods for which we "comparison shop." Furniture is an excellent example. We buy furniture infrequently and it is also an item for which we may visit several stores to compare prices, styles, and quality. Because it is a shopping good, consumers are more likely to visit a center where comparison shopping is possible (higher order center). The cost of a long-distance shopping trip as a proportion of total cost is much lower on a high-priced good, and consumers are usually willing to pay this minor cost to obtain the satisfaction and utility of greater selection.

Omaha-Council Bluffs, but all dry cleaning was done locally. This is also true of the rural residents of each center's hinterland. Notice, however, that higher order centers like Red Oak and Atlantic are able to attract consumers over greater distances than lower-level Griswold. Consumers probably combine their dry-cleaning trips with other types of shopping travel.

Figure 3.45 shows primary purchase trips for groceries (village-level, convenience good). Urban residents make almost all grocery purchases locally. Rural residents make a distinction among the orders of centers, but once again are making multipurpose shopping trips.

We do not expect reality to exactly replicate the geometric precision of the central place model because the normative constraints are not met even in the most homogeneous areas of the United States. Central place theory is a model which helps us to better understand and predict spatial patterns of consumer behavior. We must keep in mind that human beings are not economic optimizers, but do, to a limited extent, adhere to the principle of distance minimization. We can only understand the maps of consumer behavior in southwestern Iowa within the context of central place theory, and the accuracy of our understanding is amplified by reference to the model. That is the great utility of any model.

Summary

We have considered the central place model from the standpoint of man's spatial organization of tertiary activity. We constructed the basic central place model within highly constrained conditions, holding constant all variables except for the frictional effects of distance, and produced an orderly tertiary economic landscape. We outlined the assumptions, content, limitations, and extensions of classical central place theory. The chapter ended with examples of central place hierarchies in the United States, and we observed that actual conditions distort and transform theoretical networks of central places.

Central place theory stems from classical economic theory. In the study of central places, geographers have relied on three concepts to explain the spatial equilibrium of central places: (1) threshold, (2) range, and (3) hierarchy. Central place activities are arranged into a hierarchy according to the functions they perform. High order places, the metropolitan wholesaling cities, weld regions of a national market exchange economy together. Within each metropolitan trade region there is a chain of lower-order centers—smaller cities, towns, villages, and hamlets—that function as markets for the distribution of goods and services. The central place system may be regarded as a multiple system of nested centers.

The theory of central places is not a dynamic theory. It does not explain the forces that promote the growth and change of centers at specific locations. However, concepts of central place theory have been used for planning purposes. Many underdeveloped countries, for example, have primate city distributions. Western regional science usually recommends that planners streamline urban systems. They are advised to develop a "balanced" hierarchy of urban centers that link central cities with interstitial areas. Central place notions have been used to design new market centers in the polders of the Netherlands, and to find new locations for shopping centers in cities, and for services such as educational and medical systems.

KEY WORDS

administration principle
central function
central place
centrality
complementary region
convenience good
establishment
functional size
functional unit
hierarchical marginal good
Law of allometric growth
linear market
marketing principle
mercantile model
nearest neighbor analysis
rank-size rule
range of a good
settlement-building function
settlement-forming function
shopping good
threshold
traffic principle
urban multiplier

SUGGESTED READINGS

Primary Sources

Christaller, W. (1966), *Central Places in Southern Germany,* Englewood Cliffs, N.J.: Prentice-Hall (transl.).

Lösch, A. (1954), *The Economics of Location,* New Haven: Yale University Press.

Berry, B. J. L. (1967), *Geography of Market Centers and Retail Distribution,* Englewood Cliffs, N.J.: Prentice-Hall.

Von Boventer, Edwin (1970), ''Towards a United Theory of Spatial Economic Structure'' in Robert D. Dean et al. (eds.), *Spatial Economic Theory,* New York: The Free Press, pp. 325–55.

Settlement Hierarchies and Their Structures Haggett, P. (1965), *Locational Analysis in Human Geography,* London: Edward Arnold, Chapers 4 and 5.

Empirical Studies

Berry, B. J. L. (1961), ''City Size Distributions and Economic Development,'' *Economic Development and Cultural Change* **9**, 573–88.

______(1967), *Geography of Market Centers and Retail Distribution,* Englewood Cliffs, N.J.: Prentice-Hall, Chapters 1, 2, and 6.

Berry, B. J. L., H. G. Barnum and R. J. Tennant (1962), ''Retail Location and Consumer Behavior,'' *Regional Science Association, Papers and Proceedings* **9**, 65–106.

Berry B.J.L., J. R. Simmons and R. Tennant (1963), ''Urban Population Densities: Structure and Change,'' *The Geographical Review* **53**, 389–405.

Borchert, J. R. Minneapolis (1963), *Trade Centers and Trade Areas of the Upper Midwest,* Urban Report 2, Upper Midwest Economic Study, University of Minnesota Press, 14.

Vance, James E., Jr. (1970), *The Merchant's World: The Geography of Wholesaling,* Englewood Cliffs, N.J.: Prentice-Hall, Chapters 3, 4, and 5.

4 Manufacturing

Introduction

Various types of manufacturing exhibit quite different patterns. Some types of manufacturing are scattered; others are concentrated at a few locations. Orderly principles underlie these patterns. This chapter is concerned with introducing and amplifying those principles. Manufacturing patterns are the result of complex forces including environmental, economic, political, and cultural factors. We will concentrate our attention on the *spatial* forces which influence locational patterns of manufacturing.

Chapter Objectives

Primary: Examine the major forces which control patterns of manufacturing.

Secondary:

1. Discuss in detail the model of industrial location developed by Alfred Weber.
2. Introduce some important modifications of Weber's model.
3. Consider the effects of changes in technique on Weber's model.
4. Consider the effects of scale changes on industrial location.
5. Discuss the implications of demand on patterns of manufacturing.
6. Introduce the concept of locational interdependence.

The Nature of Manufacturing

Manufacturing involves: (1) bringing together raw materials to a processing point; (2) changing the form of these raw materials; and (3) distributing a finished product.

Gathering raw materials at a point and distributing a finished product require movement. Classical locational theory is an attempt to discover locations that will minimize the transportation costs of raw material gathering and finished product distribution. Changing the form of a raw material involves all factors of production (land, labor, capital, and management skills) that vary widely in cost from point to point. All three steps of the manufacturing process, therefore, have a spatial or locational dimension.

Changing the form of a raw material increases its utility or value. Flour milled from wheat is more valuable than raw grain. This increase is termed *value added* by manufacturing. Bread, in turn, is worth more than flour. Value added may be quite low in an industry engaged in the initial processing of a raw material, but a few ounces of steel and glass changed into a watch yield a high value added (table 4.1). The cost of labor or the availability of skills plays an important role in high value-added manufacturing; the cost of raw materials is the key variable in others. The relative importance of factors is called *orientation*. Terms such as ''raw material-oriented'' or ''market-oriented'' are used throughout this chapter to specify the key variable for a given industry.

Uneven Distribution of Raw Materials

One of the key constraints of our initial model of agricultural production was the assumption of evenly distributed resources. Points of manufacturing (cities) would develop even if all resources were ubiquitous. Manufacturing would operate at selected points and incur only two kinds of cost: (1) production costs which involve the interrelationships among the other factors of production (labor, capital, and technical skills) and demand; and (2) the cost of distributing the finished product to dispersed markets.

TABLE 4.1 Value added by manufacturing as a percentage of total value of shipments

Industry	Percent
Food	30
Textiles	41
Apparel	48
Lumber and wood products	43
Furniture	53
Paper products	46
Printing and publishing	67
Chemical products	56
Petroleum products	20
Leather products	50
Stone, clay, and glass products	58
Primary metal products	39
Fabricated metal products	52
Nonelectrical machinery	57
Electrical machinery	57
Instruments	67

Source: *1972 U.S. Census of Manufactures.*

One of the most obvious features of reality, however, is the fact that resources are *unevenly* distributed across space. This is especially true of the raw materials required for heavy manufacturing. Even those industries that use "producer's goods" as their raw material face an uneven distribution of material inputs. Manufacturing is therefore usually concerned with a third kind of cost: *assembly costs* or the price which must be paid to bring raw materials together from diverse locations to a single production point. Assembly costs are the main concern of classical industrial location theory.

> *Producer's goods:* "raw materials" created by manufacturing rather than coming directly from the resource base. A firm that assembles electronic calculators may purchase all its raw materials (integrated circuits, plastic, light-emitting diodes) from other manufacturers. Such a firm inputs only producer's goods.

The Simple Weberian Model: Assembly Costs

Classical location theory is founded on the work of Alfred Weber, who attempted to determine the patterns of manufacturing that would develop given a certain set of normative constraints. Weber began by assuming that transportation costs are a linear function of distance. This simplification of transportation costs constitutes one of the major criticisms of Weberian analysis, but we will preserve this assumption throughout this chapter. Transportation costs as they exist in reality and their effects on the Weberian system will be considered in detail in chapter 5. Weber also implied that the demand for a product is infinite at a given price. Each producer can sell as many units as he produces at a fixed price. He can sell none at a higher price, and charging a lower price will not affect the total demand for the product. The producer's strategy is therefore to produce the product at the lowest possible cost, thus maximizing revenue. For this reason, Weber's system is called a "least-cost approach."

> Alfred Weber (1868–1958) was a German economist who taught at the University of Prague from 1904 to 1907 and the University of Heidelberg from 1907 to 1933. His *Theory of the Location of Industries* was published in 1909 and has become the standard treatise on many aspects of industrial location. Subsequent general theories of industrial location have been modifications or extensions of Weber's general theory.

Weber's theory is also a "general theory" in that it can be applied to all politico-economic systems and all types of industries. He was concerned with identifying "those forces which operate as economic causes of location" represented in each case by savings in cost as a result of producing in one place rather than some other (Weber 1929, pp. 17–18). These forces are called *location factors* (see box).

Weber also distinguished between "general" factors which apply to all industries (transport costs, labor, and rent) and "special" forces which operate only on a specific industry. General and special factors are further subdivided into "regional" and "local" forces. Regional forces determine the general locational framework of manufacturing and include transportation and labor costs. Regional forces are, according to Weber, the result of spatial variations in raw material and labor costs. Local forces, on the other hand, cause the pattern of manufacturing to deviate from the optimum patterns produced by regional forces alone and tend to be economic in origin. Economies of scale and the high rent brought about by competition are examples.

> *Location factor:* any of the forces that operate as a cause of industrial location.

Transportation sets the general regional pattern of manufacturing. This pattern is in turn distorted by spatial variations in the cost of labor. The final solution must consider the effects of local factors. Weber's approach is to consider each set of forces in sequence, which increases the complexity of analysis.

Weber's Raw Material Classes

The first cost faced by manufacturing is the cost of assembling raw materials. Weber approached this problem by devising a simple classification system for raw materials. First, they are classified by their frequency-of-occurrence: (a) ubiquitous raw materials are universally distributed and, therefore, always have a transportation cost of zero; (b) *localized* raw materials are found only at specific locations. Transportation costs on localized raw materials are a function of the distance they must be moved. Second, Weber classified raw materials on the basis of the amount of weight lost during processing: (a) *pure* raw materials lose no weight in processing; a 150-pound transmission entering an auto-assembly plant as a raw material adds 150 pounds of weight to the finished automobile; (b) *gross* raw materials lose weight during processing. Weber deals with weight loss through a material index that measures the ratio of raw material to finished product weight. The index is the weight of the raw material divided by its processed (finished) weight. Pure raw materials have a material index of one. Weight-losing raw materials have a material index greater than one. The production of pure copper in the United States is an example. One hundred tons of copper ore are required to produce one ton of copper, so the material index for copper is 99. Fuels have the highest material index; none of their weight enters the weight of the finished product.

We are now ready to consider the effects of transportation costs for a number of different kinds of raw materials. For each case we must examine: (a) the cost of assembling raw materials (*RM*); (b) the cost of distributing the finished product (*FP*); and (c) total transportation costs (*TTC*). The optimum location in the Weberian system occurs where total transportation costs are minimized. All the cases with their final solutions are given in table 4.2.

Ubiquities Only

Only *localized* raw materials can attract production, and ubiquities merely add to the pull of the market. In all cases, we are assuming the existence of a single market point. Ubiquitous raw materials occur everywhere so the cost of their assembly is always zero. Only finished product costs are important, and they are reduced to zero with a location at the market point. This is illustrated by figure 4.1. Raw material costs (*RM*) are the line 0-0. Finished product distribution costs rise steadily away from the market. The cost line *FP* also marks total transportation costs that are minimized at the market.

TABLE 4.2 Solutions to Weber's locational problems

Material Classes	Location
Ubiquities only	Market
Localized and pure	
One pure	Anywhere between source of raw material and market
One pure and ubiquities	Market
More than one pure	Market
More than one pure and ubiquities	Market
Localized and weight losing (gross)	
One weight losing	Source
One weight losing and ubiquities	Source or market depending on relative size of input
More than one weight losing	Indeterminate (mathematical solution)
More than one weight losing and ubiquities	Indeterminate (mathematical solution)

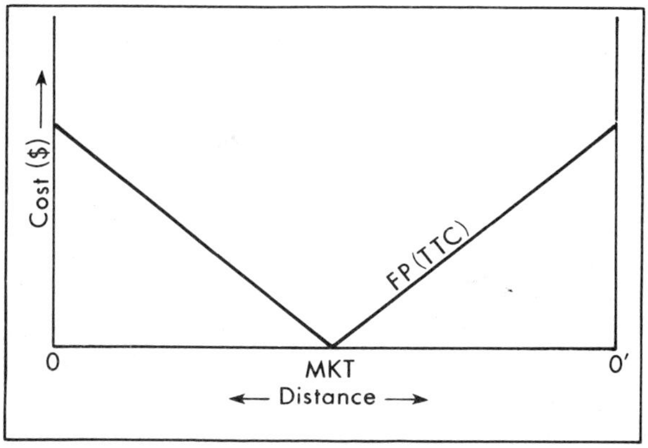

FIGURE 4.1 Weber's model: ubiquities only.

Localized, Pure Raw Materials Figure 4.2 illustrates costs given one pure localized raw material and a single market. The material is localized at *RM* and the market is at *M*. The line *RM* gives the assembly costs which increase as a function of distance from the source of the localized raw material. Similarly, the line *FP* gives the distribution costs for the finished product. Total transportation cost (*TTC*) is the sum of *RM* and *FP*. At *RM*, *TTC* = \$7.00 (*RM* = \$0, *FP* = \$7.00, *TTC* = \$7.00). At 0, *RM* = \$3.50, *FP* = \$3.50, so that *TTC* = \$7.00. Total transportation costs are exactly \$7.00 everywhere along a straight line between mine and market, so that manufacturing can locate anywhere along this line and minimize costs.

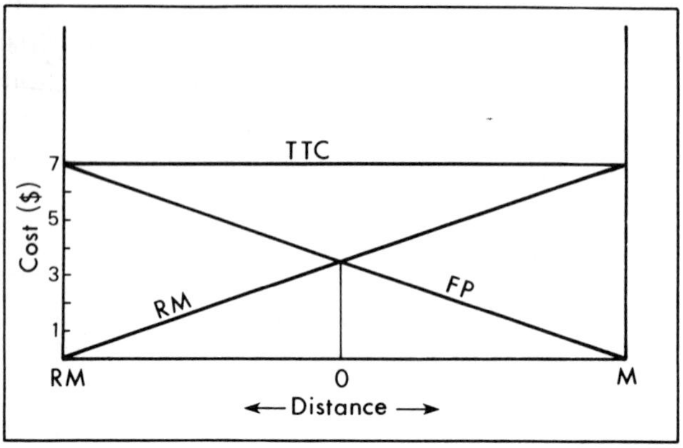

FIGURE 4.2 Weber's model: one pure, localized raw material.

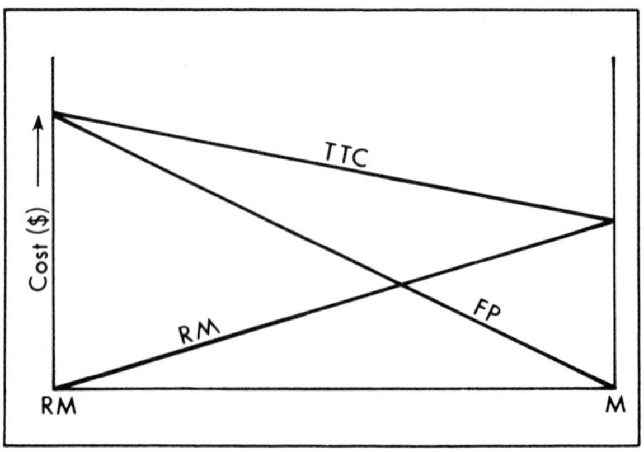

FIGURE 4.3 Weber's model: one pure, localized raw material plus ubiquities.

One Pure Localized Raw Material plus Ubiquities Figure 4.3 shows the assembly costs for the localized raw material (*RM*) are minimized at *RM*. Ubiquitous assembly costs are zero everywhere and finished product distribution costs are minimized at *M*. Ubiquitous raw materials, once processed, add to the weight of the finished product so that total transportation costs (*TTC*) are minimized at the market (*M*). In other words, this location avoids the necessity of moving the ubiquitous material in its processed form. The optimum location is at *M*.

Figure 4.4 shows the pattern of bottled and canned soft drink manufacturing in the United States in 1963. This type of manufacturing uses one pure raw material (syrup concentrate) and water which is an ubiquitous raw material. The map shows a very high association between soft drink manufacturing and population, indicating that the industry is market oriented. Such a location pattern removes the need to move the ubiquitous raw material (water) which also makes the largest contribution to the weight of the finished product.

Several Pure, Localized Raw Materials Figure 4.5 shows the solution for two pure, localized raw materials, but the outcome is the same for more than two. Once again, the single market is at *M*; one pure raw material is localized at RM_1,

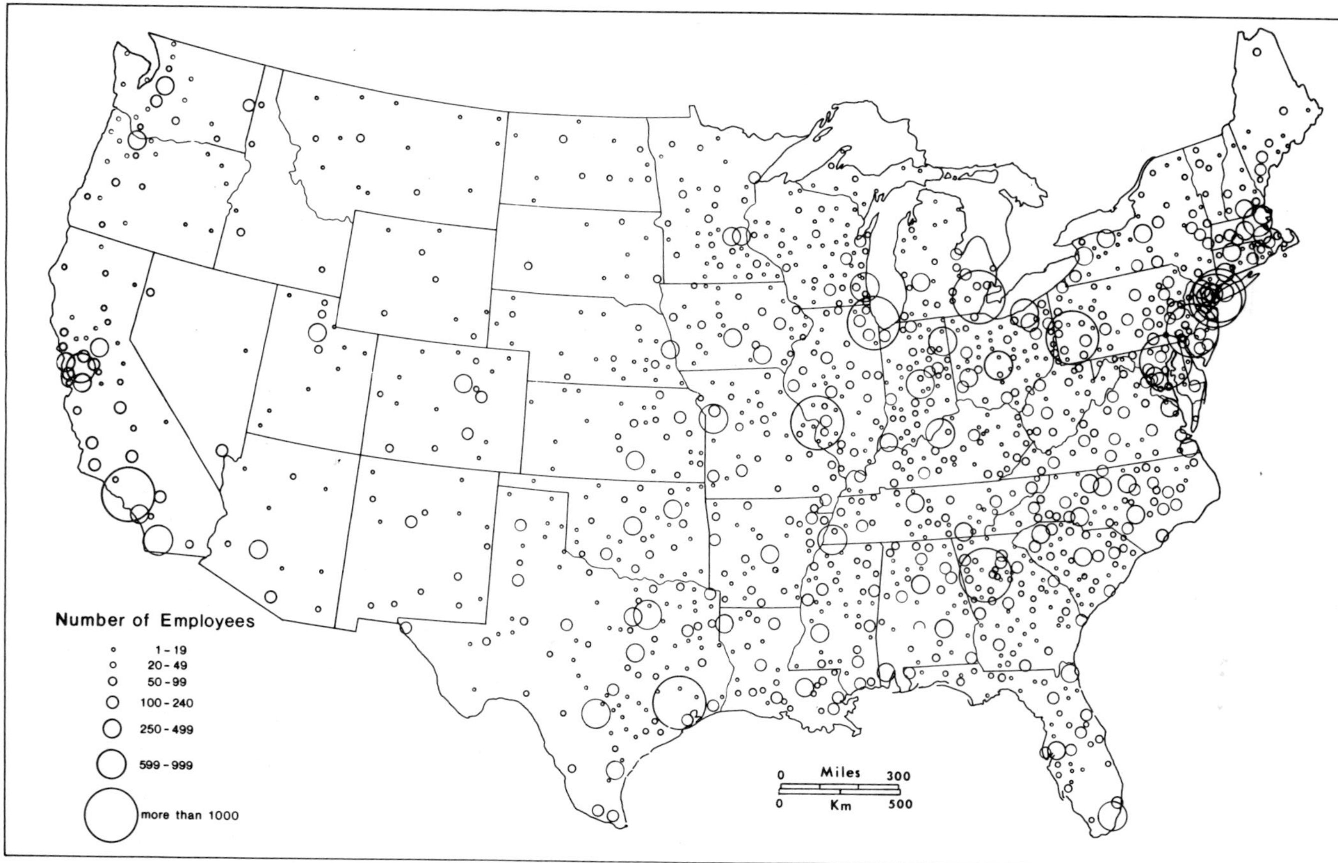

FIGURE 4.4 Location pattern of bottled and canned soft drink manufacturing, 1963.

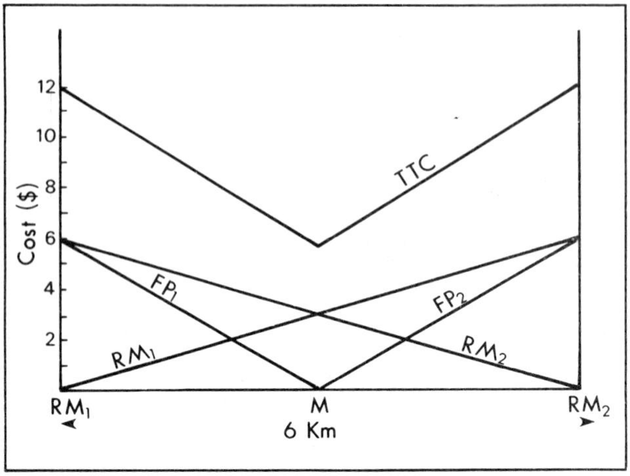

FIGURE 4.5 Weber's model: two pure, localized raw materials.

and the other is localized at RM_2. The transportation cost for each raw material is given by the lines RM_1 and RM_2. Assume in figure 4.5 that equal amounts of each raw material are used and that transport costs are $1 per ton-km. Consider a location at RM_1: RM_1 = $0, RM_2 = $6 (one ton moved six km), but we have a finished product which weighs *two* tons (both raw materials are pure). It will cost us $6 to ship the finished product back to *M* (two tons shipped three km @ $1 per ton-km = $6) so that total transportation costs (*TTC*) at RM_1 equal $12. The same total transportation costs are also true of a location at RM_2. At *M*, however, total transportation costs equal $6 (one ton of RM_1 moved three km + one ton of RM_2 moved three km @ $1 per ton-km = $6). Total transportation costs are minimized at the market. Such a location eliminates the need to "back-haul" a raw material.

Several Pure, Localized Raw Materials plus Ubiquities This case is illustrated in figure 4.6. Remember that ubiquities always add to the pull of the market. We are assuming in figure 4.6 that equal parts of RM_1, RM_2, and the ubiquitous raw materials are used so that the finished product weighs three tons (assuming an input of one ton each of the raw materials). Finished product distribution costs at RM_1 and RM_2 are now $9. Localized raw material costs (RM_2) equal $6, finished product distribution costs (FP_2) equal $9 (three tons moved three km), and total transportation costs equal $15 at RM_1 or RM_2 while they equal only $6 at *M*. The pull of the market is considerably strengthened by the addition of ubiquitous raw materials.

Figure 4.7 shows the distribution pattern of ready-mixed concrete production in the United States in 1963. This industry is a good example of the use of pure raw materials plus ubiquities. The industry uses portland cement (pure), aggregate (pure and often ubiquitous), and water (ubiquitous). Weberian theory indicates that costs are minimized at the market. The pattern presented in figure 4.7 shows a very high correlation between ready-mixed concrete production and the population distribution of the United States, indicating market orientation.

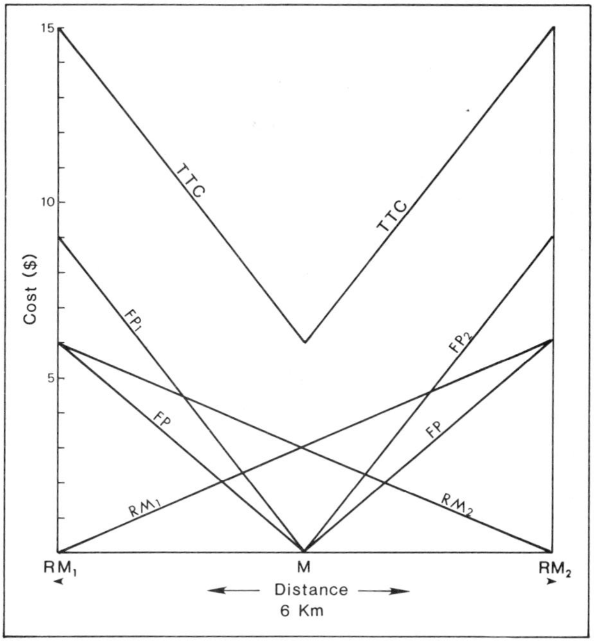

FIGURE 4.6 Weber's model: several pure, localized raw materials plus ubiquities.

Weight-Losing Raw Materials

Weight-losing raw materials have a material index greater than 1. We now need to consider several cases involving localized raw materials that lose weight in processing.

One Localized, Weight-Losing Raw Material Figure 4.8 illustrates this particular situation. Assume that the raw material (located at *RM*) loses one-half its weight in processing ($MI = 2$). Each unit of the raw material shipped to the market (*M*) costs $10 (line *RM*), but each unit of the finished product shipped from the mine costs only $5. Total transportation costs (*TTC*) are minimized at the raw material source. Copper concentration in the United States illustrates this situation. Copper ore has a high material index (99), and concentration always takes place very near copper mines. Such a location eliminates transportation costs paid to move waste.

One Localized, Weight-Losing Raw Material plus Ubiquities The solution to this case depends upon the ratio of weight lost through processing to the weight of the ubiquitous material. Two extreme cases are illustrated in figures 4.9A and 4.9B. In figure 4.9A, the weight-losing raw material is a fuel and all its weight is lost in the manufacturing process. Assume that one ton of fuel (localized at *RM*) and 1000 pounds of the ubiquitous raw material are required to produce 1000 pounds of the finished product. Total transportation costs are minimized at the source. Figure 4.9B illustrates a weight-losing raw material with a material index of 2 (one-half of

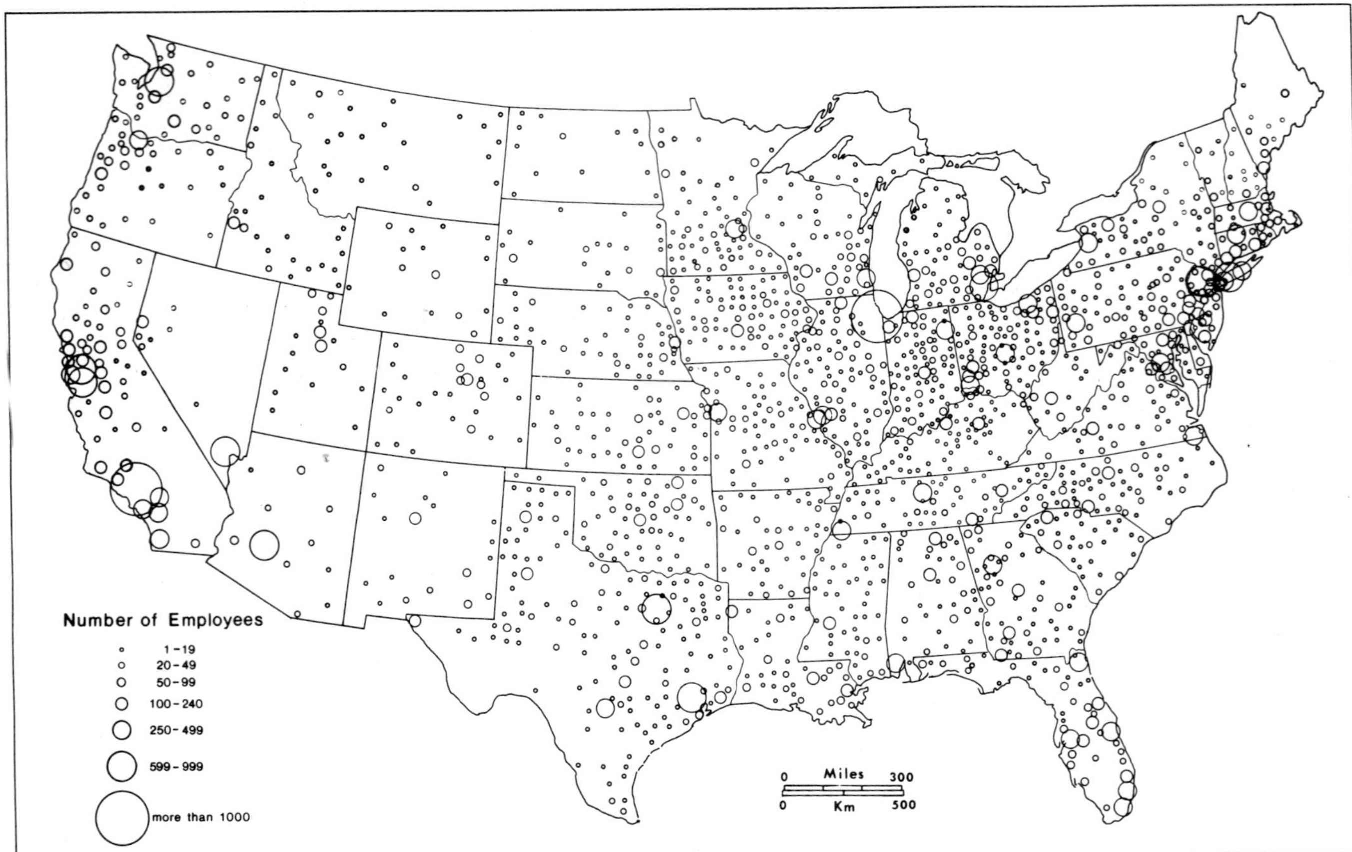

FIGURE 4.7 Location pattern of ready-mixed concrete production, 1963.

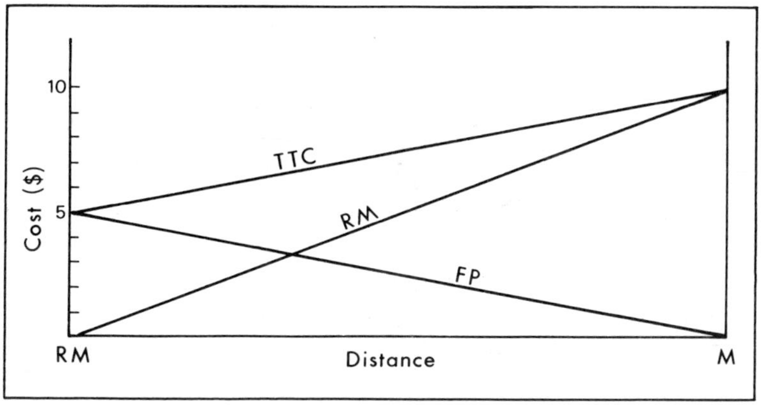

FIGURE 4.8 Weber's model: one localized, weight-losing raw material.

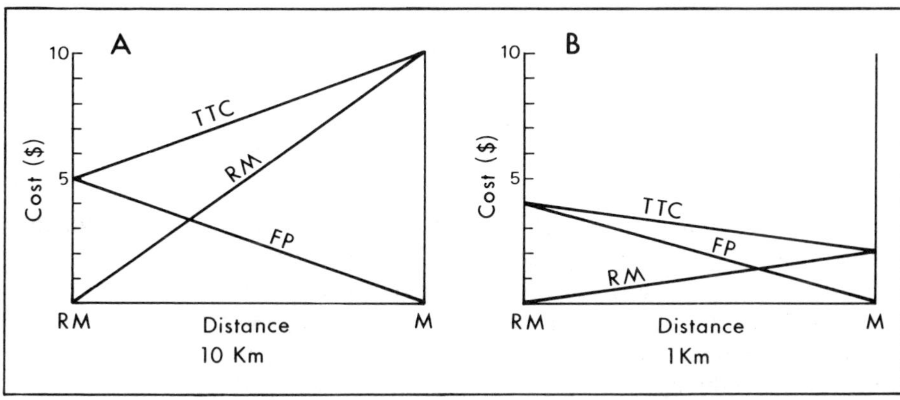

FIGURE 4.9 Weber's model: one localized, weight-losing raw material plus ubiquities (A) Optimum location at raw material source; (B) Optimum location at market.

its weight is lost in processing), but let us assume that the ratio of ubiquitous raw material to localized raw material (after processing) is 3:1. Two tons of the localized raw material plus three tons of the ubiquitous raw material are processed into a finished product weighing four tons. At *RM*, total transportation costs are $4 (weight of the finished product), but at M, total transportation costs are $2 (weight of the localized raw material required for one unit of the finished product). Total transportation costs are minimized at the market (M). This last ratio *typifies* commercial brewing. Barley and hops are the localized raw materials that lose weight in processing, but the major ingredient by weight (water) is ubiquitous. Brewers tend to be market rather than raw material oriented.

Several Localized, Weight-Losing Raw Materials The solution becomes more complex when several weight-losing raw materials are considered. There are several mathematical solutions, but a simple mechanical analogue known as the "Varignon frame" simplifies the problem. The localized raw material sites are located on a map mounted on a board (figure 4.10). Holes are drilled in the board at each site. A pulley (to reduce friction) is located at each hole. Each raw material is

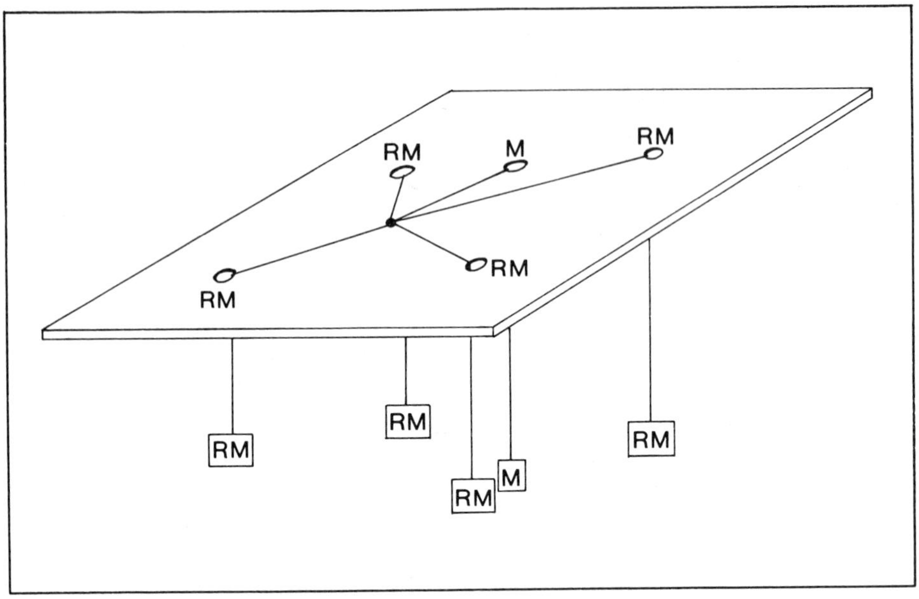

FIGURE 4.10 The Varignon frame.

simulated by a weight proportional to the total weight of the raw material required to produce one unit of the finished product. Cords are run from the weights through the pulleys (raw material sites) and tied together into a single knot. When the weights are released, the final location of the knot will be the optimum location. Finished product distribution costs are simulated by a weight (equal to finished product weight) running through a hole and pulley at the market point (M). Ubiquitous raw materials can be simulated by adding to this weight.

This type of analysis has often been applied to the steel industry which processes several weight-losing raw materials (Kennelly 1954–55).

Extensions of Weber's Model: Transportation Costs

Isard's Contribution

Walter Isard (1955) modified the transportation emphasis of the Weberian model in two ways. Transportation costs in Isard's analysis are treated as just another input cost rather than considering them to be distinct from other factors of production. This treatment brings into focus the *total* location problem. Second, Isard used the technique of *substitution analysis* (essentially marginal analysis from economics) to deal with the location problem. An example of a partial application of this analysis is presented in figure 4.11. Two pure raw materials are required for a manufacturing process. These raw materials (RM_1 and RM_2) are localized on two islands (I_1 and I_2. A partial application of substitution analysis involves determining the optimum location for the plant along the mainland coast. The transportation cost for each

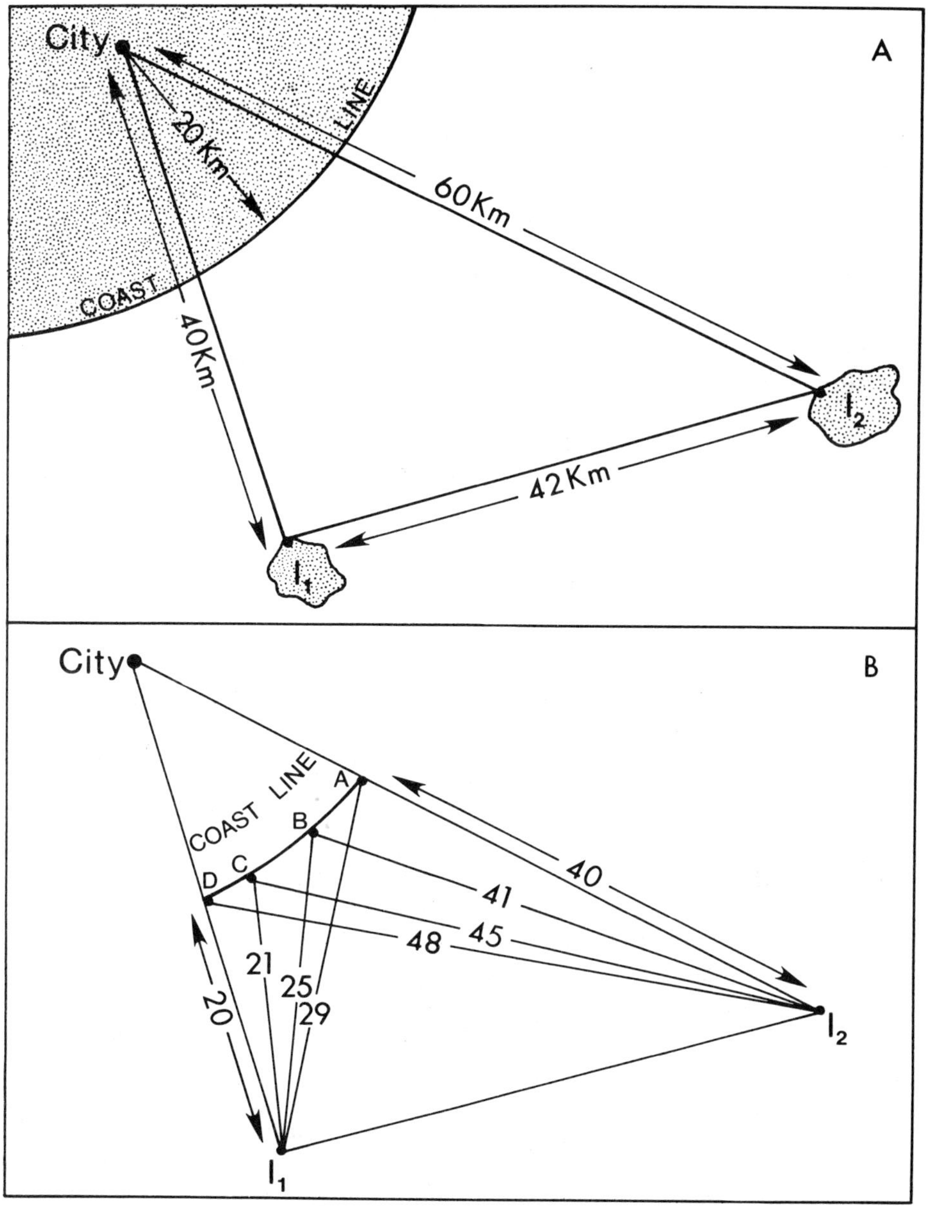

FIGURE 4.11 Substitution analysis: (A) Location map; (B) Costs from I_1 and I_2 to selected points along coast. (Continued on p. 138.)

input can be determined for any point along the coastline. At point A (figure 4.11B), for example, the cost of shipping one unit of RM_1 (from I_1) is \$29, and the cost of one unit of RM_2 is \$40. As we move along the coastline, we must pay more and more for each unit of RM_2 (transport inputs) and less and less for each unit of RM_1. In Isard's terms, we are *substituting* transport inputs on RM_2 for transport inputs on

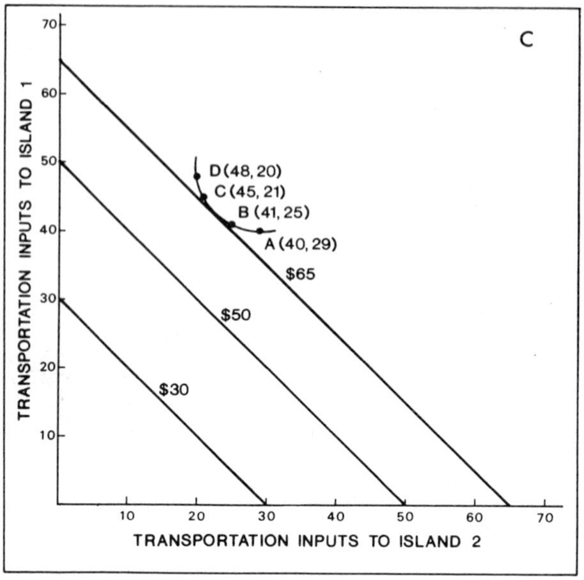

FIGURE 4.11, cont. (C) Lowest isocost line ($65) tangent to coastal shipping cost curve.

RM_1. The problem is to determine the lowest possible transportation costs for one unit of each input and the location at which that minimum occurs. In figure 4.11C, the coastline ABCD has been mapped onto a graph of cost. The vertical axis graphs transport inputs ($) for RM_1 and the horizontal axis gives transport inputs for RM_2. The straight lines drawn on the graph are called transformation lines. Consider the line which intersects the axes at $30. At the point $30,$0, we can spend $30 on RM_2 and $0 on RM_1. As we move back along the line we spend more and more on RM_1 and less and less on RM_2 until the point $0,$30 is reached. Midway along the line we spend $15 on each input. We are assuming that we need one unit of each raw material to produce the finished product. Thus, we have to move to a transformation line of a higher value ($) to obtain a whole unit of RM_1 and RM_2. If we spend $69 total, we can obtain a unit of each raw material. We will spend $40 for RM_1 and $29 for RM_2 (Point A). There are, however, an infinite number of transformation lines that can be drawn and we are interested in minimizing total transportation costs. The transformation line which is just tangent to the substitution curve solves the problem. The plant should be located at the point of tangency ($65). We have consistently referred to this example as a *partial* solution. A total equilibrium solution would have to consider the locational costs of all other inputs including finished product distribution costs, but we have introduced the basis for a more rigorous analysis.

Space-Cost Curves

Another extension of the basic Weberian system involves the use of space-cost curves developed by David Smith (1966). Assume that equal amounts of two localized, weight-losing raw materials are required to produce one unit of the finished product. The material index of each is 2, so that one ton of RM_1 and one ton of RM_2 yield a one-ton finished product. In figure 4.12A, a series of concentric

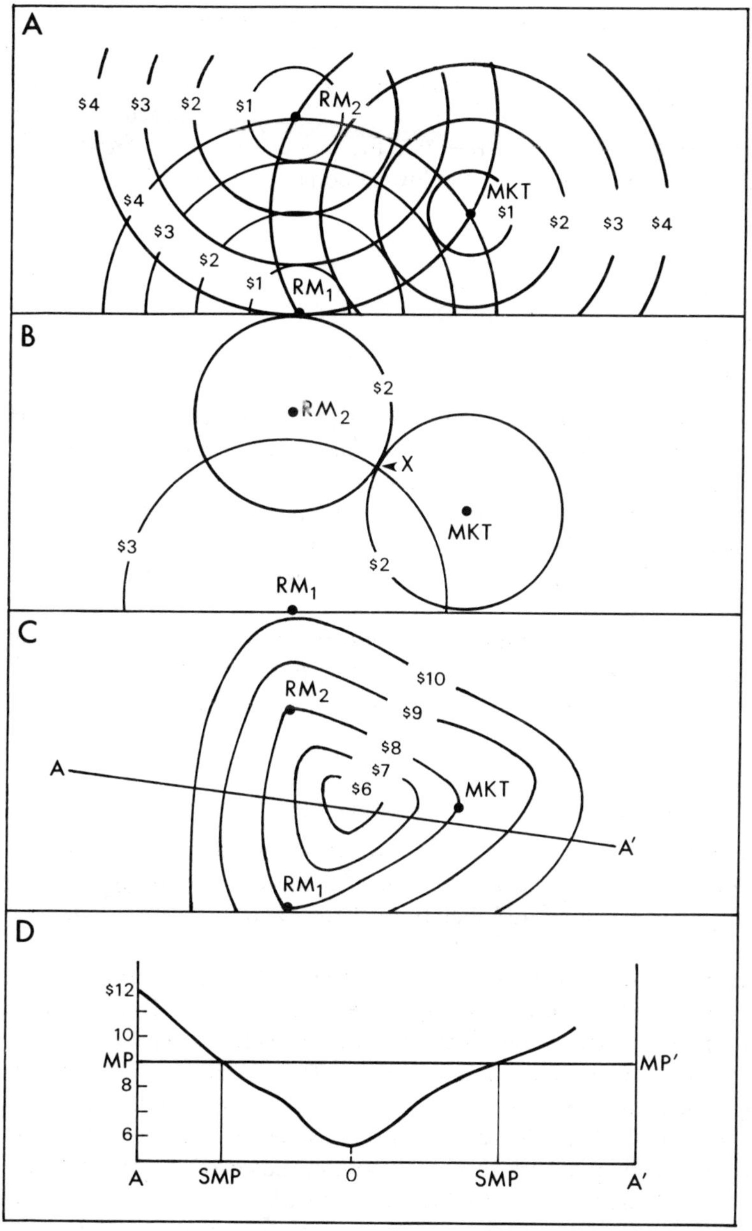

FIGURE 4.12 The development of a space-cost curve: (A) Isotims; (B) Total cost to a point; (C) Isodapanes; (D) Space-cost curve along line A-A′.

circles have been drawn around each raw material source and the market point. These are iso-cost lines for each transport input (called *isotims* by Weber).

Total transportation costs are the sum of all costs to all three points. At point X (figure 4.12B), it costs \$3 for RM_1, \$2 for RM_2, and \$2 for transporting the finished product. We can find total transportation costs for as many points as we want and connect points of equal value to produce total cost isopleths which Weber termed *isodapanes*. If we visualize figure 4.12C in three-dimensional terms, we have mapped a depression. Smith then assumes that the market price for the finished product is a spatial constant (*MP-MP'* in figure 4.12D). The intersections of the space-cost curve and the market price line give the *spatial margins to profitability* and the optimum location (0) occurs at the lowest point on the space-cost curve.

Distortions of the Isotropic Surface: The Effects of Localized Resources

We have modified the assumption of the completely isotropic surface assumed in chapters 2 and 3 when we consider the effects of *localized* resources in the Weberian model. This is the beginning of a transition from a normative to a descriptive model of reality. Once localized resources are allowed, the regular patterns implied by central place theory will be distorted to minimize the pull of nonubiquitous resources. The natural environment (localized resources) has distorted the ideal patterns of an isotropic surface.

Geography has traditionally paid much more attention to the distorting effects of the environment. While attempting to concentrate on the effects of space, the fact that the uneven distribution of resources does play a considerable role cannot be ignored.

The Secondary Sector versus the Tertiary Sector

We must constantly keep in mind the differences between the secondary and tertiary sectors of the economy. The particular set of forces that controls the location of manufacturing may be quite different from those controlling the location of central places.

The function of the tertiary sector is to provide and distribute goods and services. The secondary sector processes raw materials into finished products. Those products do not generally flow directly to consumers, but are channeled through the tertiary sector in the form of retail and wholesale trade. The tertiary sector is almost completely concerned with maximizing access to a market while minimizing distribution costs. We can think of the tertiary sector as being completely "market oriented." The orientation of the secondary sector, however, varies with the industry in question. Some types of manufacturing, as we have seen in the Weberian model, are market oriented. If all industries were of this type, the pattern of manufacturing would match the pattern of central places. Some industries, however, have a cost structure so dominated by localized input costs that they are "raw material oriented," thereby distorting the pattern.

This distortion is illustrated by figure 4.13. Point I is the "ideal" location for a given order of central place. The shaded area is a major resource deposit. City A was established to exploit that resource and has become a center of manufacturing. City A also supplies central functions to the surrounding area. Because of its initial

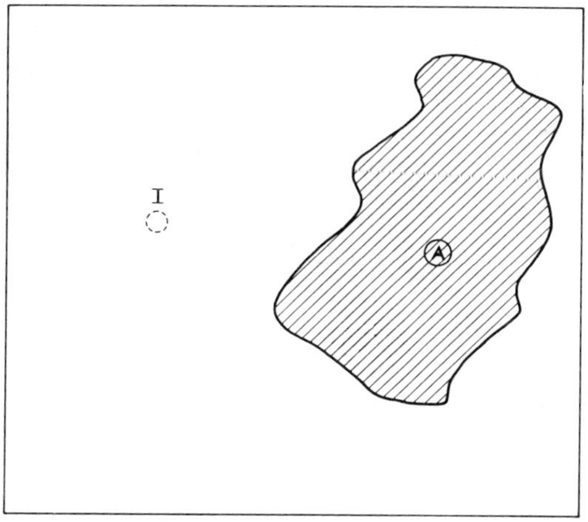

FIGURE 4.13 Distortion produced by localized resources.

establishment and growth, it has superceded the establishment of service functions at a more ideal location (I). The purely spatial pattern has been "distorted" by the uneven distribution of resources. Real-world patterns are evolutionary and are not the result of decisions made by optimizers. Most real-world decisions do not result in optimum locations. We will discuss spatial decision making in chapter 6, but should note here that locational decisions, once made, generate *inertia*. The inertia (investment in the nonoptimal site) may be great enough to keep the pattern distorted even if more optimal locations are discovered in the future. In the 1970s we certainly have the analytical skills required to locate state capitals at the centroids of state populations. The investment we have in most existing state capitals precludes us doing so. There is a tension between ideal spatial patterns and the patterns produced by localized resources. As technology (especially transportation) improves, ideal spatial patterns become more possible, but the inertia imposed by past actions exerts a constant brake on their attainment.

Changes in Cost

To illustrate the effects of a change in the cost of an input on the location pattern, we assume that two localized inputs are required to produce the finished product represented in figure 4.14. Let RM_1 be a localized source of power such as coal (mine), and RM_2 another localized raw material. We are ignoring finished product distribution costs in this model, so total costs are the sum of the two transport cost lines for the raw materials. At 0, for example, RM_1 costs \$5, RM_2 costs \$7, so that total cost is \$12. At 0′, RM_1 costs \$10, RM_2 costs \$6, and total cost is \$16. We can find total costs for all points between 0 and 0′ (the line TC_a). Suppose that electricity is offered (technological change) at a spatially constant price of \$5. The new total cost curve will be TC_b (same as TC_a left of X). The optimum location in the first case is 0_1, but the optimum location shifts to 0_2 with the introduction of electricity.

Whether or not the plant will actually shift depends upon the inertia (investment) at 0_1 and the potential savings at 0_2. Inertia, in many cases, is the more powerful force. Alexandersson (1961), for example, determined that the basic pattern of steel production in the United States remained relatively stable from 1948 to 1959 because it was cheaper to expand existing facilities than to construct completely new ones at different locations, even though the new plants might represent more optimum locations if inertial investments were ignored.

The second set of costs faced by manufacturing involves production costs. After raw materials have been assembled at a point, their form must be changed in the manufacturing process. Production costs include labor, capital, and technical and managerial skills. All these are necessary for production and exhibit spatial variations in both quantity and quality.

The Cost of Labor: Locational Impacts

Labor inputs are required for all forms of economic production, but the relative contribution of labor to value added by manufacturing varies considerably from industry to industry. Table 4.3 gives the relative importance of the labor input for selected industries in the United States. Both the supply and demand for labor vary across space, but those industries in which labor costs play a major role are much more sensitive to locational variations in the cost of this input. The real cost of labor is determined by the relative *productivity* of labor rather than the dollar cost of wages and fringe benefits. It is the labor cost *per unit produced* rather than per hour that is of prime importance in manufacturing. Table 4.4 gives some hypothetical data illustrating differences in labor productivity. Notice that the labor cost per unit produced is lower in Plant B even though the hourly total of wages and fringe benefits is higher.

Remember that Weber considered the cost of labor to be a regional factor controlling patterns of manufacturing. The initial pattern is set by transportation costs and then distorted by spatial variations in the cost of labor. Weber's model assumed that there is an infinite amount of labor available at different points, but variation in the cost of labor among the points.

Weber's analysis of the problem is given in figure 4.15. The product in question involves two localized raw materials distributed to a single market (M). Isodapanes (TTC) are shown in the figure. Total transportation costs are minimized at Point T ($4). As we move away from T, total transportation costs increase. At Point L, labor costs are $2 per unit less than at T. This unit labor savings is then used to determine the value of a *critical isodapane*. No savings in total unit cost will result if the increased transportation costs encountered at another point are greater than the labor savings of that point. The move, in other words, must not exceed $2 per unit. Transportation costs at T ($4) plus labor savings at L ($2) give the amount which cannot be exceeded ($6). Point L lies inside this critical isodapane ($6) and is clearly an economic move. A point on the critical isodapane would result in zero savings, and points outside the line represent higher total costs. In this way, within the limits established by critical isodapanes, variations in labor costs distort the pattern established by general transportation costs.

TABLE 4.3 The relative importance of labor

Industry	Contribution of Labor Costs*
Food products	7.0
Tobacco products	6.8
Textiles	17.1
Apparel	19.6
Lumber and wood products	16.5
Furniture	20.5
Paper products	15.3
Printing and publishing	18.1
Chemicals	8.3
Petroleum products	3.7
Rubber products	17.2
Leather products	21.3
Stone, clay, and glass products	18.7
Primary metal products	15.7
Fabricated metal products	18.4
Nonelectrical machinery	17.3
Electrical machinery	16.5
Transportation equipment	13.6
Instruments	14.4

*Labor costs ($) as a percentage of value of shipments ($).

TABLE 4.4 Variations in labor productivity (hypothetical data)

Plant	Total Hourly Wages and Fringe Benefits (Per Worker)	Output Per Hour in Units (Per Worker)	True Labor Cost Per Unit (Productivity)
A	$5.50	100	5.5¢
B	$7.80	200	3.9¢
C	$4.20	76	5.5¢

Equilibrium conditions should balance regional differences in the supply and demand for labor in the United States where mobility is high. Labor is theoretically a *mobile factor of production*. A high demand for labor in one place and an excess supply of labor in another should be brought into equilibrium through labor migration. Such migration has certainly occurred in the United States. Massive rural to urban migration responsible for urbanization in the United States is an example.

The response of labor, as in all factors of production, is not instantaneous. Labor, especially skilled labor, is relatively immobile (notably in the "short run"). Labor has a degree of inertia. People are reluctant to pull up stakes, leave familiar places, family, and friends, and perhaps lose local invested capital (homes, vested retire-

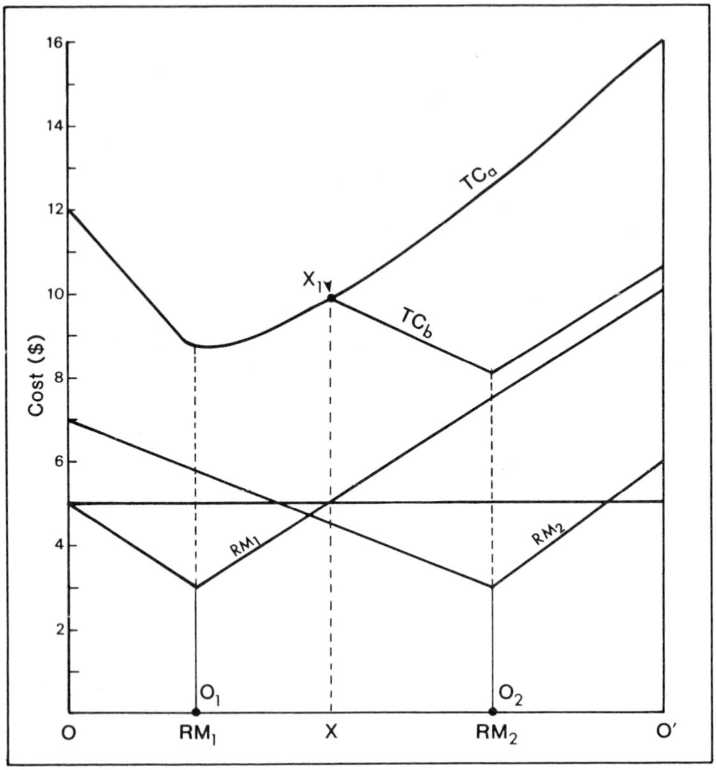

FIGURE 4.14 Changes in cost: technological innovation.

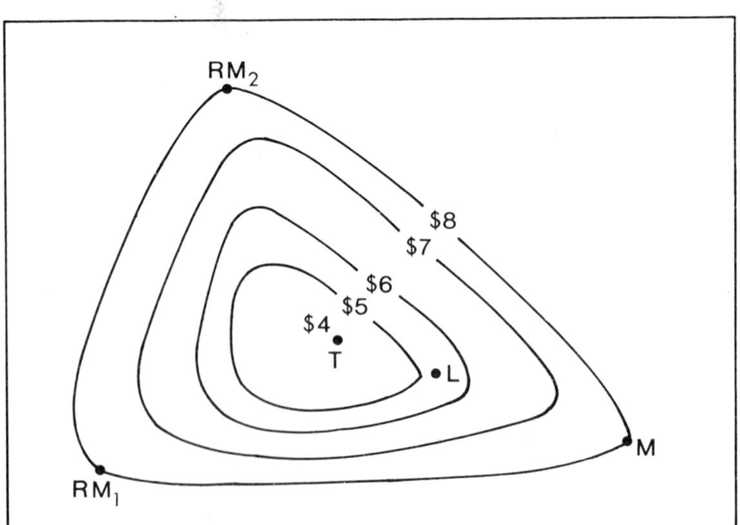

FIGURE 4.15 Critical isodapane for labor.

ment plans), and move to unfamiliar places even if jobs are plentiful in another area. They tend to sit out short periods of unemployment or to accept a smaller net income than could be earned elsewhere because of this inertia. Social policies such as unemployment compensation have reduced the plight of the unemployed and underemployed a great deal in this century. Total mobility in the United States has increased, but mobility in response to changing employment conditions by labor has probably declined.

The lack of instantaneous adjustment in labor demand and supply has resulted in regional variations in the cost of labor in the United States. These variations are illustrated in figure 4.16, a chloropleth map of the average hourly earnings of production workers in the United States. Wage rates tend to be highest in the more densely settled areas, the prime manufacturing states, and in the more urbanized areas. Wage rates are lower in the South and plains states.

Factors Affecting the Cost of Labor The map in figure 4.16 immediately suggests several factors which might affect the cost of labor in the United States. The level of industrialization seems to be a primary factor. Older, established industrial areas have higher wage rates, but because of higher skill levels may also be more productive. You must remember that figure 4.16 does not show productivity. Other factors involved include the level of unionization and the "industrial mix" of an area. Areas having a higher proportion of high wage industries will have higher wage rates than those that do not. The cost of living is another determinant of wage rates. If the cost of living is low, as in the South, workers do not have to earn as much to maintain an adequate standard of living. Other factors determine the *productivity* of labor and include the general educational level of the population, attitudes toward work, the commitment of state and local governments to training programs, and the job alternatives in the area.

Labor migration in response to supply/demand differentials is difficult to document adequately because it involves so many individual decisions. The response of individual industries to labor cost variations in the United States, however, has been the subject of numerous studies. Among the best known are the movement of textile manufacturing from New England to the Southern Piedmont and the similar migration of the shoe and leather industries to the southern midwest.

Locational Impacts of the Cost of Capital

Capital takes two forms: (1) fixed capital—money invested in buildings, equipment, and other tangible stocks; and (2) liquid capital—money used to pay wages and meet other operating costs. Theoretically, liquid capital is the most mobile factor of production because its transportation costs are almost zero. Millions of dollars can be transferred across the United States almost instantaneously through the banking system. Fixed capital is much less mobile. Capital invested in buildings and other heavy equipment is obviously immobile and has been a primary reason for the previously mentioned stagnant pattern of steel production in the United States.

Any successful type of manufacturing has an assured supply of liquid (operating) capital stemming from revenues. Most types of manufacturing, however, require large amounts of fixed capital initially to establish the operation or periodically to

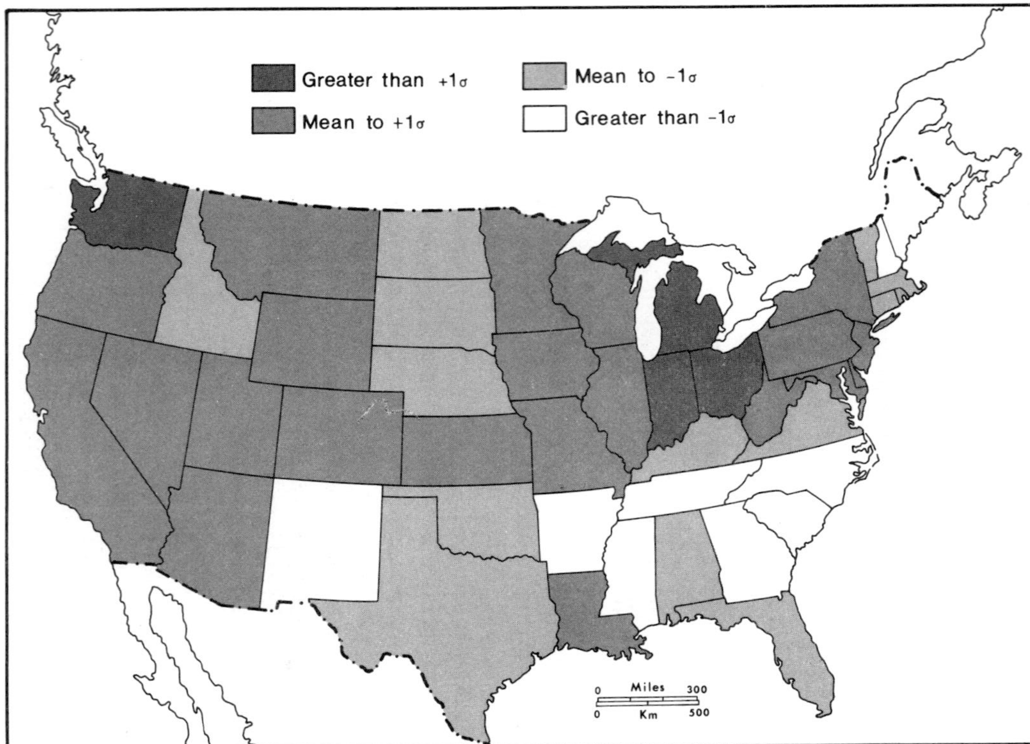

FIGURE 4.16 Variations in average hourly wages of production workers, 1974.

expand, retool or replace outdated equipment, or to branch out into new products. The cost of this capital (interest) must be paid from future revenues in the form of interest and dividends. Investment capital is not uniformly distributed nor does it display great mobility.

Investment capital can come from a variety of sources: personal funds, family and friends, lending institutions, and the sale of stocks and bonds. Most capital in the United States comes from the latter two sources. The total supply of investment capital is a function of total national wealth and the proportion of total income that is saved. Savings become the investment capital for future expansion.

Whether or not a particular type of manufacturing or a given entrepreneur can obtain an adequate amount of investment capital at an acceptable price (interest rate) depends upon several things. First, the supply of capital in both a national and local context is important. There are times when the national supply of capital is low, postponing less profitable investments. There are also regional differences in the supply of capital. Surplus capital tends to be concentrated in the older, more developed, and wealthier areas of the country. As long as profitable investments remain there, investment may be inadequate in areas of capital deficit. Second, the demand for capital determines the price of capital. As long as the demand for capital remains high in one area (such as an established industrial area), interest rates may preclude investments in less profitable regions and industries. Finally, capital can always be obtained if the user is willing to pay a high enough interest rate. Beyond supply and demand considerations, *investor confidence* is the prime determinant of whether or not capital can be obtained at an acceptable rate. Investor confidence in a particular industry may be present in one area of the country and lacking in another. There are many examples of entrepreneurs who failed to raise investment capital in one area of the country only to find it available in their home area (most notably Ford in Detroit and Douglas Aviation in Los Angeles).

Entrepreneurship and Technical Skills

Management and technical skills are required for any type of production process. Entrepreneurs are the primary agents responsible for the specific industrial pattern in the United States. The general (Weber's regional) pattern is determined by the localization of other factors of production, subsequent transportation costs, and spatial margins to profitability. Ford Motor Company was established in Detroit primarily because it was Henry Ford's home town and he was able to obtain risk capital there, but any town in the Midwest accessible to the raw materials necessary for auto production (especially steel) could have supported automobile production. On the other hand, had Ford attempted to manufacture automobiles at a large scale in Butte, Montana, he would have failed. Hunker and Wright's study (1963) found that a majority of the manufacturing plants in Ohio were located in the home towns of their founders. The Midwest and the rest of the American Manufacturing Belt establish the regional pattern of possible successful locations for most types of manufacturing, but the specific locations chosen within these margins are determined by the individual decisions of entrepreneurs.

Management should be, theoretically, much more mobile than labor because fewer people are involved and the higher incomes of managers should make moving less of a financial burden; but management skills, like labor, still tend to be highly concentrated. Figure 4.17 shows that the corporate headquarters of the 500 largest corporations in the United States are concentrated in the most densely urbanized areas of the country. The high incomes of managers allow them to enjoy the advantages of American urban life while escaping the liabilities through suburban living. The educational level of management makes the cultural attractions of large cities important also. Considerable financial inducements are necessary to persuade top managers to move to rural or less urbanized areas.

Technical skills refer not to those required in the production process (i.e., labor skills), but rather to those necessary for continued innovation in terms of both new products and processes. These skills in the United States are usually referred to as research and development (R&D). Research and development are much more important in some industries than in others. Industries such as wood products, textiles, and food have changed very little in the past decade while others, such as electronics have undergone sweeping changes. The proliferation of electronic calculators at lower and lower prices is a case in point. The amount of innovation necessary can be measured by the percentage of total value added by manufacturing that the industry spends on research and development (table 4.5).

Research and development skills tend to be localized also and focused on major research university clusters and established areas of innovation. Two of the major growth industries of the past two decades, electronics and aerospace, have been heavily influenced by government action. The prime customers and suppliers of capital for both these industries have been the federal space and defense programs. As such, governmental action has played a role in determining the major growth areas for the relatively footloose electronics industry. The location of military aircraft production was basically established during World War II, but specific locations have waxed or waned as a function of government contracts in subsequent years.

TABLE 4.5 Research and development funds as a percentage of net sales: 1974

Industry	Percent
Food products	0.4
Textiles and apparel	0.4
Lumber and wood products	0.6
Paper products	0.7
Chemicals	3.2
Petroleum refining	0.5
Rubber products	1.7
Stone, clay, and glass products	1.5
Primary metals	0.5
Fabricated metal products	1.1
Machinery	4.0
Electronic equipment	6.9
Motor vehicles	3.7
Aircraft and missiles	12.5
Professional and scientific instruments	5.4

Source: National Science Foundation.

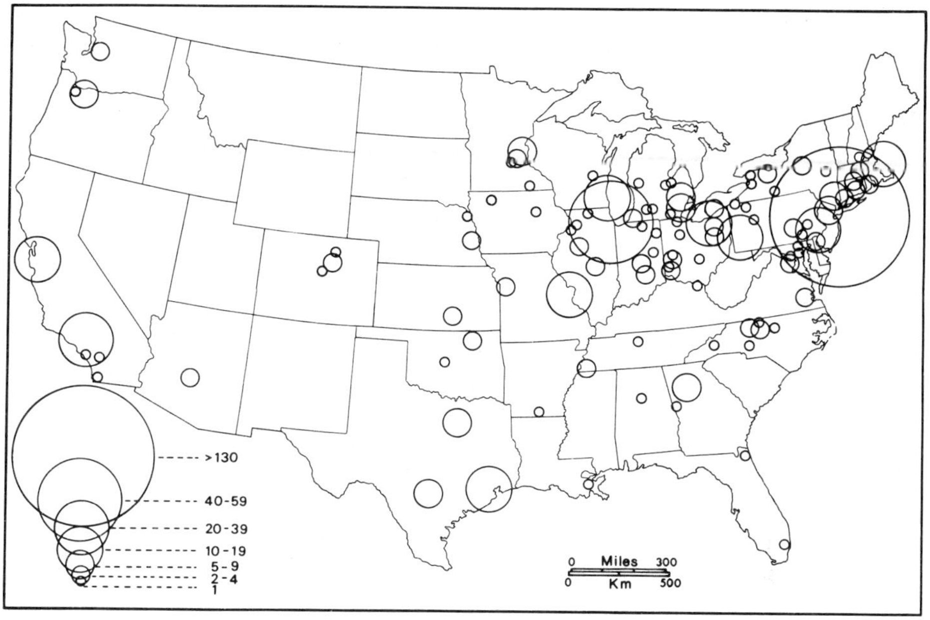

FIGURE 4.17 Corporate headquarters: 500 largest corporations, 1976 (Source: *Fortune* Magazine).

A Variable Cost Model

We must now examine in greater detail the influence of production costs on location. Smith (1966) pointed out that the establishment of any manufacturing plant involves three mutually interdependent decisions: (1) scale—the size of the operation which will determine the volume of total output; (2) technique—the particular *combination* of inputs that will be used to produce an output; and (3) location. In this section we are primarily concerned with location as a function of input costs and thus are holding the influence of technique and scale constant, but will consider them in subsequent sections.

We are also assuming that variations in demand, if they exist, are solely a function of price. These assumptions allow us to portray three general industrial location cases, shown in figure 4.18. In Case I, market price (revenue) is a spatial constant and costs vary across space. The optimum location is the lowest point on the space-cost curve and the spatial margins are located where costs equal revenue. Total revenue (demand) exhibits spatial change in Case II while costs are a spatial constant. The optimum location is the highest point on the revenue curve and the spatial margins to profitability are again where costs equal revenue. Variations in both cost and revenue across space are shown in Case III. The optimum location (0) will be where revenue exceeds costs by the greatest amount. For all three cases we can show that: (a) both curves determine the spatial margins to profitability; (b) the

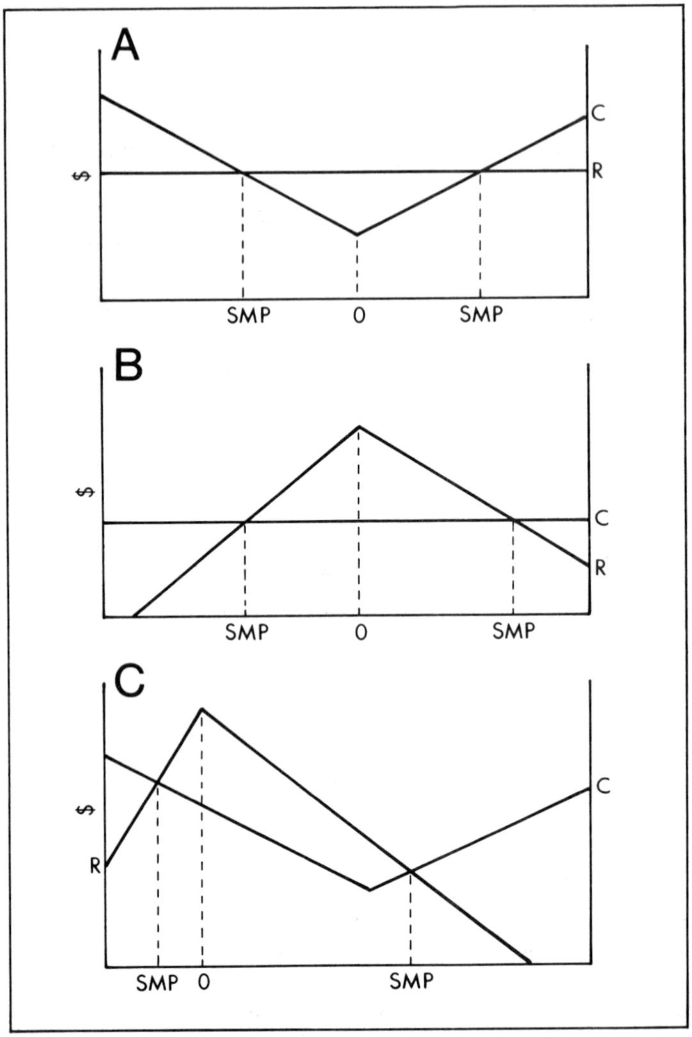

FIGURE 4.18 Spatial margins to profitability: (I) Cost variable, revenue constant; (II) Revenue variable, cost constant; (III) Revenue and cost variable [Modified from Smith (1971), *Industrial Location*, New York: John Wiley & Sons.]

variable with the steepest gradient determines the optimum location; and (c) the slope of the curve indicates the relative importance of locational costs.

Spatial margins to profitability are important because they allow us to incorporate *suboptimal* behavior. Profits are possible anywhere within these limits. The three graphs in figure 4.18 make a general statement about locational viability. Defining these margins in reality and determining specific locations to be occupied within them, however, is a much more difficult problem. We can still make one generalization about real-world patterns within spatial margins to profitability. Relatively clustered industries must face rather limited spatial margins to profitability and high location costs. The situation is illustrated in figure 4.19. Remember that any kind of cost and/or revenue may be the critical factor determining the spatial margins to profitability.

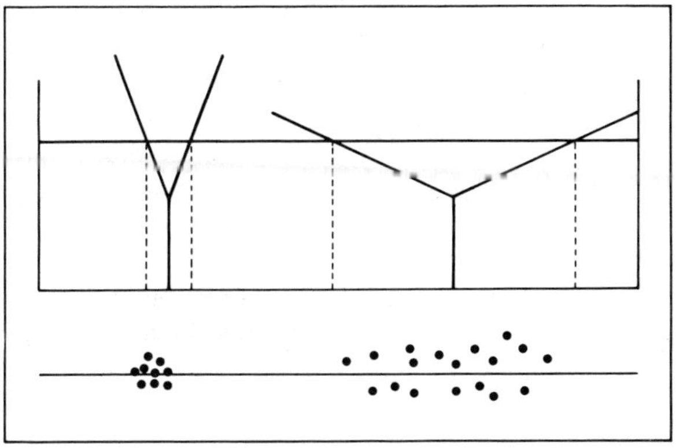

FIGURE 4.19 Spatial margins to profitability and clustering.

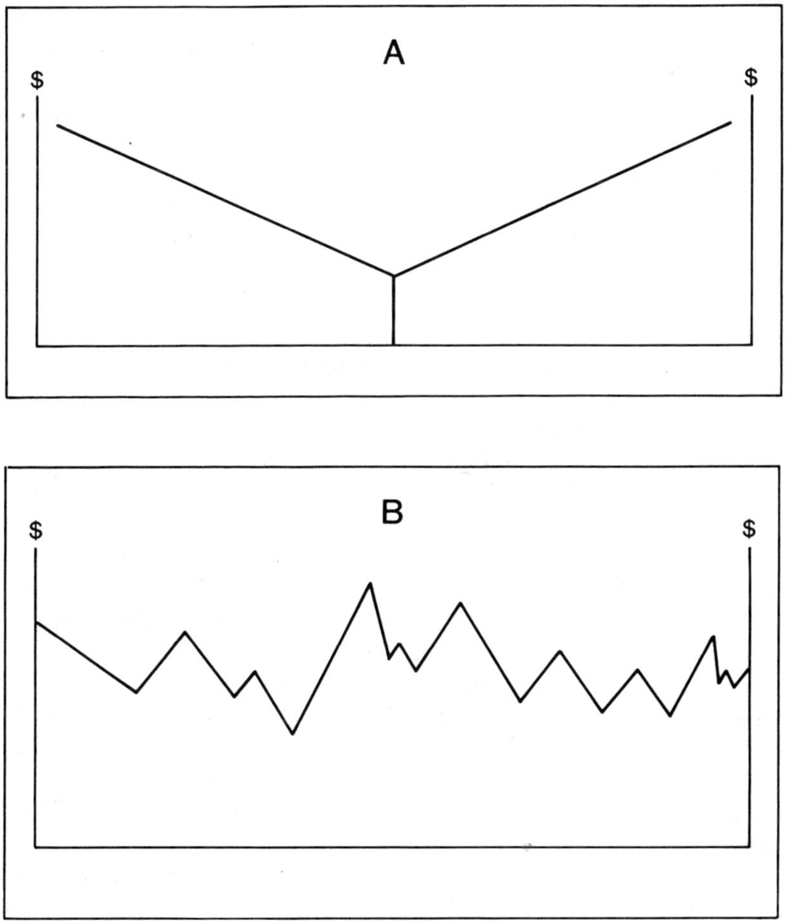

FIGURE 4.20 (A) Transfer charges; (B) Spatially variable costs.

Weber's theory is preoccupied with both transportation costs and with finding least-cost (optimal) locations. A more general theory should consider total cost and the possibility of suboptimal decisions. Location theory has focused on transportation costs because they are easily calculated and can be treated as fairly simple functions of distance. The locational effects of other kinds of cost are much more difficult to conceptualize. Isard (1956) has suggested that locational factors can be divided into three general classes on the basis of their geographic occurrence.

1. *Transfer charges:* costs that can be portrayed as a regular function of distance from some given point. The cost of acquiring a raw material from a single mine is an example of this kind of cost and is illustrated in figure 4.20A.
2. *Spatially variable costs:* costs that vary across space (labor, power, capital, management skills), but do not vary *systematically* with distance from a point (figure 4.20B).
3. *Aspatial costs:* factors that can influence costs but are independent of location, such as scale changes.

Geography has dealt with the problems associated with irregular variations in costs in a normative way through the use of models assuming an isotropic surface. Problems also can be dealt with in two ways. First, they can be *conceptually* reduced. The cost of any input can be thought of as varying over distance in terms of dollars per kilometer. The least-cost point for labor can be determined, for example, and costs rise everywhere from this point. The exact *form* of the change may, of course, vary with direction. Second, the practical aspects of the problem can be dealt with by determining the cost of an input at a large number of points and mapping variations in costs as a *surface*. The surface can be regularized by such techniques as trend surface analysis (see box). Each variable can be viewed as spatially continuous and the sum portrayed as a surface of total cost.

Smith (1966) extended Weber's analysis to all types of cost through conceptualization. He assumes that *each input* has a least-cost point. Least-cost points for materials may be mines or the factories of parts producers. There is a least-cost point for the particular kind of labor required and there is a point at which finished product distribution costs are minimized. Each of these points exerts a certain "pull" on location (remember the Varignon frame). The relative weight of all these pulls determines the least-cost location.

Smith also paid a great deal of attention to the distinction between basic and locational costs. Basic costs are the minimum paid regardless of location and represent the lowest point on the cost surface of a particular input. The basic cost for labor, for example, would be the minimum wage. Locational costs are those incurred in overcoming distance. Figure 4.21 illustrates the two kinds of cost. We assume that there are some workers who will accept the minimum wage. Their location represents the lowest point on the labor cost surface and basic cost. Away from that point workers demand more than the minimum wage, but the additional amount takes the form of locational costs. Suppose an industry is covered by a national union wage-rate. The dollar amount paid to workers is the same everywhere. We might assume that ubiquitous basic costs prevail, but we must remember our previous discussion of productivity. Basic costs are found at the point

Trend surface analysis is a statistical method used to "smooth" or discover the general trend of a complex surface. Just as regression involves fitting a line through a scatter of data points, trend surface analysis is concerned with fitting a surface (or plane) through a set of data points.

Figure A below represents a complex surface, such as wage rates in an area. Figure B shows the smoothed surface or general trend resulting from the application of trend surface analysis.

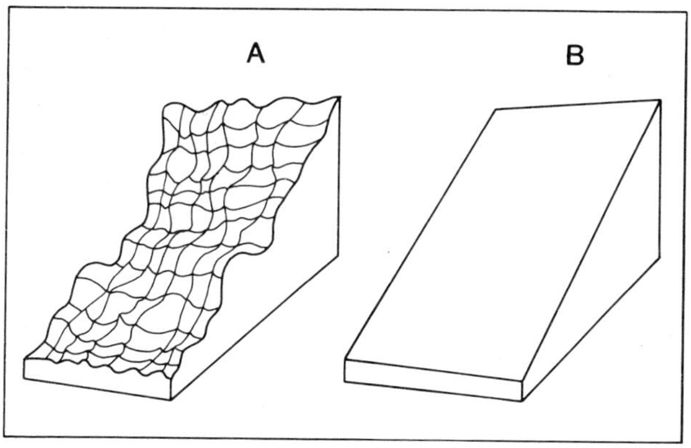

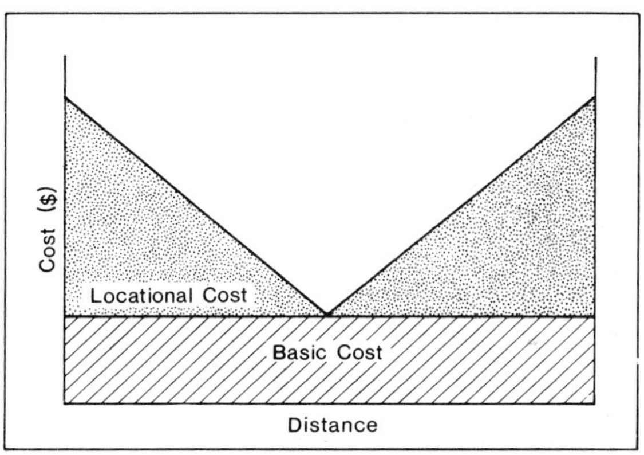

FIGURE 4.21 Basic and locational costs [After Smith (1971), *Industrial Location,* New York: John Wiley & Sons.]

of *highest* labor productivity. This represents the lowest *real* labor costs. As productivity falls away from that point, real labor costs rise, producing locational costs. The total cost of any input is the sum of locational and basic cost. The relative pull of a given input depends on: (a) the slope of the (locational) space-cost curve; and (b) the percentage contribution of an input to the total cost of output. An input that accounts for a large proportion of total basic cost or has large variations in location cost should have the greatest influence on plant location.

Basic Cost: the minimum cost of an input; the cost that must be paid at the least-cost location.
Locational Cost: all costs above basic cost. Locational costs vary with location and may rise as a function of the distance from the least-cost location.

The Model

Using a simple model, let's examine spatially variable costs. We assume that a particular product requires three inputs with locational costs—a raw material, labor, and power. All other inputs have zero locational costs and do not

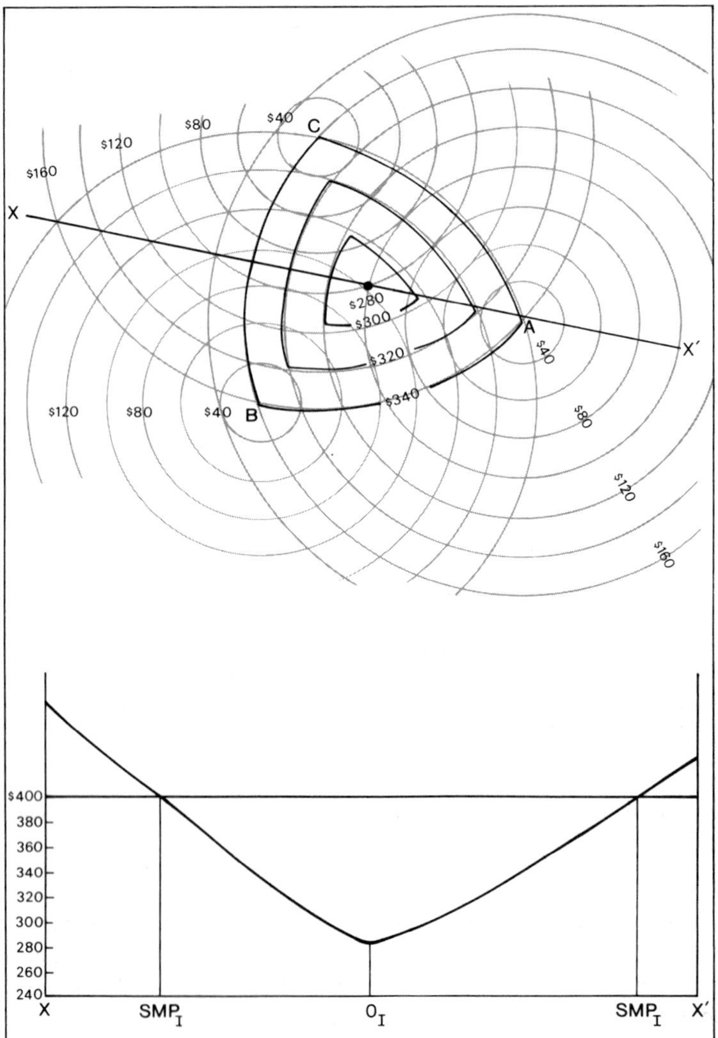

FIGURE 4.22 The variable cost model: Case I.

influence the choice of sites. In figure 4.22, the locational costs for the raw material, labor, and power are minimized at A, B, and C respectively. Consider Case I in table 4.6. Equal amounts (B) of each input are required. In each case we are dealing with the *cost* of the input so that in Case I, $20.00 will purchase the required amount of each input at the least-cost source. We must pay at least $60.00 in *basic cost*. Now we must determine the *locational cost* of each input. In Case I, locational costs are $.10 per dollar per kilometer. Moving away from A for one kilometer will raise the cost of each dollar's worth of the raw material $.10 so that the locational cost of the required quantity at one km is $2.00 ($.10 X $20.00 = $2.00). The total cost of that input at one km is $22.00.

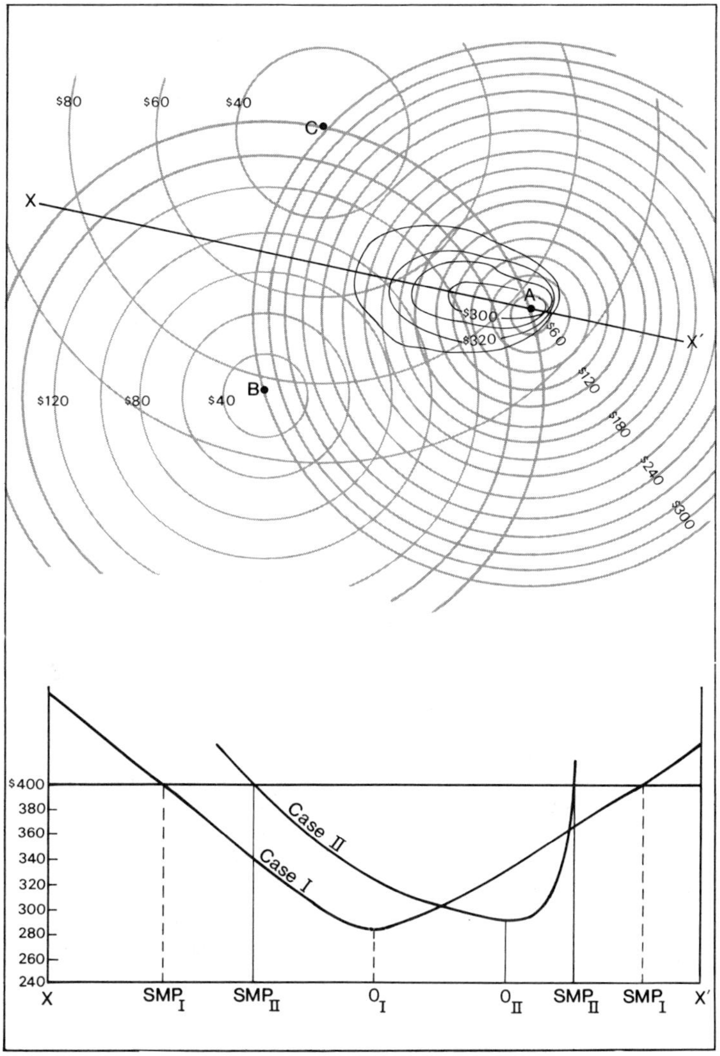

FIGURE 4.23 The variable cost model: Case II.

In figure 4.22, isocost lines are drawn around each input source at \$20 intervals. Remember that basic cost is \$20 at A so that the first isocost line is \$40 and occurs 10 kilometers from A (\$20BC + \$20LC = \$40; see table 4.6). Notice that the isotims for each input are exactly the same. We can interpolate isodapanes (total costs for all inputs) from the isotims (heavy lines in figure 4.22) and draw a space-cost curve along the line X-X′. Assuming a spatially constant market price of \$400, the optimum location is at 0_I and the spatial margins to profitability are SMP_I.

Case II examines the effect of variations in locational cost. The same amount (in dollars) of each input is required, but there are different locational costs in terms of the per kilometer cost per dollar unit. This produces a different set of isotims (figure

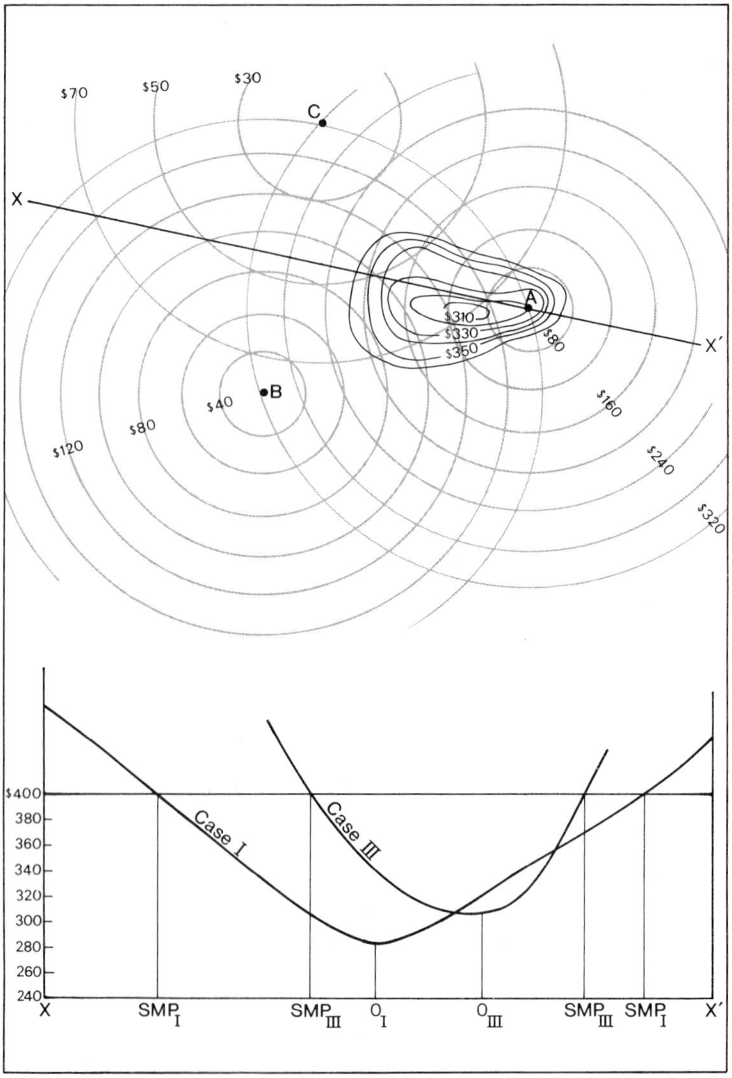

FIGURE 4.24 The variable cost model: Case III.

4.23). Basic costs are still $20 at all three input sources, but the total cost (BC + LC) rises to $40 at only 6.5 kilometers from A, and at 10 kilometers from C. The slope of a space-cost curve for input A is much steeper than for input C, and input B is intermediate. The space-cost curve for the isodapanes (sum of input costs) in figure 4.23 is shifted from its position in Case I (the space- cost curve from figure 4.22 is also shown in Case II). The optimum location (0) and the spatial margins to profitability have shifted toward A. Case III illustrates the effect of differences in basic costs. Notice in table 4.6 that the quantity (B) of the material input required has increased while the required quantity of power has declined. The cost per dollar unit per kilometer (C) is the same for all inputs, but the increased quantity of the raw material leads to increased locational costs. Figure 4.24 gives the new set of isotims for Case III. The basic cost of the raw material at A is $40 and the first $20 isocost line would be $60 ($40 + $20) and would occur at 5 kilometers from A. (Many of the isotims around A have not been drawn to avoid clutter.) The isotims around B and C are the same as for Case II. The locational costs of A are now much steeper. The space-cost curve has now shifted toward A, the optimum location is now 0_{III}, and the spatial margins to profitability are considerably smaller than in Case I.

TABLE 4.6 Basic and locational costs of inputs (variable-cost model)

Case	Input	Least Cost Source	Basic Cost of Quantity (B) Required Dollars (C) (BC)	Locational Costs Per Dollar Unit Per Kilometer (C) (C)	Space-Cost Curve Gradient (L) Dollars Per Kilometer (C) (LC)	Distance Between Total Cost Isolines at $20 Intervals ($20/LC)
I	Material	A	20	.10	2.00	10.00
	Labor	B	20	.10	2.00	10.00
	Power	C	20	.10	2.00	10.00
II	Material	A	20	.15	3.00	6.50
	Labor	B	20	.10	2.00	10.00
	Power	C	20	.05	1.00	20.00
III	Material	A	40	.10	4.00	5.00
	Labor	B	20	.10	2.00	10.00
	Power	C	10	.10	1.00	20.00

This simple series of examples should demonstrate that locational costs can occur *either* because of high transportation costs per unit *or* because a large quantity (basic cost) is required even though the per unit locational costs are low. This last point is illustrated by coal which has had a profound effect on past industrial locational patterns for heavy industry. Coal is relatively cheap to move on a per ton basis, but the quantity (basic cost) of coal required in some types of manufacturing has produced high locational costs and pulled the industry toward coal deposits.

The Locational Effects of Technique

Smith also explored in great detail the locational effects that technique might have. A decision made about any one of the three mutually interdependent factors (location, technique, and scale) may completely determine the limits of the remaining two. We will discuss scale in the next section, but technique can have a very important effect on the locational decision and warrants consideration here. Technique is the *combination of inputs* used to produce a finished product. A certain amount of land (resources), labor, and capital is required to produce any product, but (within limits) we may substitute labor for capital, or labor for land, or similar combinations.

The locational effects of technique can be illustrated with a very simple model. Assume that only two inputs with locational costs are required to produce a product. All other inputs have zero locational costs. One input is labor, whose locational costs are minimized at L in figure 4.25A, but remember that we still must pay the *basic* cost of labor even at L. Labor costs rise (per unit of labor) as we move away from L. The second input is a raw material, whose locational costs are minimized at M. Let us further assume that the finished product of our imaginary industry is a refined metal. The ore is of highest quality at M, but the metal can be mined everywhere in figure 4.25. Basic costs for the raw material are lowest at M because less processing is required for the purer ore. As we move away from M, costs rise because of the additional processing costs (i.e., more units of labor, more power, etc., are required to produce the refined metal from the lower-grade ore).

We can now determine the total costs of labor (L) at any point (j) with the following simple equation.

$$\mathrm{TC}_{Lj} = (BC_{\mathrm{L}} + LC_{\mathrm{L}} d_{Lj})\, Q_{\mathrm{L}}$$

where

BC_{L} = the basic cost of labor,
LC_{L} = the locational costs of labor per unit per kilometer,
d_{Lj} = the distance from L to j,
Q_{L} = the quantity of labor required to produce a given output.

When $j = \mathrm{L}$ (at L), $\mathrm{TC}_{Lj} = (BC_{\mathrm{L}})Q_{\mathrm{L}}$ because locational costs at L are zero. The same type of equation holds for the total cost of the raw material:

$$\mathrm{TC}_{Mj} = (BC_{\mathrm{M}} + LC_{\mathrm{M}} d_{Mj})Q_{\mathrm{M}}$$

Let us also assume that only two points are under consideration—M and L. Therefore, the total cost ($\mathrm{TC}_{\mathrm{LM}}$) for both inputs is:

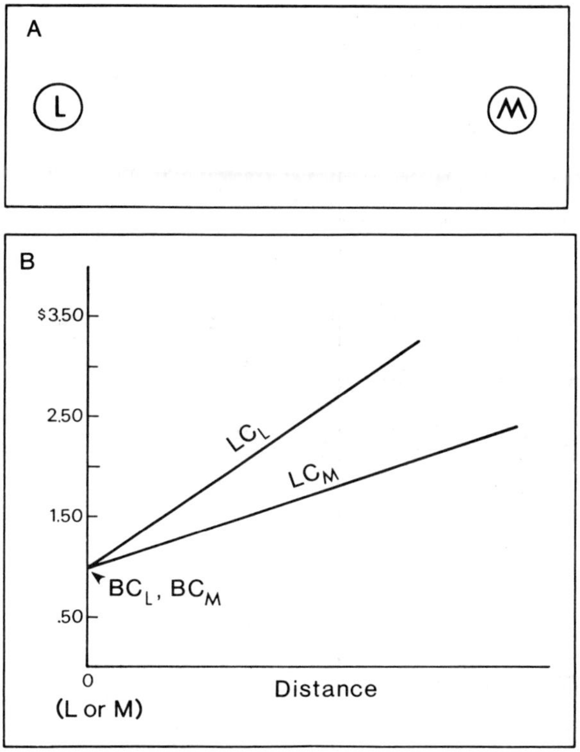

FIGURE 4.25 (A) Input locations—basic cost; (B) Location cost variations.

$TC_{LM} = (BC_L)Q_L + (BC_M + LC_M d_{Mj})Q_M$ if the location is at L (j = L)

and

$TC_{LM} = (BC_L + LC_L d_{Lj})Q_L + (BC_M)Q_M$ if the location is at M (j = M)

We are also assuming that the basic costs of each input are identical, but that the locational costs of labor increase at a greater rate than those of the material as a function of distance. This assumption is illustrated in figure 4.25B. If the basic cost of both labor and the material is $1 per unit and we spent a total of $100, what combination can be purchased if the plant is located at L? Figure 4.26A shows all possible combinations of labor and material that can be purchased for $100 at L. We could, for example, obtain 100 units of L and zero units of M. At L, the locational costs of M must be paid in addition to the basic cost, so that if we spend zero on L, our $100 will buy us only $75 worth of M. This would be the equivalent of $75 spent for the pure ore at M, or we might say that the quality of the ore has declined 25% at L. The line in the figure shows all other combinations. For example, if we spend $50 on labor we can obtain $37.50 units of the material. The possible combinations of L and M that can be purchased for $100 at M are shown in figure 4.26B. That sum obtains 100 units of M ($0 spent on L), but only 50 units of labor (if $0 is spent on M). Suppose that wage rate at L is $1 per hour; $100 buys 100 man-hours. If the rate rises to $2 per hour at M, $100 buys only 50 man-hours of

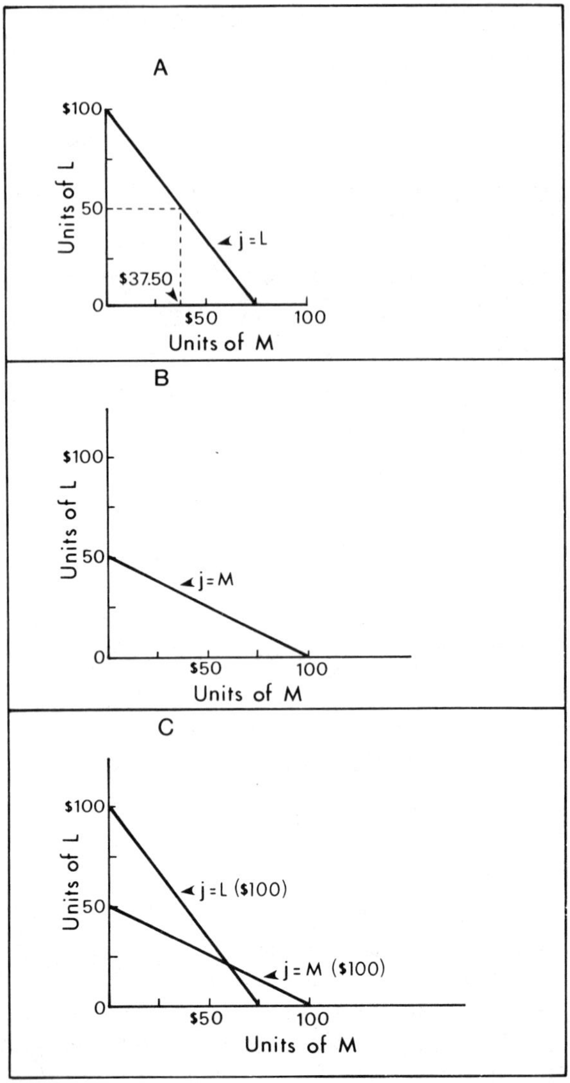

FIGURE 4.26 (A) Input combinations for j = L; (B) Input combinations for j = M; (C) Input combinations for j = L and j = M.

labor. Both *iso-outlay curves* are shown in figure 4.26C. The difference in their slopes is the result of different *locational costs*.

Now assume that $100 (basic cost) of the two inputs are required to produce 10 units of the refined metal. We cannot produce 10 units of refined metal by using 100 man-hours of labor and zero units of ore; the output cannot be produced by using 100 units of the pure ore and zero units of labor. Some of both inputs must be used, and our total costs for 10 units of refined metal will be *greater than* $100 because locational costs must be paid on one of the inputs. The $100 basic cost represents the *quantity* (*Q*) required to produce 10 units of refined metal in *man-hour and pure ore equivalents* ($Q_L + Q_M = \$100$). Further assume that at least 30 man-hours ($Q_L \geq 30$) and the equivalent of $30 worth of pure ore ($Q_M \geq 30$) are required to produce the desired output. These are the *technical restraints* involved:

$Q_L \geq 30,\ Q_M \geq 30,\ Q_L + Q_M = 100$

We could use 30 (basic) units of labor and 70 (basic) units of the material or vice versa and, within the technical limits, unitary (one-to-one) substitution is possible. Consider the following proposition very carefully. A unit of cheap labor (within the technical limits) used to mine and process low-grade ore produces the refined metal at exactly the same cost (per unit of refined metal) as the more expensive labor mining and processing the higher grade ore. This is illustrated in figure 4.27. The technical limits of labor (T_L) and the material (T_M) are shown as lines parallel to their respective axes. Beyond the technical limits of, say, labor (30 man-hours) we can add an infinite amount of ore and not produce the desired output. The same argument applies to the technical limits of the material. Between T_L and T_M, however, the line is at 45° and represents unitary substitution. As we move from T_M to T_L, we are substituting purer ore for more expensive labor at a *one-to-one ($) rate*! The $100 iso-outlay line from figure 4.26 has been drawn in figure 4.27. We cannot produce 10 units of the refined metal for $100, but we can draw an infinite number of iso-outlay lines on the figure, all of which will have the same *slope*. Notice that the $108 iso-outlay line is the *lowest value* line that touches the substitution curve. This determines total cost ($108), the optimum location (L), and the combination of labor and material used (technique). We should use 70 units of

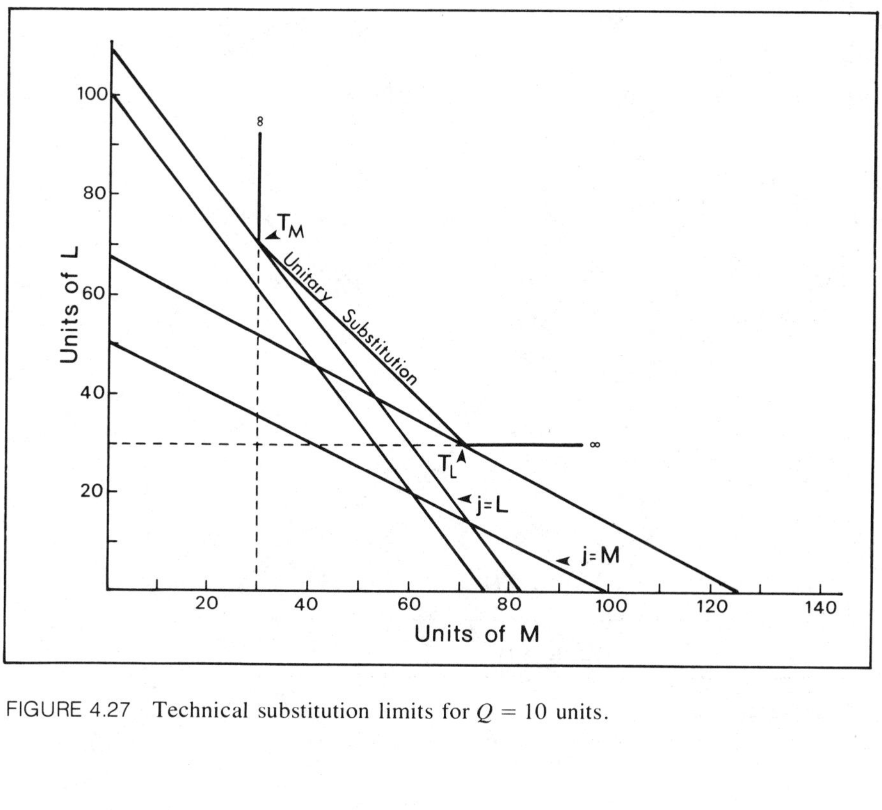

FIGURE 4.27 Technical substitution limits for $Q = 10$ units.

labor (basic cost) and 30 units (basic cost) of the low-grade ore at L. Remember that 30 units of the low-grade ore are equivalent to \$30 worth of the pure ore at M and not the quantity in the physical sense (weight or volume). More ore must be mined and more processing is required, but it is the (value) equivalent to \$30 spent at M. The strategy, given this set of assumptions, is to locate at the input source with the *highest locational cost*, use as much of that input as the technical restraints will allow, and use as little of the other input as technically feasible to minimize its locational costs.

Let us examine the locational effects of a change in technique and scale. Suppose that we want to increase our output to 20 units. The total basic cost for 20 units is \$160 ($Q_L + Q_M = \$160$ for 20 units). This is a change in scale and represents economies of scale (10 units @ \$100 = \$10 per unit; 20 units @ \$160 = \$8 per unit). Suppose that new technical limits now come into play. At least 30 units of labor are always required to produce even the smallest amount of refined metal, but to produce larger and larger outputs, more and more (equivalent) units of the ore are required. Therefore, for 20 units:

$Q_L \geqslant 30$, $Q_M \geqslant 80$, $Q_L + Q_M = \$160$.

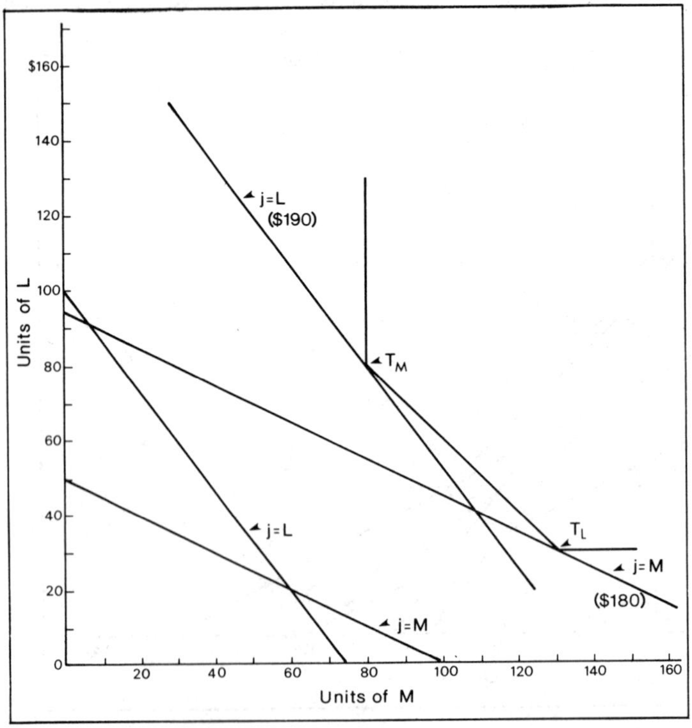

FIGURE 4.28 Technical substitution limits for Q = 20 units.

The new substitution curve is shown in figure 4.28. The technical limits of labor (T_L) remain at 30, but the technical limits of the material (T_M) have shifted to 80. Unitary substitution is still possible between T_M and T_L. We now find the least-cost iso-outlay line for the substitution curve which is \$180. The optimum location is now M and we should use 130 (basic) units of M and 30 (basic) units of L. Notice that the iso-outlay line for L equals \$190. The optimum location has shifted because the locational costs of 80 units of ore are greater than the locational costs of 30 units of labor even though the *per unit* locational costs of labor are greater than the ore. The technique strategy, however, is exactly the same as in figure 4.27: minimize the locational costs of both inputs by locating at the source of the input with the highest (total) locational costs, use as much of it as possible, and use as little as is technically feasible of the input on which locational costs must be paid.

The interdependence of location, scale, and technique is clear from these examples. If we choose a particular scale of operation, location and technique are determined. Scale and technique are given if a particular location is chosen. The other decisions are fixed if we choose to operate with a given combination of inputs (technique).

Scale Considerations in Industrial Location

We must now turn to the question of scale of operation in industrial location. Scale is very important not only because it forms one of the three interdependent production decisions, but for two other reasons as well: (1) producers are concerned with the *unit cost* of production, and adjustments in scale can produce considerable variations in unit costs; (2) scale is the means by which production is "tuned" to meet demand. This tuning may be done by the state in some types of economies and by private entrepreneurs in others.

We shall initially consider the scale economies that can be realized by an individual firm, and later examine multi-firm economies that result from agglomeration.

Principles of Scale Economies

Division of Labor and Capital One of the two key ideas in mass production is the division of labor (the other is standardization of parts). Workers performing one simple part of the production process are much more efficient than those who carry out all phases of the process. Adam Smith described the efficiencies in his analysis of two pin factories. In the first factory, each worker made the entire pin—cut wire to the proper length, sharpened one end, stamped out a head, and soldered the head to the sharpened wire. In the second factory, one worker cut wire, a second did nothing but sharpen, another stamped heads, and a final worker performed the last phase of the production process, which greatly increased average productivity per worker.

Division of labor speeds up production and makes possible the use of relatively unskilled labor. A worker can be taught one simple task in a short time, while the skills required to master the entire operation may take years. Division of labor, however, requires a large scale in that more workers are generally necessary. A larger scale also makes possible the use of very specialized equipment (capital) which may only be available in large unit sizes or whose cost is only justified in large operations.

The efficiencies of labor division also apply to management. The owner of a small firm has to do the accounting, advertising, sales, and labor relations as well as manage production. As the firm increases in size, these roles can be handed over to specialists who are better trained to handle them.

The scale of a firm can be measured in many ways such as gross sales, size of capital investment, and others, but the most common measure is the number of employees. Capital, once invested in machinery or buildings, becomes fixed capital and only produces income when it is in operation. A firm using three shifts of workers makes a much more efficient use of its fixed capital than one employing a single shift. The three-shift firm is three times larger in scale (measured by employees), yet its fixed capital investment may be no more than the single-shift firm.

The Massing of Reserves This principle states that large operations can maintain proportionally smaller inventories than small-scale firms, thereby reducing unit costs. Assume that a particular type of production requires a large, expensive, and complicated piece of machinery. The entire production process must stop if the machine breaks down. A plant shut-down even for an hour is an expensive proposition. Workers are idled, but must be paid while waiting, and other operational costs continue. A firm in this industry must maintain a reserve (inventory) of spare machine parts to prevent long-term shut-downs. Firm A has only one machine in operation, but must maintain an inventory of almost one whole machine in equivalent spare parts. A capital investment of almost two machines must be counted as part of the cost of each unit. Firm B has ten machines in operation, but because it is unlikely that the same part will fail on all ten at the same time, it must maintain a reserve of parts only slightly larger than the smaller firm.

Suppose each machine costs $10,000 and the parts inventory that must be maintained is worth $8,000. Figure 4.29 shows the decline in (proportional) inventory cost as a firm increases in scale from a one-machine operation to ten. Total

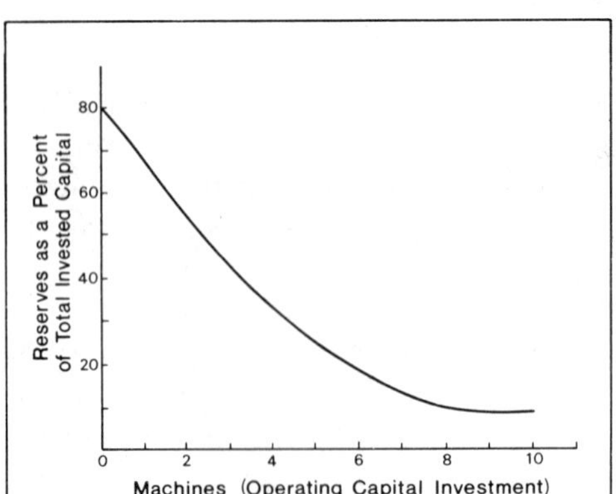

FIGURE 4.29 The massing of reserves.

capital investment is part of unit cost. As a firm increases in size, massed reserves lower unit costs.

Imperfectly Divisible Multiples This principle of scale economies is much like our prior discussion of technique and involves the possibilities of input combinations. Many inputs do not allow unitary combinations (one-to-one increases in scale).

Consider the manufacture of hammers. Assume the machine (or process) that produces hammer heads can manufacture 300 heads per hour, and the machine (or process) that manufactures hammer handles can produce 400 an hour. If we run both machines for one hour, we will have 300 complete hammers and 100 extra handles at the end of the hour. The production of hammers in this example involves imperfectly divisible multiples (400/300 does not produce a whole number).

One way to attack the problem is to run the head machine for the entire hour, but to shut down the handle machine after 45 minutes. During the shut-down costs (labor, power, rent) go on, however, in the part of the plant devoted to handle production. A second strategy is to increase the scale of the plant until we hit some unitary combination of head and handle machines. Suppose we increase the number of head machines to four and the number of handle machines to three. Now we produce 1200 heads and handles per hour. We have "tuned" the scale to reduce unit costs.

It is easy to see the kinds of savings that result from this principle, such as in automobile manufacturing where perfectly divisible multiples may be reached only in very large operations.

Bulk Purchases This principle implies that large firms pay much less for material inputs than small firms. Stated quite simply, General Motors can obtain tires for a much lower unit price than the individual dealing with the same tire company because GM buys millions of tires per year.

Possible Scale Economies

The economist portrays scale economies as a curve of long-run average costs (*LAC*) which graphs these costs (per unit) as a function of scale. A typical *LAC*

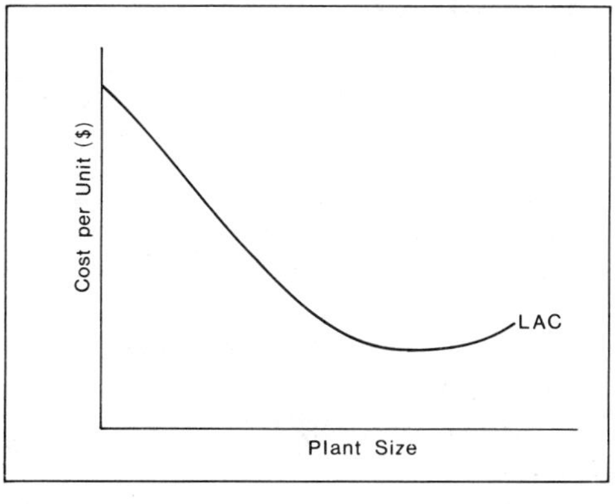

FIGURE 4.30 Economies of scale (long-run average cost).

curve for a firm is shown in figure 4.30. Notice that unit costs fall (increasing marginal returns to scale), reach an optimum point, and then begin to rise. The rise in the curve is termed *diseconomies* of scale (diminishing marginal returns to scale) and occurs when a firm becomes too large to manage and operate efficiently. The general form of long-run average costs is the same for all types of production. Several possible long-run average cost curves are shown in figure 4.31. The optimum scale is very small in Industry A, very large in Industry C, and covers a fairly wide range of scales in Industry B. Firms in Industry A should be small, large in Industry C, and range from small to large in Industry B.

Possible scale economies also give some indication of how firms in a given industry may expand production. A firm in Industry A, for example, should expand

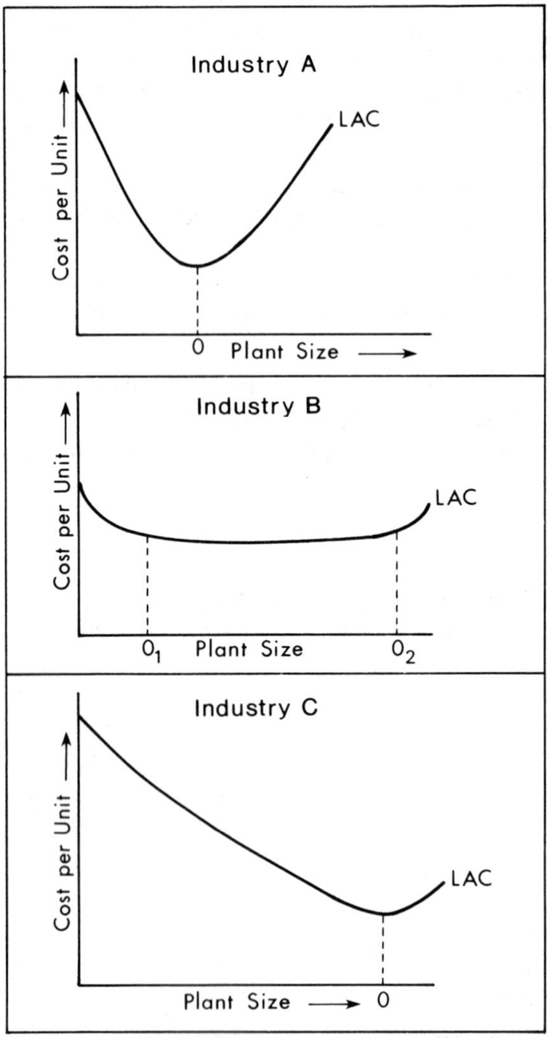

FIGURE 4.31 Variations in long-run average costs.

by building a branch plant; increasing the size of operations on the original site would produce diseconomies of scale. Firms in Industry B, however, could increase production by expanding existing plants or building new ones.

Spatial Implications of Economies of Scale

We can now examine the locational implications of intra-firm scale economies. We are ignoring the technique decision, but must once again remember that all three production decisions are interdependent.

Take the example of a company which operates two small breweries, each in a different town. The entire output of the firm is sold in the two towns. The long-run average costs (per barrel) for the firm are shown in figure 4.32A. The firm operates the two breweries at scale S_1 and costs are \$5 per barrel. The firm could reduce its cost per barrel by consolidating its operations into a single plant of scale S_2 (\$2.50 per barrel). One plant could be closed and the remaining plant doubled in size, or both plants closed and a new, larger brewery built. The firm has minimized its finished product distribution costs by manufacturing beer in each town. Additional

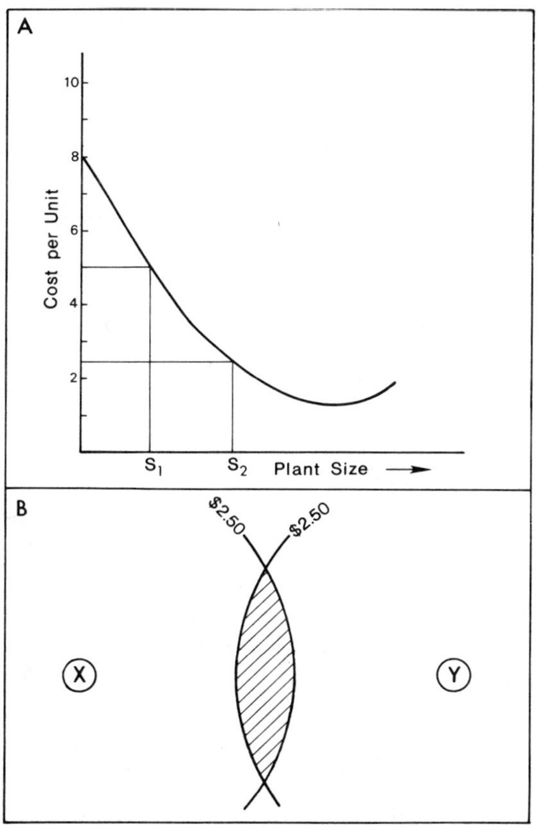

FIGURE 4.32 Spatial implications of scale economies: (A) Long-run average costs; (B) Transport cost isolines for break-even total cost with plant size of S_2.

finished product transportation costs will have to be paid if a single brewery is used. The problem to be resolved is whether or not the savings from scale economies outweigh the increased transportation costs. These two items will balance at a transportation cost of $2.50 per barrel ($2.50 *LAC* per barrel). In figure 4.32B, the iso-cost line of $2.50 per barrel from each town has been drawn. Notice that the two lines intersect, indicating that the scale savings outweigh the increased transportation costs. The larger plant can be operated in either city or in an intermediate location with a lower cost per barrel than is possible with the two small-scale plants.

Vertical and Horizontal Integration

Intra-firm scale economies imply more than simply increasing plant size. Scale refers to anything that changes the size of the firm's inputs—labor, management, capital investment, or raw materials. There are two common types of scale changes that firms use to increase their scale other than increasing plant size. Some firms may purchase raw material sources (mines, parts firms) or distribution facilities (retail outlets, advertising agencies, and trucking companies). This is called *vertical integration* because the firm is controlling more "up and down" from its initial niche in the total production process. Some large automobile manufacturing firms own iron and coal mines and produce their own steel ("down" in the process). They also may own dealerships and do their own transporting and marketing ("up" in the process). Large oil companies also tend to be vertically integrated; they control exploration, drilling, refining, and retailing.

Horizontal integration occurs when a firm gains control of more and more of a given niche of a particular industry. Shoe manufacturing has gone from over 3,500 firms in 1900 to less than 1,300 firms in 1972 as a few companies have purchased small operations. Whether vertical or horizontal integration occurs (if either occurs at all) depends upon the economies to be gained from such a move. Monopolies are somewhat regulated in the United States in an attempt to control the social cost of large-scale integration. Proposals in the seventies to break up vertically integrated oil companies are a case in point.

Inter-firm Scale Economies: Agglomeration

We have been concerned solely with intra-firm scale economies and how the expansion of a single firm can lower unit costs. Scale economies also apply to clusters of firms in the same or related industries. By clustering together (increasing the spatial scale), costs per unit can be lowered for all firms. These economies are called *externalities, agglomeration economies,* or *linkages*. Regardless of the name used, such economies take four basic forms.

1. Production linkages: These economies accrue to firms which locate near other producers manufacturing their basic raw materials. The links between producers of aircraft components and aircraft producers (clustered in southern California) and those between auto parts manufacturers and auto subassembly plants (concentrated in Michigan) provide examples. The output of one firm (or group of firms) becomes the input of another. By clustering together, distribution and assembly costs for both types of firms are reduced.

2. Service linkages: The garment industry, which includes a large cluster in New York City, is an excellent example of service linkages. The firms in the garment industry are small, but they require specialized service and maintenance activities such as the repair of sewing and cutting machines. Individually, no firm is large enough to support the development of a service industry (repair, spare parts, preventative maintenance), but collectively they can support an extensive service industry. Clustering provides the scale economies necessary for this kind of service to operate profitably, thereby eliminating down-time for individual firms.

The clustering of the Manhattan garment industry has also provided an impetus for the development of banking investment officers who deal almost exclusively with loans to this type of production. These investors have specialized in the garment industry, understand its special needs, and are much more likely to advance risk capital than investors who do not understand the industry and its unique capital requirements. This specialization could not have developed, however, if the small firms in the industry were not highly concentrated.

3. Market linkages: The garment industry also provides an example of market linkages which occur when a cluster is large enough to attract specialized distribution services. The small firms of the industry in New York have collectively attracted advertising agencies, showrooms, buyer listings, and other aspects of finished product distribution that deal exclusively with the garment trade. Firms located within the cluster have a cost advantage over isolated firms that must provide these specialized services for themselves or deal with New York firms at a considerable distance and cost.

4. Urbanization economies: Some economies are not the result of inter-firm linkages per se, but simply occur from locating in large cities. Firms in larger cities have an advantage, within limits, over similar firms in more rural areas. The city provides a market in which a small firm may sell its entire output, thereby reducing finished product distribution costs. A city is more likely to provide the specialized labor force and service industries a firm may need, and cities have the utilities (electricity, gas, and water) that industry requires. Fire and police protection are more adequately provided in urban areas. Finally, cities are major nodes on the transportation networks (road, rail, and air) that are important to many kinds of manufacturing.

Demand and Industrial Location

Thus far we have been concerned almost exclusively with the supply side of the industrial problem and have examined ways in which firms could reduce unit costs. We have implied that a firm could sell its entire output at a given market price and would be concerned only with reducing costs and increasing unit profits. This is one of the main assumptions of the economists' model of *perfect competition,* and many small firms in certain industries operate within this framework. For most firms, however, the level of demand is a very important aspect of industrial location.

Demand determines the scale of output and, in turn, determines the firm's technique and location. Concentrations of high demand certainly attract market-oriented industries and, therefore, influence location patterns. Demand is essentially a function of income and tastes—both of which change through time. Different industries must deal with different kinds of demand. Firms producing goods sold to general consumers face different locational problems than those producing a specialized product sold only to other manufacturers or to a very select group of consumers. The demand pattern in the United States facing a producer of root beer is considerably different from that facing a manufacturer of snowmobile parts.

A Demand Potential Surface

Geographers have explored the problem of demand through the concept of a *potential surface* which was extensively developed by Harris (1954). We may assume for a moment that tastes and incomes are the only factors determining demand. If tastes are uniform, the demand for a product is simply a function of income times population. If incomes are equal, the demand for a product will be high in densely populated areas and low where population is less. We could also allow income differences to play a role by weighting the population of an area by average income, total retail sales, or some other measure of the marginal propensity to consume. We also know that the price of a good is a major determinant of demand. Price can be made a simple function of distance (finished product distribution costs) if we assume that assembly and production costs are spatial constants. As always, we are holding some factors constant to simplify analysis.

What are the potential sales at Point i of a product produced at Point j? Assuming that demand is a function of population (or population weighted by income) and price (as a direct function of distance), we find:

$$D_{ij} = \frac{P_j}{d_{ij}}$$

where

D_{ij} = demand at point j for a product produced at point i,
P_j = the population of j (may be income weighted),
d_{ij} = distance between i and j.

A large population at j increases demand, but a large distance between i and j raises the price and reduces demand. We can calculate the demand potential between point i and an infinite number of points j yielding:

$$D_i = \sum_{j=1}^{n} \frac{P_j}{d_{ij}}$$

where

D_i = demand potential at i,
P_j = population of j (may be income weighted),

d_{ij} = distance between i and j,

$\sum_{j=1}^{n}$ = *sum* of demand for all points j from the first point ($j = 1$) to the last point (n).

Demand potential is computed for a large number of points and all points with same values are connected (iso-lines) to produce a map of a demand potential surface. Figure 4.33A shows the potential surface of the United States produced by weighting population by retail sales per county for a number of sample points. The actual numbers produced by this sort of calculation have only a relative meaning, so the contours are expressed as a percentage below the highest point. Away from the point, potential demand drops off in all directions as shown in figure 4.33B, a cross-section drawn from New York to Los Angeles. We might assume that demand is maximized at the highest point of the surface and potential sales would be highest there. A producer might want to get as near as possible to total demand.

The problem can, however, be viewed in another way. If all demand is concentrated at a single point, as in Weber's model, access to the market is maximized and transport costs are minimized at that point. Moving to one point, however, increases

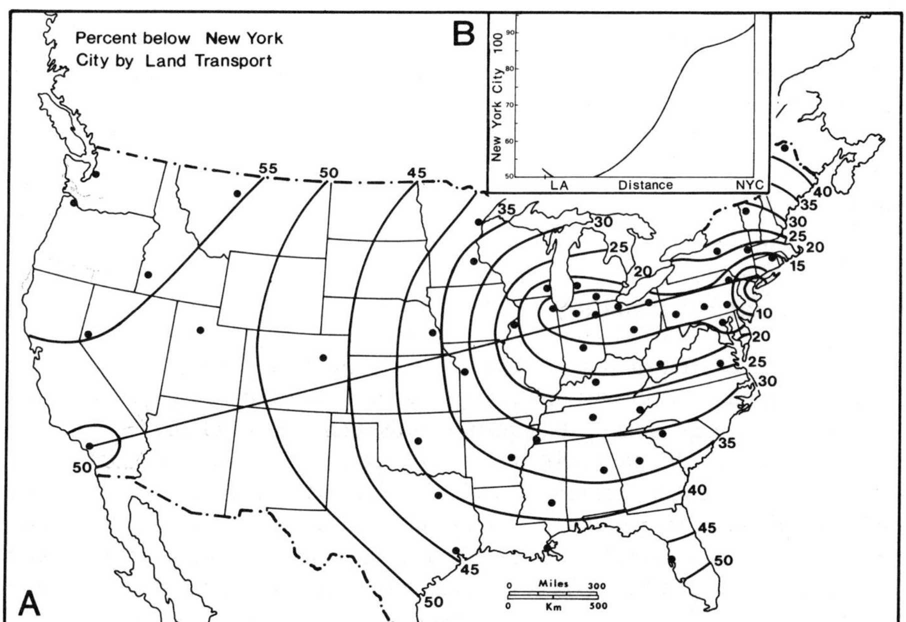

FIGURE 4.33 A. Market potential, United States [Source: C. D. Harris (1954), "The Market as a Factor in the Localization of Industry in the U.S.," Figure 4, reproduced by permission of the *Annals* of the Association of American Geographers, **44**]; B. Cross-section from New York City to Los Angeles (inset).

transportation costs (raises prices and lowers demand) to other points if demand is spread among a number of places. This is illustrated in figure 4.34. Moving from Point B to Point C raises transportation costs to other points. A location at New York City maximizes the distance to a large part of the country.

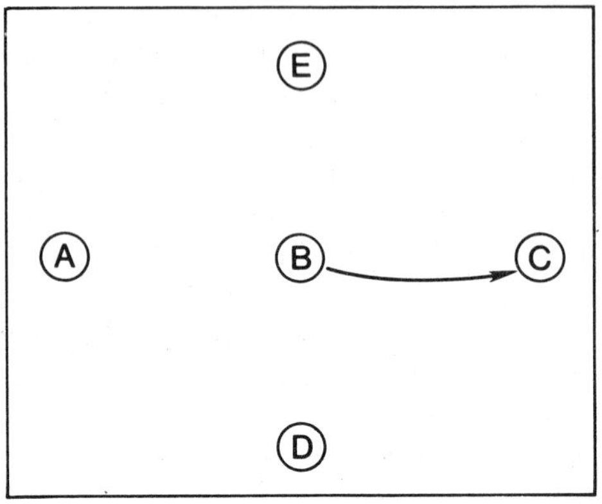

FIGURE 4.34 Changes in aggregate transportation costs.

A Transport Cost Surface

We can conceptualize a *transport cost surface* in much the same way as we did the demand potential surface:

$$TC_i = P_j d_{ij}$$

where

TC_i = total transport costs at i,
P_j = the population of j (weighted),
and d_{ij} = the distance from i to j.

Notice that in the transport cost equation we *multiply* by distance, while in the demand potential equation we *divide* by distance. A large distance will *lower* the value on the left-hand side of the equation in the demand model and *increase* it in the transport model. Figure 4.35A shows a transport cost surface based on the same sample of points as the demand model. The lowest point on the transport cost surface would be in the geometric center of the United States if population (and per capita income) were evenly distributed. The uneven distribution of population minimizes total cost at Fort Wayne, Indiana and total cost rises in all directions as shown in the New York-Los Angeles cross-section in figure 4.35B.

The problem is to determine the best location. Is it the highest point on the demand potential surface or the lowest point on the transport cost surface? Harris (1954) summed the problem neatly with a simple example. The West Coast comprised 11 percent of the U. S. market in 1954, but accounted for only 5 percent of the sales from Chicago firms (as a percentage of total national sales), yet the West Coast accounted for 22 percent of the total transport costs incurred by Chicago firms. The potential model is very useful because it allows us to visualize variations in demand. The more localized the market, the more nearly the optimum points on both surfaces coincide, but only for the distribution part of the manufacturing decision. We would still have to examine the surfaces for assembly and production costs.

The same model can be applied to industries that serve a more limited market. Figure 4.36 shows the potential demand surface faced by manufacturers. Roughly 80 percent of all manufacturing in the United States uses some raw materials that have been processed by another producer. Some types of manufacturing sell their entire output to other manufacturers, machine tools being an example. In figure 4.36, the sample points have been weighted by employment in manufacturing. Figure 4.37 shows the transportation cost surface for the same producers.

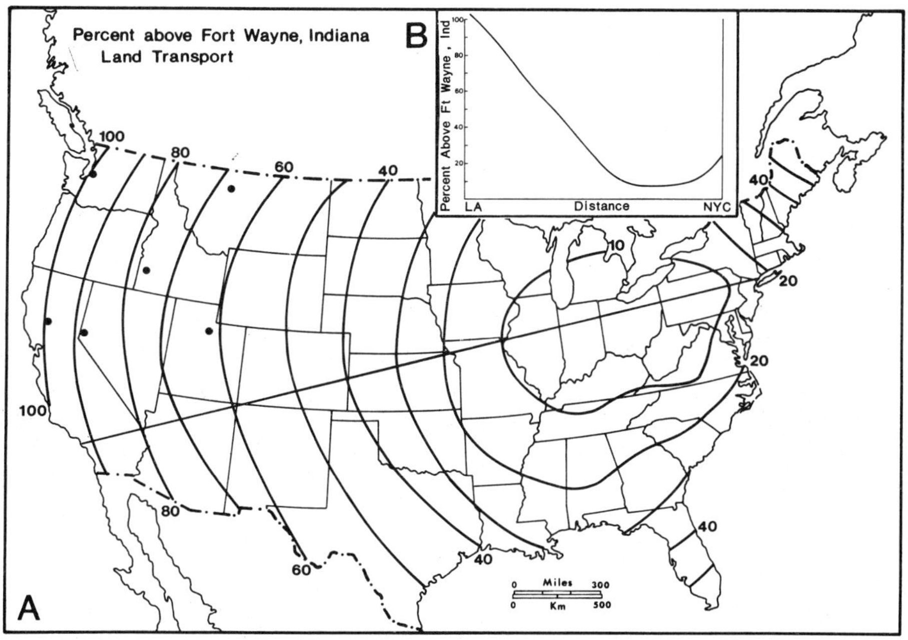

FIGURE 4.35 A. Transport cost to the national market [Source: C. D. Harris (1954), "The Market as a Factor in the Localization of Industry in the U.S.," Figure 7, reproduced by permission of the *Annals* of the Association of American Geographers, **44**]; B. Cross-section from New York City to Los Angeles (inset).

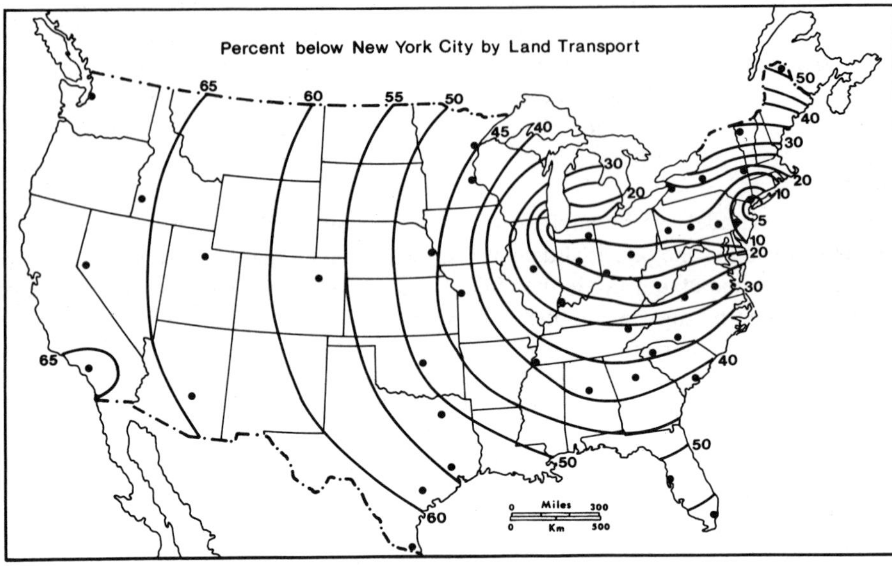

FIGURE 4.36 Manufacturing potential [Source: C. D. Harris (1954), "The Market as a Factor in the Localization of Industry in the U. S.," Figure 28, reproduced by permission of the *Annals* of the Association of American Geographers, **44**].

Throughout much of this chapter we have assumed that demand (revenue) was a spatial constant and that optimum location for production was at the point of minimum cost (figure 4.38). This figure assumes that we can sell as many units as we produce at the constant price and that revenue per unit and total revenue are maximized. Notice in figure 4.38 that we minimize cost, and maximize the profit per unit and total profit at Point 0. The reverse argument holds when price is a spatial constant and revenue varies across distance (figure 4.39). At Point 0, we maximize the profit per unit, total revenue, and total profit. We have also considered a situation in which both revenue and cost are spatial variables (figure 4.40) and the optimum location occurs where the positive distance between revenue and cost is maximized. All three figures assume that the value of revenue and/or cost *at any given point* is constant. We can sell an infinite number of units at a price of R in figure 4.38, for example. This assumption has been made to simplify analysis and to concentrate our attention on spatial variations in cost.

Let us complicate matters by making demand a function of *price*. We are also assuming that economies of scale and technique changes are not possible. At a given

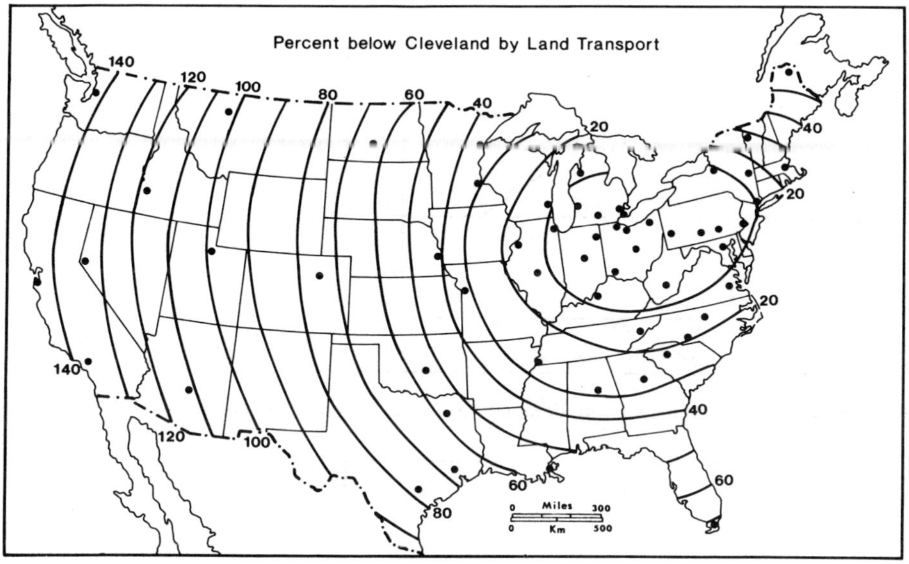

FIGURE 4.37 Transport cost to the national manufacturing market [Source: C. D. Harris (1954), "The Market as a Factor in the Localization of Industry in the U. S.," Figure 29, reproduced by permission of the *Annals* of the Association of American Geographers, **44**].

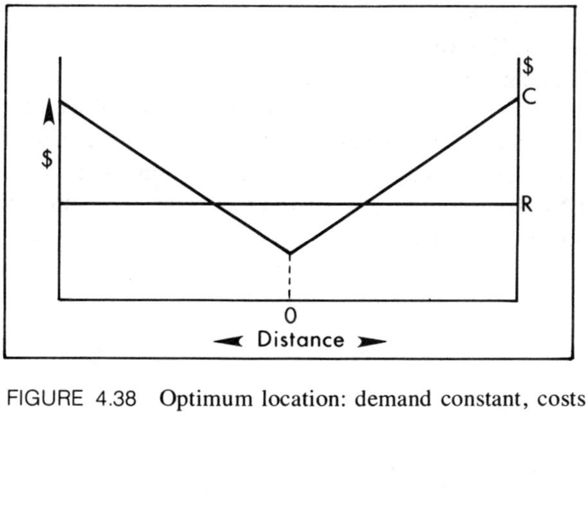

FIGURE 4.38 Optimum location: demand constant, costs variable.

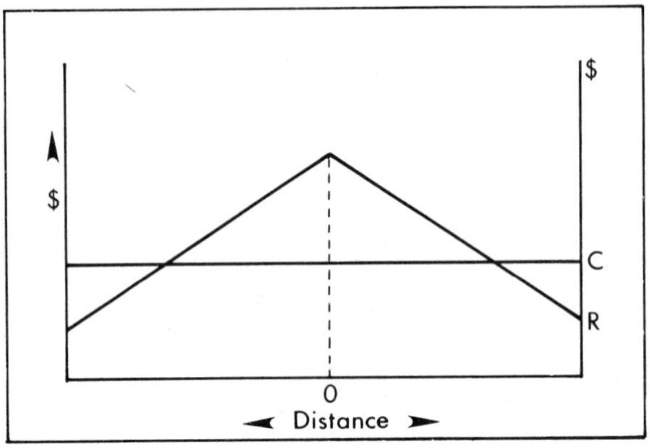

FIGURE 4.39 Optimum location: demand variable, and cost constant.

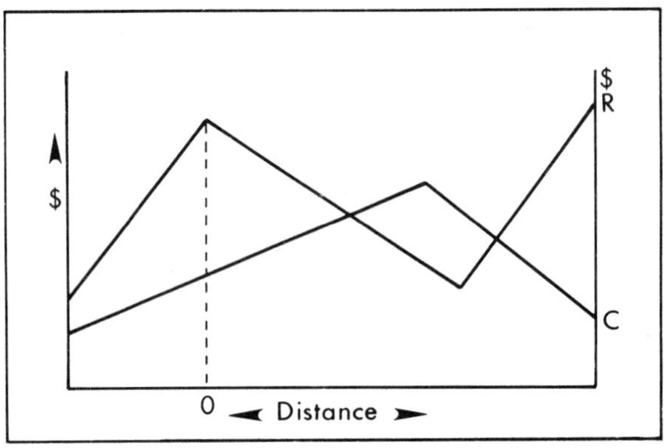

FIGURE 4.40 Optimum location: demand and costs variable.

point, the quantity produced and the particular input combination have no effect on the cost per unit. Consider figure 4.41A, the demand curve for a particular good. The quantity demanded (Q) is $Q = 20 - \text{price}$. At a price of \$20, 0 units will be purchased, and at a price of \$0, 20 units will be demanded per individual per unit of time. At a price of \$10 per unit, 10 units will be demanded. This curve illustrates *unitary price elasticity*. A one-unit change in price brings about a one-unit change in the quantity demanded. Let us also assume that transportation costs on this product are \$.10 per kilometer from 1 to 20 units. It costs \$.10 per kilometer to ship any number of units up to 20. Demand then becomes:

$$Q = 20 - (\text{MP} + .10d)$$

where

MP = market price,
and d = distance.

With a market price of \$10 and a distance of 10 kilometers,

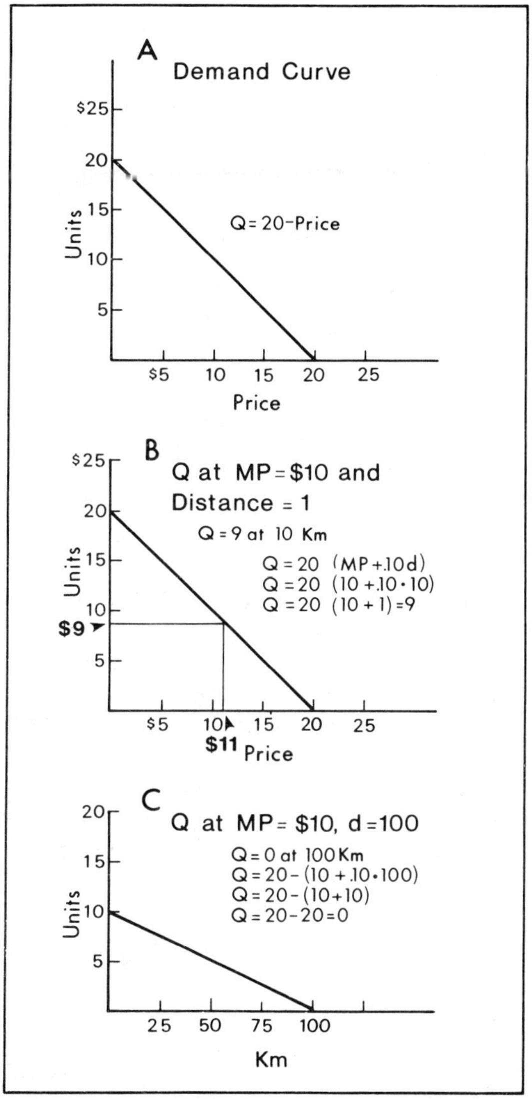

FIGURE 4.41 (A) Demand curve (unitary elasticity); (B) Q with a market price of $10 at a distance of 10 kilometers; (C) Q with a market price of $10 at a distance of 100 kilometers.

$$Q = 20 - (10 + 1)$$
$$= 9$$

so that at 10 kilometers from the plant, Q would drop to 9 units (figure 4.41B), and with a market price of $10, the edge of the market area would be reached at 100 kilometers ($Q = 0$, figure 4.41C).

We can now apply this idea to a linear market in which the population density is one person per kilometer and costs are minimized at $5 (Point 0 in figure 4.42). At

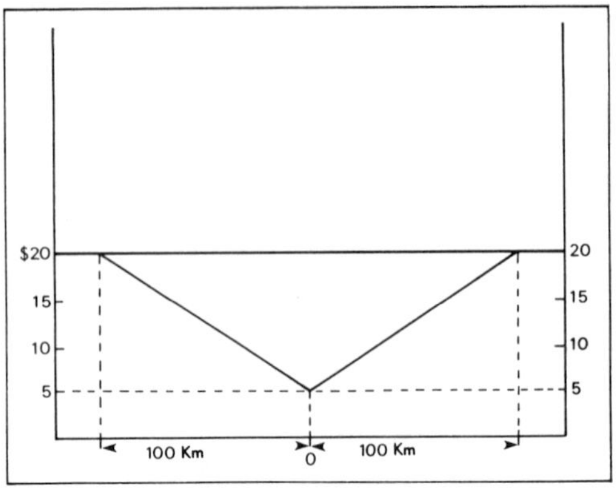

FIGURE 4.42 Demand and market area ($Q = \$20 - \$5 + \$.10d$).

what market price will profits (total) be maximized if we locate the plant at 0 given the above assumptions? The market price limits at 0 are \$5 and \$20. Below \$5, a loss is incurred and above \$20, $Q = 0$. We can calculate the total demand for any price very simply as in figure 4.43. The area OAB in the figure is the total number of units sold with a price of \$14 per unit and a total transportation cost of \$.10 per kilometer. Now consider table 4.7. At a price of \$14, 360 units are sold with a total revenue of \$5040 (360 units @ \$12 each) and total costs are \$1800 (360 units @ \$5 each). Total profit is \$3240 (\$5040 – \$1800). Total profits increase as we lower the price to \$13 and demand increases (table 4.7). We assume that each producer is operating a *spatial monopoly*; competition for the same market area is disallowed. Economics provides a ready answer for the problem at hand. The price (output) that maximizes profit is one at which *marginal revenue equals marginal cost*. Marginal revenue is the addition to total revenue brought about by a one-unit change in output. In table 4.7, we go from an output of 360 to one of 490 units, as the price falls from \$14 to \$13. This is much more than a one-unit change in output so we have to calculate *average marginal revenue* (AMR):

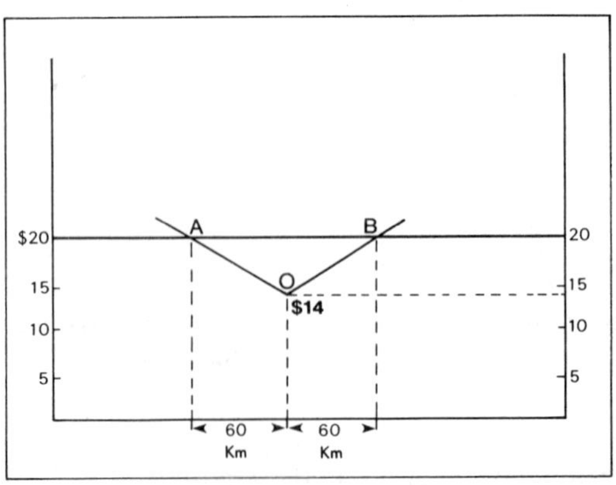

FIGURE 4.43 Calculation of total units sold.

$$\text{AMR} = \frac{\Delta \text{TR}}{\Delta Q} = \frac{6370 - 5040}{490 - 360} = \frac{1330}{130} = \$10.23$$

Average marginal cost (AMC) must be calculated in the same way:

$$\text{AMC} = \frac{\Delta \text{TC}}{\Delta Q} = \frac{2450 - 1800}{490 - 360} = \frac{650}{130} = \$5.00$$

A thousand units are sold when the price equals $10 and marginal revenue equals marginal cost. This is the output at which total profit is maximized. The data from table 4.7 are graphed in figure 4.44. Notice that the point of maximum profit is not the point at which total revenue is maximized. The locational and pricing strategy of a producer in this situation is shown in figure 4.45A. He produces at a cost of $5 per unit, sells at a price of $10 per unit, and his market area extends 80 kilometers in either direction from the production point. This solution is quite different from figure 4.38, not in terms of optimum location, but in terms of the volume and price of output. Notice that the spatial margins of production are determined not by cost, but by demand at a given price.

TABLE 4.7 Revenue, cost, and profit data (unitary elasticity, cost = $5)

Cost	Price	Units Sold (Q)	TC	TR	MR*	TP	MC**
5.00	14.00	360	1800	5040	—	3240	—
5.00	13.00	490	2450	6370	10.23	3920	5.00
5.00	12.00	640	3200	7680	8.73	4480	5.00
5.00	11.00	810	4050	8910	7.24	4860	5.00
5.00	10.00	1000	5000	10000	5.00	5000	5.00
5.00	9.00	1210	6050	10890	4.23	4840	5.00
5.00	8.00	1440	7200	11520	2.73	4320	5.00
5.00	7.00	1690	8450	11830	1.24	3380	5.00

$$*\text{MR} = \frac{\Delta \text{TR}}{\Delta Q}$$

$$**\text{MC} = \frac{\Delta \text{TC}}{\Delta Q}$$

Now let us consider the case of a producer who locates at a point other than that of least cost (figure 4.45B). This producer faces a $12 per unit cost. The relevant data are given in table 4.8. Profits are maximized at an output of 225 units, but the total profits for a producer faced with these unit costs are considerably smaller than for the producer in the previous example (figure 4.45A).

The same line of reasoning can be applied to goods that are price inelastic. An inelastic demand curve is shown in figure 4.46. A unit change in price produces a change in demand that is greater than one unit. The elasticity of demand in figure 4.46 is 2; so,

$$Q = 20 - 2(\text{MP}) \qquad \text{where MP} = \text{market place}$$

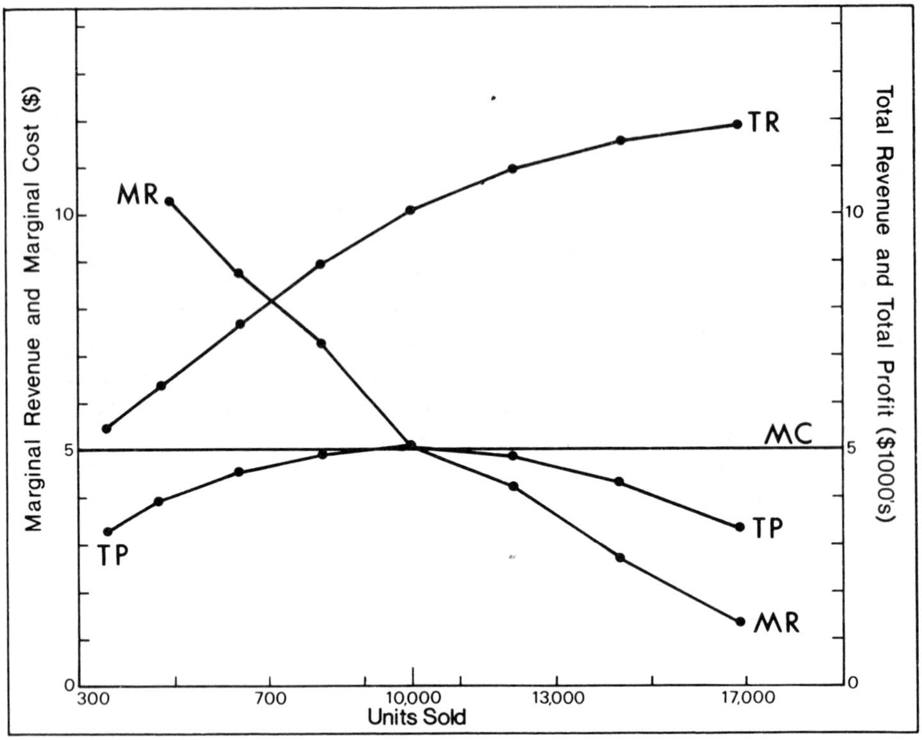

FIGURE 4.44 TR, TP, MR, MC for good with unitary price elasticity.

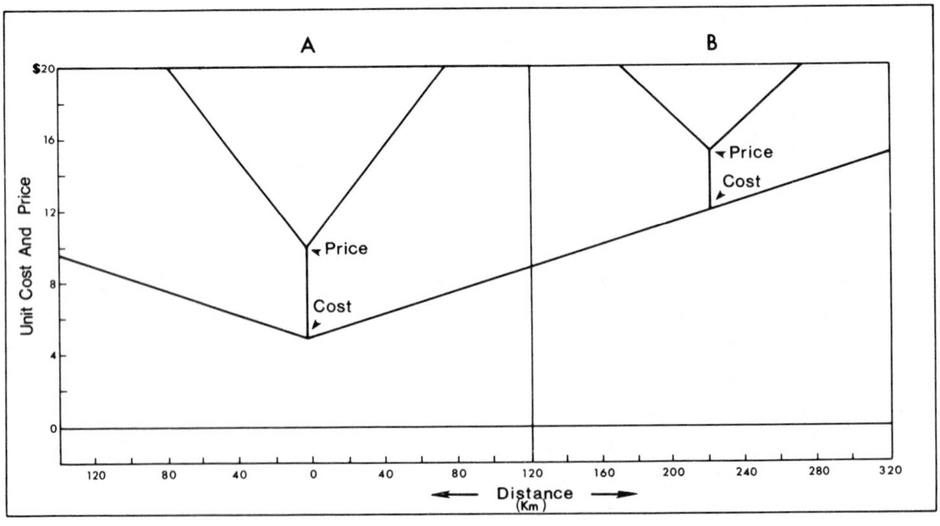

FIGURE 4.45 (A) Pricing strategy at minimum cost point ($5); (B) Pricing strategy at cost of $12.

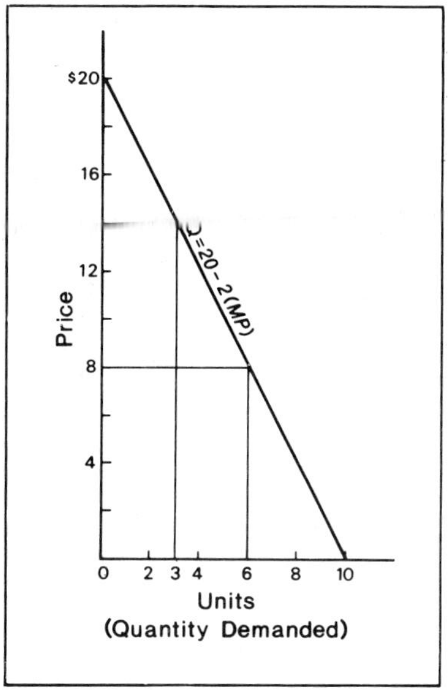

FIGURE 4.46 Price inelastic demand curve ($Q = 20 - 2\text{MP}$).

TABLE 4.8 Revenue, cost, and profit data (unitary elasticity, cost = $12)

Cost	Price	Units Sold (Q)	TC	TR	MR*	TP	MC**
12.00	17.00	90	1080	1530	—	450	—
12.00	16.00	160	1920	2560	14.71	640	12.00
12.00	15.00	250	3000	3750	12.22	750	12.00
12.00	14.50	302.5	3630	4386.25	12.00	756.25	12.00
12.00	14.00	360	4320	5040	11.36	720	12.00
12.00	13.00	490	5880	6370	10.23	490	12.00
12.00	12.00	640	7680	7680	8.73	0	12.00

$*\text{MR} = \dfrac{\Delta \text{TR}}{\Delta Q}$

$**\text{MC} = \dfrac{\Delta \text{MC}}{\Delta Q}$

Let us retain all of the assumptions of our previous example including a constant transportation rate of $.10 per kilometer and constant unit cost of $5. Data are listed in table 4.9 and are graphed in figure 4.47. Total profit is maximized at 390 units sold at $7 each, and the market area and total profits are much smaller than under unitary elasticity. The producer's market area is graphed in figure 4.48.

We can now turn our attention to a more complicated case in which potential revenue varies across space as a function both of demand and of population density. Population density varies from a low of 4 people per kilometer to a high of 52 in figure 4.49. Notice also that costs vary along this line from a high of almost $8 to a

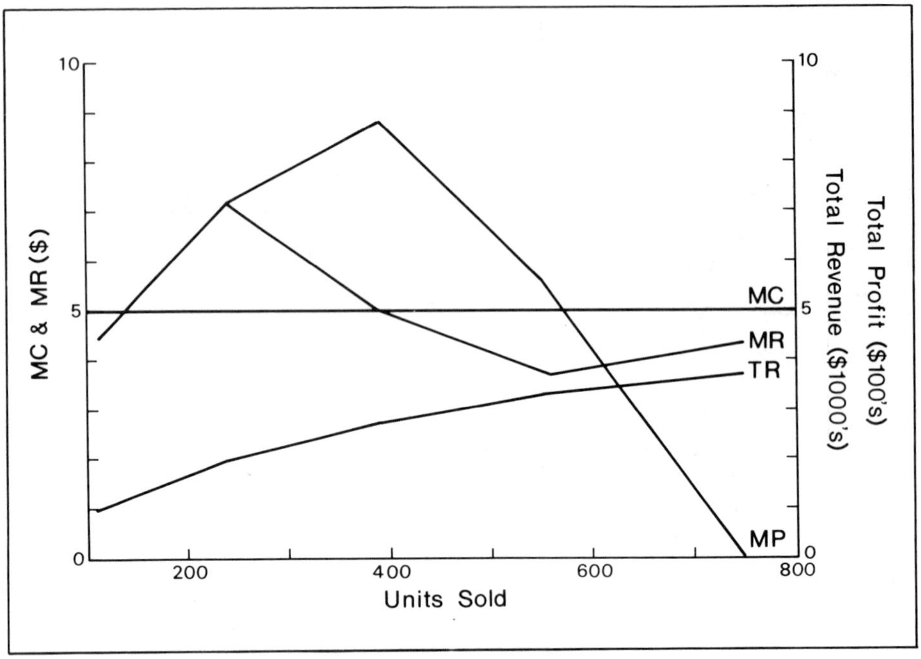

FIGURE 4.47 TR, TP, MR, MC for price inelastic good.

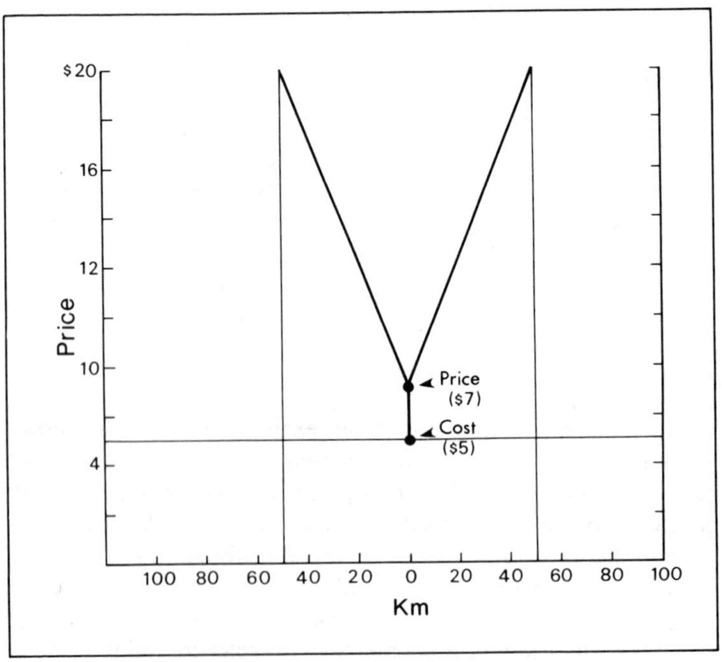

FIGURE 4.48 Market area of inelastic good.

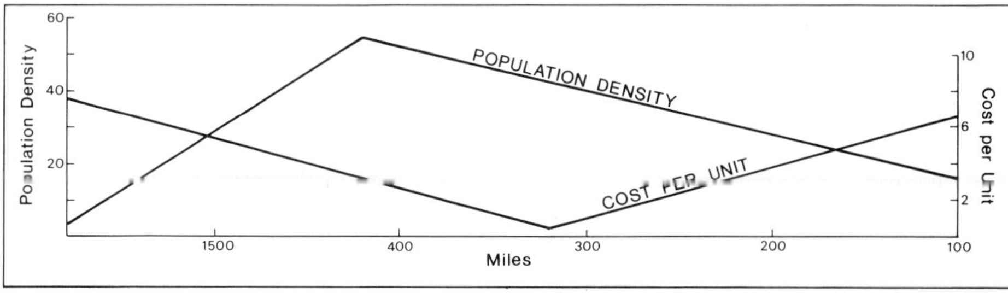

FIGURE 4.49 Variation in production cost and population density.

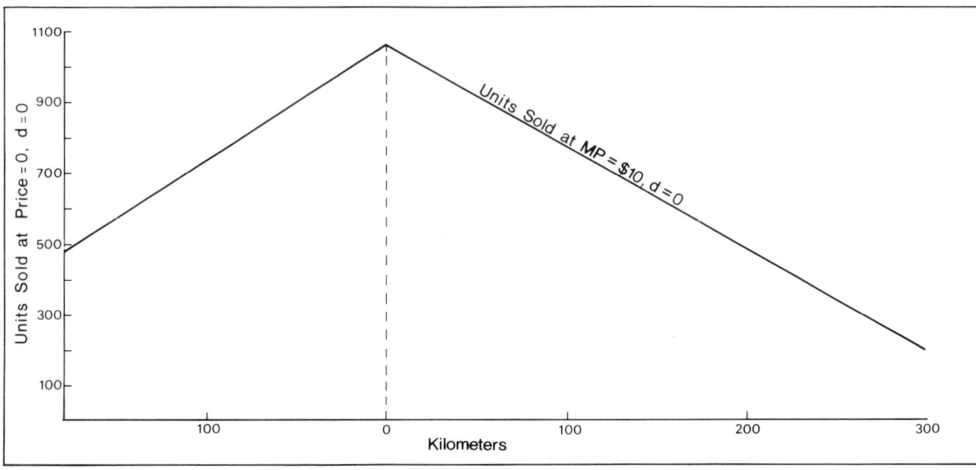

FIGURE 4.50 Variations in demand as a function of population density (MP = $10, d = 0).

low of $.50 per unit. What output should be produced and what is the optimum location if we assume unitary elasticity for the product in question? We will consider the two most obvious production points: a) the point of minimum unit cost; and b) the point of potential maximum sales. Figure 4.50 graphs potential sales for every point along the linear market at a market price of $0. We are assuming the same (unitary) demand curve as figure 4.41 in which $Q = 20 - \text{MP}$. The potential sales are calculated at each point along the market line so that distance (transportation cost) is always zero. Total sales at Point 0 are 1040 units (20 × 52 people). There is great spatial variation in demand along the linear market. Potential sales will be maximized at Point 0 at any price within the demand limits. The cost per unit at Point 0 for a market price of $12 and a transportation cost of $.10 per kilometer (for 1–20 units) is shown in figure 4.51. The line X–Y (through B) is the potential units sold for all points along the market line (MP = $12 and d = 0). At Point 0, 416 units can be sold at $12 (20 − $12 = 8 × 52 people at Point 0). Demand declines away from 0 because of the higher prices caused by transport costs ($.10$d$). Demand falls to zero at 80 km from Point 0 because:

$$Q - 20 - (12 + .10 \times 80) = 0$$

TABLE 4.9 Revenue, cost, and profit data (inelastic good)

Cost	Price	Units Sold (Q)	TC	TR	TP	MR*	MC**
5.00	9.00	110	550	990	440	—	—
5.00	8.00	240	1200	1920	720	7.15	5.00
5.00	7.00	390	1950	2730	780	5.00	5.00
5.00	6.00	560	2800	3360	560	3.70	5.00
5.00	5.00	750	3750	3750	0	4.33	5.00

$$*MR = \frac{\Delta TR}{\Delta Q}$$

$$**MC = \frac{\Delta TC}{\Delta Q}$$

Total units sold are calculated from the area of OEBW. A total of 32,800 units will be sold at Point O (table 4.10). We can perform the same calculation for all relevant market prices. Total revenue for a market price of $12 is $393,600 (32,800 @ $12 each), and total cost is $90,200 (32,800 @ $2.75 each). We must now find the number of units and market price at which marginal cost equals marginal revenue. The approximate price (table 4.10) is $8.45 with 68,700 units sold for a total profit of $391,875.

The same argument can be applied to the point of minimum unit cost (Point C in figure 4.52). The same total sales curve has been drawn in this figure (MP = $12,

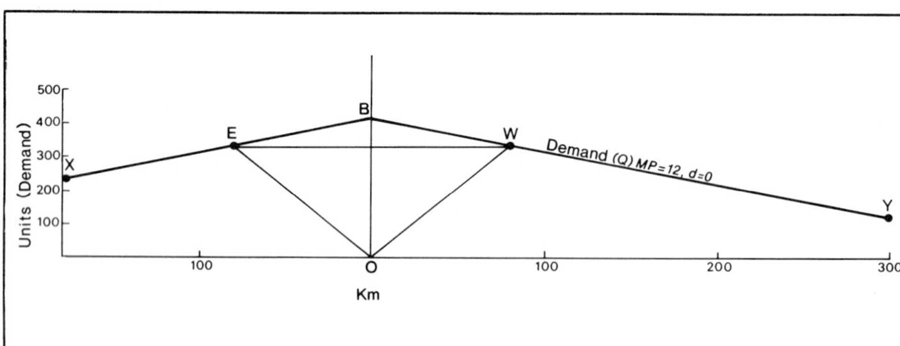

FIGURE 4.51 Demand (MP = $12 and TC = $.10 for 1-20 units) at point of maximum population density.

$d = 0$). The number of units sold at Point C is 344 (20 − 12 × 43 people) and the total number of units sold is 26,400 (area CWME). A number of market prices and the corresponding unit sales are shown in table 4.11. Marginal cost equals marginal revenue at a price of \$6.50 with 76,050 units sold. Notice that the maximum profit at Point C is greater than at Point O even though the optimum market price is lower. Point C is the optimum location for this particular example.

The analysis could be continued by introducing variations in transportation costs, economies of scale, or changes in technique, but it should be apparent that demand is a function of price and price is a function of distance from the production point. This fact means that the locational decision is much more complicated than in our initial Weberian models.

TABLE 4.10 Revenue, cost, and profit data (inelastic good at point of maximum demand)

Price	Units Sold	TR	TC	MR	TP	MC
15.00	13,000	195,000	35,750	—	159,250	—
14.00	18,600	260,400	51,150	11.67	209,250	2.75
13.00	25,200	327,600	69,300	10.18	258,300	2.75
12.00	32,800	393,600	90,200	8.68	303,400	2.75
11.00	43,200	475,200	118,800	7.84	356,400	2.75
10.00	52,000	520,000	143,000	5.09	377,000	2.75
9.00	62,700	564,300	172,425	4.14	391,875	2.75
8.454	68,700	580,800	188,925	2.75	391,875	2.75
8.00	75,400	595,200	204,600	2.64	390,600	2.75

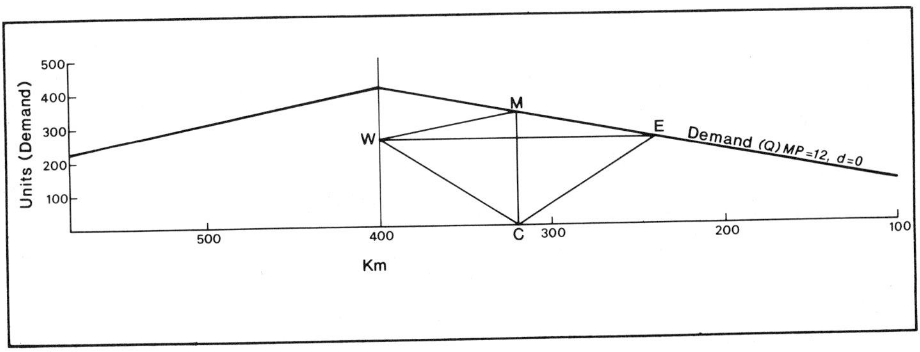

FIGURE 4.52 Demand (MP = \$12 and $d = 0$) at point of minimum unit cost.

TABLE 4.11 Revenue, cost, and profit data (inelastic good at point of minimum cost)

Price	Units Sold	TR	TC	MR	TP	MC
$12.00	26,400	316,800	13,200	—	303,600	—
11.00	34,200	376,200	17,100	7.61	359,100	.50
10.00	42,000	420,000	21,000	5.61	399,000	.50
9.00	50,600	455,400	25,300	4.11	430,100	.50
8.00	60,000	480,000	30,000	2.61	450,000	.50
7.00	70,200	491,400	35,100	1.11	456,300	.50
6.50	76,050	494,325	38,025	.50	456,300	.50
6.00	81,200	487,200	40,600	−1.38	446,600	.50

The Cost of Competition: Locational Interdependence

We must now turn to the problem of locational interdependence; the fact that competition from rival producers can dramatically lower potential revenues at a given point in space. We have assumed throughout this chapter that each producer is a spatial monopolist. The entrepreneur is the sole producer of the particular product within his market area. Profit maximization occurs, under this assumption, at the level of output at which marginal cost equals marginal revenue. The profit-maximizing strategy is quite different when nonmonopoly conditions are present.

Locational interdependence, on the other hand, implies a nonmonopoly situation. Competition in both the technical (economic) and popular sense is absent in a pure monopoly situation. There is economic competition, but none in the popular sense in the economist's model of perfect competition. The kind of market faced by spatial rivals is called an *oligopoly,* and occurs when more than one producer exists in the market, but the number is small enough so that the actions of one producer may have a considerable effect on the other. There is a lack of economic (price) competition in an oligopoly, but intense competition in the popular sense of the term.

An oligopoly usually exists when producers are considered in a spatial context. A small manufacturing plant is only concerned with the actions of other firms within the *same market area.* A producer of ready-mixed concrete in Chicago is not concerned with the actions of similar firms in Los Angeles. Even if the Los Angeles firms lower their plant price to zero, they cannot capture the Chicago market because of the transportation costs involved. The individual Chicago producer is, however, concerned with the actions of other ready-mixed firms in the Chicago area because their actions can have a considerable effect upon his profits. Locational interdependence, therefore, is a term coined basically to refer to spatial oligopolies.

The Ice Cream Vendor Analogy

A very simple oligopoly model was developed by Hotelling (1928). Imagine a stretch of beach over which people are evenly distributed. On this beach are two ice cream vendors each selling an identical product at the same price. People on the

The model of perfect competition assumes:

1. Each producer is small and there are a large number of producers; the action of an individual producer will be so small as to have no perceptible influence on price.

2. Homogeneous product; the output of one firm is indistinguishable from the output of other firms. Buyers are indifferent as to sellers.

3. Resources are perfectly mobile; production inputs cannot be monopolized by an individual firm.

4. Consumers and producers have perfect knowledge; they are optimizers. The short-run equilibrium for each producer is at the point at which marginal cost equals price. The long-run equilibrium occurs where price equals minimum long-run average cost. Each firm is characterized by a lack of "pure (economic) profits." Pure profits occur when marginal revenue exceeds marginal cost.

beach, therefore, minimize the cost of their ice cream purchases by buying from the closest vendor. Initially, the two vendors are located at the quartile points of the beach (figure 4.53A). Each person buys from the closest vendor, so that the total market area is equally divided between the two. Vendor A can temporarily increase his share of the market by shifting the location of his stand to a site immediately adjacent to Vendor B (figure 4.53B). The solid line in Figure 4.53B shows the division of the market under this condition. Vendor B's first countermove is shown in Figure 4.53C, and the final solution is given in figure 4.53D in which the market once again is even between the two vendors. Neither can gain an advantage over his rival by moving, so each must turn to other forms of competition such as advertising or product differentiation.

The Hotelling solution determines the equilibrium quantity sold by each producer and the equilibrium price, but we must assume that demand is completely inelastic at any price. If both producers charge the same price (plus the same transportation costs), total demand will be equally shared in the equilibrium situation. Hotelling assumes, in other words, that the demand of consumers at the edge of the market who must pay a higher price is the same as those near the common selling point. Both producers share the same production costs so that the common market price is that at which marginal costs equal zero. The distance to the most distant consumer is the same from both producers and neither can affect transportation costs. A producer who raises the market price will immediately lose the entire market and neither producer can lower prices to a point where costs exceed the price per unit so the equilibrium is uniquely determined. This is an optimum solution for each producer, but not for consumers because a location at the quartile points would minimize aggregate transportation costs.

Let us define the idea of a spatial oligopoly more precisely. Consider figure 4.54. A producer locates at X. Consumers pay the mill price plus transportation costs. The maximum price consumers will pay is shown by the line D = TR. Transportation costs on the product are $.10 per unit per kilometer. The producer at X need not be concerned with producers at Y and Y′. Even though their mill price is lower, they cannot encroach on his market area because of their transportation costs. He will, however, be concerned with the actions of Z and Z′ who do encroach on his potential market area. All producers must be concerned with the possibility of a

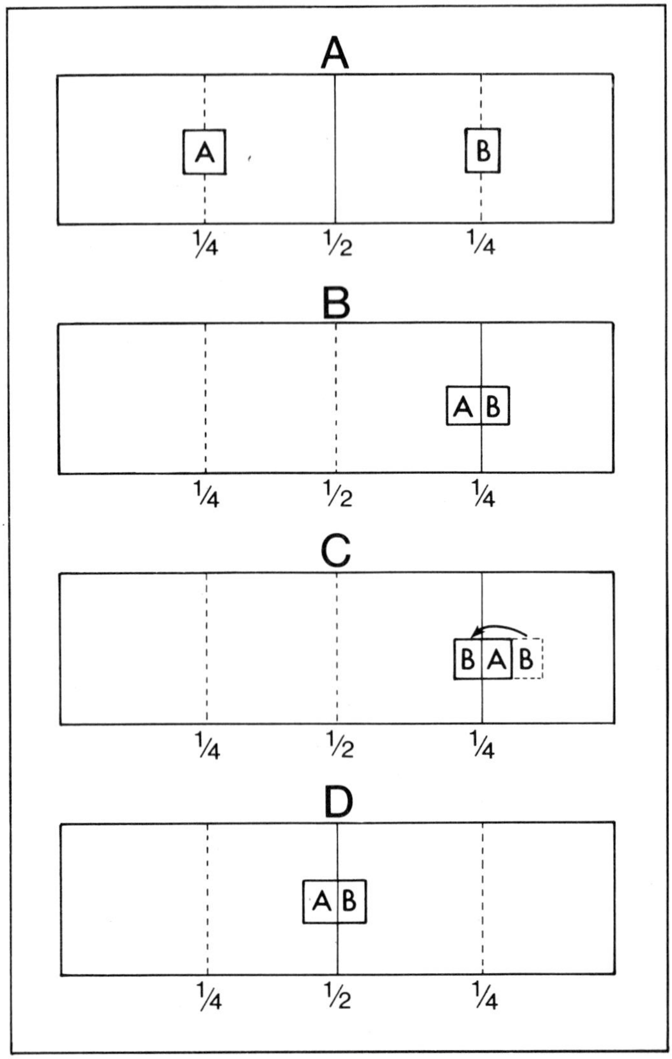

FIGURE 4.53 The Ice Cream Vendor analogy (After Hotelling 1928).

rival producer locating at any point that could capture a portion of the shared market area.

Each producer (X, Z, and Z′) will attempt to devise a strategy to minimize the possibility that rivals can increase their share of the market, thus increasing their profits.

The most important form of competition in the initial phase of a spatial oligopoly (before equilibrium) is price competition based on transportation costs. A producer is able to capture the part of the market area in which his delivered price is lowest. This outcome holds *only* if we assume that transport costs are charged to each consumer as a function of distance and *only* until equilibrium conditions are reached.

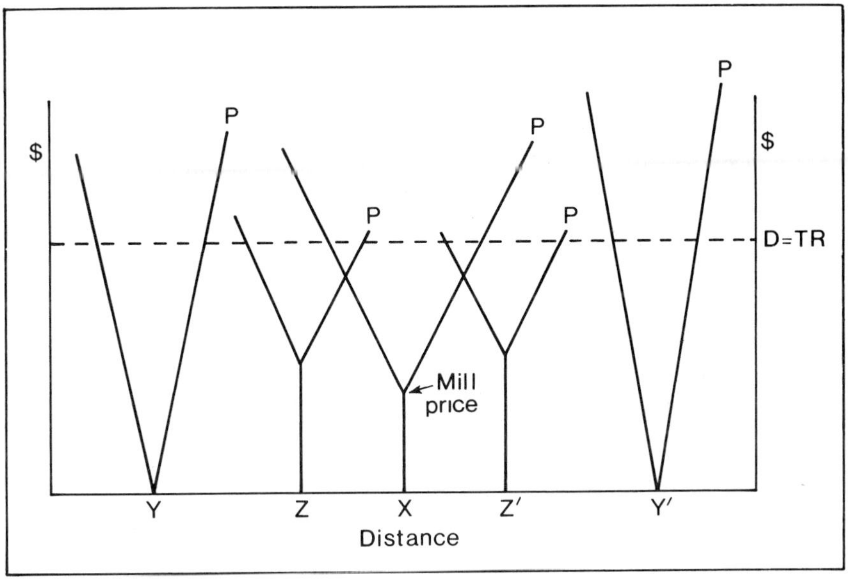

FIGURE 4.54 Spatial oligopoly.

Other transportation pricing strategies are discussed in chapter 5, but we should point out some other (nontechnical) forms of competition.

Price differentials are the only form of competition allowed in technical economic analysis, but we popularly recognize several other types. Advertising is the most important kind of nonprice competition in the United States. A second strategy is to create perceived quality differentials among products, such as the wide range of automobile types (and prices) that all bear a given producer's name. Quality differentiation divides a broad market into a group of submarkets and meets the demand for a wide variety of consumers. Design differences form a third technique of nonprice competition. Tennis racket companies, for example, continually introduce new models purported to be "superior" to last year's design and to all competition.

Nonprice competition should be the prevailing form if locational equilibrium prevails. The fact that this type of competition is the most common in the United States may imply some sort of short-run equilibrium, at least in certain industries.

Both long- and short-run locational equilibrium assume that producers can adjust instantaneously to changes in the location of competitors and other marginal changes in costs and revenues. There are a number of models beyond the scope of this book that attempt to show the equilibrium reached after a series of adjustments by spatial oligopolists. This locational inertia of reality, however, prevents this instantaneous adjustment from taking place and transportation costs prevent all factors of production from being as mobile as they are assumed to be in the models of classical economics.

Equilibrium adjustment also assumes economic rationality and perfect knowledge, which are not conditions of reality. Producers are reluctant to make major moves even if economically feasible because of uncertainty. Real spatial equilibrium, if it exists even in the short run, is the result of a trial and error process often resulting in great social costs.

Summary

The pattern of manufacturing is determined by many factors. Assembly costs occur because of the uneven distribution of raw materials required for a particular kind of manufacturing. Production costs vary because of the areal differences in the cost of labor, capital, and technical skills. Finished product distribution costs occur if a producer must sell to dispersed markets. All these costs may be collectively termed *locational* costs. Classical location theory has concentrated on finding production points at which locational costs are minimized.

Once the point of minimum locational costs is determined, however, other problems remain. The *scale* of the operation must be determined and the particular combination of inputs (*technique*) optimized. A producer must also be concerned with the actions of rival producers. The location problem, therefore, is very complex, but this complexity can be reduced with the concept of *spatial margins to profitability*. Locational costs, scale, technique, and locational interdependence together determine spatial margins to profitability. All viable manufacturing operations, by definition, must take place within these margins. How these limits are empirically determined and how locations within them are chosen requires a discussion of decision making which is the subject of chapter 6.

KEY WORDS

agglomeration economies
assembly costs
basic cost
critical isodapane
distribution costs
economies of scale
horizontal integration
imperfectly divisible multiples
isodapane
isotim
labor productivity
locational costs
locational inertia
localized raw material
market linkage
massing of reserves
material index
orientation
potential surface
production linkage
pure raw material
service linkage
space-cost curve
spatial margins to profitability
spatial monopoly
spatial oligopoly
technique
transport cost surface
ubiquitous raw material
urbanization economies
value added by manufacturing
Varignon frame
vertical integration
weight-losing raw material

SUGGESTED READINGS

Primary Sources

Weber, A. (1929), *Alfred Weber's Theory of the Location of Industries,* trans. by C. J. Friedrich, Chicago: University of Chicago Press.

Smith, D. (1971), *Industrial Location: An Economic Geographic Analysis,* New York: John Wiley and Sons.

Isard, W. (1976), *Location and Space-Economy,* Cambridge: The MIT Press.

Empirical Case Studies

Kennelly, R. A. (1954–5), "The Location of the Mexican Steel Industry," *Revista Geografica* **15**, 109–29, **16**, 60–77.

Isard, W. and Cumberland, J. H. (1950), "New England as a Possible Location for an Integrated Iron and Steel Works," *Economic Geography* **26**, 245–59.

Stafford, H. A. (1960), "Factors in the Location of the Paperboard Container Industry," *Economic Geography* **36**, 260–66.

Smith, D. (1971), *Industrial Location: An Economic Geographic Analysis,* New York: John Wiley & Sons, Chapter 18.

5 Transportation Costs

One of the primary forces structuring the space-economy is the "tyranny of distance": the fact that *all movement costs*. We have made a tremendous investment of both human and natural resources in overcoming the cost, time, and effort of movement. Transportation innovations have resulted in *time-space* and *cost-space convergence* (figure 5.1). Both the travel time and cost between the two points in figure 5.1 have been significantly reduced over time. If transportation costs were instantaneous and free, manufacturing would respond solely to aspatial forces such as economies of scale. Although transportation costs have been reduced, locational costs still exert a powerful influence on patterns of production, exchange, and consumption. Present-day patterns reflect a temporary balance between locational and aspatial forces (including inertia). We are entering a period of rapidly rising transportation costs which should increase the importance of locational costs.

We made two implicit assumptions about transportation costs in our consideration of models of agricultural production, services and retailing, and industrial location: (1) transportation costs are a linear function of distance; and (2) transportation costs are exclusively a function of distance (zero distance equals zero cost). These normative constraints reduced the complexity of the models, allowing us to concentrate on the idealized effects of distance. We can now relax these constraints.

The Thünen model is predicated on locational costs. Economic rent is a direct function of distance or the cost of transportation. Central place theory deals with strategies of balancing the tension between the scale economies of concentrating retailing and services at as few points as possible and the costs of consumers overcoming the distances they must travel to purchase goods and services. The least-cost approach of the Weberian model is primarily concerned with transportation costs. We assumed in all three models a very simplistic view of transportation costs. This chapter is devoted to a discussion of actual transportation costs.

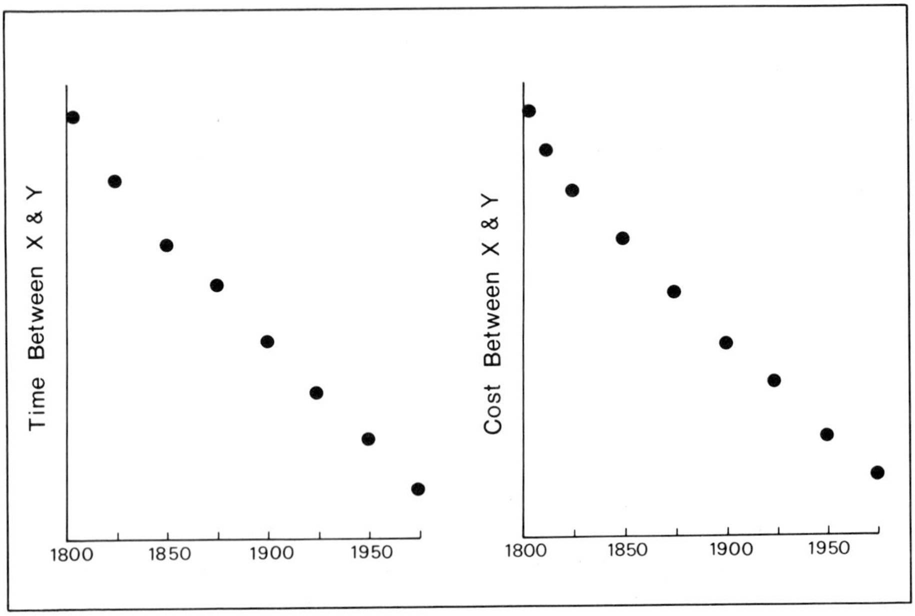

FIGURE 5.1 Time- and cost-space convergence (after Janelle 1968).

Chapter Objectives

1. Examine the structure of real transportation costs.
2. Discuss the implications of actual transportation costs on industrial location patterns.

General Properties of Transportation Costs

Figure 5.2 is a graph of the normative assumptions about transportation costs used in the first four chapters of this book. The graph is taken from table 5.1. Zero distance involves zero cost, and cost is a linear function of distance. In reality transportation costs are much more complex. Distance is the major variable affecting transportation costs, but many other factors also play a role. These additional variables distort the relatively simple patterns of our initial industrial location model.

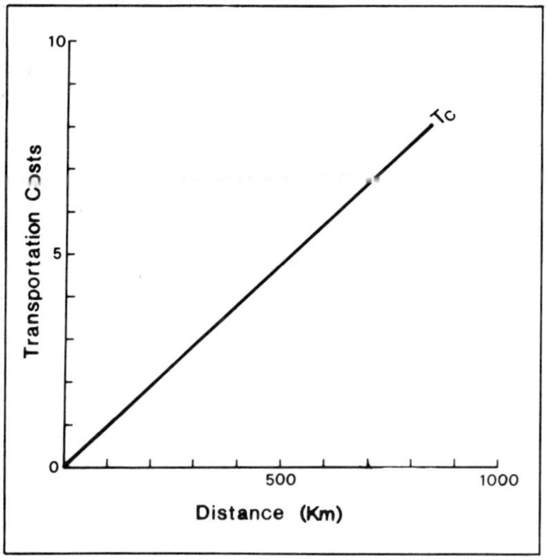

FIGURE 5.2 Linear transportation costs as a sole function of distance.

TABLE 5.1 Linear transportation costs

Kilometers	Cost ($)
0	0
100	1
200	2
300	3
400	4
500	5
600	6
700	7
800	8
900	9
1000	10

Terminal and Line-Haul Costs

Actual transportation costs can be divided into two parts: terminal and line-haul costs (figure 5.3 and table 5.2). Terminal costs must be paid regardless of the distance involved and include the cost of preparation for movement, loading and

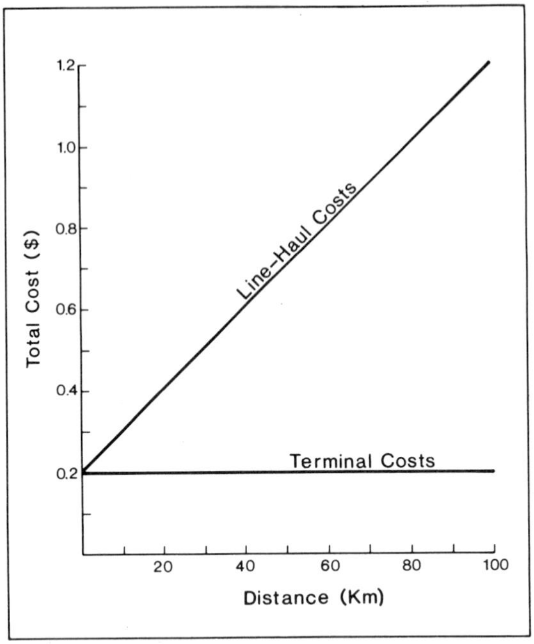

FIGURE 5.3 Terminal and line-haul costs.

unloading, capital investment, line maintenance, and other kinds of cost that are not a function of distance. Line-haul costs, on the other hand, are strictly a function of distance. For example, fuel costs are proportional to the distance a load must be moved.

Competitive differences among transportation media involve variations in terminal and line-haul costs. Figure 5.4 shows variations in terminal and line-haul costs among three different forms of transportation. Trucks have very low terminal costs because of their flexibility (they can load and unload almost anywhere) and because of the relatively low capital investment of trucking compared to other forms of transportation, but trucks have comparatively steep line-haul costs. They are not as efficient in moving freight on a ton-km basis as the other two forms of transportation. With three competing forms of transportation, trucks incur the least cost only out to the distance D_1. Rail transportation has higher terminal costs (much higher capital investment and maintenance costs), but lower line-haul costs give railroads an advantage over trucks through the distance D_1–D_2. Water transportation has the highest terminal costs, but the lowest line-haul costs, giving it an advantage over longer distances.

The distinction between terminal (often called "fixed" costs) and line-haul (variable) costs can be illustrated by rail transportation. The interest on invested capital is fixed. It is independent of the value of traffic or the distance freight must be moved. Many other expenses of a railroad are not a function of distance.

TABLE 5.2 Terminal and line-haul costs

Distance (km)	Terminal Costs ($)	Line-Haul Costs ($)	Total Transportation Costs ($)
0	.20	.00	.20
1	.20	.01	.21
10	.20	.10	.30
20	.20	.20	.40
30	.20	.30	.50
40	.20	.40	.60
50	.20	.50	.70
100	.20	1.00	1.20

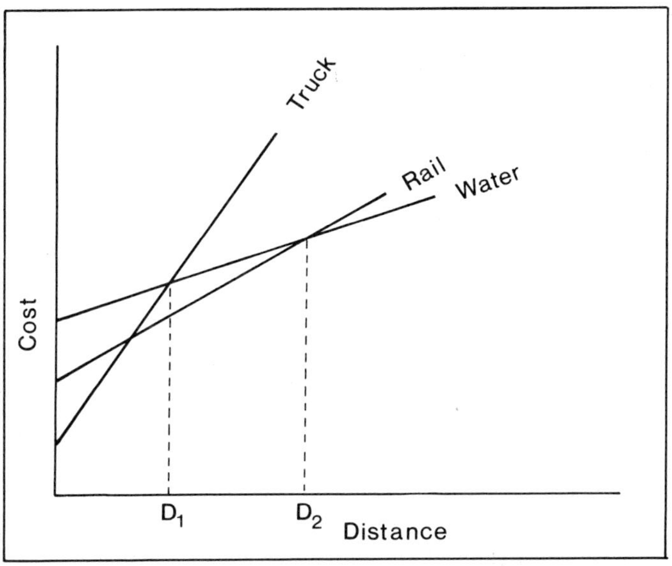

FIGURE 5.4 Variations in terminal and line-haul costs among different transport media.

Route maintenance must be continued because of constant exposure to weather which is usually much more of a factor in line deterioration than the volume of traffic. Depreciation of cars and locomotives is not solely a function of usage. Wages of crews and yard employees and fuel costs, on the other hand, tend to be proportional to mileage (ton-km or car-km). Income, which determines some taxes, is a function of the volume of traffic, but property taxes paid on rights-of-way are a fixed expense and often account for a large proportion of the tax bill of railroads. This, in part, explains the much lower terminal costs of trucks. A major share of the tax bill of the trucking industry comes from fuel taxes which go to pay for the construction and repair of the highway network in the United States, but fuel taxes are a variable expense determined by the volume of traffic and ton-km moved. Despite the nature of fixed costs for railroads in the United States, variable costs still account for 70 to 75 percent of total costs (Locklin 1972).

Curvilinear Line-Haul Costs

Figures 5.2–5.4 portray line-haul costs as a *linear* function of distance. Actual line-haul costs, however, are *curvilinear* (figure 5.5). The rate increases with distance, but at a *decreasing* rate. The distance from O to D_2 in figure 5.5 is twice the distance from O to D_1, but does not involve twice the cost (C_1 to C_2). As the distance increases, the average cost per kilometer decreases. This property of actual transportation costs is often called "economies of the long haul."

Economies of the long haul occur for several reasons. First, terminal costs are the same regardless of the distance of the trip. As line-haul costs increase, terminal costs become proportionally less of the total. This is illustrated in table 5.3; a ten-kilometer trip costs $.0550 per kilometer while a haul of 500 kilometers costs only $.0060 per kilometer. Second, line-haul *rates* are lower for longer hauls. Short hauls by rail, for example, are moved by local trains; longer hauls are made by "through" freight trains that involve fewer stops and operate more efficiently. Third, tapered line-haul costs prevent rates from restricting long-distance hauls. Rates would soon become high enough to prevent traffic if they increased in direct proportion to distance.

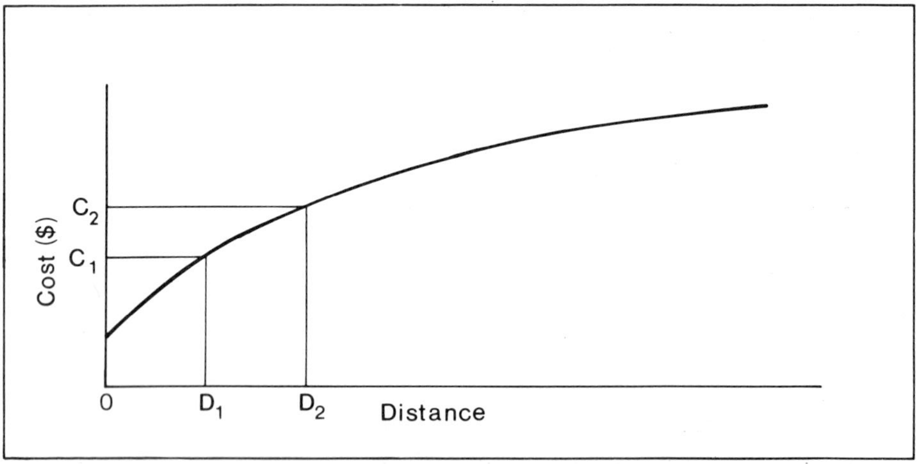

FIGURE 5.5 Curvilinear line-haul costs.

Stepped Freight Rates

Theoretically every point along a line from a given origin should pay a slightly different rate based on the actual distance involved. A given route, however, is usually divided into a number of zones because of the difficulties of computing large numbers of rates that are quoted in specific distance increments from a point of

TABLE 5.3 Effects of constant terminal costs on total cost kilometer

Terminal Cost ($)	Line-Haul Cost (Per km) ($)	Km of Haul (X)	Total Cost (Y) ($)	Cost Per km (Y/X) ($)
.50	$.005	10	.55	.0550
.50	.005	20	.60	.0300
.50	.005	30	.65	.0216
.50	.005	100	1.00	.0100
.50	.005	200	1.50	.0075
.50	.005	300	2.00	.0066
.50	.005	500	3.00	.0060

origin (table 5.4). This often gives one point a significant cost advantage over a competing point. Points X and Y in figure 5.6, for example, are very close together. Point Y should pay only slightly more for shipments from O than Point X, but because of the nature of the rate zones, Y pays a much higher price than X. Point Z pays the same price as Y even though it is much farther from the origin. Point X has a competitive advantage over Y, but Y does not have a cost advantage over Z despite the greater distance of Z.

Variations in Transportation Rates

The transportation cost curve varies among transportation modes, routes, and commodities. What determines specific rates?

Commodity Variations

The first set of factors specifically determining the cost of transportation involves the nature of the commodity. On a given mode of transportation, different commodities command different rates. The bases for differential rates can be grouped into several categories.

Loading and Packaging Costs Freight rates are generally given in cents per unit of weight. A light, bulky commodity (e. g., styrofoam insulation panels) would earn much less for the carrier per carload than a heavy commodity such as ceramic tile *if* there were a uniform rate per unit of weight. Costs for railroads, for example, are often much more a function of the number of cars handled than tonnage. The rate on light, bulky commodities must be high to obtain sufficient revenues per car. Rates can be lower on heavy-loading articles in terms of weight density or weight per cubic meter. A ton of pine lumber, for example, occupies much more space than a ton of mahogany and is charged a higher rate.

TABLE 5.4 Stepped freight weights

Distance (km)	Transportation Cost ($)
100	2.00
180	2.00
200	3.00
300	3.00
400	4.00
410	4.00
500	4.00
600	4.00
620	4.00
630	5.00
700	5.00
900	5.00

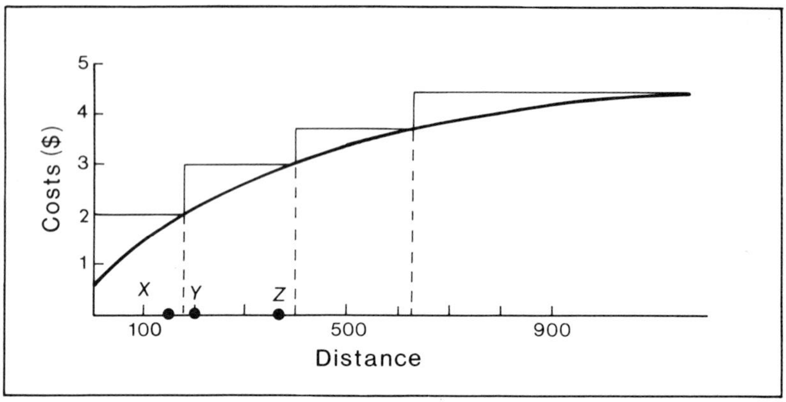

FIGURE 5.6 Stepped freight rates.

Rates generally favor "knocked-down" articles over "set-up" commodities. The parts required for a complete automobile (bodies, drive trains, engines, etc.) can be shipped for a much lower rate than a finished car. The lower rate is explained by the higher weight density of auto parts ("knocked-down") when compared to finished automobiles ("set-up").

Other commodities load lightly because of odd shapes (furniture) or because a car cannot be completely filled without damage to the commodity (melons). Some articles simply cost more to load. Wheat and coal can be loaded rapidly and cheaply by conveyor. Watermelons and television sets must be handled with great care to avoid damage. Wheat and coal require little advance preparation for shipment, but television sets and furniture require special crating and packing which add to terminal costs (figure 5.7).

Damage and Risk Variations Freight rates also vary among commodities according to the possibility of damage in transit. The carrier is usually responsible

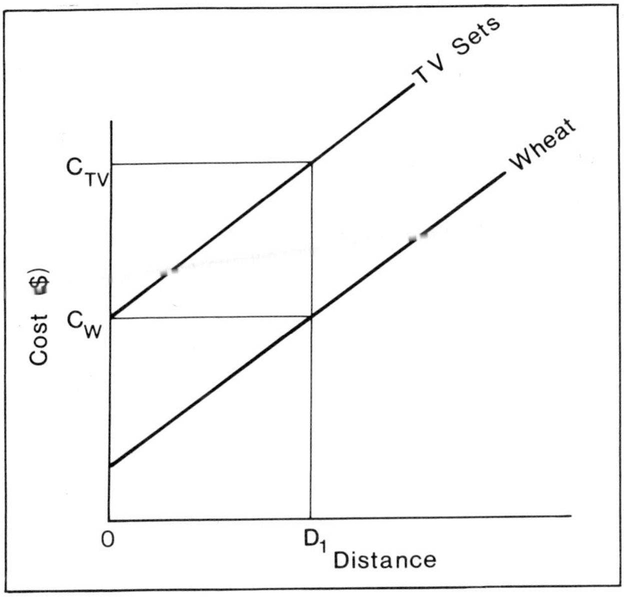

FIGURE 5.7 Variations in loading and packaging costs.

for damage during shipment and must assume a greater risk for some commodities than others. Sand, gravel, brick, and pig iron are not subject to damage, but fresh fruits and vegetables, television sets, and china are very susceptible because of perishability and/or fragility. Canned goods are charged a lower rate than food packed in glass containers.

Shipment Size The size of a shipment is another variable affecting the rate carriers charge. Some commodities are shipped in bulk while others must be carried in small quantities. Railroads charge higher rates for less-than-carload lots. Rates are lower for commodities that are transported in volume over a period of time. Carriers can better organize operations and handling methods and thus reduce costs. Increased volumes always lower costs per unit of weight because terminal charges become a smaller proportion of total costs and a high volume of a single commodity can lower line-haul costs per unit of weight. Complete trains carrying only coal or wheat are examples.

Regularity of Movement Carriers can operate at lower costs and charge lower rates if there is a regular movement over a given route. Schedules are worked out more easily and vehicles and labor needs can be planned. Irregular movements increase rates. This is often true for seasonal movements of fruits and vegetables. Large numbers of railroad cars have to be supplied over a short period of time. These cars may have to stand idle for much of the time or be diverted from other routes which disrupts regular service.

Special Equipment and Service Carriers have to provide special equipment and/or services for some commodities. Refrigerated cars cost more to operate and maintain than ordinary boxcars. Large computers require special cushioning and isolation from vibration forcing a higher rate. Special terminal facilities or sidings have to be maintained for other articles such as livestock. Perishable commodities require rapid transfer. Any of these special services can command a higher freight rate on the commodity involved.

Elasticity of Demand Goods that have a high value per unit of weight may bear a higher transportation rate. Television sets have a very high value per unit of weight when compared to coal. A high freight rate on television sets will account for only a small percentage of the total cost of the item. A slight rise in the transportation rate per ton of coal, for example, may mean a significant rise in the total cost per ton at the delivery point. Carriers generally charge what the market will bear and may exercise considerable flexibility in setting rates within the limits imposed by the Interstate Commerce Commission. Commodity A in figure 5.8 illustrates transportation price inelasticity (television sets). An increase in the rate from P_1 to P_2 produces only a slight change in the quantity of shipments. Commodity B (coal), however, exhibits a great change in the quantity of shipments with only a small change in the transportation rate (P_1 to P_2).

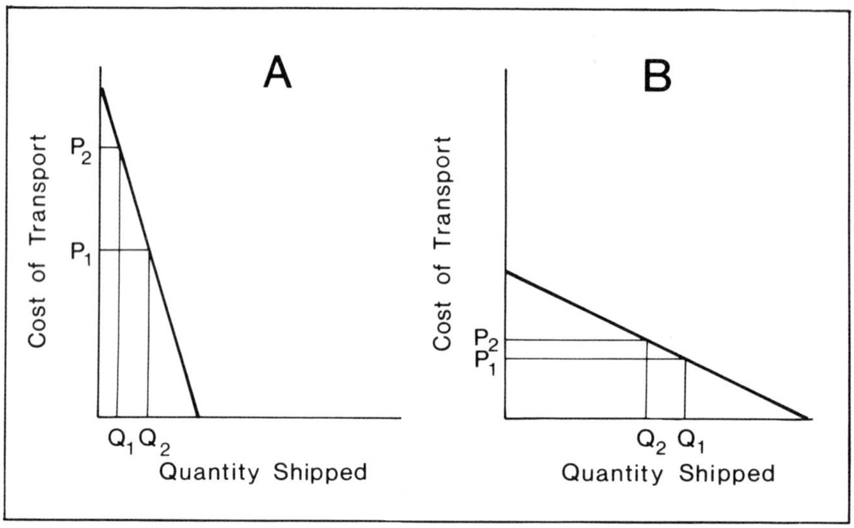

FIGURE 5.8 Demand elasticity for transportation.

The value of an article does not completely determine a commodity's ability to bear a higher freight rate. Transportation services are not purchased simply for the sake of consuming ton-km. Assume two products each with a very high value per unit of weight. One product is produced at Points A and B; the second is produced only at A. The product produced at A may be able to bear a high freight rate from A to B, but the commodity produced at both locations will not be shipped from A to B even if a very low rate is offered. Transportation is a means of distributing localized commodities. The most localized commodities can usually bear higher rates within the framework of loading, shipment size, and damage and risk characteristics.

Carrier and Route Variations

The characteristics of carriers and routes form a second set of factors determining specific rates.

Carrier Competition Higher transportation rates can be charged when there is only one possible carrier for a given commodity. Where competition between carriers is possible, rates tend to be lower. This is illustrated in figure 5.9. Both water and rail transportation are available between A and B, but only rail shipments are possible between A and C. The railroad can charge a much higher rate between the land-only points than it can between A and B where competition lowers the possible rate.

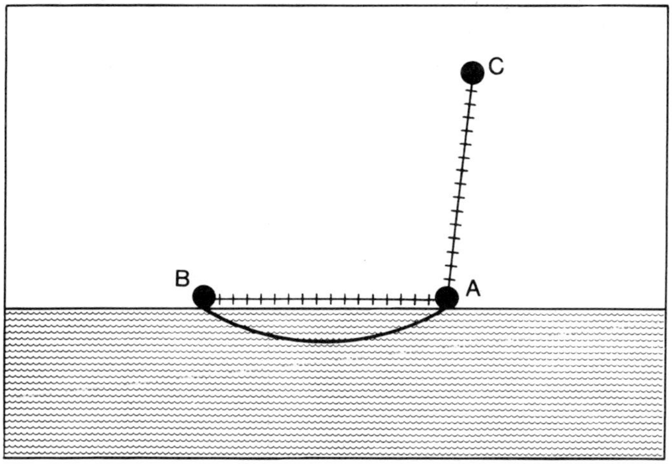

FIGURE 5.9 Carrier competition.

Route Demand High demand for transportation over a particular route can lower transportation rates. High demand lowers both line-haul and terminal cost per unit. The air-shuttle between New York and Washington, D. C. is an example. Demand for this trip is so high that much lower rates per passenger can be charged than over routes of similar distance where demand is less. High volume lowers the terminal costs per passenger (ticketing, baggage handling, landing fees, and other terminal operations) that must be paid regardless of the number of passengers. Fully loaded aircraft mean lower line-haul costs per passenger. Both reduce the total cost per person and may stimulate even higher demand.

Back-hauling Many carriers face heavy demand only in a specific direction. Consider the large volume of produce shipped from Florida to New York. Trucks must often return empty for the next load. The cost of the total trip, however, is used to determine the transportation rate. Because the carrier must make the return trip anyway, he is willing to charge very low rates on the ''back-haul.'' Any revenue on the back-haul is preferred to returning empty. Rates are higher where there is little or no possibility of back-hauling and most often occurs in the transportation of raw materials from isolated resource areas to production points. The distribution of finished products, however, generally involves traffic between existing centers creating a reciprocal flow and lower rates.

Real Transportation Costs and Location Theory

A consideration of the true form of transportation rates and the variations in rates that occur because of commodity differences and carrier and route variations highlights the complexity of transportation costs. Our initial models were based on linear transportation costs, but we must now relax that assumption to determine the effects of complex transportation costs on the space-economy. This section concentrates on the effects of real transportation costs on industrial location theory (especially modifications of the Weberian model).

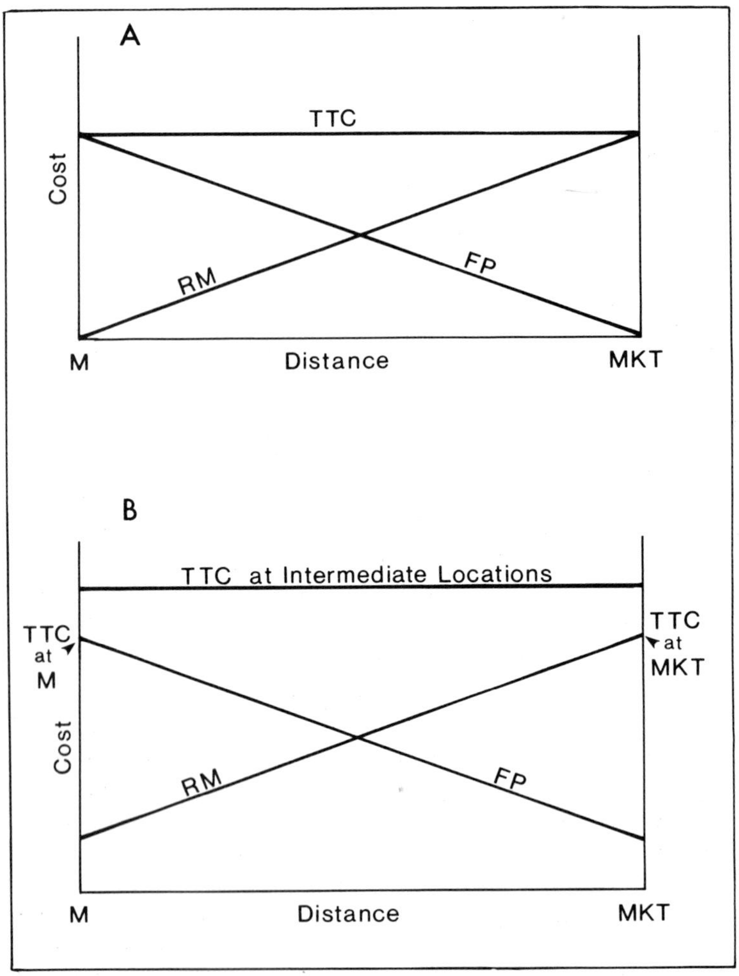

FIGURE 5.10 Weber's model: the effects of terminal costs.

Terminal Costs and Weber's System

Figure 5.10A shows the Weberian solution for one pure raw material localized at M and sold as a finished product at MKT. Terminal costs are zero and line-haul costs are linear. What happens to the Weberian solution when terminal costs are added? The solution is given in figure 5.10B. We must always pay at least *one* set of terminal costs because either the raw material or the finished product must be moved. At either the mine or the market, one set of terminal costs is paid, but at any intermediate location, *two* sets of terminal costs must be paid. This raises total transportation costs by an amount equal to one set of terminal costs. Mine or market locations have a clear advantage because terminal costs do not favor intermediate points.

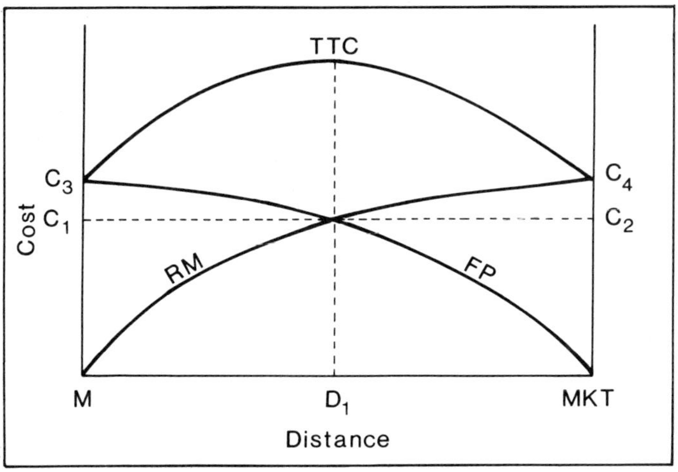

FIGURE 5.11 Weber's model: the effects of curvilinear line-haul costs.

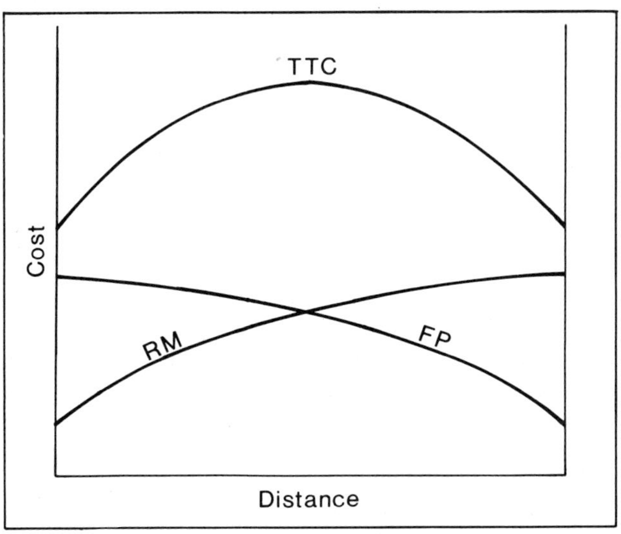

FIGURE 5.12 Weber's model: terminal and curvilinear line-haul costs.

Curvilinear Line-Haul Costs and Weber's System

Curvilinear line-haul costs also favor terminal locations. We have eliminated terminal costs in figure 5.11 for simplification. Remember that curvilinear line-haul costs favor the long haul. Shipping the raw material from M to D_1 costs C_1; shipping the finished product from D_1 to MKT costs C_2. Shipping the raw material all the way to MKT, however, only involves a cost of C_4 (twice the distance, but not twice the cost). Again, total transportation costs are minimized at either mine or market. The Weberian solution with both terminal costs and curvilinear line-haul costs is shown in figure 5.12.

Variations in Commodity Rates and Weber's System

Raw materials tend to be easier to load and are less subject to damage and risk than finished products. As a very general rule, transportation rates are lower on raw materials than finished products and favor *market* locations. This is illustrated in figure 5.13 where linear transportation costs are retained for simplicity. The lower raw material transportation rate minimizes total transportation costs (TTC) at the market.

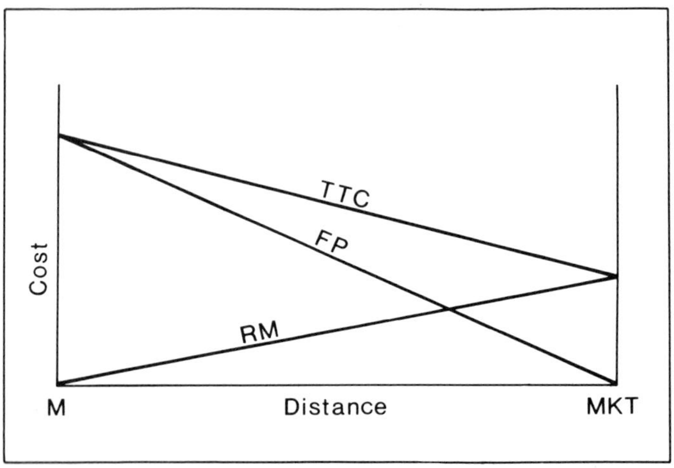

FIGURE 5.13 Weber's model: variations in commodity rates.

Curvilinear Line-Haul Costs and Market Areas

The market areas of two competing firms with linear transportation costs are diagrammed in figure 5.14. Firm A has lower production costs, but both face the same terminal and line-haul costs. With linear transportation costs, the market boundary between the two occurs at D_1. The situation changes, however, when curvilinear line-haul costs are introduced (figure 5.15). Because of long-haul economies, A is able to capture some of B's market area.

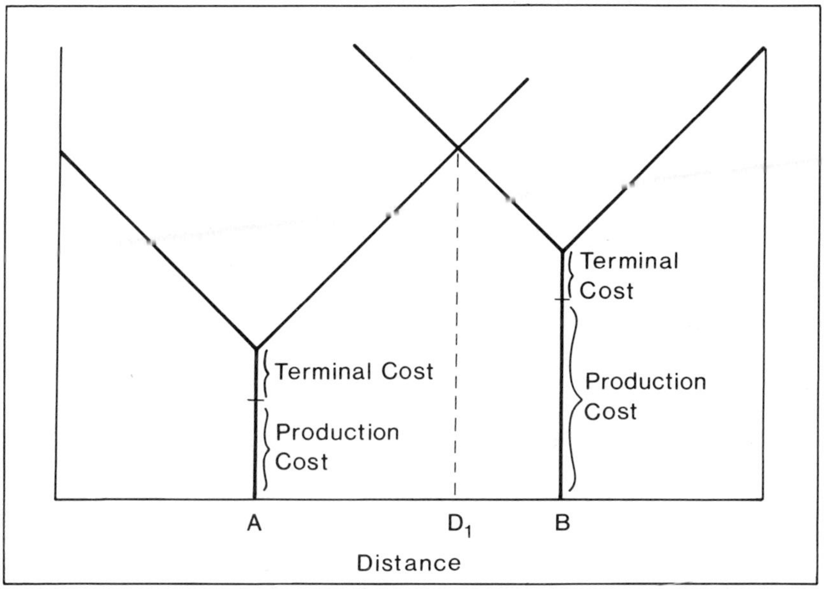

FIGURE 5.14 Market areas with linear line-haul costs.

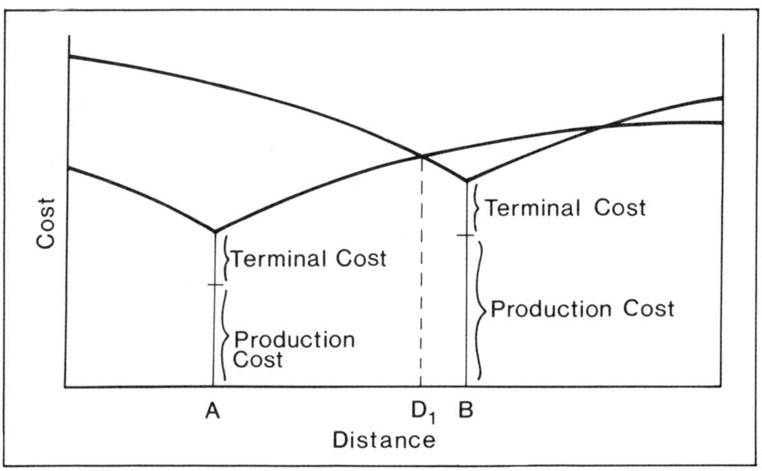

FIGURE 5.15 Market areas with curvilinear line-haul costs.

Break-of-Bulk Points

Terminal costs must be paid whenever a commodity is loaded or unloaded. This is unavoidable when transportation media must be changed. A change in carrier must occur, for example, when goods produced in the interior of the United States are shipped to Europe—land transportation to water. Materials moved from A to C in figure 5.16 are subject to terminal costs at the intermediate location B. Point B is called a "break-of-bulk" point.

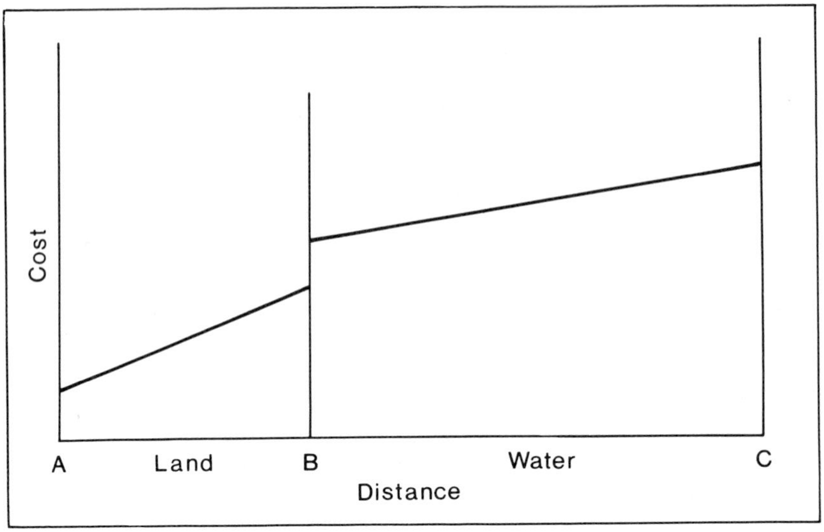

FIGURE 5.16 Break-of-bulk point between land and water transportation.

Transportation costs usually disfavor processing at intermediate locations because of additional terminal costs, but these must be paid anyway at break-of-bulk points. Processing, such as flour milling, often takes place in port cities because of this fact. Wheat comes to the city by inland transportation and is milled into flour before being loaded onto ocean carriers. Petroleum refining is another example of processing that often takes place at port break-of-bulk points.

Rate-Break Points

Transportation rates are not continuous, but are divided into stepped zones. Figure 5.17 shows three freight-rate zones. Costs are \$3 per ton in Zone 1, \$5 per ton in Zone 2, and \$6 per ton in Zone 3. A wheat-growing region is located at W and a market for flour is located at M. The cost of shipping from W to M is the

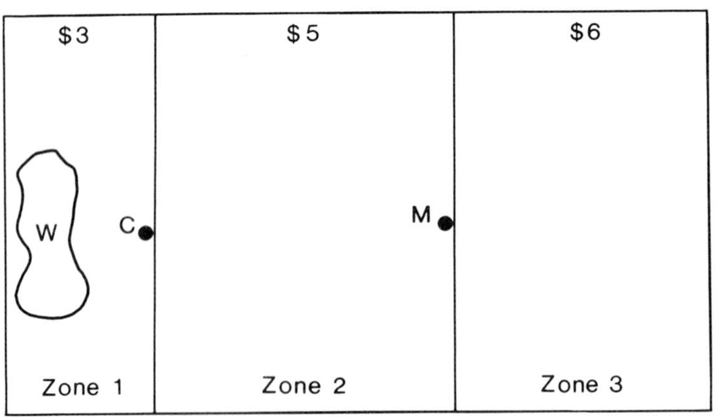

FIGURE 5.17 Rate-break point.

composite of the two rates ($8 per ton). A city (C) may have an advantage for flour milling because of its location at the rate-break point. The distances moved at the $3 and $5 rates are maximized and processing takes place at the intermediate point C. Such a location may compete favorably with mills located in the wheat area or at the market.

Pricing Strategies

Thus far we have portrayed the transportation rates charged by producers as being a function of distance from the production point. This is called freight-on-board or FOB pricing. The consumer pays the plant price plus the cost of transportation. Consumers close to the plant pay less than more distant consumers (figure 5.18). Many producers adopt a pricing strategy known as cost-insurance-freight or CIF pricing where each consumer is charged production costs plus a flat mark-up to cover transportation charges. CIF pricing is illustrated in figure 5.19. Each consumer is charged a CIF price of C_1. Consumers from A to B are charged more than the actual cost of transportation. Consumers from X to A and B to Y are charged less than the actual cost. Nearby customers subsidize the distribution costs of more distant consumers.

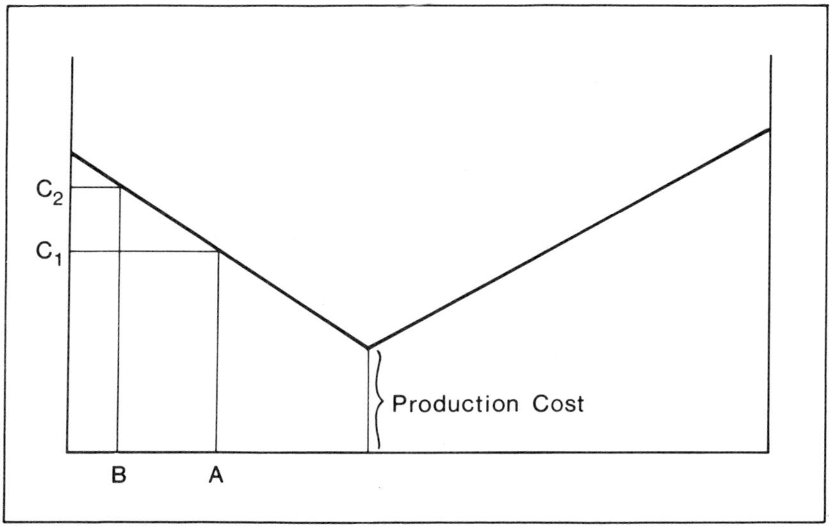

FIGURE 5.18 FOB pricing.

What effect does CIF pricing have on the market areas of producers? The FOB prices of producers A and B are shown in figure 5.20. The market area boundary is at X_1 with FOB pricing. If B adopts a CIF pricing strategy, the market area boundary shifts to X_2. Producer A can, of course, counter by also adopting CIF pricing. Each consumer then pays the same price to each producer and price-competition disappears. Producers must now compete through other means such as advertising. For finished products in the United States, CIF pricing tends to be the rule rather than the exception. This is especially true of consumer goods such as

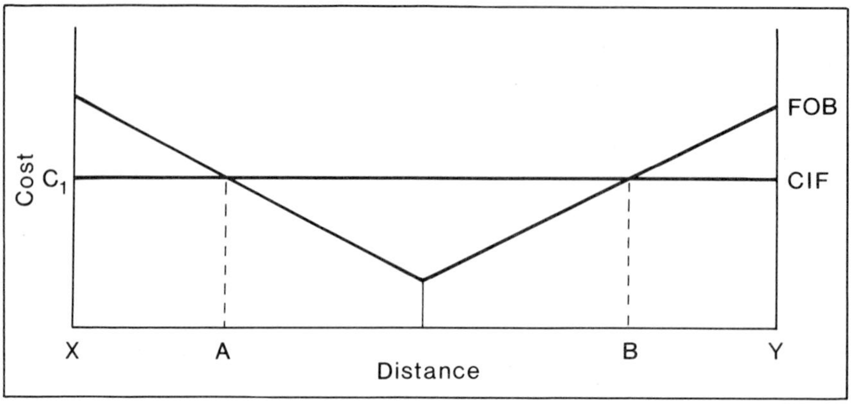

FIGURE 5.19 FOB and CIF pricing.

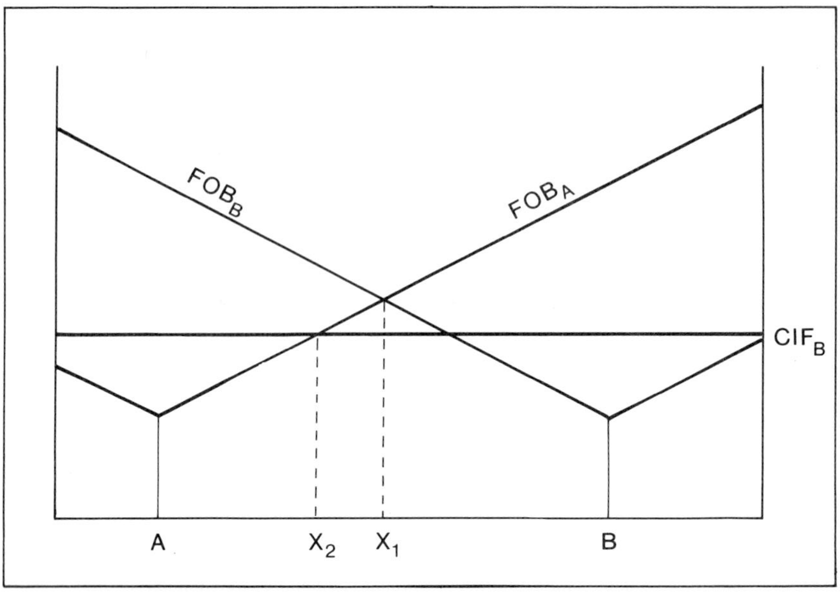

FIGURE 5.20 The effect of CIF pricing on market area boundaries.

clothing, liquor, and small appliances which are offered at a uniform price throughout the United States.

Conclusion

In reality, transportation costs are complex, but must be considered to obtain an understanding of production, exchange, and consumption patterns. Differential commodity rates were implied in the three-crop Thünen model. Decreasing transportation rates have favored the growth of higher order central places over the lowest order places. As a result, the hamlet has almost disappeared from the American landscape as an economically viable entity in the central place sense. Many hamlets have retained their residential roles, but have lost central functions. The effects of actual transportation costs are best illustrated by modifications of the Weberian model of industrial location.

The net effects of terminal and line-haul costs, differential commodity rates, carrier and route variations, and tapering variable costs can be summarized in four points.

1. Actual transportation costs tend to favor *terminal* locations (raw material source or market) over intermediate locations.
2. Transportation rates tend to be lower for many raw materials than for finished products favoring production at market locations.
3. Transportation rates tend to be lower where the demand for transportation is high. High demand, in turn, increases the supply of transportation opportunities (routes and carriers). This tends to favor developed areas.
4. Transportation is required only for *localized* commodities which are produced at few locations and demanded at others. High transportation costs, however, can make the cost of local production competitive with localized production plus transportation costs, giving rise to a ubiquitous production pattern of some commodities with high transportation costs. Ice cream, commercial ice production, fluid milk, and concrete products are examples. In other words, high transportation costs outweigh the scale economies that might accrue to large-scale production at a few points and give rise to a ubiquitous pattern of production.

KEY WORDS

back-hauling
break-of-bulk point
CIF pricing
cost-space convergence
curvilinear line-haul costs
FOB pricing
line-haul cost
stepped freight rates
terminal cost
time-space convergence

SUGGESTED READINGS

General Sources

Taaffe, E. and Gauthier, H. (1973), *Geography of Transportation,* Englewood Cliffs, N.J.: Prentice-Hall.

Lowe, J. and Moryadas, S. (1975), *The Geography of Movement,* Boston: Houghton Mifflin.

Eliot Hurst, M. E., ed. (1974), *Transportation Geography: Comments and Readings,* New York: McGraw-Hill.

Janelle, D. G. (1969), "Spatial Reorganization: A Model and A Concept," *Annals* of the Association of American Geographers **59**, 348–64.

——— (1968), "Central Place Development in a Time-Space Framework," *Professional Geographer* **20**, 5–10.

Overview of Part 1

Four patterns introduced the first part of this text (Figure 1). We now have the basis for a better understanding of these patterns. Part A shows two contrasting agricultural regions separated by a distinct boundary. The boundary must represent the intersection of two bid-rent curves. The bid-rent curves may be a function of transportation costs to a distant market, specific environmental conditions, or a combination of the two. Both distance (which necessitates transportation costs) and fertility are factors controlling the pattern. Economic conditions, however, must also be considered. Production will not take place even under the most desirable distance/fertility conditions if there is no demand for the product. Conversely, high demand can expand production into high cost distance/fertility conditions.

Part B shows a pattern of settlements mapped according to size. The regularity of the size and spacing of these settlements can be understood within the context of central place theory. Lower order centers squeeze in among higher order centers by capturing a market area sufficient to meet the threshold of their hierarchical marginal good. A maximum number of consumers is served from a minimum number of centers. The pattern is efficient. An alternative strategy would be to offer all goods at a single point, but this would maximize aggregate consumer travel costs and excess profits on most goods. A second alternative would offer all goods at all points which would minimize the scale economies of retailing and services and aggregate consumer travel distances. The costs of both alternatives would be very high in terms of either lost scale economies or consumer travel costs. The central hierarchy is a compromise between these extremes.

Part C is a map of primary manufacturing centers. These locations can be understood in terms of Weberian theory. The production points

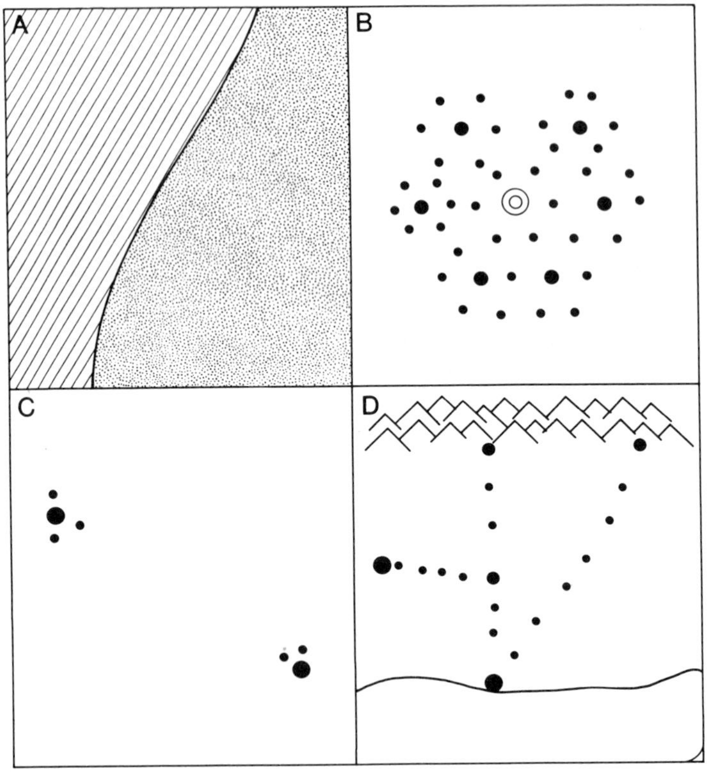

FIGURE 1 Hypothetical economic landscape patterns.

may represent least-cost locations near localized resources, low-wage labor pools, or they may represent points whose past investment (inertia) has induced large-scale economies.

Part D is a map of centers whose patterns must be understood in other terms. The large center on the sea coast may be a break-of-bulk point while inland centers may be nodes on major transportation arteries. Other centers may represent localized amenity resources that give rise to resort and specialized recreation centers.

The economic landscape is a composite of many patterns and can be broken down into component parts to increase our understanding with recourse to the models we have developed.

Lösch proposed that the economic landscape is a function of three variables: (1) transportation costs; (2) economies of scale; and (3) agriculture's need for space. Even if the earth's surface were completely homogeneous in terms of the physical environment, it would be differentiated into a pattern of transportation routes, production points (cities), and individual farms as a result of the interplay among these three variables.

Let us ignore agriculture's need for space for the moment and consider the implications of transportation costs and scale economies. If transportation were instantaneous and free, production would take place at random points at the optimal scale for each kind of production. No point would have an advantage over another in terms of the cost of any input. All inputs could be purchased at their basic cost. Suppose there were transportation costs, but no economies of scale. There would be no advantage to a division of labor or the specialization of production. An individual could produce his own food, fiber, and manufactured goods for exactly the same cost as large-scale operations. With no economic incentive, all production would take place at the individual or household level, minimizing transportation costs. The results are intermediate with the existence of both transportation costs and scale economies. The balance between the two creates a series of production points. Discrete production points necessitate transportation routes that are straight lines on a homogeneous surface minimizing the distance among points.

Scale economies require individual farms with the quantity of land in each farm adjusted to fit between the intensive and extensive margins of production. Patterns arise on a completely homogeneous surface for these purely economic reasons.

The heterogeneity of the earth's physical environment adds to the complexity and obviously plays a major role in structuring patterns of production, exchange, and consumption. These patterns, however, are economic events and are primarily the result of economic forces. Environmental space distorts the ideal patterns that economic forces and the abstract properties of space would produce if the earth's surface were completely homogeneous.

Other factors also contribute to the complexity of economic forces. The models considered thus far assume the existence of an optimizing population. Optimizers consider all possible outcomes of a given action and an infinite number of possible actions instantly. The real world, however, is inhabited by fallible human beings and we can never be sure that any action is optimal. We make decisions through a trial-and-error process. A decision resulting in positive economic rewards is usually considered correct even though other courses of action might have been more successful. Human beings are also concerned with values other than purely economic ones. We make many decisions which are not optimal in an economic sense, but which satisfy personal, social, and ethical goals. Such decisions, however, may have economic consequences and further distort landscape patterns.

Another complicating factor is the fact that economic landscapes are evolutionary. Patterns created by optimizers should never undergo any evolutionary stages. The optimizer's landscape should go from completely undifferentiated to optimal without any intervening stages, but real landscapes must change within the structure imposed by past actions. Past decisions create tremendous inertia. The capital invested at a point in the past, for example, may be so great as to preclude the establishment of production at an optimal location. Resources exploited in the past are not available for today's production. Transportation nets shaped by past action have a profound influence on present flows and future development. Labor pools formed by past job opportunities do not easily shift to labor-short areas. Inertia exerts powerful restrictions on the evolution of the economic landscape.

part 2

Nonoptimal Decision Making and Evolutionary Systems

6 Decision Making

Introduction

A working knowledge of the classical location models introduced in Part 1 is necessary for an understanding of more dynamic models which incorporate suboptimal human decision making. We assumed in Part 1 that the economic landscape was the work of optimizers. Optimizers can foresee instantaneously the outcomes of all possible actions and always act to maximize profits. The landscape created by optimizers does not go through any intermediate adjustment stages, but rather goes from undifferentiated to optimal instantaneously.

Real economic landscapes, however, are created by fallible human beings. We cannot foresee the outcomes of all possible actions; our knowledge is imperfect. Neither do we have the ability to synthesize large amounts of information instantaneously. Real economic landscapes are the result of a trial-and-error process. They are evolutionary, and the economic landscapes of tomorrow are strongly structured by existing patterns of production, exchange, and consumption.

Decision makers who have created the existing economic landscape are not optimizers. To gain a better understanding of real-world patterns we must utilize a model of the decision maker called the *satisficer*. Satisficers make decisions which are "good enough" or satisfactory. A correct decision is one which results in profits or, at least, zero loss. These decisions may be optimal, but only if decision makers are lucky enough to choose an optimal location. Satisficers may choose suboptimal locations even when more profitable locations are known if they are strongly motivated by noneconomic factors.

Satisficers, armed with imperfect knowledge, face a dynamic world. Even in the best of situations, only a few possible locations can be considered. A good location today may diminish in profitability tomorrow because of the actions of competitors. Satisficers may forego known higher profits elsewhere in order to gain noneconomic rewards of operating in given locations. This concept is often termed *psychic income*. Psychic income is the noneconomic satisfaction which may come from operating in one's home town, in a specific physical environment, or away from other environments such as high-crime urban areas. Any understanding of the economic landscape of reality must incorporate this view of human decision making.

Chapter Objectives

1. Examine some of the forces which control nonoptimal decision making.
2. Outline some of the models which have been developed to consider the spatial effects of nonoptimal decision making.
3. Compare optimal economic landscapes with those created by satisficers.

The Behavioral Matrix

A conceptual approach to the problem of nonoptimal decision making involves the use of a "behavioral matrix" (Pred 1967), as shown in figure 6.1. The origin of

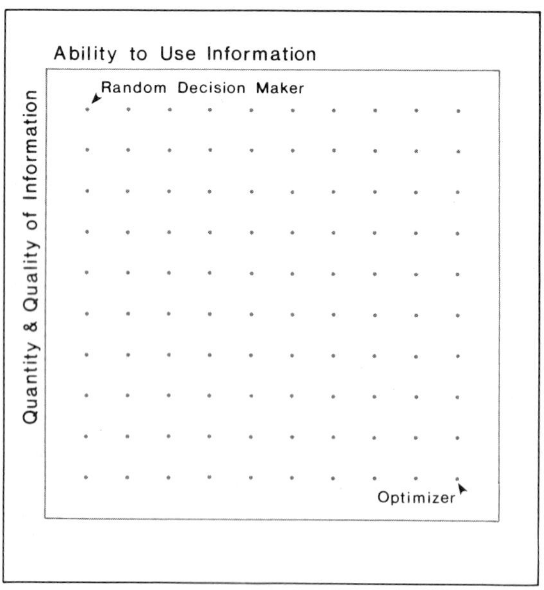

FIGURE 6.1 A behavioral matrix [Source: Pred (1967), "Behavior and Location: Foundations for a Geographic and Dynamic Location Theory, Part I," *Lund Studies in Geography, Series B*, 27.]

the matrix is the top, left-hand corner. The reliability and quantity of information increases to the right and the ability and speed with which that knowledge is utilized increases downward. A perfect optimizer would be located in the extreme lower, right-hand corner. A purely "random" decision maker would be located at the origin. Large corporations with extensive data resources and personnel equipped to synthesize information about possible decisions may occupy the lower right quadrant. The small businessman with limited resources may occupy the upper left quadrant. Each decision maker occupies some point on the behavioral matrix.

An elementary application of the behavioral matrix is shown in figure 6.2. The iso-lines shown in the figure represent spatial margins to viability. Any location chosen within those margins is a viable location. Decision makers in the lower right quadrant of the behavioral matrix are most likely to choose viable locations, but they may also select nonviable sites and disappear from the landscape. Decision makers from the upper left quadrant are more likely to choose nonviable locations, but they may be lucky enough to select viable or even optimal sites.

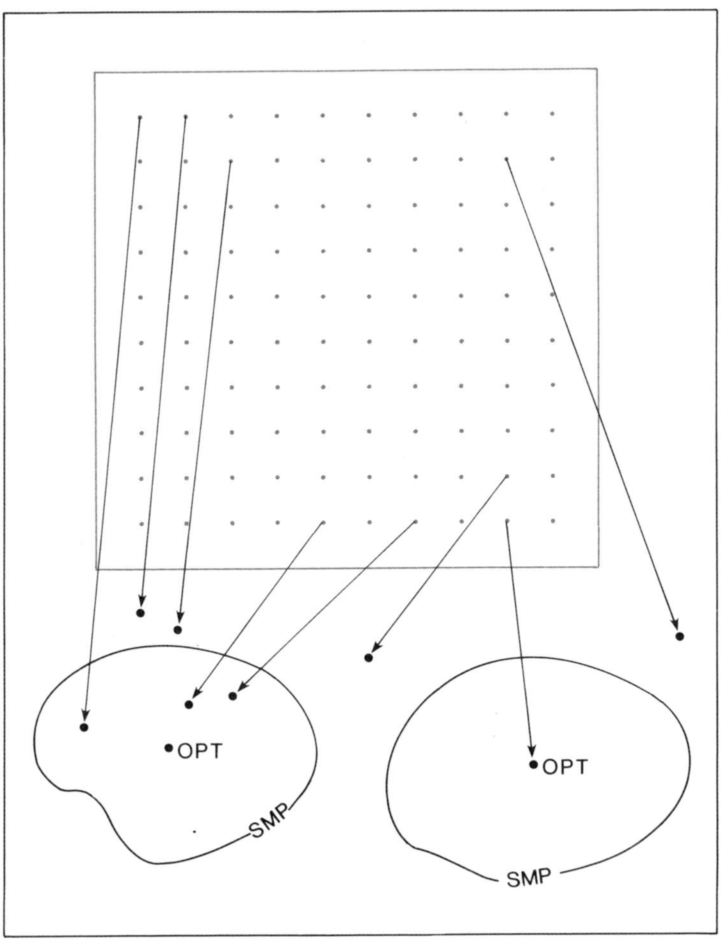

FIGURE 6.2 A behavioral and locational choice [Source: Pred (1967), "Behavior and Location: Foundations for a Geographic and Dynamic Location Theory, Part I," *Lund Studies in Geography, Series B*, 27.]

Agriculture

The behavioral matrix can be applied to the Thünen model of agricultural land use. The optimum crop in a given location is a trial-and-error process. The Thünen model helps us to understand the *prevailing* form of agriculture especially when the environmental aspects of Ricardian rent theory are added. Within the prevailing pattern of agriculture, however, there may be individual farms or larger subregions where other forms of agriculture predominate. This may result from suboptimal decision making, as illustrated in figure 6.3. Better decision makers have, with few exceptions, chosen the more profitable form of agriculture for a given location. Less knowledgeable decision makers have, in many cases, chosen less profitable, but still viable forms of agriculture. Most of the less

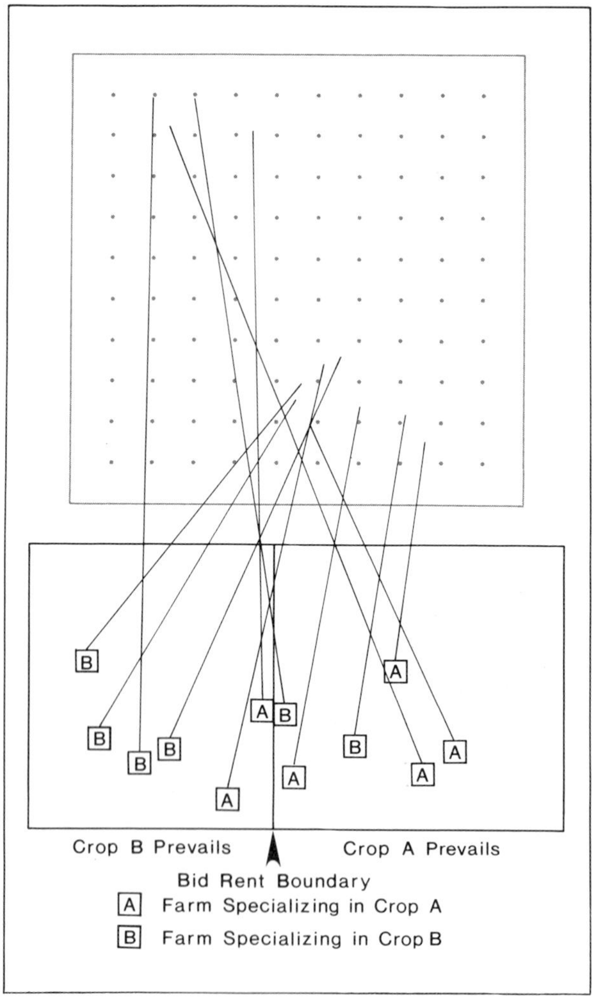

FIGURE 6.3 A behavioral matrix and agricultural regions.

profitable decisions occur near the boundary of the two prevailing crops where the decision is less clear-cut and information often conflicting.

Many types of agriculture and farming practices are the result of cultural biases that often prevail even in the face of precise economic information. The horse-powered agriculture of Amish farms in the midst of tractor-based farming, the persistence of wheat farming on the margins of dry lands during the 1930s, and the continuation of tobacco as a secondary crop in parts of the South are examples. Residual farms surrounded by suburban housing at the margins of cities are another example. How can they persist in the face of much more profitable forms of land use? The answer is partly the result of the time period involved and partly the result of the basis of agriculture. Residual farms cannot persist in the *long-run,* but for a short period of years they can hold out in the face of much higher income that would result from selling the land for housing purposes. The owner must reap psychic income from remaining in farming. The psychic income from such action outweighs the pecuniary income from selling. Land is the basis for agricultural wealth. A farmer who owns the land controls the means of production and can persist in the face of more competitive forms of land use. No beginning farmer, however, could afford to buy a residual farm for agricultural purposes. The same is true of secondary forms of agriculture in the midst of more profitable types of farming. We must assume, however, that such decisions produce some sort of favorable results in the short-run.

Environmental Space: A Game Theory Approach

Environmental conditions provide a partial explanation for broad patterns of prevailing agricultural conditions. The boundary between wheat farming and livestock ranching, for example, is basically a function of precipitation. If rainfall could be predicted with extreme accuracy over the long-run, the boundary between the two types of agriculture would be much less transitional. The uncertainty of environmental conditions always plays a considerable role in agricultural decision making. Some areas are too dry for wheat, whereas other areas always have enough moisture. In a middle zone between wet and dry, however, some years will support wheat while others will bring severe losses to any agriculturalist attempting to grow it. Farmers in this middle zone may practice only ranching, risk everything on wheat with its potentially high rewards or losses, or mix the two types of agriculture as a hedge against the uncertainty of the environment.

Environmental decision making has been approached in a game-theoretic framework (Gould 1963). Although the environment is uncertain, we do have some notion of the probabilities of normal and extreme conditions based on past experience, and these probabilities can be used to develop a strategy of action using game theory. Two abstract examples of the use of game theory will be given. The values of both environmental conditions and net incomes per hectare in the examples are hypothetical, but real values could be provided through field work. We will first assume that farmers want to maximize their net income per hectare with a minimum of uncertainty. We further simplify the problem by assuming only two environmental possibilities: drought and abnormally wet years.

The first example involves only two possible types of agriculture: wheat and livestock ranching. The net income of each type is shown in figure 6.4. Wheat

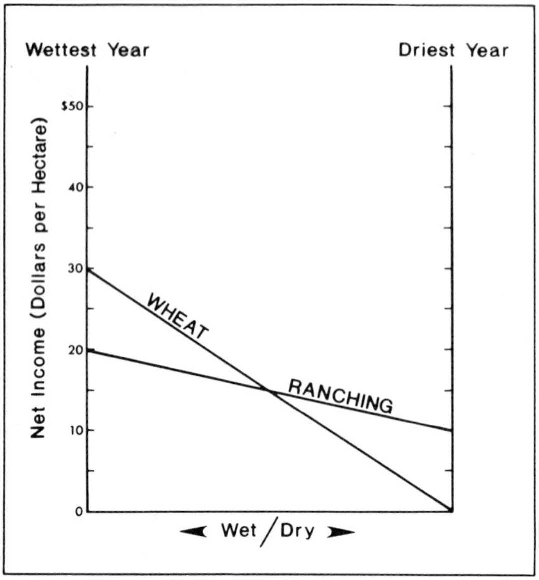

FIGURE 6.4 Wheat and ranching yields: extreme years.

ranges from $30 per hectare in the wettest years to zero in the dry years; livestock ranching yields a net income per hectare of $20 in the wet years and $10 in the dry years. These values can be placed in matrix form as in figure 6.5 yielding a "two-person-two-strategy-zero-sum game." The agriculturalist represents one person in the game and the environment the opposing player . The two types of agriculture are the two strategies. The game is a "zero-sum" game because the "pay-off" to one player is exactly the value "lost" by the opponent. In figure 6.5, for example, let us assume that the farmer chooses the strategy of ranching. If the "environment" chooses the strategy of a wet year, it will "lose" $10 ($20 – $10) compared to a dry year strategy, but the farmer will gain $10 over a dry year. In the matrix of figure 6.5, the value of $10 is a minimum value of a row and a maximum value in a column. This is called a "saddle-point" or minimum-maximum point in game theory. The "minimax" can also be seen in figure 6.4 in which the value of $10 is the lowest point on the curve that produces the best outcome in the driest year (ranching). The farmer will always win by practicing livestock ranching and the environment will always "lose." The environment will "win" some of the time if a strategy of wheat farming is chosen.

The second example considers a more humid area in which four strategies are possible: (1) livestock ranching based on natural vegetation; (2) wheat farming; (3) corn with all income based on the sale of corn as grain; and (4) feeder livestock with all income derived from animals fattened on corn. Which strategy (or combination of strategies) will yield the highest net income per hectare over the long-run with the least risk? The graphical solution to this question is given in figure 6.6. The lowest point on the uppermost boundary in the figure gives the two crops on which farmers should concentrate (corn and livestock). "Mixed farming" is a combination of corn-for-grain and feeder livestock. The two crops are then placed in a pay-off

ENVIRONMENT'S STRATEGIES

FARMER'S STRATEGIES	Wet	Dry
Ranching	$20	$10
Wheat	$30	$0

$10 is a row minimum and a column maximum

FIGURE 6.5 Pay-off matrix: wheat and ranching.

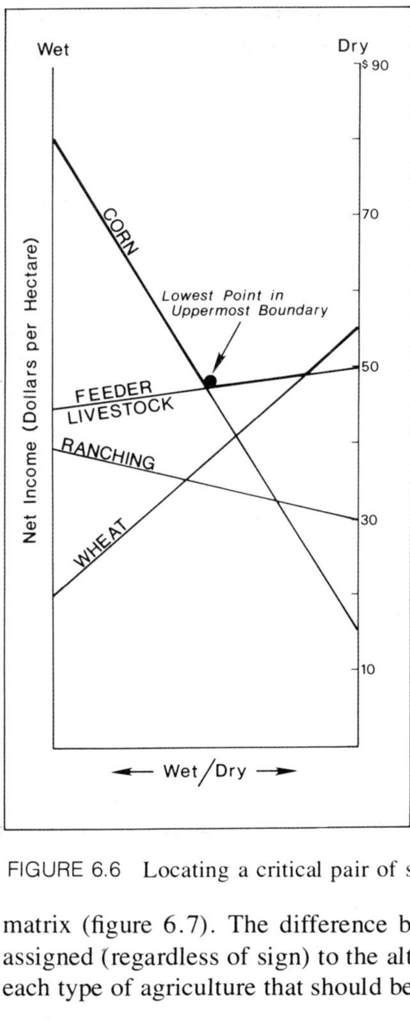

FIGURE 6.6 Locating a critical pair of strategies.

matrix (figure 6.7). The difference between each pair of values is calculated and assigned (regardless of sign) to the alternate strategy to determine the proportion of each type of agriculture that should be planned for sale. Corn should be the primary

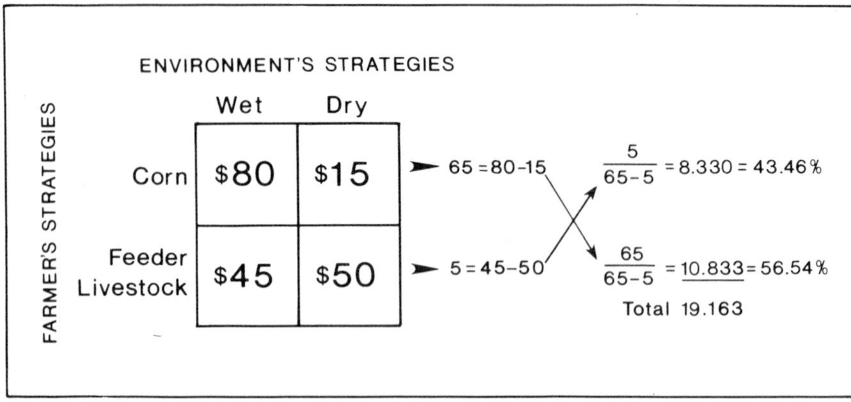

FIGURE 6.7 Pay-off matrix: corn and feeder livestock.

cash crop 43.46 percent of the time and feeder cattle should account for sales 56.54 percent of the time. The type of agriculture that will be the primary sale item must be planned ahead. Feeder cattle must be purchased early in the year for fattening and a farmer cannot switch from feeder cattle sales to sell corn for grain without first dumping livestock on the market or losing his total investment in the cattle by not feeding them at all.

How should the pay-off matrix (figure 6.7) be used? Should corn be the sole source of income 43.46 percent of the years and feeder cattle the remainder? Should total income be based on these proportions each year? In game theory terms and over the long-run, it makes no difference. Assume that dry years occur 50 percent of the time and the farmer uses 43.46 percent of his land for corn (for grain) and 56.54 percent for feeder cattle (figure 6.7) each year. If the year is dry, total income per hectare will be $30.21; if the year is wet, total income per hectare will be $64.78 (see figure 6.8). The average income per hectare over the long run will be $47.50. The same average will result if the land is used exclusively for corn for 43.46 percent of the years, and

ASSUME:	Dry years occur 50% of the time. 43.46% of land used for corn for grain 56.54% of land used for feeder livestock
WET YEAR:	Corn=$34.77=($80.00 • 43.46%) Livestock=$25.44=($45.00 • 56.54%) Total (per hectare)=$60.21
DRY YEAR:	Corn=$6.52=($15.00 • 43.46%) Livestock $28.27=($50.00 • 56.54%) Total (per hectare)=$34.79
AVERAGE =	$47.50 = $60.21+$34.79÷ 2 (dry years occur 50% of the time).

FIGURE 6.8 Determination of long-run average income per hectare.

for feeder livestock for the remainder. The individual farmer, however, must be concerned with short-run results. A very low income will result in a dry year if corn is the sole source of income and will be below average ($45 per hectare) in a wet year if all income is derived from feeder livestock. We assume that each farmer desires at least an "average" income each year and will therefore obtain the best results if the specific proportions of each type of agriculture are adopted every year.

Game theory provides only a framework within which the problem of uncertainty can be approached. We must assume that patterns of production are the result of a trial-and-error process that has been modified over time. Agriculture is always a gamble and there are random shocks caused by environmental extremes even in technologically advanced nations such as the United States. The water shortages and severe winter of 1976–77 are examples.

The Diffusion of Technological Innovations

The margins of a particular kind of agriculture can shift because of (1) changes in demand which can shift the boundary into less profitable areas if demand is high and diminish the area of the crop if demand falls; and (2) changes in technology that allow the crop to shift into areas once limited by environmental conditions. We have used the example of hybrid corn, a technological innovation which shifted the margins of corn-based agriculture. Less than one-third of the corn planted in the United States in 1940 was of the hybrid variety, but by 1954 almost 90 percent was hybrid and the percentage was over 97 percent in the north central states which constitute the heart of the Corn Belt. The use of hybrid corn increased the yield per hectare by as much as 20 percent and made the use of mechanical harvesters much more efficient, but the greatest benefit of hybrids was the great increase in the speed of maturation. Older varieties of corn required at least 140 days for maturation while the hybrids mature in as little as 90 days. Rapid maturation made corn a viable crop in formerly marginal areas and a marginal crop in areas where it could not be grown for grain before the introduction of hybrids. In other words, the environmental margins of the crop were shifted northward in the United States. Roepke (1959) found that the introduction of hybrids resulted in (1) an increase in the intensity of corn production in the core region of the Corn Belt; (2) a significant increase in the intensity of production in areas formerly marginal for corn; and (3) little change in the amount of production in areas newly marginal for corn. Roepke also found evidence that Corn Belt type farming had shifted northward into southern Wisconsin. The introduction of hybrid corn, therefore, produced a change in the pattern of agricultural production in the United States. Other technological innovations have wrought similar changes in the patterns of the economic landscape.

Because changes in technology induce changes in agricultural patterns, we are interested in the forces that control the spread and adoption of technological innovations. Innovations are not adopted instantaneously by all potential users. The rate of adoption does, however, follow a rather consistent and predictable sequence. Once the innovation is introduced in an area, it is accepted very early by a small percentage of the potential users. A short period of rapid adoption then follows and tails off over time once the rate of adoption has reached 90 percent or more. The change in the cumulative percentage of adoption is shown in figure 6.9 which is a generalization of acceptance curves for most types of innovation.

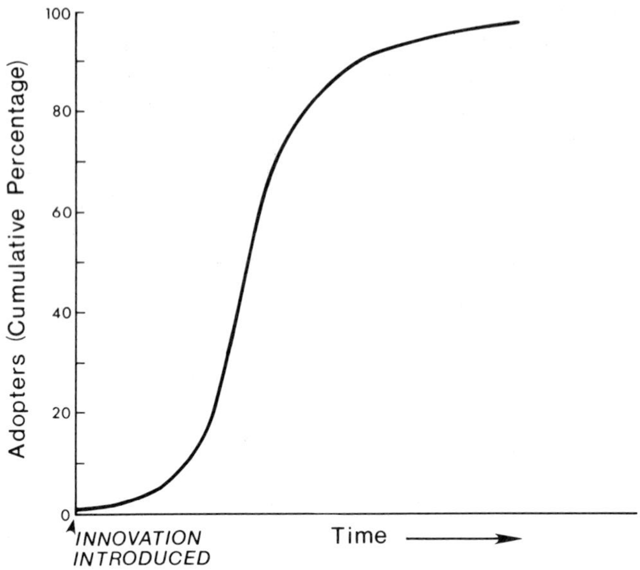

FIGURE 6.9 Adoption of an innovation over time.

The technique geographers have used to analyze the process of technological innovation adoption in a spatial context is *simulation*. It is assumed that an innovation *diffuses* outward from an initial core. The core is a given distribution of people who have already accepted the innovation. The problem then becomes one of determining the key variable(s) which controls the diffusion or spread of the innovation. As with all models, there are numerous factors which cannot be or are not included among the variables selected for controls. These other factors that might influence the spread of innovation are considered to interact *randomly* in the diffusion model. This is the first model we have considered that attempts to represent real decision making by suggesting that people behave randomly within a given set of rules.

Most of the initial work in geography on the simulation of diffusion was done by Hägerstrand (1953). The Hägerstrand model assumes that innovation spreads through personal contacts and that the frequency of personal contact is an *inverse* function of distance. The problem, therefore, is to determine the exact form of the relationship between distance and the frequency of personal contact. Hägerstrand first applied the techniques of simulation to an analysis of the diffusion of a government subsidy program in Sweden. The government program was designed to encourage farmers to improve pastureland and to discourage grazing in open woodland. Figure 6.10 shows the number of acceptors in the area of Hägerstrand's study in the first year after the introduction of the subsidy program in 1929. Personal contact was especially important in promoting the acceptance of the program in the 1930s before the widespread use of radio, television, telephones, and automobiles in rural areas. Hägerstrand used the distances over which area people migrated as an estimate of the distance/personal contact relationship. Most migrants settled rather

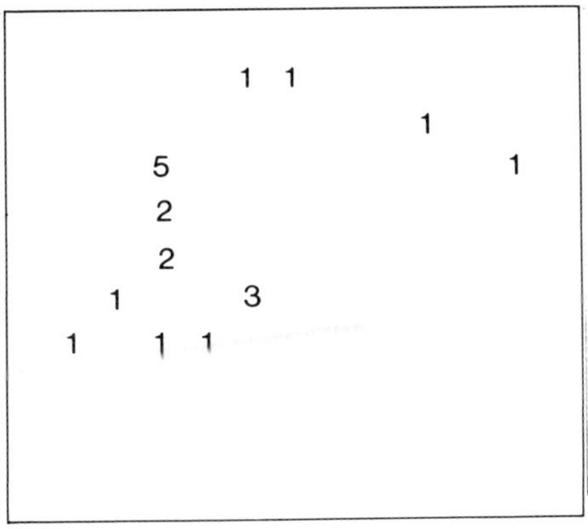

FIGURE 6.10 Initial acceptors in 1929 [Adapted from Hägerstrand (1965), "A Monte Carlo Approach to Diffusion," *European Journal of Sociology* **6**, 43–67 by permission of author and publisher.]

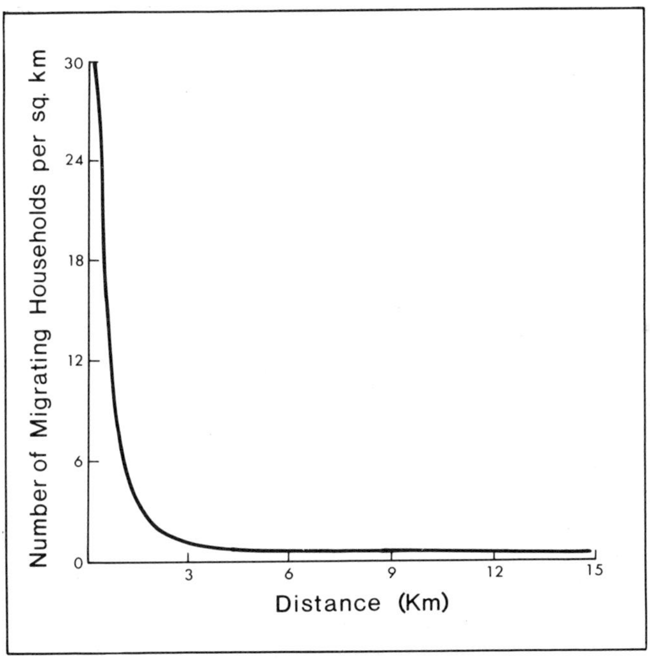

FIGURE 6.11 Migration as a function of distance.

close to home and, as distance increased, the number of migrants declined. The distance-decay curve is shown in figure 6.11.

The migration/distance curve was then used to develop a "mean information field" (MIF) that gives the probability of personal contact from a given point in all directions. The MIF is calculated by rotating the migration/distance curve 360° (figure 6.11). The MIF developed by Hägerstrand was an area 25 kilometers by 25 kilometers (figure 6.12A) in which the value of each cell was determined by the curve in figure 6.11. For example, a cell whose center is 10 kilometers from the center square has a value of 0.167 (interpolated from figure 6.11). These values were then translated into migrant households per cell by multiplying by 25. The value 0.167 (10 kilometers from center) is an estimate of the number of migrant households per square kilometer. Each cell contains 25 square kilometers so that 0.167 times 25 is an estimate of the number of migrating households from the center cell (4.17 in figure 6.12B). The distance-decay function overestimates the number of migrants at very short distances, so the value of the center cell was determined by using the actual number of migrants over this distance. The result is figure 6.12B. The values in figure 6.12B were then converted into probabilities by dividing each value by the sum of all values (figure 6.12C). The probabilities in figure 6.12C sum to 1.00. The probabilities were then accumulated from 0.0000 to 0.9999 with the interval assigned each cell determined by its respective probability (figure 6.12D). Each of the corner cells in figure 6.12D, for example, has a probability of .0096 and an interval of 96.

A

.095	.139	.167	.139	.095
.139	.299	.543	.299	.139
.167	.543		.543	.167
.139	.299	.543	.299	.139
.095	.139	.167	.139	.095

B

2.38	3.48	4.17	3.48	2.38
3.48	7.48	13.57	7.48	3.48
4.17	13.57	110.00	13.57	4.17
3.48	7.48	13.57	7.48	3.48
2.38	3.38	4.17	3.48	2.38

C

.0096	.0140	.0168	.0140	.0096
.0140	.0301	.0547	.0301	.0140
.0168	.0547	.4431	.0547	.0168
.0140	.0301	.0547	.0301	.0140
.0096	.0140	.0168	.0140	.0096

D

.0000 .0096	.0097 .0236	.0237 .0404	.0405 .0544	.0545 .0640
.0641 .0780	.0781 .1081	.1082 .1628	.1629 .1929	.1930 .2069
.2070 .2237	.2238 .2784	.2785 .7215	.7216 .7762	.7763 .7930
.7931 .8070	.8071 .8371	.8372 .8918	.8919 .9219	.9220 .9359
.9630 .9455	.9456 .9595	.9596 .9763	.9764 .9903	.9904 .9999

FIGURE 6.12 Calculation of a mean information field.

The simulation proceeds by centering the mean information field over an acceptor and drawing a random number. Suppose the first random number drawn is 0.6000. We then assume that information on the farm subsidy is passed from an initial acceptor to someone living in the center cell (figure 6.13). This process is repeated for each initial acceptor. Given the probabilities, most information (and therefore new acceptors) will be passed to people living a very short distance from someone already using the innovation, but the possibility of drawing any random number from 0.0000 to 0.9999 allows the innovation to diffuse to more distant farmers. The

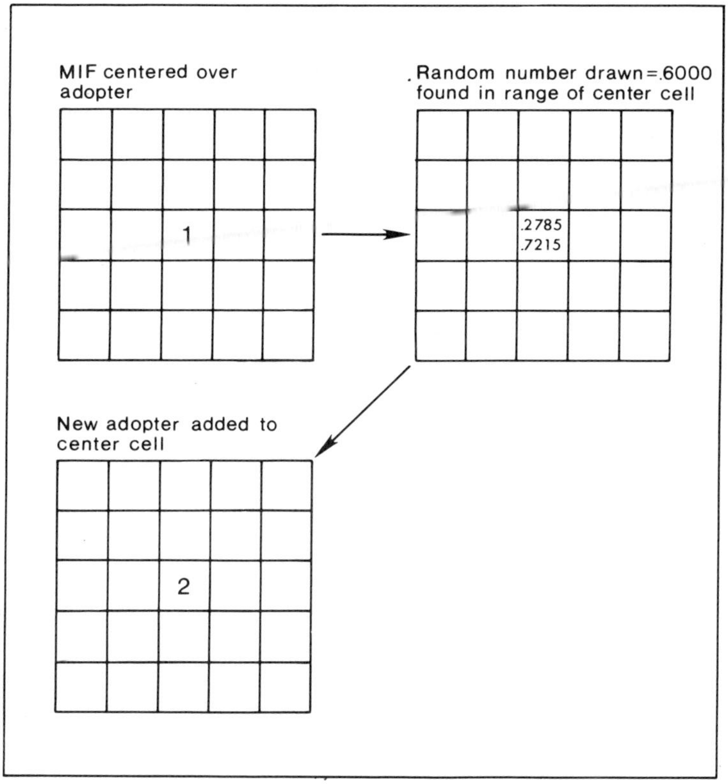

FIGURE 6.13 The simulation process.

process is continued for a series of rounds with the mean information field centered on all acceptors from the preceding round. Figure 6.14 shows the actual and simulated pattern of acceptance for three years. There are differences, of course, but simulation does predict the actual pattern of diffusion of this particular innovation quite well.

The diffusion model can be modified to simulate nonuniform transportation routes and variations in population density. Furthermore, all farmers do not accept new ideas instantly, but the model can be altered to account for the relative speed of acceptance. We may decide that a given cell must be "hit" two or three times before the innovation is accepted. A cell's probability can be changed to reflect accurately its population density and movements in certain directions limited to simulate the inadequacy of transportation routes.

New technology is one of the prime forces operating to change agricultural patterns. Innovations may allow the farmer to increase the gross income per hectare, lower the cost per hectare, or both. New technology may lower the risk the farmer must face in terms of weather or soil fertility. Hybrid corn is an excellent example of an innovation that allowed the expansion of a higher net income agriculture into a new area and lowered the risk farmers faced from shortened growing seasons. Irrigation systems lower risk, while herbicides, pesticides, and fertilizers increase yields per hectare. To understand how patterns of agricultural production change, we must have some understanding of how innovations spread and the diffusion model increases that understanding. The diffusion model also allows us to simulate

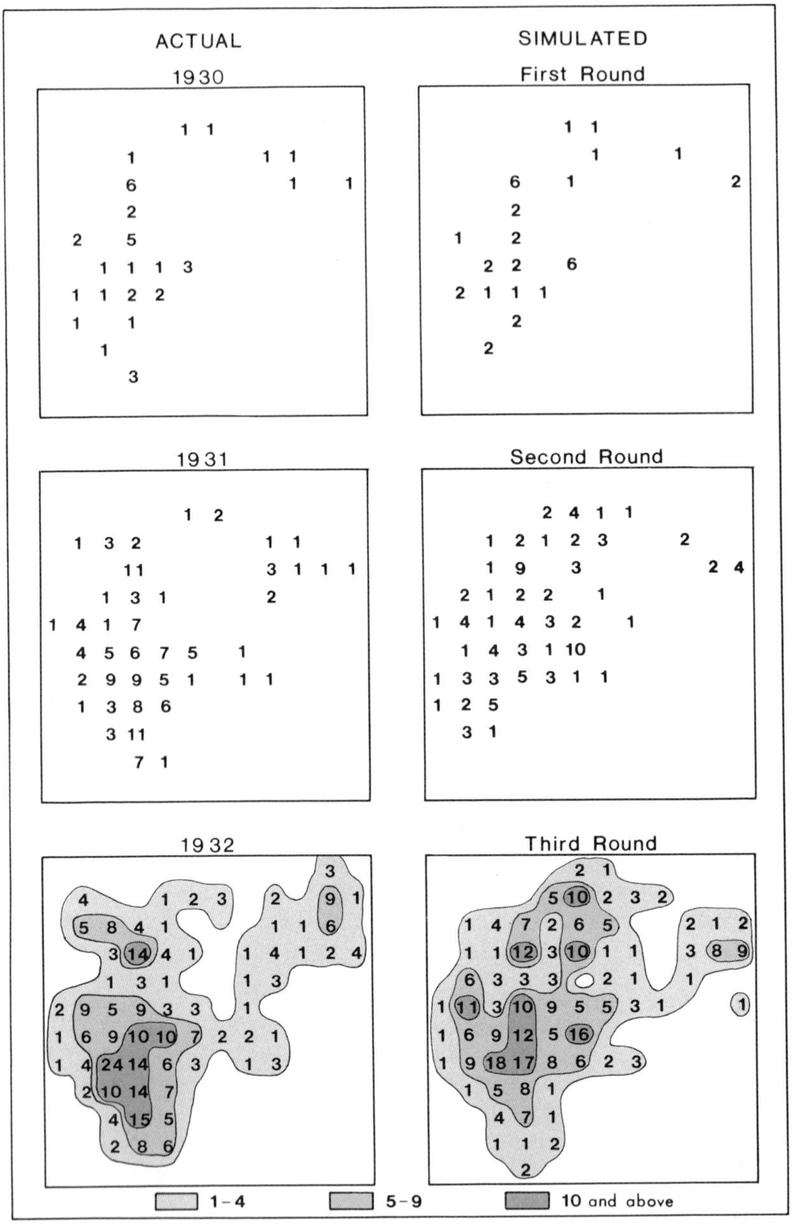

FIGURE 6.14 Actual and simulated patterns. [Adapted from Hägerstrand (1965), "A Monte Carlo Approach to Diffusion," *European Journal of Sociology* **6**, 43–67 by permission of author and publisher.]

nonoptimal human decision making and portrays the landscape as evolutionary rather than instantaneous, which is typical of descriptive (as opposed to normative) models.

Agricultural patterns also shift in response to changes in demand. The growing importance of meat in the American diet over the past hundred years has resulted in increased emphasis on feeder livestock in the Midwest. Many agricultural pattern shifts take years to occur and reflect slowly changing demand, the spatial restraints on the diffusion of information, and the unwillingness of farmers to accept new risks. Modern agriculture requires a large capital investment. Machinery may be so specialized that it can be used for only one particular kind of agriculture, creating inertia.

Catastrophe Theory: Possible Applications

Some agricultural boundary changes are much more rapid. The rate-of-acceptance curve in figure 6.9 represents a continuous or "smooth" process. The gradual migration of an agricultural boundary is the same type of phenomenon, but a sudden boundary shift is a discontinuous or "abrupt" process. "Catastrophe theory" is a new technique that has widespread applications in many areas of geography. Catastrophe theory is capable of dealing with abrupt or discontinuous phenomena. In this section, we present a very elementary application to a geographic event. Catastrophe theory deals with events not only numerically, but also visually by representing discontinuous events with certain geometric shapes. The rapid shift of the western boundary of wheat production as the prevailing form of agriculture is illustrated in figure 6.15. Rainfall increases along one axis and risk increases along the other. The surface of the graph is folded, however, to produce a "cusp." A movement from the upper surface of the cusp to the lower surface is a discontinuous event or catastrophe. The upper surface represents wheat farming and the lower surface represents livestock ranching. Wheat farming expanded westward during the early part of the twentieth century in the United States into land that was climatically better suited to livestock ranching. The expansion was a gradual process made possible by abnormally wet years (increasing rainfall) which lowered risk. This is represented by the smooth progression from livestock ranching to wheat farming along the continuous edge of the graph in figure 6.15.

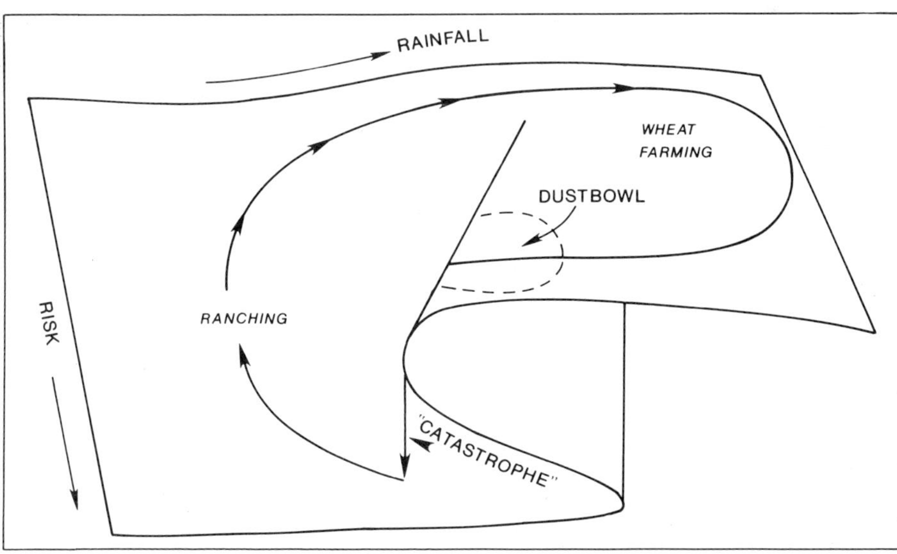

FIGURE 6.15 A "cusp" catastrophe surface.

Wheat was planted using ''dry farming'' techniques which proved to be disastrous in the long-run. As rainfall declined and conditions moved toward the drought of the 1930s, the risk involved in wheat farming increased. The drought and dry farming techniques resulted in the Dust Bowl conditions experienced throughout much of the plains states during that time. Farmers held out as long as possible in an attempt to amortize their investment in wheat farming equipment and land mortgages. Finally, the situation was no longer tenable and agricultural conditions shifted almost instantly from wheat agriculture to ranching and the western boundary of wheat cultivation (as the prevailing form) retreated many km eastward. This shift is represented by the drop from the upper part of the cusp to the lower part.

A rapid change in the type of agriculture always involves risk because of the new and different kind of investment required but, as rainfall remained low, the amount of risk represented by livestock ranching declined. The same process could be repeated if abnormally wet conditions prevailed over a long period of time. The smooth transition from ranching to wheat farming would occur because of the relatively high income per hectare for wheat farming compared to ranching, but the transition would be smooth because there are no conditions inducing rapid change.

The smooth (continuous) part of a catastrophe cusp has all the elements of both game theory and innovation diffusion. Game theory deals with the final result of a long trial-and-error process which attempts to minimize risk. Diffusion deals with the spread of information over time and space. If a wheat farmer has a good income per hectare over a period of years, the information spreads most readily to adjacent land-holders who may adopt this type of agriculture. This passage of ''successful'' information leads to a gradual and continuous migration of an agricultural boundary over a period of years. The cusp part of the catastrophe model, however, deals with the discontinuous or abrupt change that can occur under very adverse conditions. Game theory and diffusion theory in many cases represent evolutionary and short-run solutions to the problem of the best type of agriculture in an area while catastrophe theory may represent a long-run solution and simulate conditions that require an either-or decision.

The agriculturalist engaged in ''mixed farming'' often faces an either-or decision. He can concentrate his investment for the year on feeder livestock or on corn grown for grain. Which is chosen depends upon the relative price of each, but once committed, the farmer cannot easily change back to the alternative type of agriculture during the year. This is represented by the ''swallow-tail'' surface in figure 6.16. The lower surface on the right represents corn for grain while the lower surface on the left represents an investment in feeder livestock. The middle of the upper surface represents equality between the price of feeder livestock and corn grown for grain (potential net income per hectare). The price of corn increases relatively to the right and the net income of feeder livestock increases to the left. The other dimension of the upper surface represents time, with the outermost edge of the surface being the exact time the decision must be made as to which type of agriculture will be chosen. As we move along the time axis, we come closer and closer to the time at which some decision must be made. The individual farmer swings to the right or left of the equality line depending upon the relative prices of

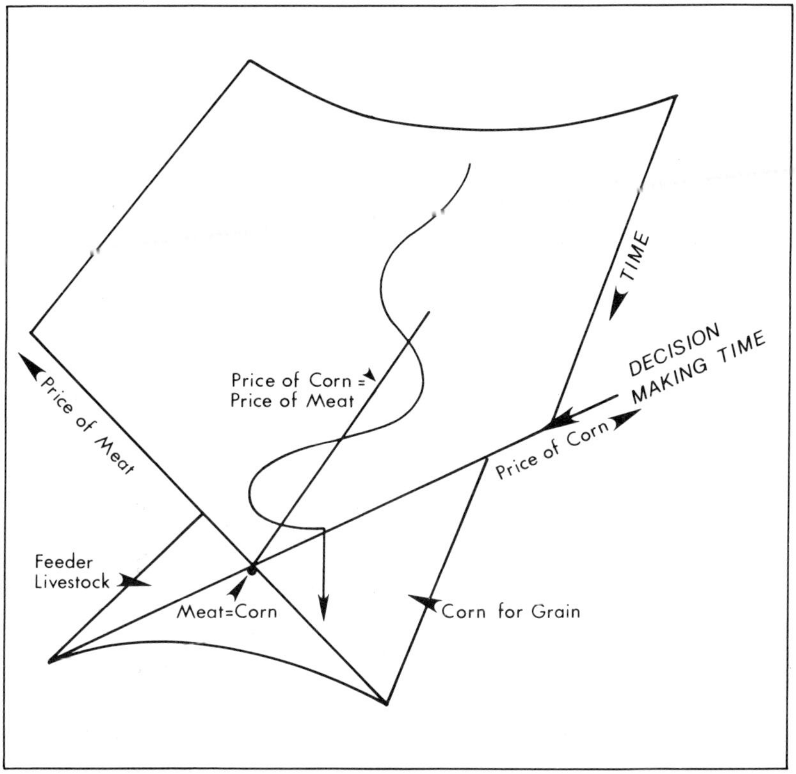

FIGURE 6.16 A "swallow-tail" catastrophe surface.

corn and feeder livestock. At the decision-making time, there is an abrupt shift to one of the two lower surfaces (agricultural types). Movement from the corn-for-grain surface to the feeder livestock surface is not possible.

These two elementary examples represent some possible applications of catastrophe theory to geographical problems. Some elements of the theory are especially applicable to decision making and explaining sudden trends or shifts in patterns.

The Size and Spacing of Cities

A partial explanation of the size and spacing of cities was discussed in chapter 3. The normative assumptions of the central place model include: (1) an even distribution of population *and* resources; and (2) instantaneous adjustment of the hierarchy to produce a stable system. These two assumptions produce a static and precise geometric arrangement of cities in terms of size and spacing. The size and spacing arrangement of cities in reality, however, is the result of many complex forces. An understanding of the arrangement of urban places must take into account the following factors:

1. The economic and social conditions which allow and/or encourage the concentration of all economic activities in settlements. The central place model deals only with central functions, but settlements are also the localization points for most manufacturing and other settlement-building activities.

2. The spatial or geographic conditions that influence the spacing and size of settlements. This includes the heterogeneous nature of the physical environment that determines transportation routes, the economic base of an area, and the distribution of resources.

3. The fact that the development of the urban pattern is an *evolutionary* process in which the structure of the past exerts a powerful influence on subsequent growth and change.

4. Recognition of the fact that the urban system is the result of human decisions based on imperfect knowledge. This last point forces us to recognize the elements of uncertainty and indeterminancy that play a major role in the formation of the urban system.

Central place theory deals primarily with the economic links between a settlement and its hinterland, whereas industrial location theory treats activities that serve national or regional markets and depend upon a complex of localized and ubiquitous raw materials, transportation routes, labor supplies, and management skills as well as variations in demand. The settlement-building aspect of manufacturing has been a key factor in urban growth and change. Urbanization has been primarily the result of migration: cities have grown because the population has migrated from rural areas in response to changing employment opportunities. Today, interurban migration is a prime force promoting the differential growth of cities.

The evolutionary aspects of the urban system are also very important. The present settlement is the result of complex historical forces. We must recognize that: (1) technology changes; (2) urban populations and the physical aspects of cities are constantly being modified; and (3) social and economic conditions often undergo radical change after a locational decision is made. Technological change is extremely important. Transportation innovations change our evaluation of distance. Hinterlands expand or contract as transportation costs change. Technology forces a constant reevaluation and assessment of the variable resource base. An area that had no resource base on which to develop at one time period may be a rapid growth area in another time period because changing technology allowed the exploitation of a localized resource.

We must also take into account the uncertainty and indeterminancy of human decisions. Human decisions are rarely perfect. At a given point in time, there may be many possible locations for a level of central place, many viable locations for a particular type of manufacturing, or many settlements to which an individual might migrate in search of employment. Once a decision is made, however, it affects subsequent decisions. Faced with many alternatives, the decision maker chooses the action he thinks has the greatest probability of success, but the probability is determined by the information available and the circumstances under which the decision is made. The actual choice may be considered a "random" action strongly conditioned by the probabilities of the moment. There are also many other smaller forces whose net effect may also be considered random. In this section, we are concerned with the random and cumulative effects of human decision making.

In chapter 4, we dealt briefly with the "distortion" of ideal locations (in the sense of central place geometry) by the existence of localized resources. Thus human decision making plays a role in all aspects of the urban system because central places, manufacturing, transportation routes, and migration are all the result of human action. The initial sites of many settlements were chosen for reasons that had nothing to do with spacing geometry. Many settlements were initially located to take advantage of natural routeways such as mountain passes, stream fords, or the head of navigation on rivers. Others were located for completely random reasons such as where the horse died on the way west. Whether or not such settlements survived (and their ultimate hierarchical level) depended upon the subsequent development of the region including the size and spacing of other centers. Settlements that were able to exploit a localized resource base might have become the highest level central place in an area simply because of the large population and consequent central functional size initiated by the population supported by manufacturing. This is illustrated in figure 6.17. Point I is the ideal location for the highest order central place in the region shown. The shaded area represents a localized power resource such as coal. The isoline is a spatial margin to viability for the highest order central place in the region. Because of the spacing geometry, we must assume that places outside that isoline can never attain the highest level. The first settlement in the area is located at A to exploit the resource base. That city prospers, increases in population through migration, and grows in functional size. A subsequent settlement locates at I, but is a pure central place. Because of the early growth and subsequent size of A, it assumes the primate central place role in the region. The

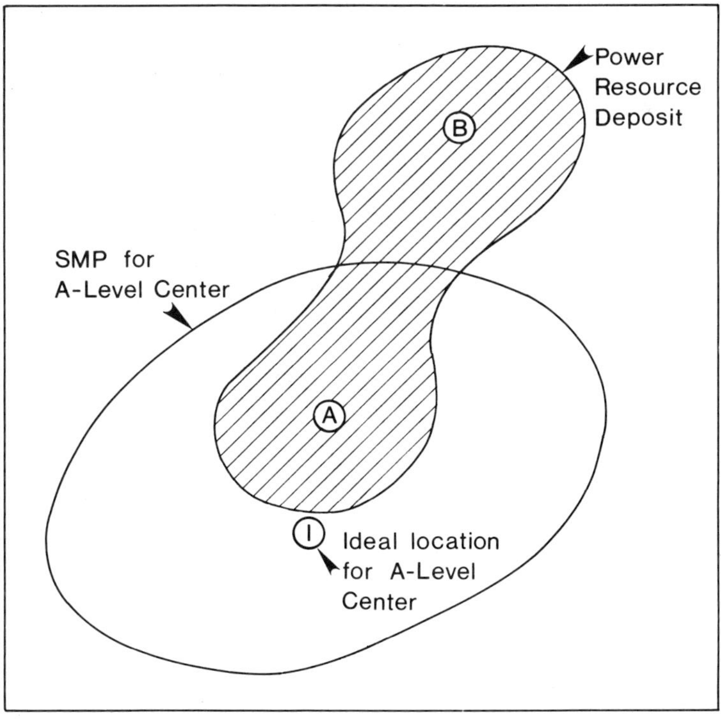

FIGURE 6.17 Actual and ideal locations: distortion by localized resources.

final pattern is the result of both the unpredictability of human decision making and the evolutionary nature of the urban system. We are assuming that the localized resource can only support one large manufacturing city. The initial site chosen for development could have been at I which would have optimized the spacing arrangement of the highest order central places, or at point B. Point B, however, is outside the spatial margins to viability for A-level centers and could never have developed to that level. Its population would be supported by manufacturing (resource exploitation) and lower-level central functions.

Morrill (1963) developed an extensive model incorporating all aspects of a developing urban system including the "randomness" of human decision making. The model uses the same approach as the simulation introduced in our discussion of the diffusion of innovation. Human decisions are assumed to be random within probability restraints. Probability or stochastic models must be used when it is necessary to evaluate an indeterminate situation. A range of possibilities is built in rather than various forces converging to a unique solution. Certain possibilities are given a higher probability than others, but the final choice is determined by the drawing of random numbers as in the diffusion model. This type of simulation is called a "Monte Carlo" model and was first used extensively in geography by Hägerstrand. The probabilities used in Morrill's analysis were determined by prior developments and the random choices of a given stage were used in turn to establish probabilities for subsequent stages. In this section, Morrill's model is discussed extensively to demonstrate the effects of both random decision making and the structures imposed by development over time.

Morrill began by defining a study region, dividing it into component areas, and choosing time periods (figure 6.18). To simulate the development of a real urban system, we would have to collect information on net growth rates during the chosen time period, the demand for new transportation, the amount of economic activity which could be supported, and the number of migrants that an economic activity would be likely to attract. For our example, these levels can be chosen arbitrarily.

The first step in the model is to assign transportation routes. In figure 6.19, for example, point C can be connected by several possible links. Possible connections may be limited by assuming that any alternate route can be only a given percentage longer than the shortest possible route or certain routes can be excluded from consideration by physical barriers. Each possible route is then given a probability of being chosen based on its distance, the population of the areas through which it passes, and the costs of building such a route. A specific route is then chosen by random numbers to simulate the uncertainty of human decision making. Transport routes are important because a place, once connected, has a much better chance of becoming a higher order central place and of attracting other settlement-building economic activities.

The second step in the model is the assignment of noncentral place (settlement-building) activities such as manufacturing. The demand for these activities is determined by population, income, resources, and other factors. The total number of plants and their output would be determined from our economic analysis of the area if we were simulating a real urban system. The possibility of each sub-area in the study region attracting manufacturing is then determined. All sub-areas may be

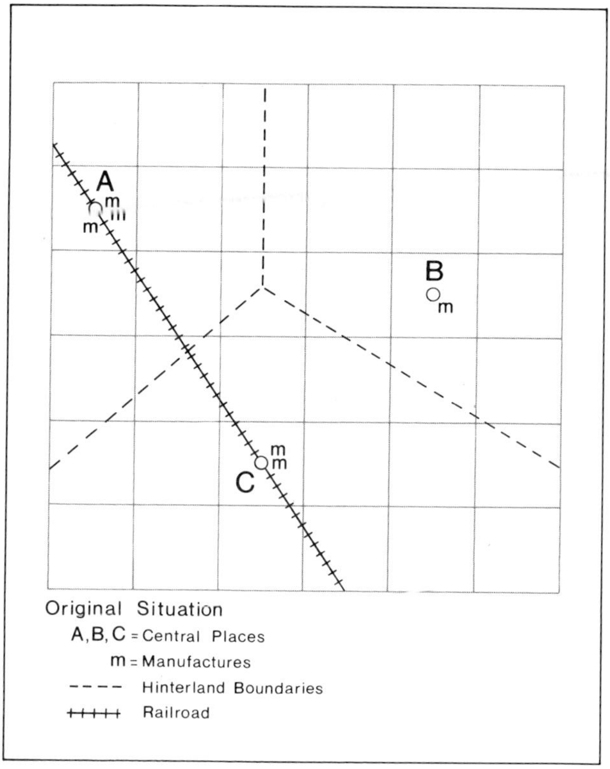

FIGURE 6.18 The simulation of an urban system: original situation.

considered possibilities or we may exclude some areas from analysis because the cost of production is prohibitive or because they lack the necessary labor force or resource base. The probability of each sub-area attracting a manufacturing plant is then determined. Ineligible areas have a probability of zero. Eligible areas have probabilities determined by resources, transportation links, labor force, and other factors considered by traditional industrial location theory (figure 6.20). The total number of manufacturing plants required to meet the demand of a given time period is then assigned using the Monte Carlo technique as in figure 6.21.

The assignment of central place activities is the third step of the Morrill model and determines which areas will be successful in capturing a local hinterland as the economy of the study area grows and is able to support more and more central functions. The probability of a place attaining a given level in the central place hierarchy is strongly conditioned, however, by the presence or absence of transportation connections and manufacturing. The assignment of central place activities involves determining the total number of central places of a given level that can be supported in the region by dividing the total population of the area by the threshold of each central function. The possibility of new central places is conditioned by the minimum hinterlands (thresholds) of existing central places. Higher order central functions can be added at successively fewer central places and their thresholds met

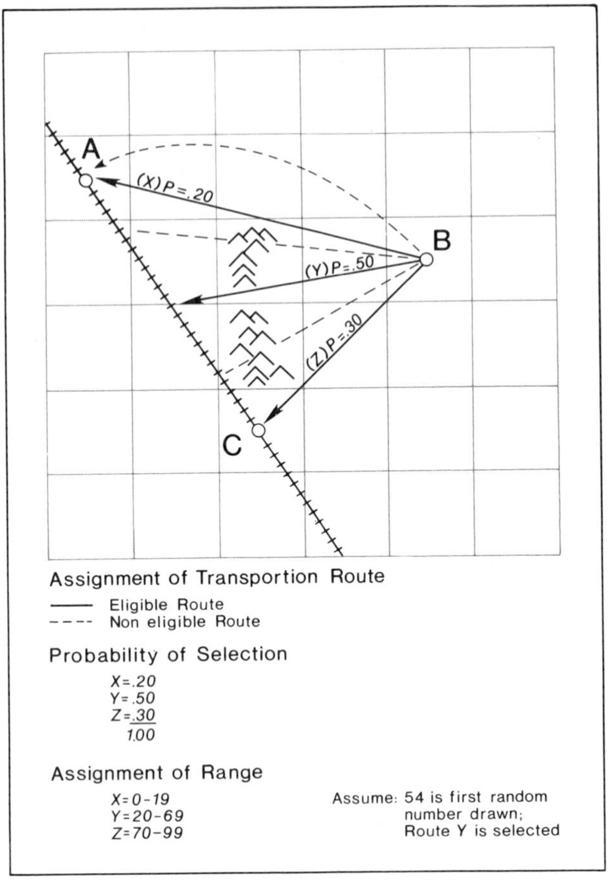

FIGURE 6.19 The simulation of an urban system: assignment of transportation routes.

by the consolidation of smaller hinterlands. Lower order central places, on the other hand, can only squeeze in if sufficient threshold populations can be found for them within the limits imposed by existing central place hinterlands. Any hinterland, old or new: (1) must contain at least a threshold population for the good in question; and (2) cannot overlap the hinterland of an existing center. A given place has the possibility of becoming a central place of several different levels. Once the level is determined, however, the hinterland of the place is limited by the necessary threshold market area required by that level.

The probability of a settlement's becoming a given level of central place is dependent upon many factors including the population of the place, manufacturing activities, and transportation connections. A place that is not in the best geometric position for a given level may succeed: (1) because the resident population supported by manufacturing requires a certain range of service functions; and (2) because of superior connections via the existing transportation network. Each settlement and its theoretical hinterland is assigned a probability based on these criteria (figure 6.22).

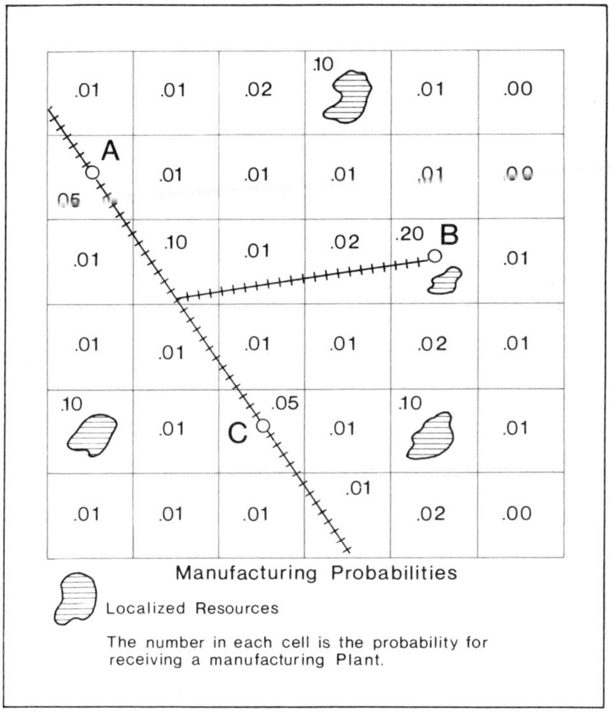

FIGURE 6.20 The simulation of an urban system: assignment of manufacturing probabilities.

Monte Carlo simulation is then used to determine which points actually succeed as central places of a given level. The selection of the first central place eliminates many others from consideration because hinterlands of a given level must be mutually exclusive. All possible central places contained in the first hinterland selected are eliminated. In figure 6.23 the first random number chosen, 20, selects hinterland 1 (place X) and eliminates the possibility of places Y and Z becoming places of the same level.

The Monte Carlo process continues until all possible hinterlands have been selected. Some areas may remain outside the theoretical hinterland of a chosen central place and are assigned to the nearest viable central place. The process is then repeated for higher levels of the hierarchy, but, to be selected, a place must already be a central place of the next lower order. Prior simulation, therefore, sets rigid limits on the next step of the simulation process.

The fourth step of Morrill's model is a simulation of migration that redistributes population and provides the basis for urban growth and decline. The expected volume of migration from a given area is determined by employment conditions, resource base, and socioeconomic characteristics. The probability of other areas receiving migrants from a source area is then determined by three factors: (1) the distance from a source region; (2) the attractiveness as determined by growth and employment potential; and (3) previous migration from the source region (friend/

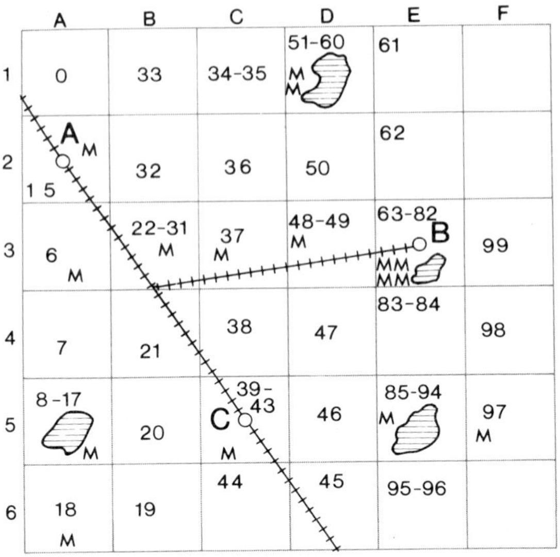

Assignment of Manufactures
(16 Plants to be assigned)
M = Manufacturing Plant

Random Numbers Drawn	Plant Assigned to Area
59	D1
82	E3
37	C3
06	A3
23	B3
18	A6
49	D3
74	E3
63	E3
87	E5
77	E3
53	D1
97	F5
12	A5
41	C5
02	A2

FIGURE 6.21 The simulation of an urban system: assignment of manufacturing plants.

family contacts). Each area is then assigned a probability range for attracting migrants from a given source region and Monte Carlo simulation is used to assign migrants. The sequence of the model is shown in figures 6.24A through 6.24D. The losses or gains of a given area through migration are used to adjust the level of urban development in each area to give a constant feedback.

Morrill's model is an important departure from the static and geometric central place models of Christaller and Lösch because of its built-in flexibility and its evolutionary (feedback) elements. We have presented the model in a very abbreviated form, but the required data for a given area can be collected and the model run to determine whether or not it adequately results in an urban system corresponding to reality. The most important feature of the model is the incorporation of nonoptimal and indeterminate human decision making.

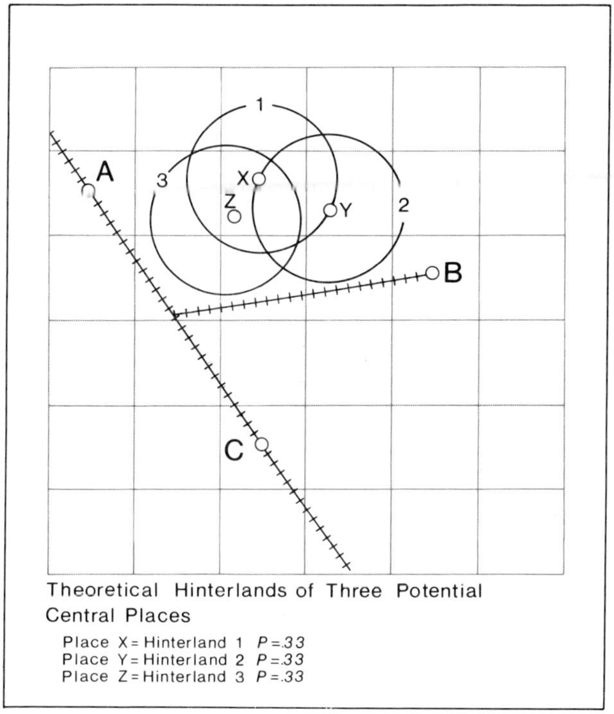

FIGURE 6.22 The simulation of an urban system: theoretical central place hinterlands.

Manufacturing

Manufacturing requires a decision to operate at a particular scale with a particular input combination at a given location. This decision must be made without perfect knowledge. The reliability of an individual decision depends upon the location of the decision maker within the behavioral matrix. We have dealt with the problem of industrial decision making in a limited way in the discussion of the location of settlement-building functions in Morrill's model of the urban system. In this section we will explore the industrial decision-making process in greater detail.

A study of locational behavior is one part of the problem of understanding the patterns of the economic landscape. We discussed in chapter 4 the *structure* of viable locations—the conditions that make certain locations viable and/or optimal and other locations nonviable. With a perfect knowledge of this structure, the optimizer would choose only optimal locations. The concept of spatial margins to viability was introduced to allow the inclusion of suboptimal decision making. The second part of the problem is a consideration of how actual locational decisions are made. These are two quite different aspects of the same problem. The first aspect is concerned with economic forces, while the second is concerned with the behavioral aspects of decision making.

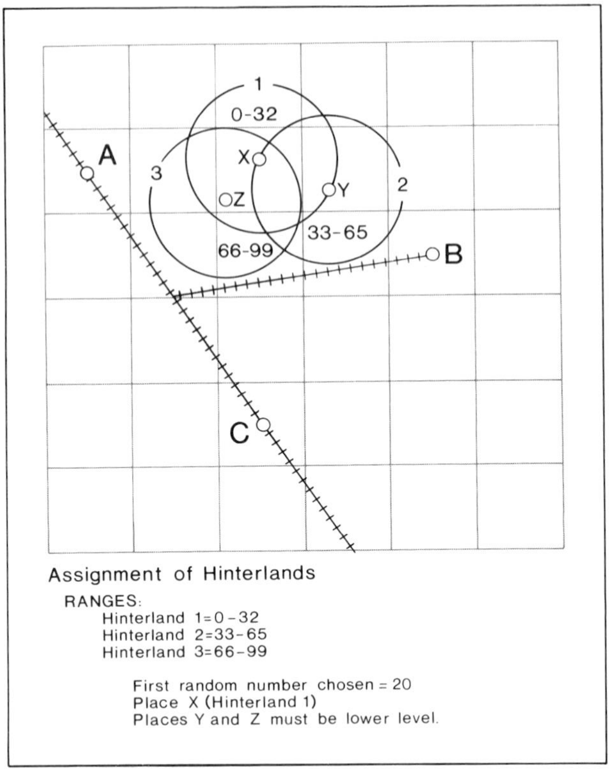

FIGURE 6.23 The simulation of an urban system: assignment of central place hinterlands.

Deterministic models that make up much of location theory ignore decision making. We do not have to be concerned with the decision-making process of optimizers. Their behavior is completely predictable. If an optimal location exists, the optimizer will always choose that particular point. The behavioral matrix introduces a stochastic element in an attempt to simulate nonoptimal behavior. Stochastic models determine the *probability* of a certain outcome. The behavioral matrix determines the probability of a decision maker's choosing a viable (or optimal) location from the individual's store of information and ability to use that information. The behavioral matrix assumes that the store of knowledge (and ability) is information about the economic structures that determine the viability of a given location or many possible locations. A third approach assumes that all industrial location decisions are made by individuals who fall in the extreme upper left-hand corner of the behavioral matrix. In other words, they have no relevant information (or ability) concerning the spatial structure of economic viability. The actions of these decision makers can be characterized as completely random. A question is then raised concerning the difference between the industrial landscape created by perfect knowledge and one created by random decision makers, or the difference between random decision makers and those possessing some information (and ability) concerning the spatial structure of viability.

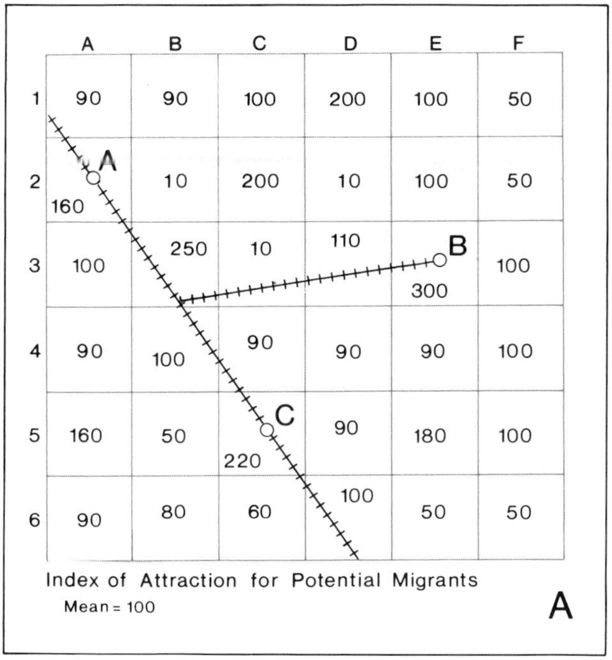

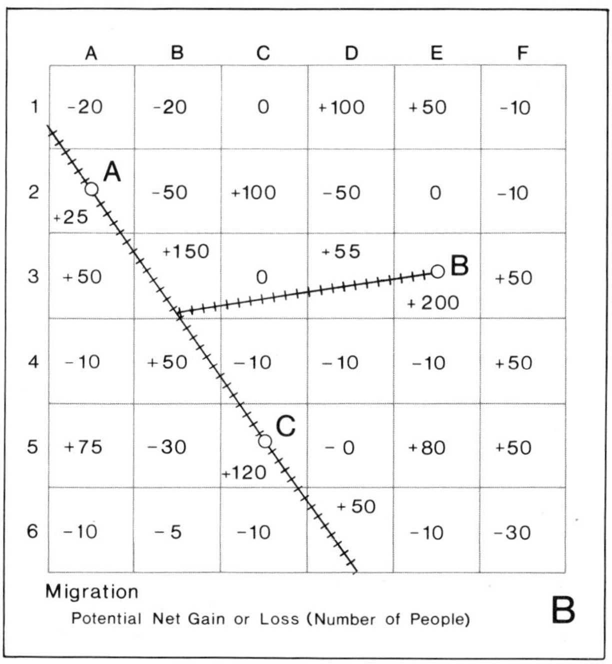

FIGURE 6.24 The simulation of an urban system—migration: (A) Indexes of attraction; (B) Potential gains or losses; Parts (C) and (D) on next page.

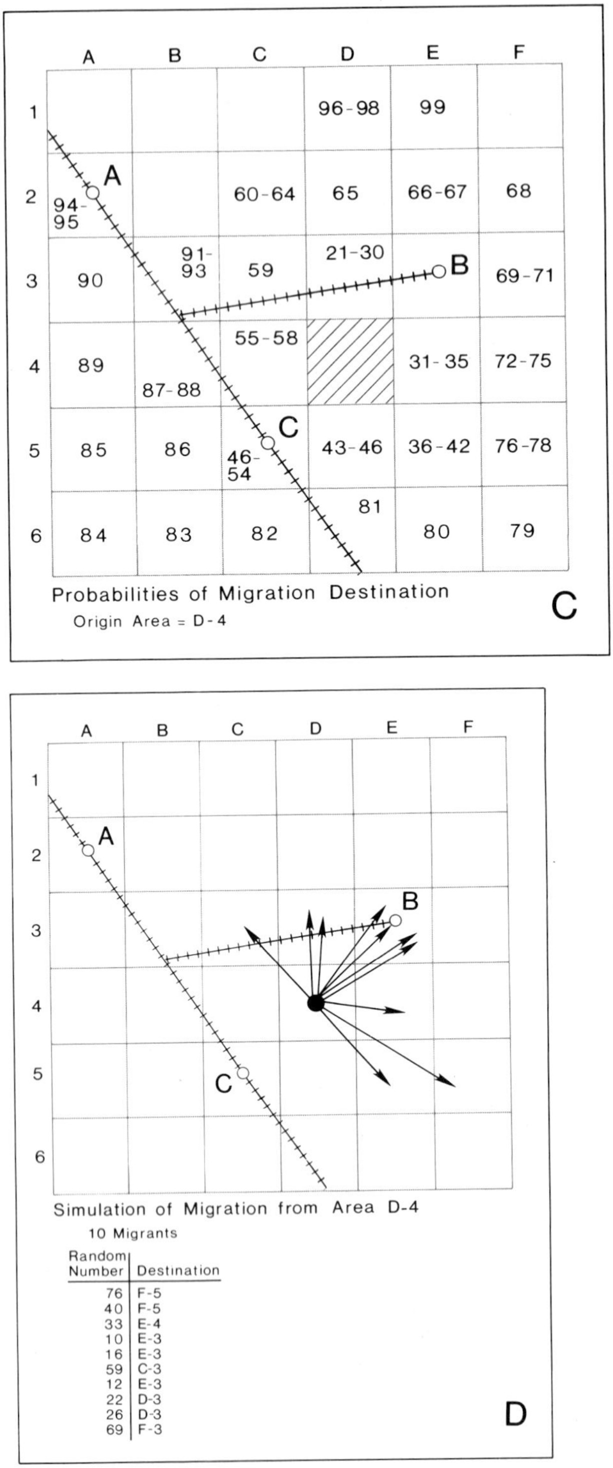

FIGURE 6.24 cont. (C) Migration probabilities; (D) Assignment of migrants from area D-4.

Alchian (1950) and Tiebout (1957) explored this question in detail. The following discussion is based mostly on Alchian's ideas and terminology. His major points are as follows.

1. If the number of random decisions is large enough, the probability of some decision makers' selecting viable and optimal locations is also large. Alchian likened the process to betting on a horse race. Some bettors may use the most rational handicapping system possible and select the winning horse. Other bettors may select the same horse for "nonrational" reasons, such as its name or a lucky number. If we know nothing about the decision-making process, both bettors are correct in the sense of perfect foresight. Therefore, it does not matter whether the decision-making process is rational in the economic sense or completely random in that viable locations will be chosen if enough random decisions are made.

2. Individual behavior based on foresight and rational motivation does not necessarily imply a *collective* pattern of behavior different from collective random action. Judgments differ even when based on the best available evidence and each individual personally weighs each variable, but the aggregate set of actions may be indistinguishable from a set of random actions.

3. Even if all decision making is random, we can still specify the conditions and structures determining viability. With a knowledge of the viability structure, the types of locations that will be more viable relative to other types can be stated even if the decision makers themselves do not know the locational conditions of success or try to achieve them by readjusting locations. If they do know the conditions, there will be a tendency toward a locational equilibrium. This point can be illustrated with the following example. Suppose that the location pattern of the plants in an industry is fixed for a given period, but during that period the potential viability of many locations is altered (perhaps through differential migration). Some plants will be located closer to the new, but unknown, optimum locations. These firms now have a greater probability of survival and growth. Such locations will prosper relative to others and will come to dominate the locational pattern. Survival conditions may push the location pattern of the set of survivors toward the unknowable optimum location pattern by either repeated trials or survival of more of those who happened to be near the optimum locations (as determined subsequently). If this new viability structure lasts very long, the pattern will be different from that which prevailed or would have prevailed under other spatial economic structures. Even if the viability structure cannot be forecast, the locations having a higher probability of success may be stated, given alternative potential viability structures. If a consideration of past patterns rather than the prediction of future patterns is the task, a critical variable in facilitating survival can be identified, even though the individual decision makers were not aware of it.

4. Prediction of viable locations does not assert that every (or any) firm change its location. It only asserts that the pattern of a new *set* of locations, or possibly a set of new locations, will differ from the pattern produced by a preceding viability structure. As the conditions of viability and optimality change, some firms that were once optimal may now be merely viable and vice versa.

5. A final implication that can be drawn from the random hypothesis is that empirical investigations such as questionnaires may be incapable of evaluating the hypothesis that traditional location factors exert a "pull" on an industry or "cause"

certain location patterns. Suppose that for a certain industry the presence of low-wage labor is the critical (structural) variable determining viable locations. We poll the founder of each plant in order to validate this hypothesis. Each plant founder, however, asserts that the presence of low-wage labor had absolutely no influence on his choice of a plant site. Nonetheless, those who chose locations near pools of low-wage labor have a greater probability of success and, through time, a pattern in harmony with those conditions may evolve. Questionnaires may reveal that the location decision of each entrepreneur was different and based on amenity (noneconomic) factors. In this example, the spatial margins to profitability were determined by economic-demographic conditions (low-wage labor pools) that are independent of the decision-making process, but a researcher using questionnaires might conclude that the differential pattern of amenities determined the pattern. In fact, the pattern is the result of subjective (noneconomic) decisions which founded plants on sites coinciding with viable space-economic conditions. Only successful plant founders are polled; the ones who chose nonviable sites have disappeared from the landscape. This is not to suggest that individuals do not consider spatial-economic conditions, only that it is not necessary. To produce a given location pattern, a particular viability structure is required as well as a group of participants who submit various locations for the structure's selection and adoption. Noneconomic reasons for locational decisions are numerous and difficult to quantify. They may be considered as random, as in Morrill's model of urban system evolution.

The congruency between an economic landscape produced by optimizers and one produced by the random process can be amplified by a simple simulation model. In figure 6.25, the spatial margins to profitability for a particular industry have been drawn. These margins are very small and the exact center of each viable area represents the optimum location for a manufacturing plant in the industry. The spatial margins to viability and the optimum locations are determined by economic conditions that are independent of locational decisions. In other words, we are

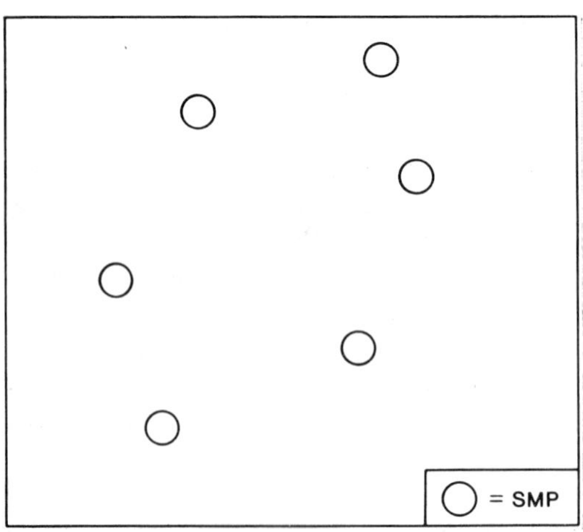

FIGURE 6.25 Spatial margins to profitability for industry X.

ignoring the possible changes in profitability that might result from locational interdependence.

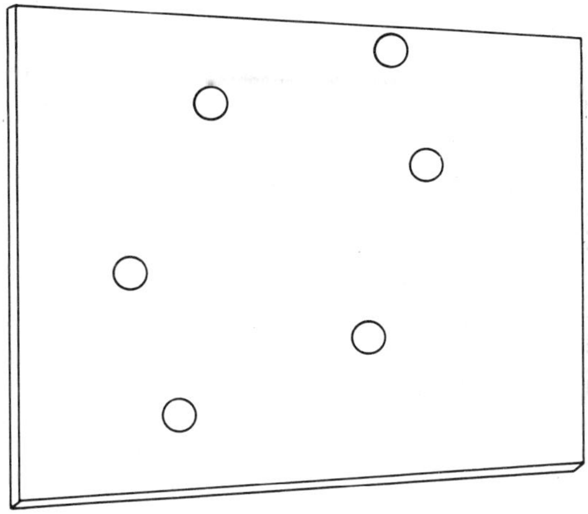

FIGURE 6.26 Map covered by plywood sheet (holes correspond to spatial margins to profitability).

A sheet of plywood is placed over the map and holes cut in the covering sheet matching the spatial margins to profitability on the map below (figure 6.26). With only six possible viable locations, we are assuming that only six manufacturing plants (one in each area) are required to serve total demand. The decision-making process is simulated by throwing darts at the plywood sheet, removing the sheet after all darts have been thrown, and observing the resultant pattern. The actions of optimizers are simulated by the darts champion of an English pub. He is given only six darts to throw and the resulting pattern is shown in figure 6.27. The actions of random decision makers are simulated by someone with little experience at darts who is given a hundred darts to throw. The pattern produced by random action is shown in figure 6.28. The actions of optimizers and random decision makers have produced exactly the same pattern. The process in reality, of course, is much more complicated than this simple example basically because of the problem of locational interdependence. The structure of viable locations is constantly altered each time a new producer establishes a production site, but, if demand is stable, the final outcome is much the same. We cannot be sure that current producers are in *optimal* sites, however, only that they are in viable sites during the current period.

Even producers who pay careful attention to the spatial structure of economic conditions can never be sure they have selected an optimal site even though they may be certain of its viability because of the large amount of information facing most producers. Shortages of time and money preclude the examination of all possible sites. A producer may identify one set of spatial margins to profitability and the optimum location within these limits. This is a "local" solution to the location problem, while the "global" solution may present locations where higher profits are possible as illustrated in figure 6.29. A producer examines only the area to the right of the vertical line. Within that area he determines the spatial margins to profitability

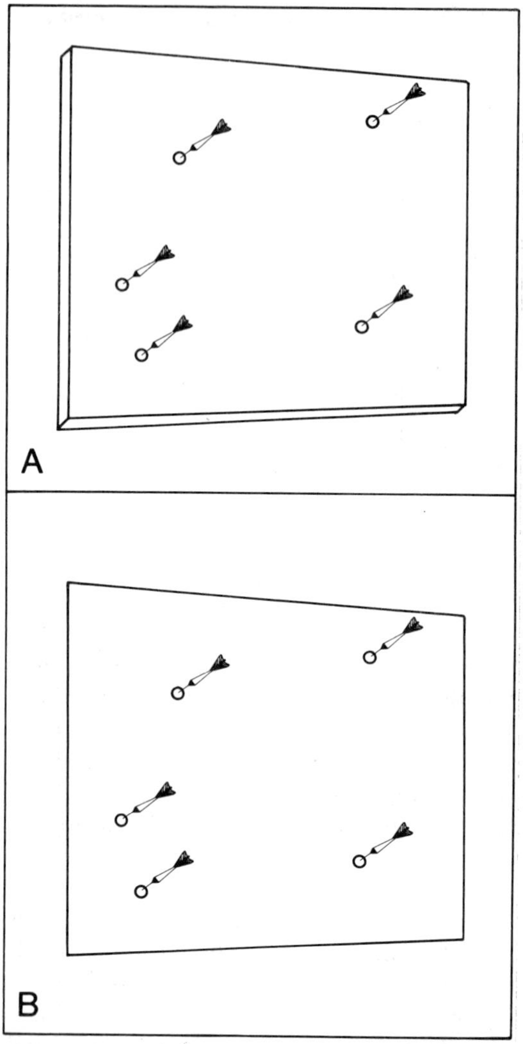

FIGURE 6.27 (A) Simulation by optimizer; (B) Resultant pattern.

and selects an optimal location. In a global sense, however, more profitable locations are possible. Total demand may be met by an aggregate of locations that are merely viable rather than optimal.

Summary

Most models of the economic landscape have assumed the existence of optimizers who produce rigid location patterns based on perfect knowledge. Such models are *deterministic* in that a given set of data always yields a specific pattern. In reality, however, a behavioral approach must be used to deal with patterns of production,

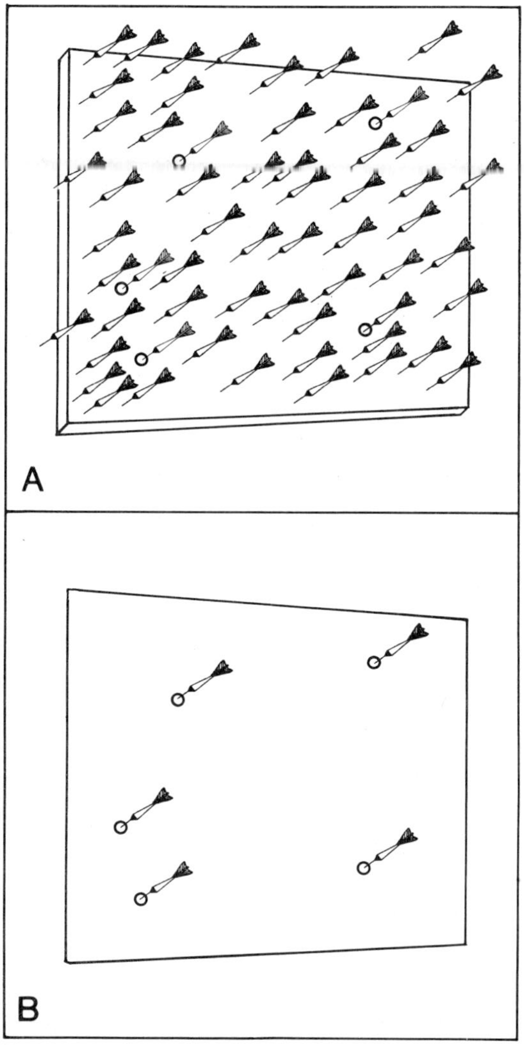

FIGURE 6.28 (A) Simulation by satisficer; (B) Resultant pattern.

exchange, and consumption. Human decisions are merely satisfactory choices and are often made with noneconomic motives in mind. This forces a reliance on *stochastic* models that specify only the probability of a certain set of actions producing a particular pattern. Monte Carlo simulation is an excellent example of a stochastic model. We have demonstrated, however, in this chapter that the patterns produced by nonoptimal decision makers may not be appreciably different from those produced by optimizers if the limits of choice are small and if the number of individual decision makers is large enough. The problem is complicated by the actions of other producers and the fact that the decisions of today are strongly limited by the conditions imposed by past actions. Real economic landscapes are therefore *evolutionary* in that each stage of development is structured by previous stages. The evolutionary nature of the economic landscape is the subject of the following chapter.

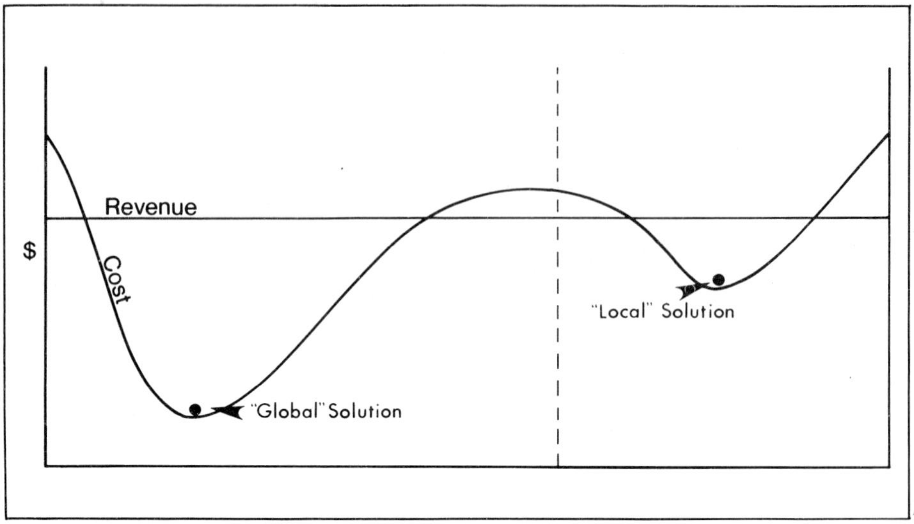

FIGURE 6.29 "Local" and "global" solutions.

KEY WORDS

behavioral matrix
game theory
global solution
local solution
mean information field
Monte Carlo simulation
psychic income
saddle-point
satisficer
simulation
spatial diffusion
zero-sum game

SUGGESTED READINGS

Spatial Diffusion

Gould, P. (1969), *Spatial Diffusion,* Commission on College Geography, Resource Paper No. 4.

Hägerstrand, T. (1967), *Innovation Diffusion as a Spatial Process* (trans. and postscript by A. Pred), Chicago: University of Chicago Press.

Behavioral Aspects of Locational Decision Making

Pred, A. (1967), "Behavior and Location: Foundations for a Geographic and Dynamic Location Theory, Part 1," *Lund Studies in Geography, Series B*, 27.

———(1969), "Behavior and Location: Foundations for a Geographic and Dynamic Location Theory, Part 2," *Lund Studies in Geography, Series B,* 28.

Catastrophe Theory

Zeeman, E. C. (1976), "Catastrophe Theory," *Scientific American* **234**, No. 4, 65–83.

Simulation of an Urban System

Morrill, R. L. (1965), "Migration and the Spread and Growth of Urban Settlement," *Lund Studies in Geography, Series B*, 26.

Game Theory

Gould, P. (1963), "Man Against His Environment: A Game Theoretic Framework," *Annals* of the Association of American Geographers **53**, 290–97.

Random Decision Making

Alchian, A. A. (1950), "Uncertainty, Evolution, and Economic Theory," *Journal of Political Economy* **58**, 211–21.

Tiebout, C. M. (1957), "Location Theory, Empirical Evidence, and Economic Evolution," *Papers* of the Regional Science Association **3**, 74–86.

7 Development

Introduction

This chapter deals with the evolving space-economy. How does the economic landscape change and develop? We cannot answer this question without the concept of time and without having a sense of its passage. Time sets limits to the arrangement of economic activities on the earth's surface, but like space, it is passive or neutral; it does not determine patterns of economic activities. Time can be likened to the denominator of a fraction. The numerator is the number of economic events observed. Change may be viewed in terms of change over time and rates of change.

Problems of change and development are complex; the frequently voiced complaint that we do not have a single overall and accepted theory is evidence of that complexity. The discussion of the often conflicting ideas about the evolution of the space-economy begins with a definition of development. We then provide a brief history of the ideas and events molding the development of the world's political economy. The next four sections deal with (1) the measurement of economic performance and directions of economic change; (2) stages of growth models; (3) center-periphery relations; and (4) basic objectives of development. The chapter ends with a review that places the ideas contained in this book in perspective.

Chapter Objectives

1. Present a brief history of the world's political- and space-economy.

2. Outline the major models that have been constructed to explain development.
3. Discuss in detail stages of growth and center-periphery models.
4. Bridge the gap between static equilibrium models developed in Part 1 and dynamic disequilibrium models.

Defining Development

What does development mean? Until recently it has been treated as a synonym of *economic growth*. *Development* has been defined as a "rapid rise in total and per capita income, sustained over a considerable time and affecting most segments of a society, together with related demographic, economic, and technological changes" (Conkling and Yeates 1976, pp. 257–58). In the 1970s, few scholars subscribe to such a view. The popular trend has been to define development in terms of progress towards the realization of an assortment of welfare goals..

Seers (1972), for example, pleaded for a definition of development based on human well-being. He asked:

> Why do we confuse development with economic growth? . . . Development means creating the conditions for the realization of human personality. Its evaluation must therefore take into account three linked economic criteria: whether there has been a reduction in i) poverty; ii) unemployment; iii) inequality. (p. 21)

He showed that some countries have experienced not only rapid growth of per capita income, but also increases in poverty, unemployment, and inequality. He pleaded for measures of development at the family level based on nutrition, health, infant mortality, access to education, and political participation. "One cannot really say that there has been development for the world as a whole when the benefits of technical progress have served minorities which were already relatively rich" (1972, p. 33).

In this chapter our task is not to advocate policies to reduce social and economic injustice, but to introduce ideas about development that may help us to understand the organization of the economic landscape. Therefore, we prefer to adopt a holistic, goal-free definition. Development is the whole process of change. Such a comprehensive definition implies that the development of the economic landscape has both positive and negative dimensions.

History of the World's Political Economy

It is instructive to look at the history of the world's political economy by tracing ideas and events from the age of mercantilism through the period of monopoly capitalism.

Financial Capitalism

In the sixteenth century, an age of nascent capitalism, rulers of respectable European states were mercantilists. According to mercantilists, the first task of government was the central direction of the economy and the rapid accumulation of gold and silver in the royal exchequer. Szentes, who described the early modern period as the "heyday of merchant capital," (1971, p. 137) said:

> This pursuit of profit, as production was still carried on on a feudal basis, took the form of commercial profit-making, the acquisition of tangible money, of gold [and silver]. But to get rich in commerce, to get hold of more money, of gold is possible only if the exchange is uneven, if one party always wins while the others constantly lose. But the possibilities of a lasting and repeated uneven exchange are very limited within the society of a given country, so the activity of merchant capital was directed from the beginning to the *outside,* to foreign countries. The ideology of merchant capital, *mercantilism,* points to foreign trade as the source of a country's enrichment and sees the way to increase the nation's wealth in importing as much gold as possible into the country, while exporting as little as possible, preferably nothing out of it. (1971, p. 137)

These motives were heightened by rivalries among West European nation-states. To the mercantilist, there existed a finite amount of trade in the world, and, as a consequence, the struggle was to obtain the largest share.

Although many causes other than economic undoubtedly led to overseas expansion, the commercial factor was significant from the late fifteenth century onward when national wealth was believed to be the basis of national strength. Commercial expansion found its expression in economic nationalism. This phenomenon arose first in Portugal and Spain, and then, early in the sixteenth century, it became a characteristic of northwest Europe. From many rival harbors, especially Antwerp, Amsterdam, and London, a commercial network spread out to embrace parts of subsaharan Africa and its adjacent Atlantic Islands, the West Indies, the Americas, Indonesia, and parts of Asia.

Early capitalism drew nearly the whole world into an interdependent economic system. Europe was enriched by the lands where Europeans traded, but their trading activities impoverished these lands. Although the home market promoted economic growth, it was the overseas market that made possible European industrial revolutions.

Economic Liberalism and Industrial Capitalism

In the age of mercantilism, the economic landscape was cluttered with obstacles to the free-play of European economies. Guilds limited entry into craft industries. Tariffs, exclusive trade treaties, quotas, and other barriers checked the continued expansion of international trade. Opposition to mercantilism increased in the late eighteenth century, and a climate of economic liberalism gradually emerged. As an ideology, the term *economic liberalism* is used synonymously with the classical approach to economics. The principal origin of the classical model is in Adam Smith's (1723–90) *Wealth of Nations,* published in 1776.

Smith's Vision of Progress Smith extolled the ideology of economic liberalism and refuted the doctrine of mercantilism. *The Wealth of Nations* is the basis for modern Western models of growth and regional development. It contains the paradigm or the overall model on which the location theories considered in previous chapters were built.

Smith believed in the probability of human progress in a world of laissez-faire societies. Economic liberty promised rising per capita real income. Moreover, a system of liberty could more nearly fulfill individual aspirations. There was, according to Smith, no getting over the fact that people were naturally selfish. Economic liberty would allow people to follow their own self-interest, get rich, and rise in the world by trucking and exchanging one good for another.

Thus, at the heart of Smith's vision of progress was a world of free enterprise capitalism. Central control of the economy should be vested in the "invisible hand of the market." Production should be in the hands of small entrepreneurs and independent artisans. Economic men should be freed from the shackles of meddling governments.

Smith emphasized the importance of the division of labor, that it is limited by the size of the market, and he "discovered" the principle of scale economies. In common with other classical economists, he viewed production as a function of land, labor, and capital, and considered technology and entrepreneurship to be additional variables. If impediments to growth were removed, Smith argued that an economy would experience increasing sustained growth. Each year some of the economic surplus would be used for investment and total output in subsequent years would be larger. Economic surplus is the excess amount of total output in any given time period over and above socially necessary costs required to produce that output.

Smith's ideas were developed in the first half of the nineteenth century by several British economists, particularly Ricardo (1772–1823) and Malthus (1766–1834). Except for the addition of marginal analysis in the 1870s which led to the substitution of the term "neoclassical model" for "classical model," few changes were made to the accepted interpretation of the Western economic system until the 1930s. Until then the economic system was assumed to be self-regulating or self-righting.

Views of Ricardo and Malthus Most nineteenth century British economists assumed that classical economics had universal application. They thought it could be applied to all countries and to the international economy. Ricardo, in particular, showed how an analysis of a domestic economy could be applied to international economic relationships. He argued that in a laissez-faire environment, international specialization and division of labor between the center (metropolitan countries) and the periphery (satellite countries) was advantageous to both areas. The basic argument in support of this view was embodied in his law of comparative costs under which

> if trade is left free each country in the long run tends to specialize in the production of and to export those commodities in which production it enjoys a comparative advantage in terms of real costs, and to obtain by importation those commodities which could be produced at home only at a comparative disadvantage in terms of real costs, and such specialization is to the mutual advantage of the countries participating in it. (Viner 1937, p. 438).

The *law of comparative costs* is the principle which explains that people of different countries benefit from the free flow of goods and services. It explains that the main determinant for trade is not an absolute cost advantage, but a comparative cost advantage between countries.

Assume only the United States and the United Kingdom are engaged in trade, and these two countries produce only two commodities, wheat and cloth. Assume also that the United States can produce wheat and cloth cheaper than the United Kingdom, and the difference between American and British costs is greater for wheat than for cloth, as follows:

	Cloth	Wheat
U.K.	130	120
U.S.	110	60

Although the United Kingdom has an absolute advantage in neither good, it does have a comparative advantage in cloth. The United Kingdom would benefit by specializing in the production and export of cloth. Conversely, the United States would be better off to concentrate on wheat.

Moreover, Ricardo and his followers showed how Smith's concepts of economic growth could be applied to the international economic system. They suggested that under free enterprise conditions, capital flows into areas where it is most needed. The classical model assumed that international investment "leads to the movement of capital from countries where its marginal value productivity is low to countries where it is high, and thus tends to exercise an 'equalizing effect' throughout the world inducing a rise in the world's capital resources, thereby acting as an accelerator in boosting world's real income" (Clairmonte 1960, pp. 163–64).

In contrast to Smith, Ricardo was a pessimist, and he was often concerned with the limits to growth, finding them in the finite quantity of available land for agriculture. As we saw in chapter 2, Ricardo reasoned that the most fertile land is always put to use first, and that less favored land, which yields less, is put to use as demand for agricultural products increases. Eventually a unit of land is reached that just repays the cost of production. As the extensive "margin" of cultivation is approached, production costs increase and profits fall. Ricardo relied heavily on the law of diminishing returns to show how the economic surplus would eventually become zero, and the economy would enter a dismal stationary state with expansion at an end. He did not ignore technical improvements, but thought they would offset diminishing returns only temporarily.

Malthus also considered limits to growth and introduced the problem of population into economic growth theory. He assumed that unchecked population increases at a geometric rate (2,4,8,16), but food production increases only arithmetically (2,4,6,8). On the basis of this proposition, he concluded that for a population living in a specific region and drawing food supplies therefrom, the law of diminishing returns eventually reduces productivity per head. Diminishing per capita production continues until a new equilibrium is established. Excess population is removed by what Malthus termed the positive checks of disease, famine, and war. He also admitted that there is an escape from the deadly equilibrium: moral restraint before and after marriage. He did believe, however, that if population growth is restrained in the real world, the process of capitalist accumulation could continue uninterrupted. Indeed, throughout the nineteenth century, food production did increase faster than population in Europe and North America as a result of the intensification and extension of capitalism.

Marx's Vision of Capitalist Development In the face of persistent working class poverty in nineteenth century Britain, Marx (1818–83) challenged laissez-faire economists who assumed that the capitalist system combines factors of production in an optimal fashion, and that the economy works in the best interests of everyone. Like Ricardo, Marx believed that capitalism was doomed, but to him the progress of expanding capitalism would be checked by forces endogenous to the system itself, not by exogenous constraints such as finite land. Marx's argument was on three levels: moral (injustices of capitalism), sociological (class conflict), and economic (accumulation of capital in private hands leading to economic abundance and the breakdown of capitalism). At each level of his discussion, conflict is emphasized. Out of conflict comes change, and change is a dialectical process by which socialism was to replace capitalism. Marx believed that change had an economic basis in the class division of society into workers and capitalists. He said that conflict between workers and capitalists would build until the fabric of society was torn asunder by revolution.

Marx's evolutionary model of the tendencies of capitalist development begins with a labor theory of value and ends with the doctrine of periodic business crises, unemployment, class conflict, and transition to socialism (figure 7.1). Marx noted that the value of a good is determined by the amount of socially necessary labor embodied in it. In a precapitalist society, relative values of commodities are readily calculated. If good A entails 10 hours of labor and good B 20 hours, then B has twice the value of A; that is, the two goods can be traded at the rates of 2A : 1B. In such a society, all exchange is of equivalent value.

In a capitalistic society, on the other hand, surplus value is created. Marx asked: how can one class of people, capitalists, get something for nothing? How do they acquire a portion of produced value for themselves without contributing any labor in return? Marx said that labor is a commodity, and its value is determined in just the same way as the value of any other commodity—by the amount of socially necessary labor required to produce it, which is nothing more than a worker's subsistence wage. For example, if a laborer has to work six hours to obtain a subsistence income, then that is the socially necessary amount of labor producing a worker. Suppose a worker in a factory has to work 12 hours instead of six hours to gain a job. In this case, Marx said the worker creates surplus value for the capitalist. He works six hours for himself, and another six hours for his master, and the rate of surplus value is six hours divided by six hours, or 100 percent.

Worker exploitation can be intensified and the surplus value appropriated by the capitalist increased by stretching the working day. If the work week were stabilized, an employer could expand surplus value by substituting capital for labor. The gains of an employer are short-lived, however. His competitors imitate his method of production. His rate of surplus value is driven down to its former level. The capitalist is back where he started. He is compelled to introduce more labor-saving

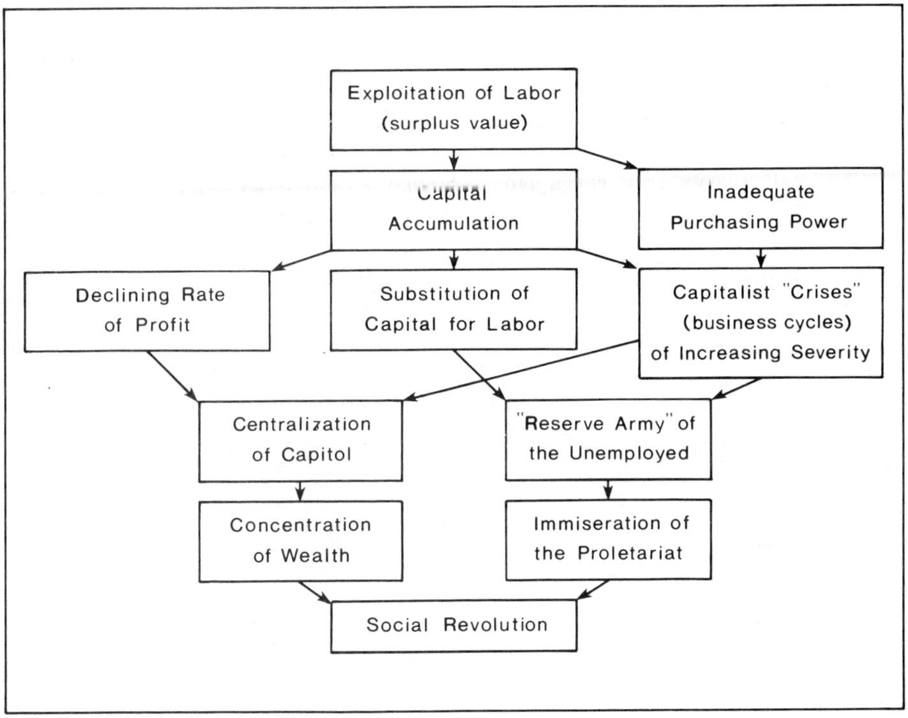

FIGURE 7.1 Model of Marx's theory of capitalist development. [From Daniel R. Fusfield (1966), *The Age of the Economist*, p. 58, fig. 1. Copyright © 1966 by Scott, Foresman and Company. Reprinted by permission.]

machinery and the cycle begins again. Marx argued that the process of introducing even more labor-saving equipment is inimical to workers. Displaced laborers form a "reserve army" of the unemployed, which keeps wages at minimal levels.

The essence of Marx's theory is that the engine that drives economic growth is capital accumulation. Economic growth is always unbalanced. The capitalist mode of production fails to achieve equilibrium because of the contradictory nature of competitive production. As a result, there are short-run cyclical crises (unemployment and declining rates of profit) that are corrected by increasing rates of accumulation through concentration (the trend toward larger, more efficient factories in each industry) and geographical extension (imperialism). Marx argued that periodic crises become more frequent and catastrophic over time. In each crisis big capitalists devour little capitalists, and individual capitalism becomes monopoly capitalism. Capitalists seek larger output and bigger profits, and they deploy bigger and better machines that replace more and more workers. The misery of workers intensifies and conditions ripen for the movement from capitalism to socialism which, according to Marx, is a higher stage of historical evolution. Thus the search for surplus value through labor exploitation leads to the growth, stagnation, and demise of capitalism.

Marxists and Imperialism Like most classical economists, Marx had little to say about underdeveloped countries. He regarded them as extensions of the capitalist core (Europe-North America) and thought that their destiny was to trace the path mapped out by modern industrial nations. World events have not supported his prediction regarding urban-industrialization in underdeveloped countries.

In the early twentieth century, Marxist writers had much more to say about underdeveloped countries. Rosa Luxemburg and Lenin elaborated theories of imperialism that explain how capitalism in the age of monopoly must find new space for continued expansion. Luxemburg argued that consumption cannot increase in a closed capitalist system and thus accumulation is impossible. She argued that the invasion of underdeveloped countries by capitalism kept the system alive. She described the "manner in which the capitalist system, by trade, conquest, and theft, swallowed up the precapitalist economies,—some reduced to colonies of capitalist nations, some remaining nominally independent—and fed itself upon their ruins" (Robinson 1951, p. 26). As Joan Robinson has said, "Few would deny that the extension of capitalism into new territories was the mainspring of . . . the 'vast secular boom' of the last two hundred years, and many academic economists account for the uneasy condition of capitalism in the twentieth century largely by the 'closing of the frontier' all over the world" (1951, p. 28).

In recent years, neo-Marxists have shown how an intensifying and expanding industrial capitalism integrated societies unevenly into a single net of world market and resource exploitation (Baran and Sweezy 1966; Frank 1970; Arrighi and Saul 1973; and Poulantzas 1975). They give special attention to a complement to the theory of imperialism. It is a theory of dependence, which considers effects of imperialism on underdeveloped countries. "Dependence" means a conditioning situation in which the economies of one group of countries are conditioned by the development and expansion of others.

Schumpeter and the End of Capitalism Schumpeter (1883–1950), a lifelong believer in capitalism, did not think capitalism would survive. In his major works, he emphasized that entrepreneurs and their innovations are the principal sources of growth and change. He did not think the Great Depression of the 1930s meant the failure of capitalism. The Great Depression indicated that the world capitalist system was in a long wave of bad times and that good times would return just as soon as innovations and technological change turned the wave upward once more. He believed in the effectiveness of capitalism in producing and distributing goods and services for all. He even thought that by 1978 capitalism could eliminate poverty in the United States, but in the process several features of capitalism would become apparent. The first characteristic is the disappearance of the entrepreneur. Technology and organization of large-scale production are important innovations of capitalism leading to big business and monopolistic markets. The second characteristic is the alienation of thinkers, writers, and teachers from adherence to the sytem. They criticize the faults of capitalism and create a climate of opinion antagonistic to capitalistic ways of life. The third characteristic is government intervention directed toward the faults of the economy—inequality of development, subsidizing agriculture, smoothing out the trade cycle. Entrepreneurial freedom of action is reduced. These three characteristics hinder the growth of the economy, and the system collapses as intellectuals predicted. Schumpeter concluded that capitalism would eventually be replaced by socialism.

Keynes and the Fall of Economic Liberalism The heyday of economic liberalism was the period 1850–1875 when Britain virtually succeeded in controlling world economy. Economic liberalism was agreeable to British conditions only after Britain became the "workshop of the world" and her industries were in no fear of foreign competition. But British hegemony was short-lived. Britain's competitive status was shaken after the onset of a world economic crisis in the 1870s. As a consequence, liberalism was gradually abandoned. The retreat of British liberalism can be explained superficially by the international trade practices of other powers, particularly Germany and the United States. More than any other factor, however, the drift from individual capitalism to monopoly capitalism made the idea of a laissez-faire economic environment untenable. Not until the world depression of the 1930s did economic liberalism come to be rejected, and not until the acceptance of Keynes' *General Theory* did the belief that the economic system was self-regulating come to be discredited.

Keynes' general theory is an analysis of the causes of unemployment. He argued that employment depends on the level of national production, which is governed by the volume of demand for consumer goods and the volume of private and public investments. He introduced the concept of equilibrium at less than full employment, which may be explained as follows: a decline in total spending caused by reduced investment reduces incomes, which in turn causes savings to decline until the desire to save is brought into balance with the desire to invest. Keynes did not think that a modern capitalist economy could sustain a high enough level of investment to maintain full employment. He advocated government control of the level of economic activity in the national interest, but he advised that the economy in general be left free to respond to the decisions of welfare-maximizing consumers and profit-maximizing producers.

Keynes presented an alternative to socialism for the nations of Western Europe and North America. His theory, which permitted government to borrow and spend the proceeds to cure an economic depression, did not amend the neoclassical paradigm to any great degree. It was designed less to alter the market exchange economies than to preserve and revitalize them. Keynesian economics became the economic mainstream until the 1970s when state capitalism appeared incapable of dealing with the twin problems of inflation and high unemployment.

In this section we have sketched the development of the world's political economy. We have reviewed the theories and visions of such giants as Smith, Marx, and Keynes. Few geographical ideas were treated. The reader may well ask: what is the purpose of learning about what was said and done before the present in a geography text on the economic landscape? The section will have served its purpose if it helps the student to understand that the development of the world's spatial economy has been a reflection of its political economy. Thus, it is not surprising that we found in Part 1 a good deal of correspondence between classical location models and reality. In the past 200 years, the dominant model for the spatial organization of North America has been free-enterprise capitalism. The pursuit of private profit has been the major force underlying the economic growth of the United States.

Directions of Economic Change

Measurements of Economic Activity

The Keynesian emphasis on the management of economies by governments required a reliable device for measuring the aggregate performance of a national economy. Most market economies now use income or product indices to measure levels of economic activity. The most familiar values are: (1) *Gross Domestic Product (GDP),* the total output of goods and services of an economy; (2) *Gross National Product (GNP),* that portion of GDP that stays at home; and (3) *Net National Product (NNP),* GNP less capital consumption allowances. Where comparisons need to be made between nations or regions, GDP per capita, which is regarded as the most important measurement of economic welfare available, is often used. The reason GDP per capita is better than total GDP is obvious; an increase in GDP over time may not mean very much if population has increased more rapidly.

Table 7.1 is an example of the use of GDP statistics and shows the enormous disparity between developed capitalist countries and underdeveloped countries. In 1969, about 650 million people in the industrial West produced six times the wealth generated by 1,550 million inhabitants of the underdeveloped world. The wealth produced by the United States alone was more than two and one-half times greater than the combined gross national products of Africa, Asia, and Latin America which had eight times the population of the United States. There is also inequality within the underdeveloped world: in 1969 Asia had a GDP of $129 billion for over a billion people; Africa, $66 billion for 310 million people; and Latin America, $137 billion for 235 million people.

TABLE 7.1 Gross domestic product at factor cost (in billions of U. S. dollars)

Region	1963	1965	1967	1969
Industrial West and underdeveloped world	1394	1649	1914	2271
Industrial West	1168	1385	1616	1914
United States	596	692	804	930
Underdeveloped world	226	264	298	357
Latin America	80	93	113	137
Africa	43	50	56	66
Asia (except Middle East)	89	104	109	129

Source: United Nations, *Yearbook of the Statistics of National Accounts,* New York, 1970.

However well income or product indices may seem to reflect international disparities, their use should be treated with caution. They hide the ways in which available income is distributed between individuals or places. There are also variations in the ways countries assess their indices. Centrally planned economies, for example, measure only material product, thereby excluding the contribution of services such as commerce and public transportation. Further, it is virtually impossible to assess the output of the indigenous sector in underdeveloped countries. Indeed, figures for underdeveloped countries are very crude and subject to wide margins of error. As an additional point, the use of product indices is misleading if the purpose is to measure society's well-being. They include the production, consumption, and discard of all environmentally harmful goals; they include, for example, the cleaning and health bills that result from pollution (Boulding 1970). Some economists advocate the use of a new indicator, Gross National Quality (GNQ). In theory, this would entail subtracting all undesirable effects from GNP. In other words, GNQ ("goods") = GNP ("goods" and "bads") − "bads." Irrespective of all these arguments, product indices provide a useful first approximation of differences in national or regional living standards.

Some researchers have placed more weight on narrower, but more accurate indices, such as per capita consumption of energy or steel. These indices, it is said, give reasonable measures of industrialization and hence levels of economic growth. Other investigators have combined sets of indices, each defining an aspect of the interlocked socioeconomic structure of nations. Berry (1960), after obtaining 43 indices for 95 countries, collapsed them into a synthetic scale of development using principal components analysis (figure 7.2 and box). By calculating component scores for each country, Berry was able to portray, on a single map, a world pattern of economic development (figure 7.3).

The use of single or multiple measures contrasting the wealth of nations gives a static image of world development. Since the pattern is always changing, comparisons ignoring time may be of limited value. Consequently, economists have devoted much effort to investigating the direction of change in international and interregional living standards. They wonder whether rich countries or regions are growing richer and the poor, poorer. Let us look at evidence from historical trends and from econometric models of growth to see if we can decide whether differences are increasing or decreasing.

Empirical Evidence

Comparisons of cross-national living standards are difficult to make for the period before the Industrial Revolution in the European-North American region. For the most recent past, the task is easier. Calculations by Patel (1964) led to the conclusion that developed countries now contribute much more as a proportion to the total world income than previously. He calculated that the proportion increased from 35 percent in 1850 to 78 percent in 1960. If current trends continue, developed countries will contribute an even greater proportion to total world income. Futurologists Kahn and Wiener (1967), who estimated that world income per capita would double by the year 2000, have predicted that the existing gap between the developed and the underdeveloped world will widen from the present ratio of 12:1 to around 18:1.

The disparity in income between the developed and the underdeveloped world is not just enormous, but becoming larger. One conclusion follows: underdeveloped

Principal components analysis is a multivariate statistical method that is widely used in geographical analysis. It involves an orthogonal transformation of a set of highly interconnected variables into a new set of independent variables or components. The first component explains a large proportion of the variance, followed by components that account for decreasing percentages of the variance.

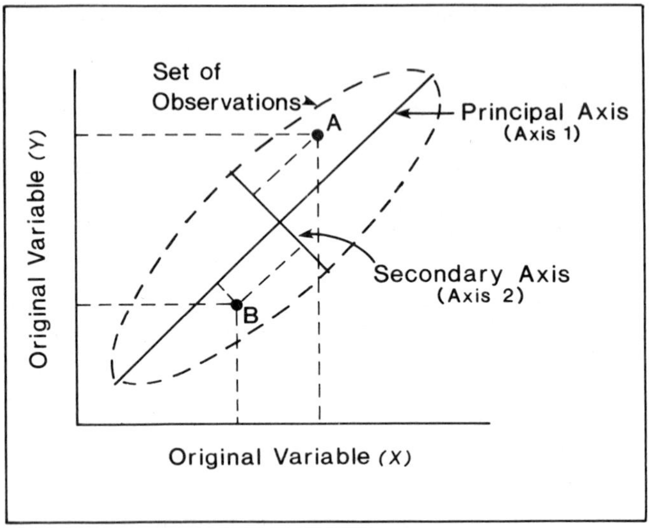

To illustrate the idea of collapsing a set of intercorrelated variables into a smaller number of composite variables, consider a simple case of two variables (X and Y) describing the characteristics of two countries (A and B). The elliptical area encloses the cluster of points for all other countries considered in the analysis. Matrix algebra permits the identification of a principal axis. The principal axis (Axis 1) is a new variable explaining more of the original variance than a second new variable (Axis 2) at right angles to it. Countries A and B may now be described in terms of the first component (Axis 1) rather than the two original variables (X and Y). For a good nontechnical introduction to principal component analysis see P. R. Gould (1967), "On the Geographic Interpretation of Eigenvalues," *Transactions of the Institute for British Geographers* **42**, 53–86.

countries, even those with rates of growth faster than the developed countries, will not be able to close the relative gap in income per capita. Myint illustrated this point with some simple arithmetic. Assume a

> . . . developed country with a per capita income of $1,000 and an underdeveloped country with a per capita income of $100, both growing at the same rate, say 2 percent per annum. The initial gap is $900. Next year, the per capita income of the developed country rises to $1,020 while the per capita income of the underdeveloped country rises to $102—thus resulting in a widening gap of $918. (Myint 1964, p. 18)

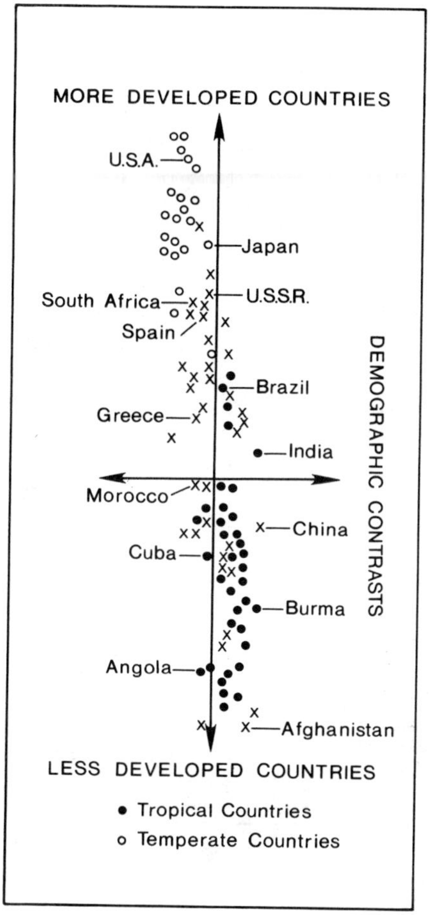

FIGURE 7.2 The distribution of countries on economic and demographic scales. [After Norton Ginsburg (1961), *Atlas of Economic Development*, Chicago: University of Chicago Press, p. 113, fig. 3. © 1961 by the University of Chicago.]

Data in table 7.2 indicate that the gap between developed and underdeveloped countries is greater than the hypothetical example given by Myint.

Contrasting explanations of the widening gap have been advanced by social scientists who have studied evidence from historical trends. Western writers have suggested two main reasons. One is that underdeveloped countries are unable to escape the "low income equilibrium trap." They are caught in a closed cycle of poverty or limiting factors characterized by low output, low incomes, low demand levels, low savings, low investment, and hence capital deficiency leading to low output (figure 7.4). The other reason is that underdeveloped countries are at an earlier, though "natural" stage of development.

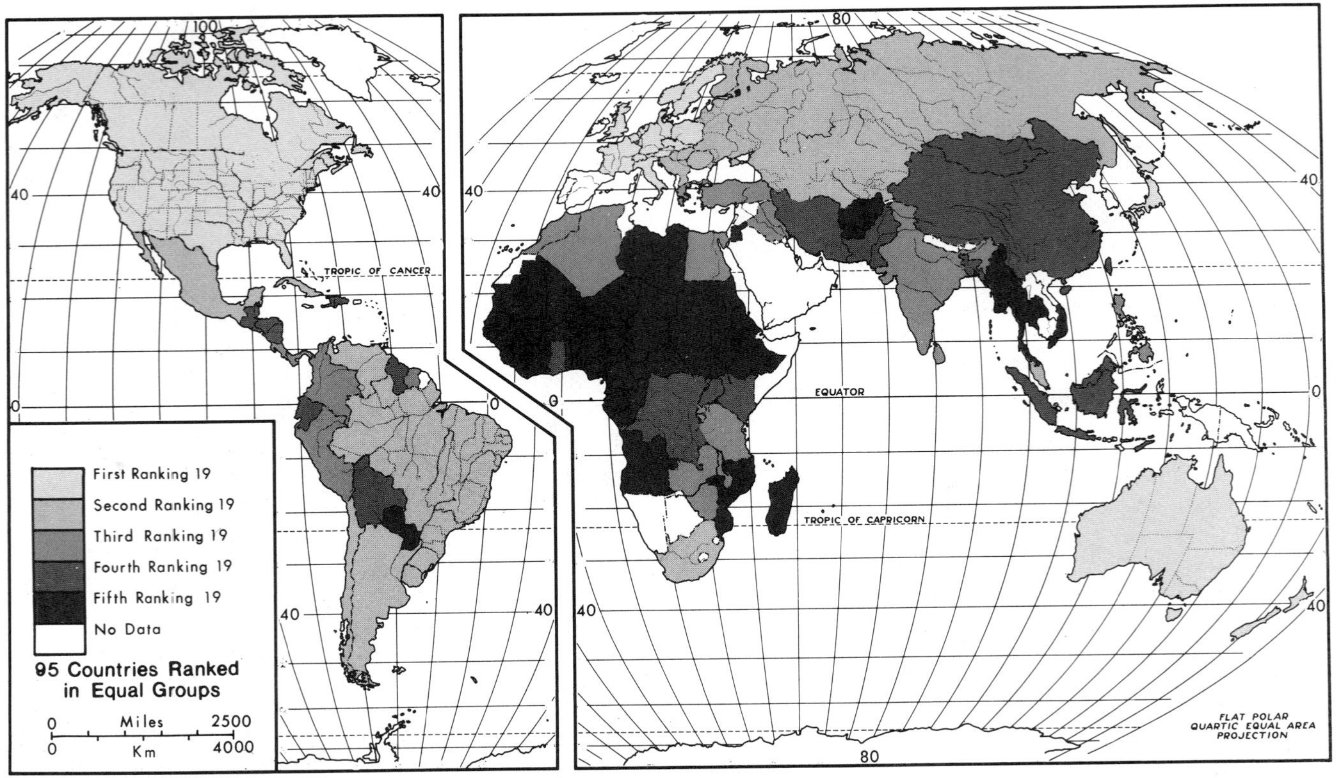

FIGURE 7.3 The world pattern of economic development based on 43 indices. [From Norton Ginsburg (1961), *Atlas of Economic Development*, Chicago: University of Chicago Press, p. 111, fig. 1. © 1961 by the University of Chicago.]

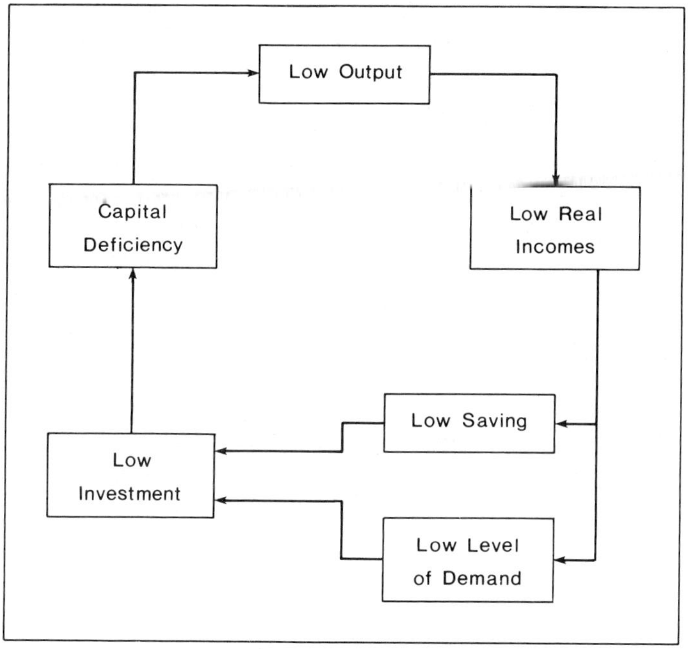

FIGURE 7.4 Closed cycle of poverty.

TABLE 7.2 Per capita national product (1968) and average annual growth rates (1961–1968)

Country	GNP Per Capita (U.S. $)	GNP Per Capita Growth Rates (%)
Developed countries:		
United States	3,980	3.4
United Kingdom	1,790	2.0
West Germany	1,970	3.4
Japan	1,190	9.9
South American countries:		
Brazil	250	1.6
Argentina	820	1.0
Colombia	310	1.4
Peru	380	3.5
Venezuela	950	1.4
Chile	480	1.8
Ecuador	220	1.2
Bolivia	150	1.8
Uruguay	520	−1.4
Paraguay	230	1.3

Source: *World Bank Atlas,* The World Bank, Washington, D. C., 1970.
Note: Only South American countries with populations of one million or more are included. It must be stressed that many of these data of GNP per capita at factor cost are approximate at best. Additional details are provided in the source cited.

Other social scientists, particularly those from underdeveloped countries, disagree with these explanations. According to them, underdevelopment "is the product of a *specific development,* which is most closely connected with, moreover derived from the development of (the) capitalist world economy" (Szentes 1971, p. 132). This observation emphasizes that developed and underdeveloped countries are on opposite sides of a single worldwide system. Thus, peripheral underdeveloped nations are dominated to a large extent by a huge macrometropolitan center, which is Europe-North America. Study of table 7.3 showing changing world energy production, flows, and consumption reinforces the image of Europe-North America as the all-consuming sink.

TABLE 7.3 World energy: production, trade and consumption

World and Region	Year	Production/Trade Million Metric Tons (Coal Equivalent)		Consumption Per Capita Metric Tons
		Total Production	Import/Export	
World	1955	3,298	−15[1]	1.29
	1960	4,311	−27	1.41
	1965	5,324	−38	1.59
	1970	7,000	−74	1.89
	1974	8,621	−668	2.05
Anglo-America	1955	1,320	+57	6.37
	1960	1,441	+118	7.80
	1965	1,767	+151	9.06
	1970	2,260	+184	10.94
	1974	2,388	+267	11.32
Western Europe	1955	571	+184	2.52
	1960	563	+284	2.57
	1965	574	+527	3.05
	1970	557	+853	3.78
	1974	625	+914	4.28
Oceania	1955	25	+14	2.86
	1960	31	+15	2.95
	1965	42	+20	3.63
	1970	71	+11	4.03
	1974	109	−15	4.54
Gulf-Caribbean	1955	190	−136	n.d.
	1960	263	−180	0.89
	1965	317	−222	0.99
	1970	357	−217	1.12
	1974	361	−188	1.25
Southern America	1955	19	+29	0.56
	1960	34	+28	0.51
	1965	49	+28	0.58
	1970	70	+36	0.71
	1974	103	+44	0.84

TABLE 7.3 (continued)

World and Region	Year	Production/Trade Million Metric Tons (Coal Equivalent)		Consumption Per Capita Metric Tons
		Total Production	Import/Export	
Middle East	1955	216	−182	n.d.
	1960	351	−301	0.26
	1965	555	−497	0.35
	1970	942	−856	0.78
	1974	1,668	−1,548	1.03
South and East Asia	1955	121	+25	0.22
	1960	165	+55	0.24
	1965	199	+146	0.32
	1970	242	+354	0.48
	1974	310	+367	0.67
Africa	1955	38	+16	0.26
	1960	58	+7	0.31
	1965	197	−101	0.32
	1970	450	−337	0.31
	1974	483	−343	0.40
Centrally planned economies [2]	1955	798	−21	0.85
	1960	1,406	−53	1.28
	1965	1,623	−90	1.45
	1970	2,051	−102	1.69
	1974	2,576	−167	1.99

Source: United Nations *Statistical Yearbook,* New York, 1955, 1956, 1960, 1961, 1965, 1966, 1970, 1971, 1975.

[1] The negative figures for world totals refer to energy in transit.

[2] Eastern Europe, China (except Taiwan), North Korea, North Vietnam and U.S.S.R.

Note: *Production data* are a summation of all major inanimate fuel and energy sources. These include coal, lignite, crude petroleum, natural gas, and hydro- and nuclear electricity; where peat used as fuel is important, it is included with coal and lignite. *Consumption data* are based on the apparent consumption of coal, lignite, petroleum products, natural gas and hydro- and nuclear electricity. Coke, manufactured gas, and electricity internationally traded are considered to have been consumed by the importing country. Comparison between coal and other sources of energy is based on a conversion to equivalent metric tons of high grade bituminous coal. The first column refers to a region's production, the second column refers to the region's import/export balance. A positive figure means that the region imports so much in addition to its own production. A negative figure means that the region exports that amount of its production to other parts of the world.

Are disparities increasing or decreasing within individual countries? Evidence seems to indicate that regional income differences are widening in many underdeveloped countries (Williamson 1965). In Canada only a small amount of convergence occurred between 1890 and 1956 (Green 1969). In post-World War II Britain there has been very little convergence despite a strong regional equalization policy (Richardson 1969). On the other hand, income data for the United States show a marked convergence trend between 1880 and 1950 (Easterlin 1960). Nonetheless, the convergence process has fluctuated and actually reversed itself in

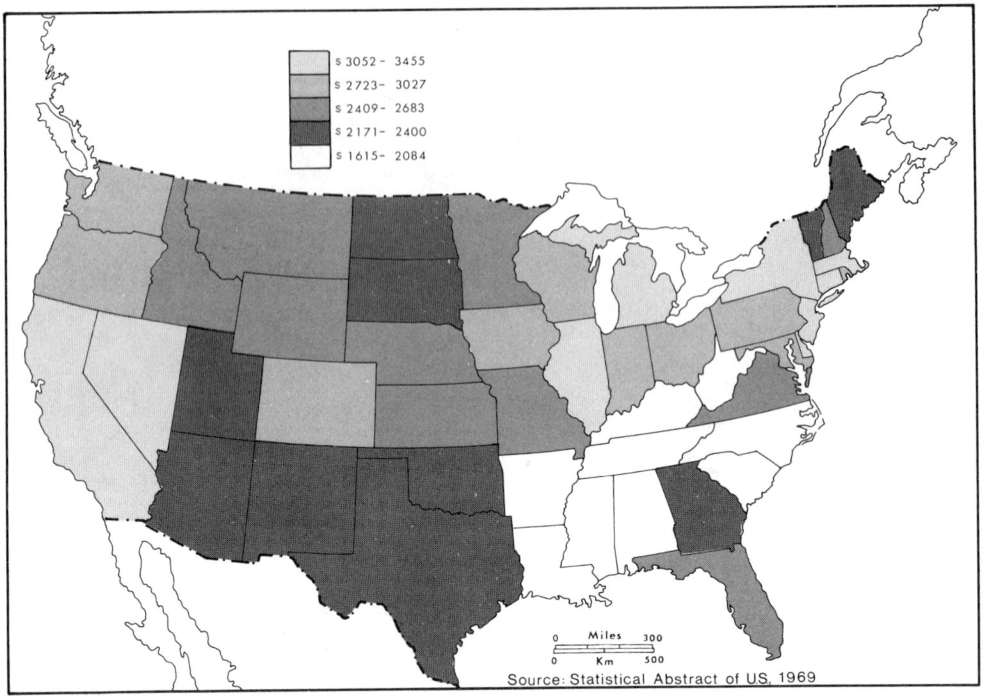

A

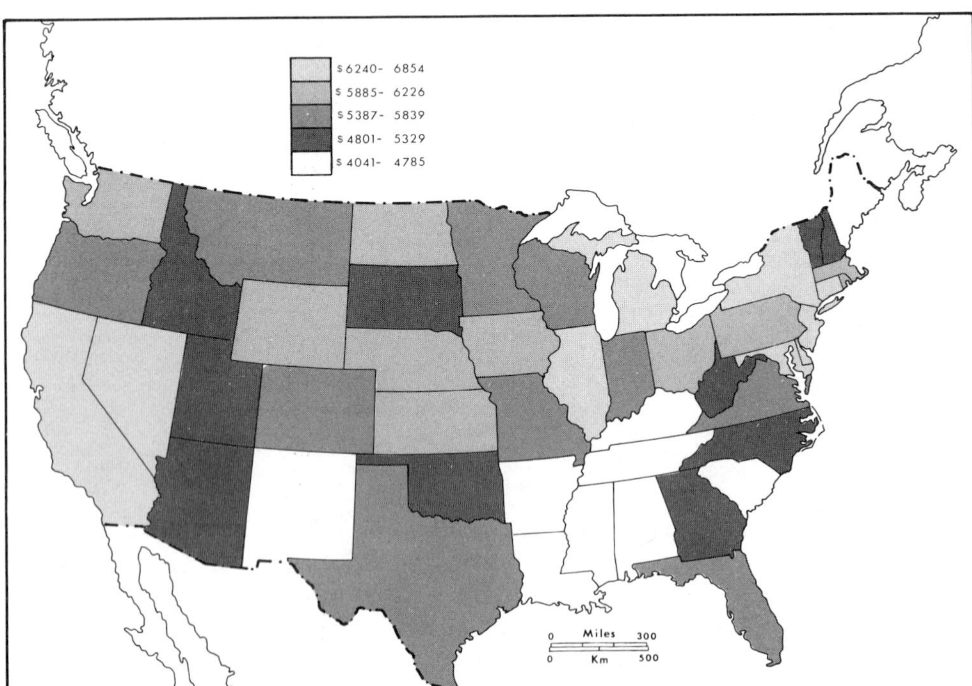

B

FIGURE 7.5 Per capita income, United States. (Source: *Statistical Abstract of U.S.*, 1976.)

the 1920s. Figure 7.5 indicates that convergence is far from complete in the United States and that the relative position of states by per capita income changed little between 1965 (A) and 1975 (B).

Theoretical Evidence

Two theoretical models, the Harrod-Domar and neoclassical approaches to the analysis of regional growth, disagree on the direction of movement. Their predictions are worth presenting. Both models are highly quantitative and contain very little realism. They shed light on variations in regional economic activity for wealthy, mature economies, but they say virtually nothing about how growth is initiated in a national economy. They assume that regions are homogeneous; that is, they ignore spatial differences within regions.

R. F. Harrod proposed a growth model in 1939 and E. Domar proposed an unrelated but similar model in 1946. The two models are usually discussed together as the Harrod-Domar model of growth. The theoretical assumptions of the model are a constant propensity to save, fixed coefficients in production, and a constant rate of growth. Additional assumptions are a single-good economy, constant returns to scale, and no technical progress. The model proposed for national growth analysis can be adopted for a regional system by taking into account interregional movements of capital and labor. For a good description of the Harrod-Domar model see H. W. Richardson (1969), *Elements of Regional Economics*, London: Penguin, pp. 47–50.

The conflict of predictions between these two econometric models is a consequence of their different assumptions. The main difference between the neoclassical model, based on traditional economic theory, and the Harrod-Domar model, based on Keynesian concepts, is that neoclassicism implies a theory of factor mobility (the possibility of substitution between capital and labor). The Harrod-Domar model *does not* contain an automatic equilibrating mechanism. Table 7.4 shows the prediction of the two regional growth models. The Harrod-Domar model predicts that interregional growth leads to divergence. Fast-growing

TABLE 7.4 Predictions of Harrod-Domar and neoclassical regional growth models

	Characteristics of Fast-Growing Regions			
Model	Level of Income	Direction of Labor	Direction of Capital	Interregional Growth
Harrod-Domar	High	Inward	Inward	Divergence
Neoclassical	Low	Outward	Inward	Convergence

Data from H. W. Richardson (1969), *Elements of Regional Economics*, London: Penguin, p. 58, table 2.

regions will have higher income levels than other regions, and they will attract a net inward movement of capital and labor. By contrast, the traditional neoclassical model suggests that the pattern of regional growth in a free market leads to convergence of regional per capita income. Fast-growing regions will have lower income levels than other regions, attract a net inward movement of capital, and experience a net outward movement of labor.

Stages of Growth Models

Historical interpretations of economic growth are represented by stages or transition models. In the last quarter-century, transition models have excited an immense amount of interest among scholars including geographers. They evolved in response to the quickening pace of world economic expansion and integration, the collapse of colonial power structures, the emergence of new social systems, and the Cold War.

Major characteristics of stages-of-growth models may be summarized as follows:

1. *Model of economic growth*. The study of economic growth has been dominated by measurements of national economic performance. A basic assumption is that material productivity is an indicator of economic welfare. This idea of progress is not a scientific concept; it is a value judgment.
2. *Conceptualizing the modern economy*. For a model of economic growth, it was necessary to fix a beginning and an end to the process. The influential ideas come from the nineteenth and early twentieth century economists, sociologists, and social philosophers who proposed ideal polarities—barter and credit, sacred and secular, organic and mechanical—which can be subsumed under the more general traditional-modern dichotomy. Table 7.5 provides a good summary of the polar distinctions between traditional (pre-industrial) and modern (urban-industrial) society. The stimulus for these polarities was provided by the history of English urbanization and industrialization.
3. *Evolutionary Schema*. An evolutionary rationale is implicit in studies examining the process of transformation from traditional to modern. It is assumed that the path of change is a unitary process governed by the linear laws of history.
4. *Achieving development*. A major idea is the transition from tradition to modernity. Study of the transitional phase has focused on identifying and analyzing the circumstances and consequences of change. The transition has been treated either with a negative emphasis in terms of removing obstacles to development, or with a positive emphasis of creating the cultural environment necessary for development.
5. *Elites*. The role of elites is considered crucial for the evolution of a modern economic society. Leadership groups—political, bureaucratic, entrepreneurial, intellectual, and military—are charged with the responsibility of providing the conditions needed for "take-off."

We begin with an examination of Walt W. Rostow's model of economic growth, the best known and most popular transition model. It has influenced policy formation and has had an all-pervading influence on studies of the process of change.

TABLE 7.5 Polar distinctions between pre-industrial and urban-industrial society[1]

	Pre-Industrial Society	Urban-Industrial Society
Demographic	High mortality, fertility	Low mortality, fertility
Behavioral	Particularistic, prescribed; individual has multiplex roles	Universalistic, instrumental; individual has specialized roles
Societal	Kin-group solidarity, extended family, ethnic cohesion; cleavages between ethnic groups	Atomisation, affiliations secondary; professional influence groups
Economic	Nonmonetary or simple monetary base; local exchange; little infrastructure; craft industries; low specialization	Pecuniary base; national exchange; extensive interdependence; factory production; capital intensive
Political	Nonsecular authority; prescriptive legitimacy; interpersonal communications; traditional bases	Secular polity; elected government; mass media participation; rational bureaucracy
Spatial (geographical)	Parochial relationships; close ties to immediate environment; duplication of socio-spatial groups in a cellular net	Regional and national interdependence; specialized roles based upon major resources and relative location within urban-spatial system.

[1] After B. J. L. Berry (1973), *The Human Consequences of Urbanization*, New York: St. Martin's Press, Inc., Macmillan and Co., Ltd., p. 13, table 1.

Rostow's Historical Scheme

In 1960, the economic historian Rostow published *The Stages of Economic Growth: A Non-Communist Manifesto*. He called his book "an economic historian's way of generalizing the sweep of modern history" (1960, p. 1). He wanted to offer a comprehensive interpretation of development as Marx did. Unlike Marx, however, he argued that the highest stage of evolution is not socialism, but developed capitalism. He developed a deterministic model using long-term data for fifteen countries and outline data for some others. He maintained that as each country develops it passes through a series of comparable stages.

The Stages of Economic Growth Rostow identified five main stages in the unilineal evolution of societies (figure 7.6).

1. *The Traditional Society*. Knowledge of modern technology and science is lacking. Productivity levels are low. At least 75 percent of the population is engaged in food production. Upper classes spend available capital on unproductive ends. Society is conservative, resistant to change, and hierarchically organized: political

power is either in the hands of a land-owning aristocracy or is embodied in a central authority supported by the military and civil servants.

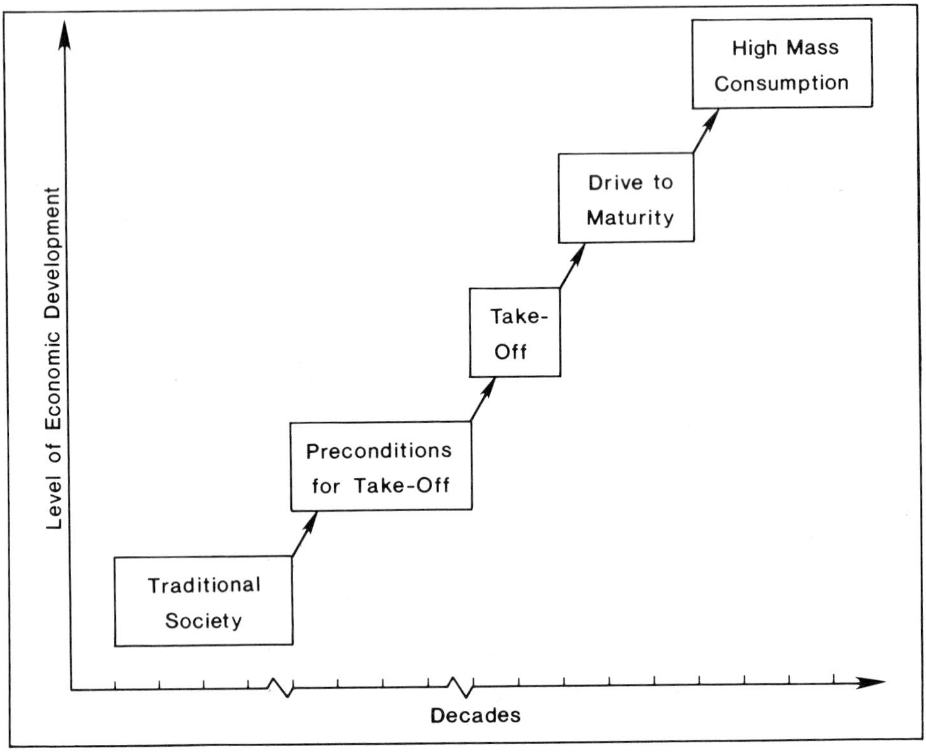

FIGURE 7.6 Rostow's five stages of economic growth.

2. *The Preconditions for Take-Off*. Radical changes overcome obstacles to growth. In general, exogenous influences stimulate the initial growth of productive investment, the installation of roads, railways, and utilities, and the emergence of a new elite. Agriculture surrenders its dominance to secondary and tertiary activities. Society develops a new mentality, a propensity to accept new techniques, and a freedom to operate for a new class of businessmen. People believe that economic growth creates conditions necessary for the attainment of certain goods, greater national power, improved social welfare, and a higher material standard of living. Rostow dated this phase in Western Europe as the seventeenth and eighteenth centuries. In the underdeveloped world, the idea of economic progress came usually with European interventionism and diffused within and through social elites.

3. *The Take-Off Stage*. The crucial third stage marks the "great watershed in the life of modern societies" (Rostow 1960, p. 7). In a critical decade or two the forces making for economic progress expand and dominate society. Growth becomes more or less automatic. The rate of effective investment and savings increases from five percent of national income to over ten percent. One or more substantial manufactur-

ing sectors expand rapidly and they become "leading sectors" of growth. A political, social, and institutional framework emerges quickly, exploiting the impulses to expansion in the modern sector and giving the growth an on-going character. "One can approximately allocate the take-off of Britain to the two decades after 1783; France and the United States to the several decades preceding 1860; Germany, the third quarter of the nineteenth century; Russia and Canada, the quarter century or so preceding 1914; while during the 1950's India and China have, in quite different ways, launched their respective take-offs" (Rostow 1960, p. 9 and figure 7.7).

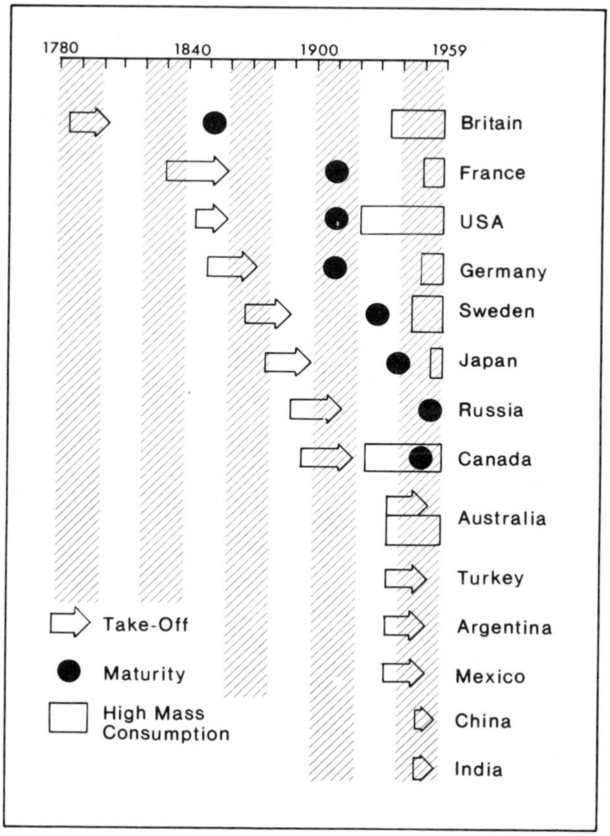

FIGURE 7.7 Stages of economic growth applied to selected countries. [From Walt W. Rostow (1960), *The Stages of Economic Growth: A Non-Communist Manifesto*, Cambridge, England: Cambridge University, p. xii.]

4. *Drive to Maturity*. The society, which becomes a force in the international economy, continues to reallocate for reinvestment a sizeable proportion of national income every year. Growth spreads from leading sectors such as iron, steel, and coal toward machine tools and electronics. Society has the technological skills and the industrial leadership necessary to produce almost anything it chooses to produce.

Historically, Britain completed the drive to maturity by 1850, the United States, Germany, and France 50 years later, and the Soviet Union after World War II.

5. *The Stage of High Mass Consumption.* Leading sectors of a technically and technologically mature society shift toward durable consumer goods and services. Per capita income is so high that a large number of people gain a command over consumption that transcends basic food, shelter, and clothing. They buy automobiles, sewing machines, and electric-powered household gadgets. Urbanization and the proportion of the population working in offices and in skilled factory jobs increase. Society turns its attention to superior objectives such as increased resources allocated to social welfare and security. The United States and Canada achieved this phase by the 1920s, Australia and Britain by 1940, and Germany, Sweden, and Japan after 1945. "The Soviet Union is technically ready for this stage, and, by every sign, its citizens hunger for it; but Communist leaders face difficult political and social problems of adjustment if this stage is launched" (Rostow 1960, p. 11).

Evaluation of Rostow's Model Rostow's model is an interpretation of the industrial revolution of the West. The first two stages are preparatory to the industrial revolution and the last two are its result. The third stage, which can only be inferred from the result of the Industrial Revolution, is the most important phase. Take-off required three conditions: (1) a rise in the rate of production investment from five percent to over ten percent of the national income; (2) the development of one or more substantial manufacturing sectors with a high rate of growth; and (3) the existence or quick emergence of a satisfactory political, social, and institutional framework to ensure continuous growth.

Rostow's model contains an implicit assumption that all countries were roughly equal in economic development initially and, in the course of time, some countries increased their output per head considerably while others lagged behind. It offers underdeveloped countries a way to escape from the "low-level equilibrium trap": if they apply the lessons of the advanced nations and accept a judicious mix of state planning and entrepreneurial laissez-faire capitalism, they will develop their resources to the point where growth becomes a self-sustaining process. The model treats underdeveloped countries as self-contained units that must generate their own transformation. It firmly establishes such phrases in the literature of development as "take-off" and "self-sustaining growth."

Rostow's model has been both very persuasive and heavily criticized. Szentes (1971) examined many of the common complaints concerning the sloppy nature of Rostow's definitions and, in particular, inveighed against Rostow's version of history. Szentes dismissed Rostow's claim that the present state of "backwardness" of underdeveloped countries is an original state or is one of the transitional stages of the natural evolution from the original primitive state toward maturity. He rejected Rostow's argument that the now developed countries were once underdeveloped. Szentes defined the word "underdeveloped" to mean not an initial state, but a condition arrived at through the agency of imperialism, which "sets up an 'internal' structure of underdevelopment" (Frank 1969, p. xxi). He agreed with Frank, who noted that Rostow's model "attributes a history to the developed countries but denies all history to the underdeveloped ones" (1967, p. 37). He considered that Rostow's model is unhistorical from another point of view:

> It simply disregards the historical fact, which by the way is truly reflected by the most typical and specific characteristics of underdeveloped countries, that the economic and political expansion of Europe since the fifteenth century has come to incorporate the now underdeveloped countries into a single stream of world history, which has given rise simultaneously to the present development of some countries and the present underdevelopment of others. (1971, p. 97)

Idealized Model of Transport Development

In the decade of the 1960s, geographers were influenced by Rostow's ideas of viewing growth processes as a series of discrete stages. One example is Taaffe,

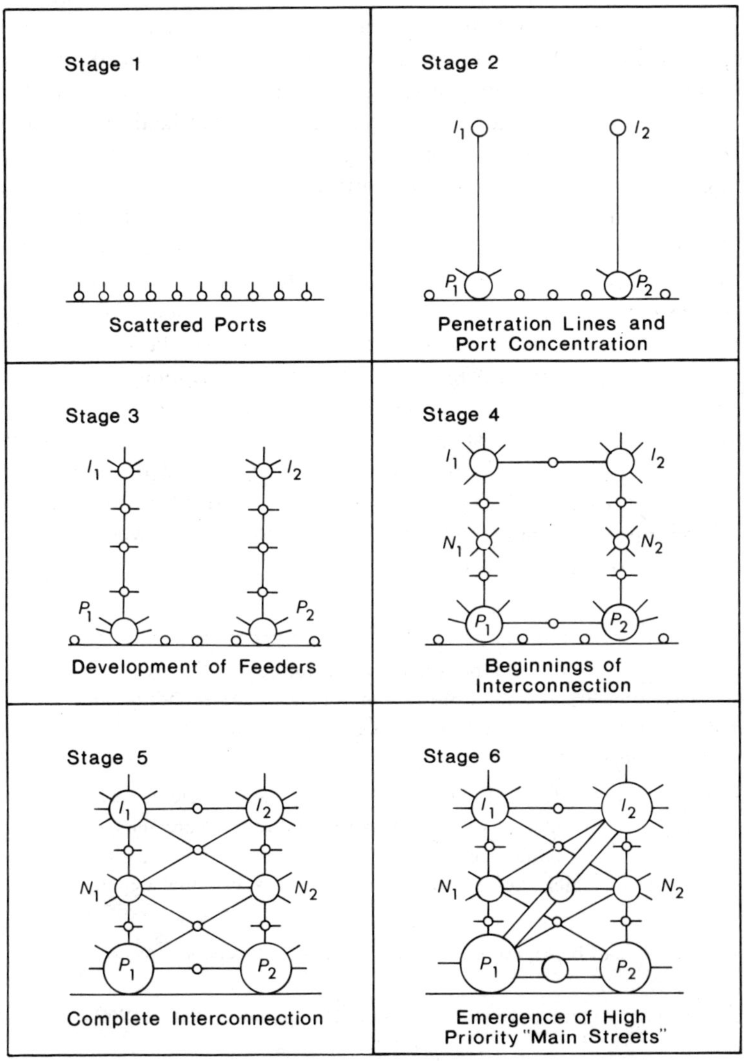

FIGURE 7.8 Model of transport development. [From E. J. Taaffe, R. L. Morrill, and P. R. Gould (1963), "Transport Expansion in Underdeveloped Countries: A Comparative Analysis," *Geographical Review* **53**, 504.]

Morrill, and Gould's (1963) model describing the growth of transport networks. Studies in Nigeria, East Africa, Brazil, and Malaya provided the basis for their model, but it is generally applicable to the United States. They assumed implicitly a macro-region with an unexploited interior. They defined the extension of transport in terms of penetration from the coast. Transport links reflect "1) the desire to connect an administrative center on the sea coast with an interior area of political and military control; 2) the desire to reach areas of mineral exploitation; [and] 3) the desire to reach areas of potential agricultural export production" (1963, p. 506).

The model illustrates through six stages the self-reinforcing interplay between the evolution of a transport network and urban growth (figure 7.8). The ideal-typical sequence begins (stage 1) with a series of small scattered ports along the sea coast. In stage 2, two major lines of penetration, which reduce transport costs, link major ports (P_1 and P_2) and their inland centers (I_1 and I_2). Feeder routes begin to develop and focus on the major ports. Agglomeration economies permit the major ports to expand their hinterlands by capturing the hinterlands of smaller adjacent ports that decline or disappear. In stage 3, feeder routes focus on major ports and inland centers and new urban centers grow at strategic points along the main routes. By stage 4 lateral route development enhances the competitive position of the major ports and inland centers. A few nodes along the original lines of inland penetration, N_1 and N_2 become focal points for feeder networks of their own, and they begin to capture the hinterlands of smaller centers on each side. Eventually a transport network interconnects all the major centers (stage 5). The last stage shows the development of high-priority linkages reinforcing the advantages of urban centers that have come to dominate the economic landscape.

The ideal-typical sequence of transport development illustrates how a space-economy tends to root itself ever more firmly as early locational decisions that shaped the system are reinforced subsequently by others. The result is an increased concentration of economic development and increased polarization between core and peripheral areas of the space-economy (see box below).

The concepts of core-region and periphery were introduced to Western regional analysis by John Friedmann. Core-regions of the space-economy are major centers of innovative change and other areas are defined as peripheral. According to Friedmann:

> . . . core regions are territorially organized subsystems of society which have a high capacity for innovative change; peripheral regions are subsystems whose development path is determined chiefly by core region institutions with respect to which they stand in a relation of substantial dependency.
>
> Peripheral regions can be identified by their relations of dependency to a core area.
>
> Core and periphery together constitute a complete spatial system. (1969, pp. 18–19)

Idealized Model of American Metropolitan Evolution

Borchert (1967), who studied the evolution of the American urban-economic system, also noted that "growth breeds growth" leading to the concentration of economic activity in core-areas of the space-economy. His stage model emphasizes ways in which changes in technology shape the economic landscape. Borchert said:

> Throughout the evolution of the present pattern of American metropolitan areas two factors, great migrations and major changes in technology, have particularly influenced the location of relative growth and decline. Both factors have repeatedly been given specific geographical expression through their relationship to resource patterns. Major changes in technology have resulted in critically important changes in the evaluation or definition of particular resources on which the growth of certain urban regions had previously been based. Great migrations have sought to exploit resources—ranging from climate to coal to water to zinc—that were newly appreciated or newly accessible within the national market. Usually . . . the new appreciation or accessibility has come about, in turn, through some major technological innovation. (1967, p. 324)

Borchert identified four epochs in American metropolitan growth separated by changes in technology considered important in the location of urban development.

1. Sail-Wagon Epoch, 1790–1830. Large American cities were ports along the northeastern seaboard (figure 7.9). Despite the destruction of formal colonial ties in 1776, port cities remained mercantile centers linking European countries with sources of raw materials. The largest cities, New York, Boston, Philadelphia, and Baltimore, were roughly the same size, but New York, with its middle location along the Atlantic strip and better location with respect to inland waterways, began to emerge as the national metropolis after 1825.

2. Iron-Horse Epoch, 1830–1870. The railroad induced major changes. It linked the coast with the interior west of the Appalachians. New York strengthened its position as the dominant center in the urban system. Inland rail and processing centers such as Cincinnati, Pittsburgh, Chicago, and St. Louis grew rapidly. Figures 7.10 and 7.11 show the diffusion of settlement and the differential growth of urban centers between 1830 and 1870.

3. Steel-Rail Epoch, 1879–1920. By 1870, the heartland-dominated structure of the American space-economy emerged. In succeeding decades differences between the heartland and other parts of the space-economy increased (figure 7.12). The hallmark of this epoch was the rapid expansion of manufacturing in heartland cities that had initial advantages of good locations with respect to agricultural and mineral resources.

4. Auto-Air-Amenity Epoch, 1920–present. In this epoch the internal combustion engine revolutionized transport and a steady shift to service employment occurred. Much new employment growth took place in the heartland, where there were already large concentrations of people to be served. Urban growth spread around heartland cities. The increased demand for amenity resources stimulated the rapid growth of cities in the Sunbelt states, but the tendency toward decentralization has had a modest impact on America's heartland-hinterland structure.

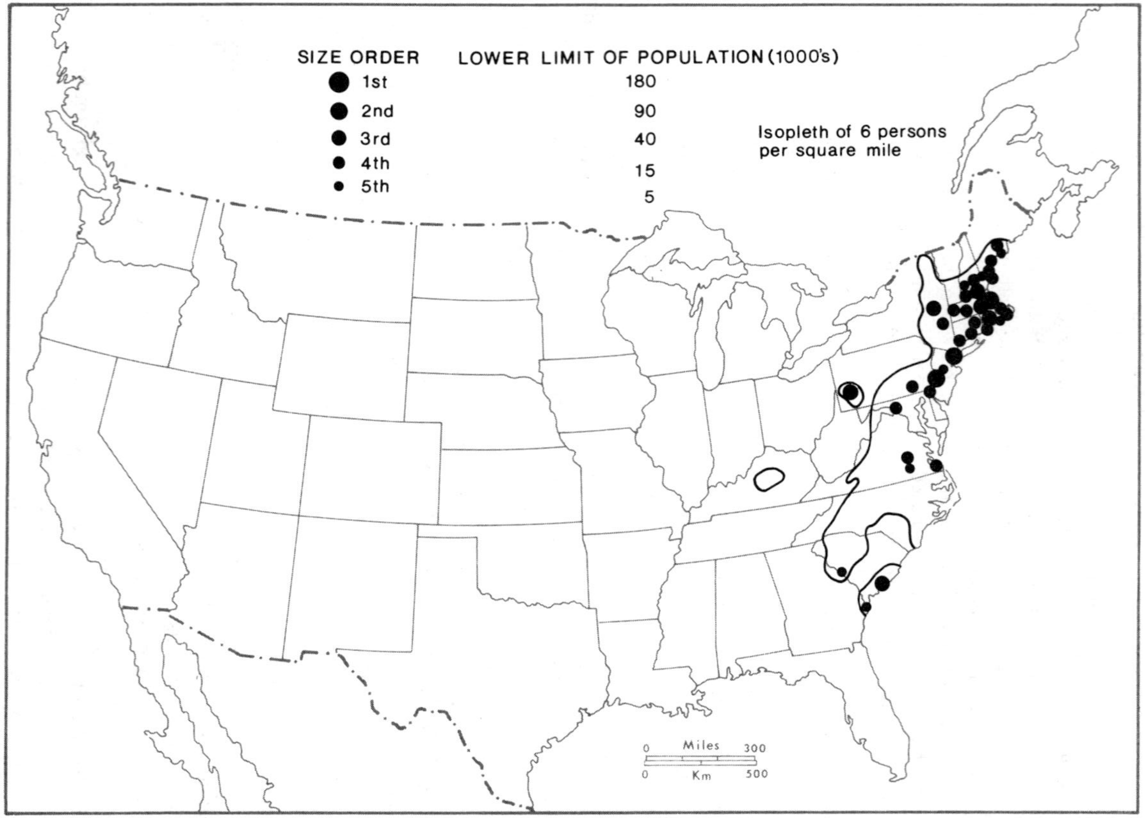

FIGURE 7.9 Distribution of major cities in the United States (1790). [From J. R. Borchert (1967), "American Metropolitan Evolution," *Geographical Review* **57**, 313, fig. 6.]

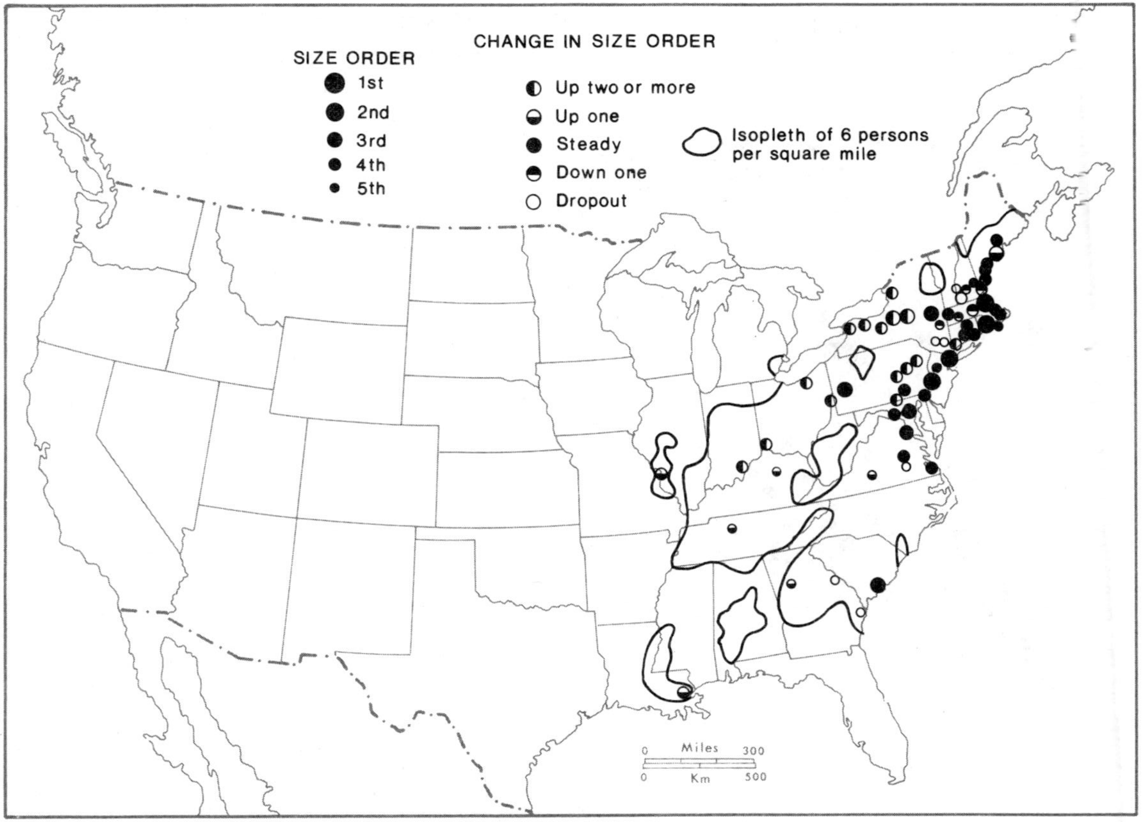

FIGURE 7.10 Distribution of major cities in the United States (1830). [From J. R. Borchert (1967), ''American Metropolitan Evolution,'' *Geographical Review* **57**, 316, fig. 7.]

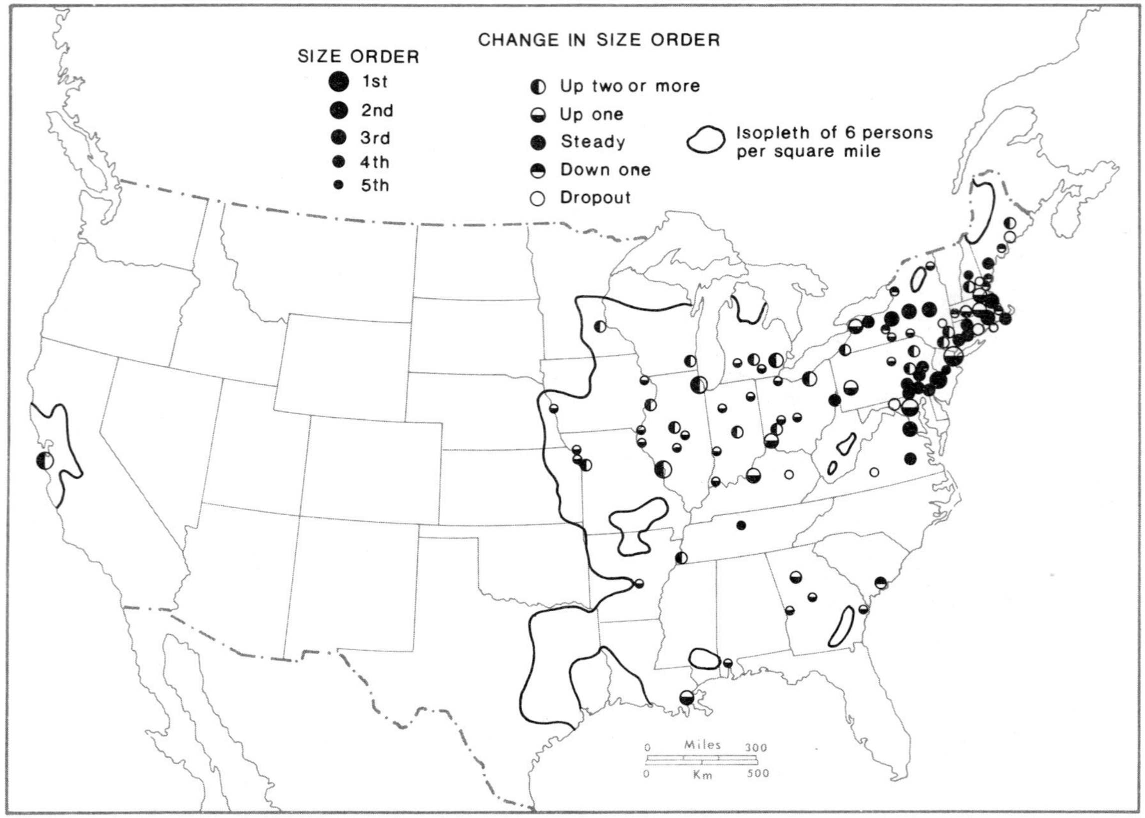

FIGURE 7.11 Distribution of major cities in the United States (1870). [From J. R. Borchert (1967), "American Metropolitan Evolution," *Geographical Review* **57**, 317, fig. 8.]

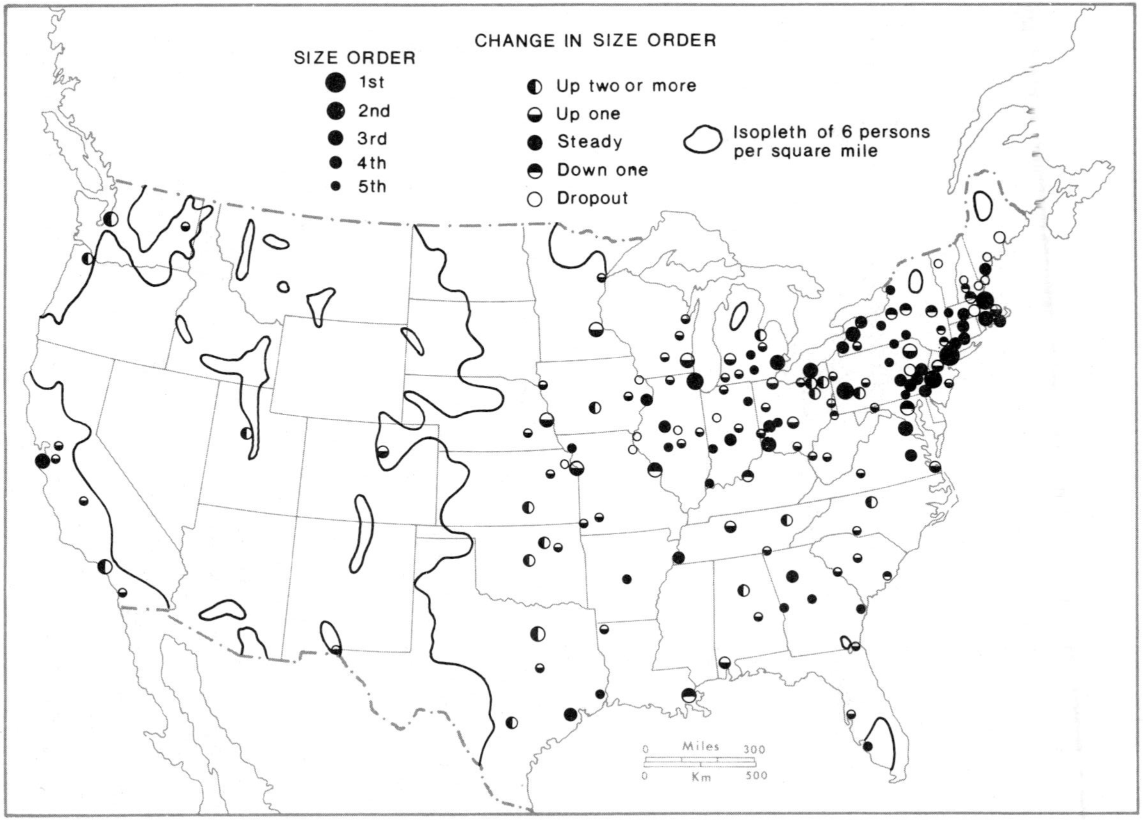

FIGURE 7.12 Distribution of major cities in the United States (1920). [From J. R. Borchert (1967), "American Metropolitan Evolution," *Geographical Review* **57**, 318, fig. 9.]

Center-Periphery Relations

Borchert's (1967) study of American metropolitan evolution suggests that classical equilibrium arguments concerning urban and regional development do not work as postulated. Equilibrium models focus on deviation-counteracting systems and hypothesize that the advantage of the center is only temporary. The underlying assumption is that economic processes steer a system "naturally" toward an optimal equilibrium state. Thus, regional development inequalities are corrected by a relatively free flow of the factors of production that eventually bring about an equalization between center and periphery. No government intervention is required in the periphery; economic development will spread automatically from center to peripheral areas. There is, however, little historical evidence to support this assumption. Polarizing effects accentuating differences between center and periphery are the norm. In this section, we explore notions of unequal development.

> The term "deviation-counteraction" refers to any process that operates to reduce inhomogeneities or differences within a system. Conversely, "deviation-amplification" refers to any process that amplifies an initial "kick" or "trigger" to growth, and increases deviation and divergence from an initial condition. For a discussion of deviation-counteracting and deviation-amplifying forces, see Magorah Maruyama (1963), "The Second Cybernetics: Deviation-Amplifying Mutual Causal Processes," *American Scientist* **51**, 164–79.

The Center-Periphery Concept

The center-periphery concept is one of the most geographical ideas presented by regional analysts. In its Marxist form, the center appropriates to itself the surplus of the periphery for its own development. The center-periphery phenomenon may be regarded as a multiple system of nested centers and peripheries. At the world level, the global center (rich industrial countries) drains the global periphery (underdeveloped countries). Warntz's maps of world income and population potential provide an effective summary of center-periphery relations at the global level (figure 7.13). The income map depicts the twin potential peaks of North America and Western Europe (the controlling power of "world metropolis"), each encircled by a steep gradient merging into an essentially homogeneous region representing the more remote economic backwaters of the world. This pattern contrasts with the population map where the highest potentials are located in underdeveloped south and southeast Asia.

Within any part of the international system and within any national unit, there is another center and periphery. The center, although of considerably less power, is of sufficient strength to appropriate to itself a smaller, but still sizeable, fraction of remaining surplus value. The center may be a single urban area, or a region encompassing several towns that stand in an advantageous relation to the hinterland. Even in remote peripheral areas there are likely to be local, regional imbalances with some areas growing and others stagnating or declining.

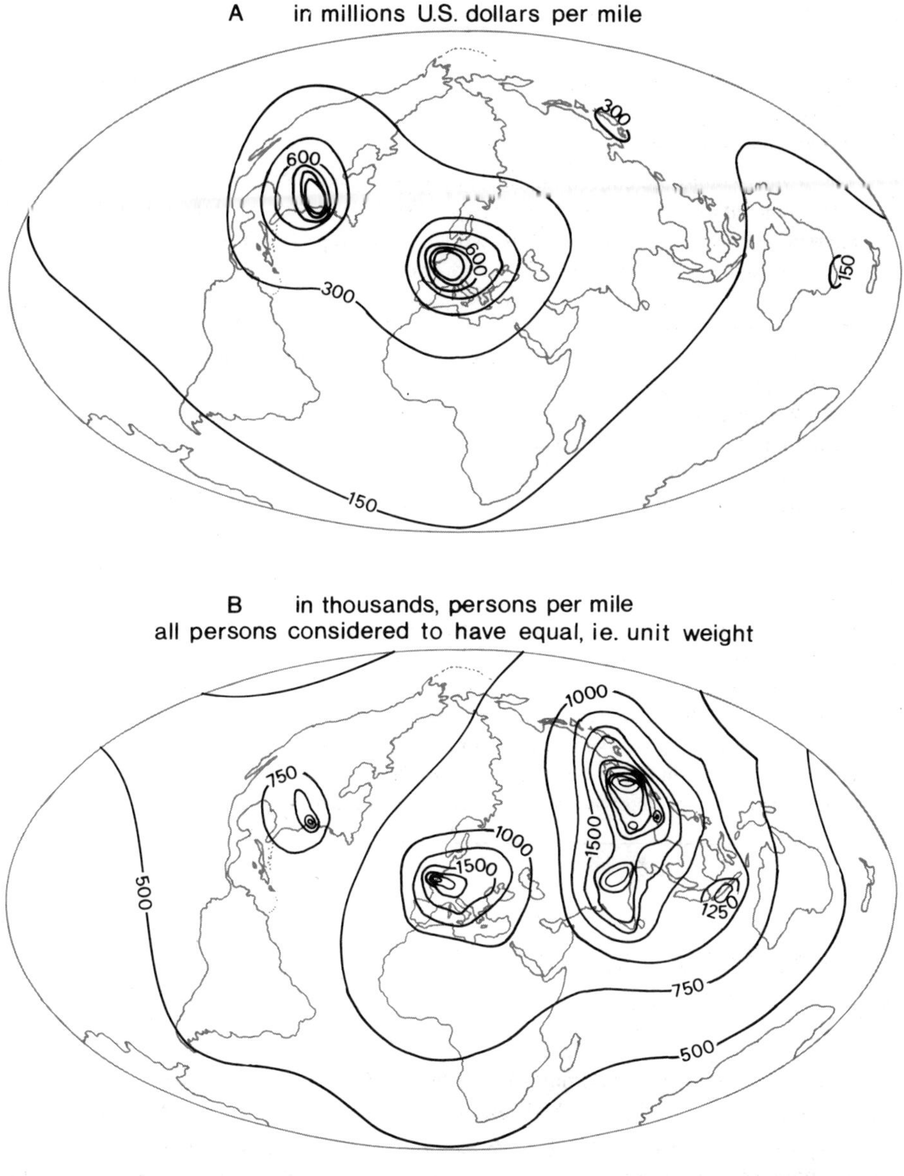

FIGURE 7.13 World income potential and world population potential for the 1960s. [From William Warntz (1965), *Macrogeography and Income Fronts*, Philadelphia: Regional Science Institute, pp. 92, 111, figs. 19, 24.]

There are reverse flows from the various centers to the peripheries—to peripheral nations, to peripheral rural areas—but these flows may accentuate further center-periphery differences. The major consequence of investment (transport and new technologies) has been an increase in the rate at which the economic surplus can be accumulated at the center (Harvey 1972, p. 7).

The center-periphery concept has been variously stated by social scientists. One view of the center-periphery phenomenon was presented by Friedmann (1966), who divided the world into a dynamic center and a stagnating periphery, and proposed four regions, as follows:

1. *Core-regions* are concentrated metropolitan economies with a high capacity for innovation and change. They exist as nested hierarchies from the national metropolis down to the hamlet. At the world level Europe-North America is the core development region in the Western world.
2. *Upward-transition regions* are peripheral to the core and suitable for resource exploitation and development. A special type of upward-transition region is the *development corridor* that exists between two major cities. An example is the corridor between Rio de Janeiro and Sao Paulo.
3. *Resource-frontier regions* are peripheral areas of new settlement. An example is settlement on the north slope of Alaska.
4. *Downward-transition regions* are stagnating or declining areas. Rural economies and uncontrolled urban settlements of the underdeveloped world are examples.

An alternative view of the center-periphery concept was presented by Frank (1969, 1970) in his schematic system of transfer of exploitation. A similar interpretation of the center-periphery structure is presented in this text. This type of dichotomy has been criticized for being too concerned with the idea of spatial dominance. It assumes exploitation occurs only at the periphery, and not at both center and periphery. It does not pay sufficient attention to relations among capitalists, workers, and peasants. According to Poulantzas, the essence of the chain of exploitation is that ''each link of this chain reflects the chain as a whole in the specificity of its own social formation'' (1975, p. 42).

Polarized Development: Models of Myrdal and Hirschman

Myrdal (1957) and Hirschman (1958) attacked equilibrium notions in economic theory and suggested basic ideas about polarized development. Myrdal viewed core-regions of the space-economy as self-reinforcing magnets of progress. Rather than deviation-counteracting forces, deviation-amplifying forces exist to increase and make more rigid the differences between center and periphery. Myrdal began his book with a discussion of the widening gap between rich and poor nations and between rich and poor people. He then sketched a model of cumulative change, arguing that during the early stages of development, increasing economic inequalities are generated through the operation of circular or cumulative upward causation (figure 7.14). He reasoned that ''change does not call forth contradicting forces'' as equalization models suggest, ''but, instead, supporting changes; which move the system in the same direction as the first change but much further'' (1957, p. 13). Myrdal said that once growth has been initiated in favored locations in a free

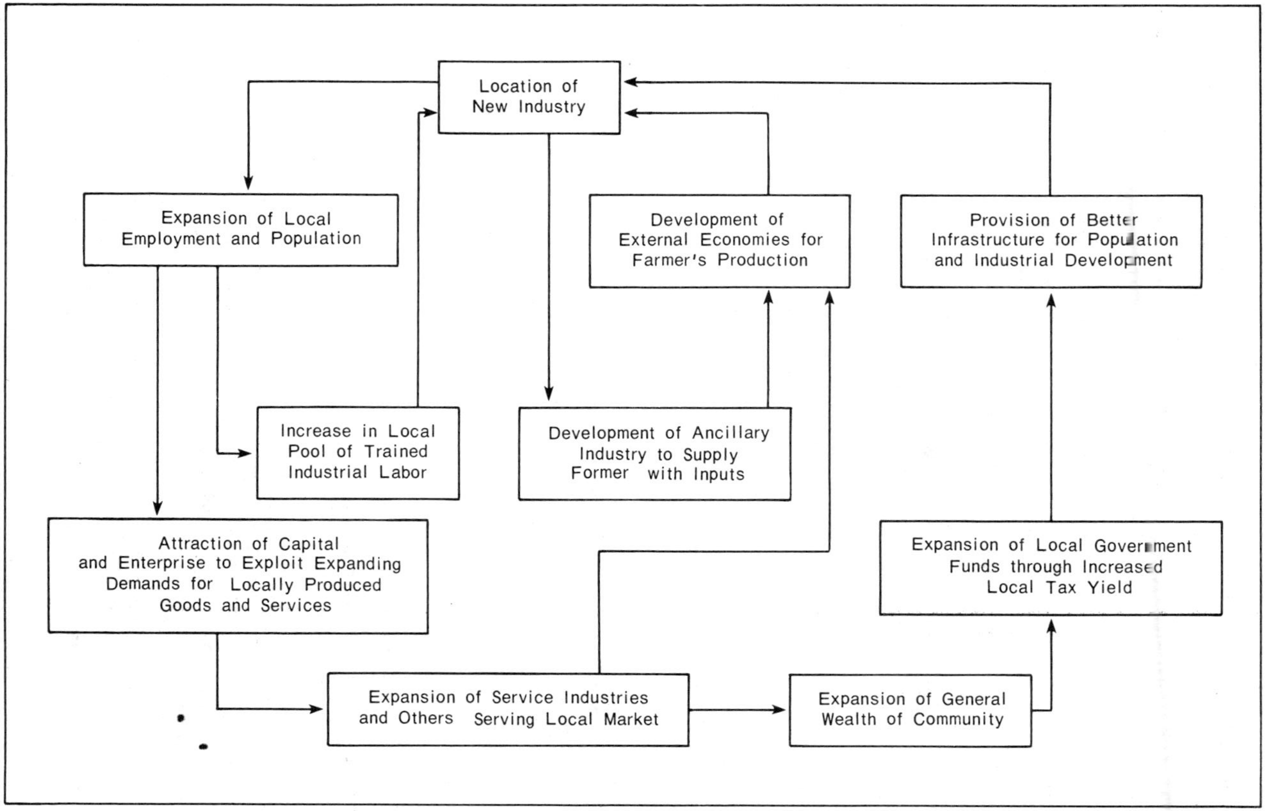

FIGURE 7.14 Myrdal's model of circular or cumulative upward causation. [From D. E. Keeble (1967), "Models of Economic Development," in Richard J. Chorley and Peter Haggett, eds., *Models in Geography,* London: Methuen, p. 258, fig. 8.4.]

economy, inflows of labor, skills, capital, and commodities develop spontaneously to support them. These flows, however, induce backwash effects, amplifying inequalities between expanding and other regions. Myrdal argued that if events follow an uncontrolled course, backwash effects perpetuate growth in expanding regions and retard growth elsewhere. For development to occur throughout a country, centrifugal spread effects of expansionary momentum must, on the average, be stronger than backwash effects.

Growing regions influence other regions through two opposing forces which, in the Myrdal model, are called "spread effects" and "backwash effects." Spread effects refer to the beneficial impact prosperous regions have on less prosperous regions. These may include increased demand for primary commodities, increased investment, and the diffusion of modern technology. Very often spread effects are restricted to areas around major centers of the urban hierarchy.

Backwash effects refer to net movements of people, commodities, and capital from lagging to growing regions. An example of backwash at the world scale is heavy profit repatriation of multinational firms. The table shows that as a result of direct U. S. overseas investments between 1950 and 1965 there was a net capital flow of $16 billion to the United States. For the years 1950–1965 the United States repatriated from underdeveloped countries nearly three times as much money as was invested.

Direct Investments Transferred to the United States (1950–1965)

	Europe	Canada	Latin America	All Other Areas
	(in billions of U.S. dollars)			
Flow of direct investments from U.S.[1]	8.1	6.8	3.8	5.2
Income on capital transferred to U.S.[2]	5.5	5.9	11.3	14.3
	+2.6	+0.9	−7.5	−9.1

Source: Harry Magdoff (1970) "The American Empire and the U.S. Economy," in Robert I. Rhodes, ed., *Imperialism and Underdevelopment,* New York: Monthly Review Press, p. 39. Copyright © 1970 by Monthly Review, Inc. Reprinted by permission of Monthly Review Press.

[1] The figures represent net capital movements of direct investments.

[2] The figures represent the sum of dividends, interest, and branch profits (not profits of corporate subsidiaries whose earnings are retained abroad) after taxes.

Myrdal recognized that backwash effects are stronger in depression than in boom, so that down-turns of the business cycle affect stagnating or regressing communities more than vigorous growth centers. He noted that spread effects in rich industrial countries have not been strong enough to draw whole national economies into a more or less equal and simultaneous expansion process.

> In the United States, for example, almost the whole of the region usually referred to as the south was until recently largely a stagnating one. Similarly, the emergence some generations ago of the great new opportunities in agriculture in the western frontier left large rural areas in New England in a decay from which some of them have not yet emerged. (1957, pp. 32–33)

Myrdal did not have any faith that laissez-faire capitalism would reduce inequalities. In his view the best hope for greater regional equality lies in government intervention and control. Governments should introduce policies that augment spread effects and offset backwash effects.

Hirschman advanced a similar model of economic development and pointed out that polarization effects are natural in the early stages of development. He argued more persistently than Myrdal, however, in favor of massive investment in the urban-industrial core-region, realizing full well that such a policy would accentuate differences between the center and the periphery.

His model shows that once an initial decision is made to locate a particular industry at a specific point, it has an initial multiplier effect (figure 7.15). New local demands are generated by the factory and by the purchasing power of its labor force. The labor force creates a demand for housing and for a set of services. The new factory attracts additional industries producing complementary goods. Linked industries either provide needed inputs (backward linkages) or purchase semifinished products (forward linkages) from the initial factory. The entire process has a cumulative, self-generating momentum; after the first cycle of growth is complete, a new round of growth is initiated at a higher threshold. As figure 7.15 illustrates, the cycles of growth can be carried through any number of times, at least until the process is arrested by diseconomies or interrupted by the competitive advantages of other growth points. Figure 7.15 also shows that the initial multiplier stimulates expansion of nonindustrial activities and they in turn trigger a second multiplier that induces further growth and still higher thresholds.

Hirschman argued that it was natural for entrepreneurs to select and to concentrate their activities at growth points. Development becomes increasingly unbalanced. Growth of the developing region—''North'' according to Hirschman's terminology—restricts the capacity for growth elsewhere—''South.'' The North attracts skilled labor and savings from the South. The income elasticity of demand is greater for Northern manufactured goods, and terms of trade turn against Southern producers of primary commodities.

The central idea of Hirschman's model is that these polarization effects are offset eventually by ''trickling-down effects,'' the equivalent of Myrdal's spread effects. Trickling-down effects include the Northern purchase of commodities produced in the South and the southward movement of capital. In addition, the North may attract enough Southern labor to ensure an increase in the South's marginal productivity of labor and per capita consumption levels. Hirschman insisted that trickling-down effects can only take place if the North needs the South for its own expansion. He presumed that if, in the course of development, inequalities between North and South do not melt away through unrestrained market forces, then the ''visible'' hand of the state would have to intervene and introduce remedial measures.

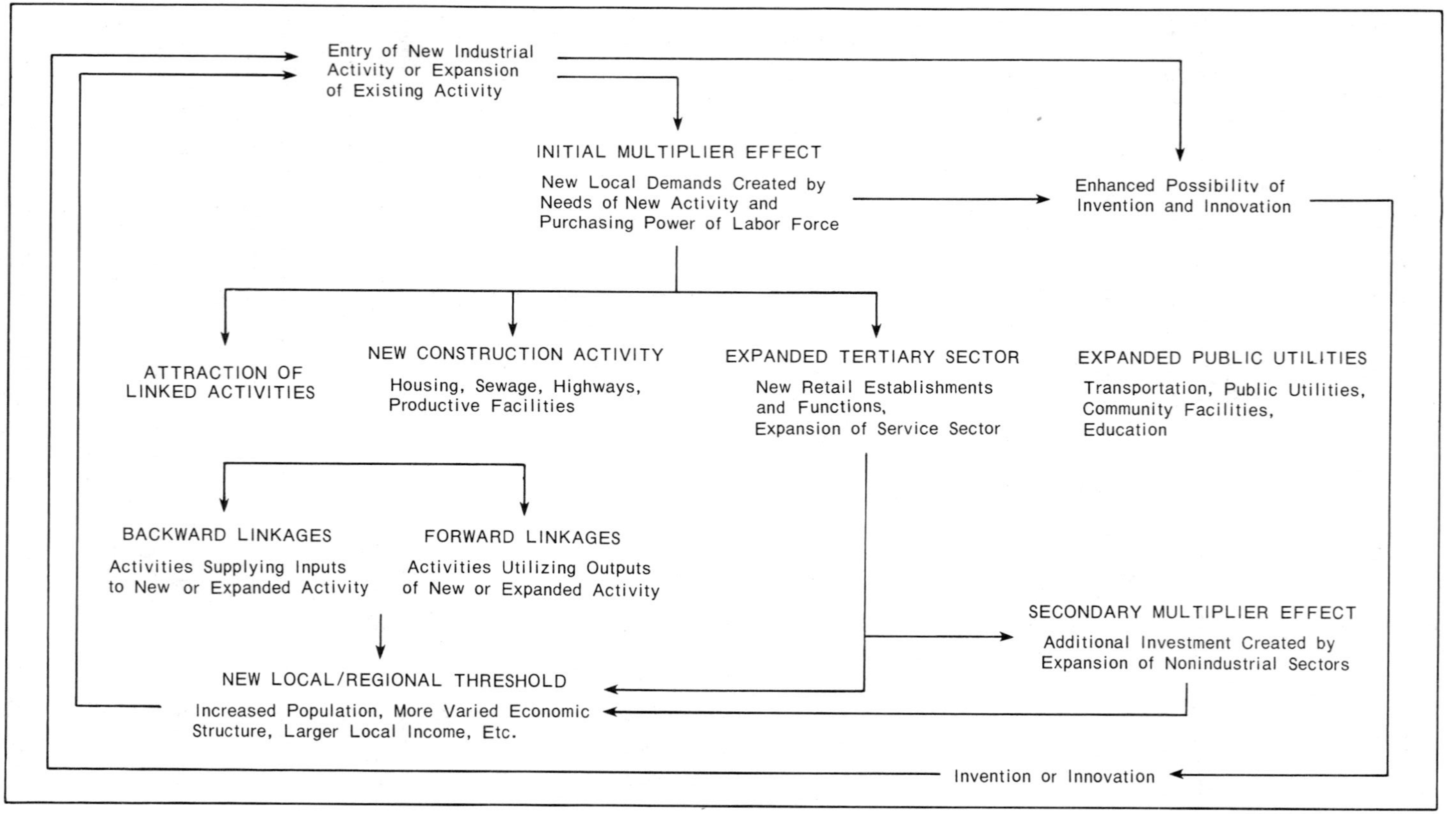

FIGURE 7.15 Initial multiplier effect and the process of cumulative upward causation. [Based on A. Pred (1966), *The Spatial Dynamics of U. S. Urban-Industrial Growth,* Cambridge, Massachusetts: The M.I.T. Press, p. 25, fig. 2.1.]

Both Myrdal's and Hirschman's models of spatial polarization of economies suggest that increasing disparities between more developed and less developed areas are typical of early stages of economic development. On the question of later convergence, Myrdal was pessimistic and did not carry his analysis beyond a discussion of the vicious cycle of backwash effects, whereas Hirschman insisted that eventual convergence is the norm.

Friedmann's Model of Regional Development

The name of John Friedmann is closely associated with the development of Western regional science. We review his work in center-periphery relations from 1964 to 1970. In an early statement on regional development Friedmann (jointly with Alonso) stated:

> Spatial patterns will change with shifts in the structure of demand and of production, in the level of technology, and in the social and political organization of the nation. The economic and social development of the nation is reflected in its patterns of settlement; its patterns of commuting and migration; and its reticulation of areas of urban influence. And if there is a spatial pattern corresponding to each "stage" of economic development, it may be further suggested that there is an optimal strategy for spatial transformation from one stage to the next. In the early period of development, marginal returns to the factors of production differ greatly between regions. With economic advancement, economic functions become more differentiated in space, and the relevant scale of many functions will increase. At an advanced stage of development, the national economy will appear as a fully integrated hierarchy of functional areas, with most of the population and activities polarized in metropolitan areas and, in effect, with national markets for labor, capital, and commodities. (1964, p. 2)

The authors then proposed their version of the center-periphery model:

> . . . centers not only grow so rapidly as to create problems of an entirely new order, but they also act as suction pumps, pulling in the more dynamic elements from the more static regions. The remainder of the country is thus relegated to a second-class, peripheral position. It is placed in a quasi-colonial relationship to the center, experiencing net outflows of people, capital, and resources, most of which redound to the advantage of the center where economic growth will tend to be rapid, sustained, and cumulative. (1964, p. 3)

Two years later, Friedmann devised a descriptive four-stage model of spatial evolution in his book *Regional Development Policy*. It draws on the nineteenth century North American experience to impose stages onto the continuum of economic growth countries are supposed to experience as they develop. Friedmann recognized the following stages of spatial evolution (figure 7.16):

1. *A pre-industrial phase* is characterized by a number of small independent urban centers spread throughout a large region. There is no urban hierarchy, the possibilities for growth are soon exhausted, and the economy tends to stagnate. Friedmann assumed the system to be in balance, because each center serves, by and large, only its local area.

2. A period of *incipient-industrialization* is characterized by a primate city (C) dominating a large region and exploiting the natural resources of its periphery (P). Local economies in the periphery are undermined as a consequence of a mass movement of would-be entrepreneurs, intellectuals, and labor to the primate city.

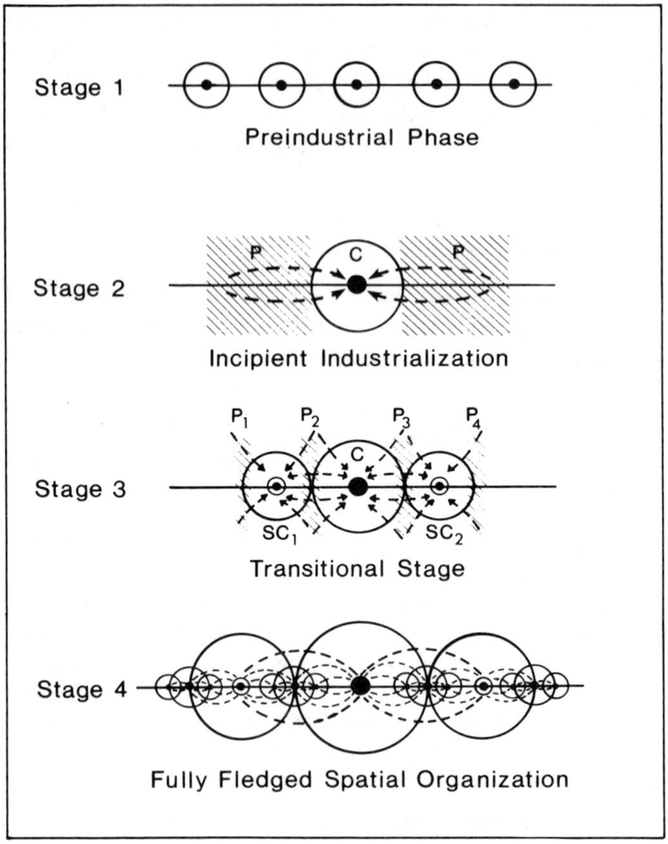

FIGURE 7.16 Friedmann's stages of spatial evolution. [From J. Friedmann (1966), *Regional Development Policy: A Case Study of Venezuela*. Cambridge, Massachusetts: The M.I.T. Press, p. 36, fig. 2.1.]

Friedmann viewed the primacy-dominated organization of space as unstable, because the system is generated by exogenous forces.

3. During the *transitional stage* toward industrial maturation the primate city (C) still dominates the large region, but not as much as previously. A hierarchy of strategically located urban centers (SC_1 and SC_2) evolves naturally or is hastened by deliberate planning, reducing the influence of the large city. Friedmann regarded the third stage as still unstable, because pockets of "backwardness" in peripheral areas persist (P_1, P_2, P_3, and P_4).

4. The last stage consists of a *full-fledged spatial organization* based on the hierarchy principle which covers the entire national territory. According to Friedmann this functionally interdependent system of cities will fulfill essential goals of internal spatial organization such as national integration, efficiency of location, maximum growth potential, and a high degree of interregional balance.

Friedmann's evolutionary model posits ultimate convergence between center and periphery. However, he stressed that empirical evidence points to persistent disequilibrium (1966, p. 14). He noted that even after 150 years of sustained urban-

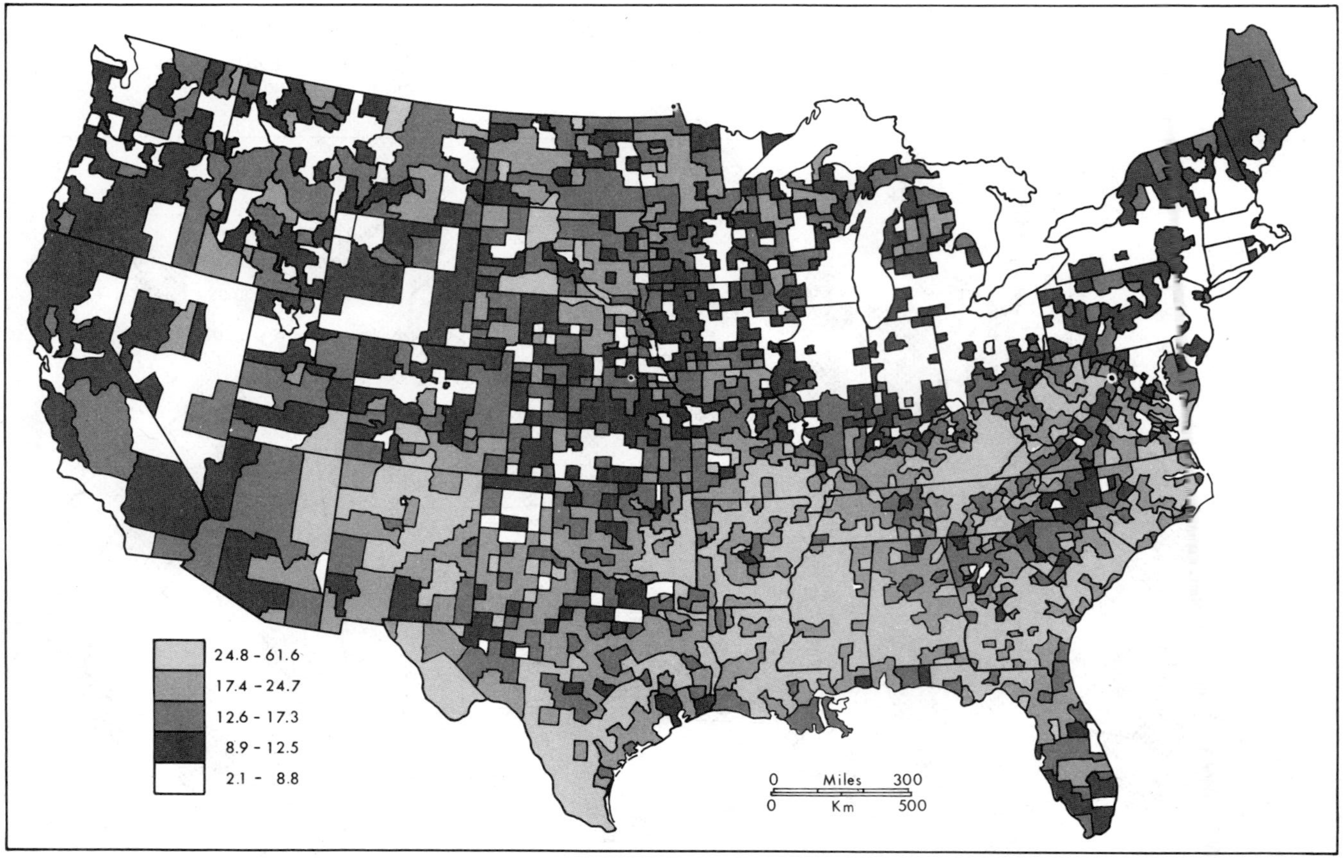

FIGURE 7.17 Percentage of families below low income level in the United States (1969). [Source: *County and City Data Book* (1972), U. S. Bureau of Census.]

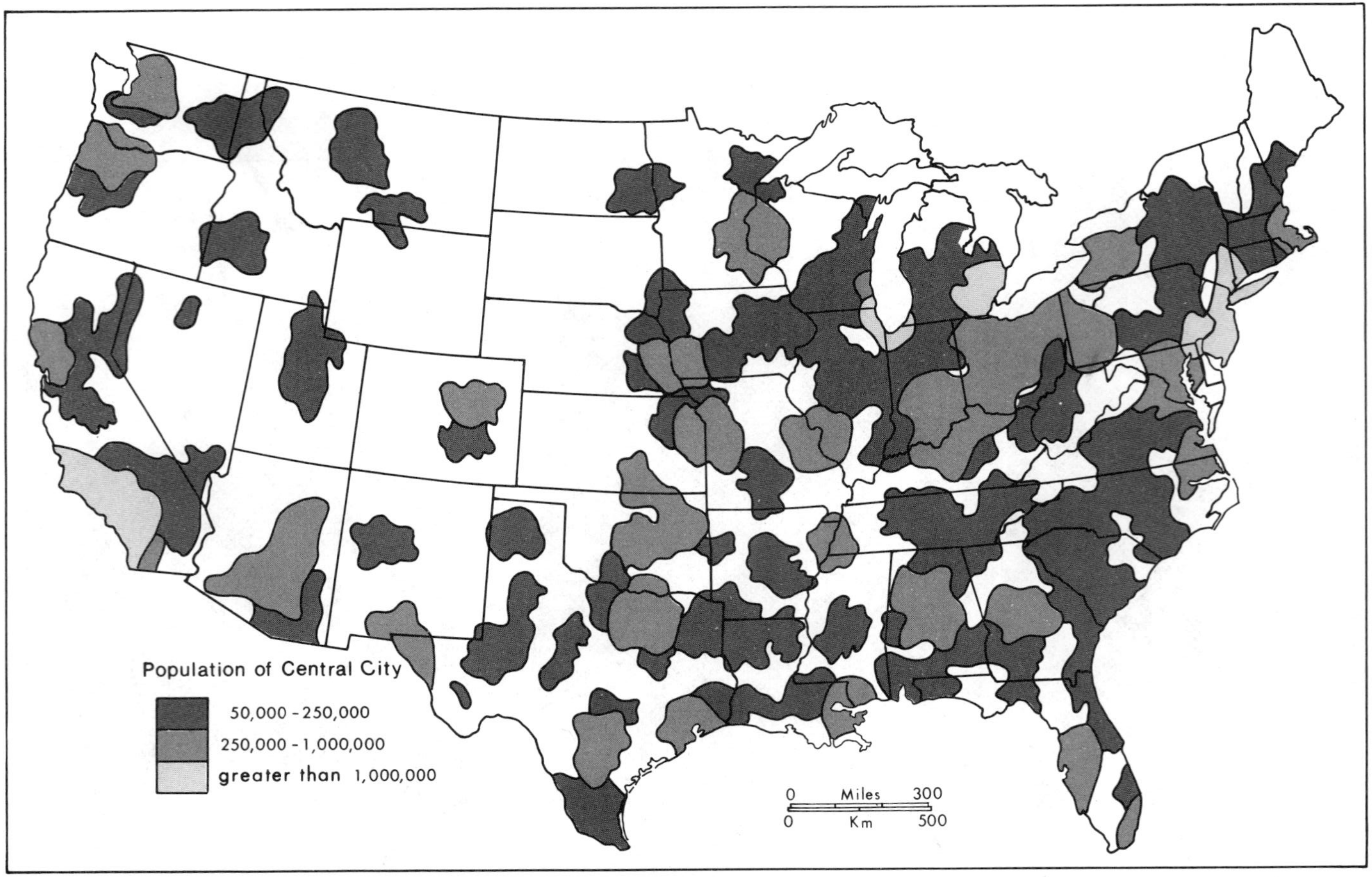

FIGURE 7.18 Extent of commuting fields in the United States (1960). [After B. J. L. Berry (1968), *Metropolitan Area Definition: A Re-evaluation of Concept and Statistical Practice*, Washington, D. C.: Bureau of the Census, Working Paper No. 28.]

industrialization, the United States still has problems of depressed and backward regions. Figures 7.17 and 7.18 demonstrate the disequalization of development in the United States. Note the inverse relationship between low income and extent of commuting fields. The heartland has the greatest complexity of interpenetrating and coalescing commuter fields and the hinterlands, with the widest spacing of metropolitan urban centers and the most extensive interurban peripheries, have the greatest concentration of low income counties.

Friedmann went on to remark that convergence is an extremely drawn out process, and will come only when a society reaches an advanced stage of the industrialization process. He suggested, however, that continued urban-industrial expansion in major metropolitan areas should lead to catalytic impacts on surrounding regions. He offered a number of propositions that reflect the on-going urban-regional development process in the United States. The propositions, which have an explicit link with central place theory and innovation diffusion theory, are as follows:

> Economic growth takes place in a matrix of urban regions through which the space economy is organized . . . . Cities organize the space economy. They are centers of activity and of innovation, focal points of the transport network, locations of superior accessibility at which firms can most easily reap scale economies and at which industrial complexes can obtain the economies of localization and urbanization. Agricultural enterprise is more efficient in the vicinity of cities. The more prosperous commercialized agricultures encircle the major cities . . . . There are two major elements in this organization of economic activities in space:
>
> (a) A system of cities, organized in a hierarchy according to the functions performed by each;
>
> (b) Corresponding areas of urban influence or urban fields surrounding each of the cities in the system.
>
> Generally one can argue the following about this system of spatial organization:
>
> (a) The size and function of a central city and the size of the urban field are proportional.
>
> (b) The spatial incidence of economic growth is a function of distance from the central city. Troughs of economic backwardness lie in the most inaccessible areas along the intermetropolitan peripheries.
>
> (c) Impulses of economic change are transmitted in order from higher to lower centers in the urban hierarchy, in a "size-rachet" sequence, so that continued innovation in large cities remains critical for extension of growth over the complete economic system.
>
> (d) The growth potential of an area situated along an axis between two cities is a function of the intensity of interaction between them. (Berry 1969, p. 288)

Friedmann became critical of his own emphasis on economic forces propelling change. In *A General Theory of Polarized Development* he sought a linkage between regional interaction theory and a theory of social change. He stated:

> The General-Theory treats economic growth as a function of changes in the structure that inevitably limit a system's capacity for expansion and, in the specific case of growth based on the application of science to problems of economic production, also of the system's capacity for continuous generation and absorption of innovations. This formulation assigns a decisive influence to the institutional and organizational framework of society and, specifically to the patterns of authority and dependency that

> result from the unusual capacity of certain areas to serve as cradles of innovation. (1969, pp. 29–30)

Adopting a non-Marxist conflict theory of social change, Friedmann reformulated his center-periphery model:

> Dominant core and dominated periphery together constitute a relatively stable spatial system in which the latter is successfully "colonized" chiefly to sustain the continued growth of the former.
>
> The further growth of core regions, however, is in the final analysis constrained by the tensions that tend to build up from the ever more visible discrepancies in the rates of expansion and modernization between core and periphery. The increasing flow of information from core to periphery, together with aroused awareness of potentially modernizing elites in the periphery of the conditions of their own dependency, produce conflict with core-region authorities over the extent of permissible autonomy. (1969, p. 30)

Friedmann identified four possible resolutions of dualism between center and periphery: (1) the suppression of peripheral elites by the center; (2) neutralization of peripheral elites; (3) replacement of center by peripheral elites; and (4) cooptation of peripheral elites by center. These outcomes lead either to further deviation-amplification or to the appearance of deviation-counteracting forces. If conflict resolution between center and periphery results in further deviation-amplification, the center becomes progressively more and more rigid vis-à-vis the periphery, and "growth without development" is the consequence.

The critical planning problem then becomes how and when to change authority-dependency relations if "progress" is to occur. There is little agreement about when to transform authority-dependency relations. It is argued that in the early stages of economic development the center works to mobilize the periphery, and therefore, the most effective development policy is to leave things as they are. Yet it is recognized that this course might create an overly entrenched center, and might decrease the likelihood of peaceful transformation.

Although the problem of when to act is unresolved, how to change is, in Friedmann's view, more clear. Several interrelated transformations are required. The transformations are isomorphic and include:

> 1. *Socio-cultural patterns.* The evolution of spatial structure proceeds from isolated "islands of innovation" to a completely "modernized" surface.
>
> 2. *Locational patterns of economic activity.* The evolution of spatial structure proceeds from intense center concentration of "modern" activities to a more dispersed pattern.
>
> 3. *Settlement patterns.* The evolution of spatial structure proceeds from primacy to log-normality in a hierarchy of central places.
>
> 4. *Political organization.* The evolution of spatial structure proceeds from a centralized to a decentralized system for making political and economic decisions. (Friedmann 1970, pp. 33–34)

These isomorphic transformations suggest a relationship between the degree of disequilibrium and the level of development. In the early phases of development, backwash effects dominate. The degree of disequilibrium reaches a peak in the middle phases of development, after which spread effects begin to propel the system toward an equilibrium state (figure 7.19).

To summarize our discussion of center-periphery relations, classical economists argue that no intervention is required in processes of spatial organization. By contrast, analysts such as Friedmann urge active intervention because of the inability of "invisible hands" to reduce disequilibrium. He advocates that planners should "act upon social and economic processes . . . to guide society towards desired objectives" (Friedmann 1967, p. 229). For Friedmann, the desired objectives were a high rate of growth and economic efficiency.

Friedmann's conception of the center-periphery model is very close to a Marxian view of the world. His notion of dominated periphery by dominant core corresponds with the idea of the center appropriating the economic surplus of the periphery for its own development. However, Marxists would prefer to view the problem of unequal development not primarily in terms of spatial relations, but of class relations. They would argue that revolutionary strategies of change are necessary to redress inequalities generated by the capitalist mode of production.

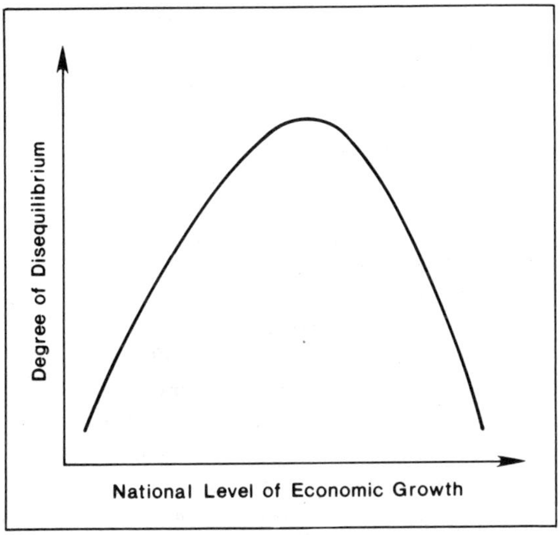

FIGURE 7.19 Relationship between the degree of disequilibrium and the level of development.

Basic Objectives of Development

The existing philosophy of development based on Western models intimates a maximum growth economy that assumes a world of unlimited waste and pollution reservoirs and indestructible ecosystems. Economists such as Schumacher (1973) and Mishan (1969) argue that economic growth should be slowed so that resources can be diverted from "growth for growth's sake" and applied to the task of creating a humanly tolerable world. An emphasis on linear economic growth increases the gap between man and nature. "Growthmania" is a road to nowhere. Ecologically minded economists and economic geographers conclude that permanent economic growth is impossible because of the presence of a condition of scarcity in nature.

A linear economic system is based on a goal of ever-increasing growth. It involves a short-run philosophy of resource use: a temporary life-style of abundant red meat, two or more cars per family, and a plentitude of energy-extravagant home appliances. According to environmentalists, a "cowboy" economy must be transformed into a dynamic steady state or "spaceship" economy. Spaceship economics recognizes earth's finiteness. It assumes that resources are exhaustible, that they must be recycled, and that input rates must be reduced to levels that do not irreversibly damage the world's life support systems. The table compares cowboy and spaceship economics.

Cowboy Economics	Spaceship Economics
Essentially infinite resources and energy.	Finite resources and infinite energy (if fusion or solar energy can be developed).
Linear flow of matter and energy.	Linear flow of energy but recycling of matter.
Increase flow rates of matter and energy and output (maximize throughput).	Stabilize flow rates of matter and energy by deliberately reducing throughput—a steady-state system with balanced inputs and outputs well below the limits of the system.
Goals of efficiency, quantity, simplification, and cultural and physical homogeneity to attain short-term stability.	Goals of quality and deliberate preservation of cultural and physical diversity to attain long-term stability at the expense of some efficiency.
Output control of pollution (consequences of second law of thermodynamics can be avoided or minimized by cleaning up output).	Input and output control (consequences of the second law of thermodynamics can be decreased in the long run by decreasing input and flow rates along with controlling output).
Continued growth provides capital for output control and redistribution of wealth (trickle down theory).	If growth continues, capital must be increasingly devoted to maintenance and repairs, thus decreasing life quality and preventing redistribution of wealth.
Free enterprise, a competitive market system, or a centralized control economy that can respond to undesirable side effects.	Market responds only if we find ways to include quality of life indicators into the price of goods and services.
Short-term view and planning.	Long-term view and planning.
Local and national outlook.	Global outlook.

Source: G. Tyler Miller, Jr. (1975), *Living in the Environment: Concepts, Problems, and Alternatives*, Belmont: Wadsworth, p. 331.

Brookfield (1975) discussed the ecological dimension of scarcity. He agreed with Marxists that social institutions in market exchange economies are geared to the maintenance of scarcity (Harvey 1972, p. 5), but dismissed the argument that scarcity can be eliminated by the adoption of a higher form of economic organization (socialism). He emphasized that scarcity is an inherent condition. Resources are naturally scarce. Space is scarce. Human labor power is scarce. All social systems, whether based on reciprocity, redistribution, or market exchange exist to allocate scarce resources. Market exchange, which expanded into a world system of developed and underdeveloped countries, "has proved extraordinarily effective" in adapting to absolute scarcity, "but at the costs of accentuating scarcity for some while easing it for others" (Brookfield 1975, p. 205). Although Brookfield felt that relative, socially determined scarcity might be eliminated by a new form of social organization, he argued that it would be capable only of ameliorating the effects of absolute scarcity.

For Brookfield, maldistribution of scarce resources underlies the whole development problem. Moreover, the organization of world space and political economy by an intrusive industrial capitalism, and a world network of cities that helps the system to function, has created a world in which resources, already unevenly located geographically, are even more unevenly appropriated and consumed socially. From at least the time of Drake's voyage on the *Golden Hind*, distortions in resource use have been increasing.

Brookfield pointed out that the study of development has concentrated on economic mechanisms of allocating and redistributing scarce resources and has neglected problems of absolute scarcity. In the social sciences of the West, theories of growth and regional development hardly acknowledge the presence of a condition of resource scarcity. Brookfield argued that it is essential to pay attention to induced scarcity, but of prime importance to pay close attention to scarcity in nature. As he said: "It is only the fact of scarcity that makes it possible to exploit scarcity" (1975, p. 207).

Summary and Conclusions

In this chapter we emphasized the tendency toward the geographical concentration of development. Progressive development concentration is primarily the result of a pattern of deviation-amplification, which is contingent upon locational advantages derived during earlier stages of growth. So long as the process of spiralling and cumulative growth operates, imbalances in regions and resources will continue in market economies. We did not pass judgment on this pattern of spatial organization, but described its result.

Classical location theory is of limited applicability when interpreting and analyzing the evolution of the economic landscape. It is concerned with maximizing profits, minimizing costs, and optimal locational behavior. From these ideas emerged deterministic equilibrium models postulating optimal patterns of agricultural land use (chapter 2), urban size and spacing (chapter 3), and industrial location (see chapter 4). These theories emphasize form and static organizational structures.

Location theory derived from classical economics is valuable to entrepreneurs and regional planners who seek normative solutions, but for those interested in interpreting the real economic landscape, it provides only partial insights. A greater understanding of the economic landscape is achieved when existing location theory is embellished by theories that take into account nonoptimal behavior and imperfect knowledge (chapter 6) and the impacts patterns of one time have on those of a later time (chapter 7). A dynamic geography of economic activity, found in the macro-spatial and synthesizing studies of Friedmann (1966, 1969, 1970) and the more specialized work of Hägerstrand (1953) and Morrill (1963), is of increasing interest to geographers.

This text made the paradigm of spatial organization the basis for organizing and presenting material. It is one of several ways of viewing the economic landscape. However, there is a danger that a paradigm, leading one to see the world in a particular way, will prevent one from seeing the world in another way. This point is illustrated in figure 7.20. The drawing by Toulouse-Lautrec is a perceptual illusion. Many people who see an old woman in the picture have difficulty in seeing a young woman and vice versa. To learn to see is to learn to impose order on stimuli. One's manner of dealing with information contains expectations as to how that information can be ordered. Economic geographies based on Marxist spaceship earth or approaches may lead to alternative views of the economic landscape.

FIGURE 7.20 Picture of ...?

KEY WORDS

backwash effects
capitalism
center and periphery
closed cycle of poverty
development
deviation-amplifying forces
deviation-counteracting forces
GDP, GNP, and NNP
economic growth
laissez-faire
law of comparative costs
law of diminishing returns
mercantilism
multiplier effect
polarized development
polarization effects
principal components analysis
regional disparities
resource scarcity
socialism
spread effects
stage models
trickle-down effects
underdevelopment
unilineal evolution

SUGGESTED READINGS

Primary Sources

Berry, B. J. L. (1973), *The Human Consequences of Urbanization—Divergent Paths in the Urban Experience of the Twentieth Century*, New York: St. Martin's Press, Inc., Macmillan and Co., Ltd.

Brookfield, H. (1975), *Interdependent Development,* Pittsburgh: University of Pittsburgh Press.

de Souza, A. R. and P. W. Porter (1974), *The Underdevelopment and Modernization of the Third World,* Washington, D. C.: Association of American Geographers Commission on College Geography, Resource Paper No. 28.

Friedmann, J. and W. Alonso, eds. (1964), *Regional Development and Planning: A Reader,* Cambridge Mass.: The M.I.T. Press.

Harvey, D. (1975), "The Geography of Capitalist Accumulation: A Reconstruction of the Marxian Theory," *Antipode* **7**, 9–21.

Pred, A. (1966), *The Spatial Dynamics of U. S. Urban-Industrial Growth, 1800–1914,* Cambridge, Mass.: The M.I.T. Press.

Readings from Other Social Sciences

Amen, S. (1973), *Accumulation on a World Scale,* New York: Monthly Review Press.

Baran, P. A. and P. M. Sweezy (1966), *Monopoly Capital,* New York: Monthly Review Press.

Barratt Brown, M. (1974), *The Economics of Imperialism*, Harmondsworth, England: The M.I.T. Press.

Frank, A. G. (1969), *Capitalism and Underdevelopment in Latin America,* New York: Monthly Review Press.

Hirschman, A. O. (1958), *The Strategy of Economic Development,* New Haven, Conn.: Yale University Press.

Kuznets, S. (1961), *Capital in the American Economy: Its Formation and Financing,* National Bureau of Economic Research: Princeton University Press.

Maruyama, M. (1963), "The Second Cybernetics: Deviation Amplifying Mutual Causal Processes," *American Scientist* **51**, 164–79.

Myrdal, G. (1957), *Economic Theory and Underdeveloped Countries*, London: Duckworth.

Szentes, T. (1971), *The Political Economy of Underdevelopment,* Budapest: Akadémiai Kiadó.

Bibliography

Aaronovitch, S. and M. C. Sawyer (1974), "The Concentration of British Manufacturing," *Lloyds Bank Review* **114**, 14–23.

Abler, R., J. S. Adams and P. R. Gould (1971), *Spatial Organization: The Geographer's View of the World*, Englewood Cliffs, N. J.: Prentice-Hall.

Ackerman, E. A. (1958), "Geography as a Fundamental Research Discipline," *University of Chicago, Department of Geography Research Paper,* 53.

Ackerman, E. A. (1963), "Where is a Research Frontier?" *Annals* of the Association of American Geographers **53**, 429–40.

Ackley, G. (1942), "Spatial Competition in a Discontinuous Market," *Quarterly Journal of Economics* **56**, 212–30.

Airov, J. (1956), "Location Factors in Synthetic Fiber Production," *Papers,* Regional Science Association **2**, 291–303.

Airov, J. (1959), *The Location of the Synthetic Fiber Industry: A Case Study in Regional Analysis,* Cambridge: MIT Press.

Alchian, A. (1950), "Uncertainty, Evolution, and Economic Theory," *Journal of Political Economy* **58**, 211–21.

Alexander, J. W. (1944), "Freight Rates as a Geographical Factor in Illinois," *Economic Geography* **20**, 25–30.

Alexander, J. W. (1954), "The Basic-Nonbasic Concept of Urban Economic Functions," *Economic Geography* **30**, 246–61.

Alexander, J. W., S. E. Brown and R. E. Dahlberg (1958), "Freight Rates: Selected Aspects of Uniform and Nodal Regions," *Economic Geography* **34**, 1–18.

Alexander, J. W. (1958), "Location of Manufacturing: Methods of Measurement," *Annals* of the Association of American Geographers **48**, 20–26.

Alexander, J. W. and Lindberg, J. B. (1961), "Measurements of Manufacturing: Coefficients of Correlation," *Journal of Regional Science* **1**, 71–81.

Alexander, J. W. (1963), *Economic Geography,* Englewood Cliffs, N. J.: Prentice-Hall.

Alexandersson, G. (1956), *The Industrial Structure of American Cities,* Lincoln: University of Nebraska Press.

Alexandersson, G. (1961), "Changes in the Location Pattern of the Anglo-American Steel Industry: 1948–1959," *Economic Geography* **37**, 95–114.

Alexandersson, G. (1967), *Geography of Manufacturing,* Englewood Cliffs, N. J.: Prentice-Hall.

Alonso, W. (1960), "A Theory of the Urban Land Market," *Papers and Proceedings*, Regional Science Association **6**, 149–57.

Alonso, W. (1964a), 'Location Theory,' *"Regional Development and Planning: A Reader,"* J. Friedmann and W. Alonso, eds., Cambridge: MIT Press.

Alonso, W. (1964b), *Location and Land Use: Toward a General Theory of Land Rent,* Cambridge: Harvard University Press.

Alonso, W. (1967), "A Reformulation of Classical Location Theory and Its Relation to Rent Theory," *Papers and Proceedings*, Regional Science Association **19**, 23–44.

Alonso, W. (1968), "Industrial Location and Regional Policy in Economic Development," *Working Papers,* 14, Berkeley: Department of City and Regional Planning and Center for Planning and Development Research, Institute of Urban and Regional Development, University of California.

Amin, S. (1973), *Accumulation on a World Scale*, New York: Monthly Review Press.

Andrews, P. W. S. and E. Brunner (1962–1963), "Business Profit and the Quiet Life," *Journal of Industrial Economics* **11**, pp. 72–78.

Appleton, J. H. (1963), "The Efficacy of the Great Australian Divide as a Barrier to Railway Communications," *Transactions of the Institute of British Geographers* **33**, 101–22.

Area Redevelopment Administration (1965), *Area Redevelopment Policies in Britain and the Countries of the Common Market.*

Armstrong, A. and A. Silberston (1965), "Size of Plant, Size of Enterprise, and Concentration in British Manufacturing Industry, 1935–1958," *Journal of the Royal Statistical Society*, A, **128**, 395–420.

Arndt, H. W. (1955), "External Economies in Economic Growth," *Economic Record* **31**, 192–214.

Arrighi, G. and J. S. Saul (1973), *Essays on the Political Economy of Africa,* New York: Monthly Review Press.

Artle, R. (1959), *Studies in the Structure of the Stockholm Economy,* Stockholm: Business Research Institute.

Atlas of Illinois Resources (1960), Section 4: Transportation, Department of Geography, University of Illinois, for Division of Industrial Planning and Development, State of Illinois.

Averitt, R. T. (1968), *The Dual Economy: The Dynamics of American Industry Structure,* New York: Norton.

Bain, J. S. (1954), "Economies of Scale, Concentration and the Condition of Entry in 20 Manufacturing Industries, *American Economic Review* **44**, 15–39.

Bain, J. S. (1968), *Industrial Organization,* 2d ed., New York: Wiley.

Baker, O. E. (1921), "Increasing Importance of the Physical Conditions in Determining the Utilization of Land for Agriculture and Forest Production in the U. S.," *Annals* of the Association of American Geographers **11**, 17–46.

Baldwin, R. E. (1956), "Patterns of Development in Newly Settled Regions," *Manchester School of Economic and Social Studies* **24**, 161–79.

Ball, C. and M. Teitz (1958), "Expressways and Industrial Location," *Traffic Quarterly* **12**, 589–601.

Ballabon, M. C. (1957), "Putting the 'Economic' into Economic Geography," *Economic Geography* **33**, 217–23.

Bannock, G. (1971), *The Juggernauts: The Age of the Big Corporation,* Indianapolis: Bobbs-Merrill.

Baran, P. and P. M. Sweezy (1966), *Monopoly Capital,* New York: Monthly Review Press.

Barbero, G. (1966), "Development Problems in Southern Italy," J. Higgs, ed., *People in the Countryside: Studies in Rural Social Development*, London: National Council of Social Service, pp. 160–72.

Barfod, B. (1938), *Local Economic Effects of a Large Scale Industrial Undertaking,* Copenhagen: Munksgaard.

Barloon, M. J. (1954), "The Expansion of Blast Furnace Capacity, 1938-1952: A Study in Geographical Cost Differentials," *Business History Review* **28**, 1–23.

Barloon, M. J. (1965), "Interrelationship of the Changing Structure of American Transportation and Changes in Industrial Location," *Land Economics* **41**, 169–82.

Barlowe, R. (1958), *Land Resource Economics*, Englewood Cliffs, N. J.: Prentice-Hall.

Barnum, H. G. (1966), "Market Centers and Hinterlands in Baden-Würtemberg," *University of Chicago, Department of Geography Research Paper,* 103.

Barratt Brown, M. (1974), *The Economics of Imperialism*, Harmondsworth, England: MIT Press.

Bater, J. H. and D. F. Walker (1974), "Aspects of Industrial Linkage: The Example of the Hamilton Metalworking Complex, Ontario," *Révue Géographique Montreal* **28**, 233–43.

Baumol, W. J. (1965), *Economic Theory and Operations Analysis,* Englewood Cliffs, N. J.: Prentice-Hall.

Beach, E. F. (1957), *Economic Models: An Exposition,* New York: Wiley.

Beacham, A. and W. T. Osborn (1970), "The Movement of Manufacturing Industry," *Regional Studies* **4**, 41–47.

Beaver, S. H. (1935), "The Location of Industry," *Geography* **20**, 191–96.

Beavon, K. S. O. and A. S. Mabin (1975), "The Lösch System of Market Areas: Derivation and Extension," *Geographical Analysis* **7**, 131–51.

Beckmann, M. and T. Marshak (1955), "An Activity Analysis Approach to Location Theory," *Kyklos* **8**, 125–43.

Beckmann, M. (1955a), "Some Reflections on Lösch's Theory of Location," *Papers and Proceedings,* Regional Science Association **1**.

Beckmann, M. (1955b), "The Economics of Location," *Kyklos* **8**, 416–21.

Beckmann, M. (1958), "City Hierarchies and the Distribution of City Size," *Economic Development and Cultural Change* **6**, 243–48.

Beckmann, M. (1968), *Location Theory,* New York: Random House.

Beckmann, M. and J. C. McPherson (1970), "City Size Distribution in a Central Place Hierarchy: An Alternative Approach," *Journal of Regional Science* **10**, 25–33.

Beesley, M. (1955), "Birth and Death of Industrial Establishments: Experience in the West Midlands Conurbation," *Journal of Industrial Economics* **4**, 45–61.

Bell, W. H. and D. W. Stephenson (1964), "An Index of Economic Health for Ontario Counties and Districts," *Ontario Economic Review* **2**, 1–7.

Berry, B. J. L. and W. L. Garrison (1958a), "Functional Bases of the Central Place Hierarchy," *Economic Geography* **34**, 145–54.

Berry, B. J. L. and W. L. Garrison (1958b), "A Note on Central Place Theory and the Range of a Good," *Economic Geography* **34**, 304–11.

Berry, B. J. L. and W. L. Garrison (1958c), "Recent Developments of Central Place Theory," *Papers and Proceedings*, Regional Science Association **4**, 107–20.

Berry, B. J. L. and W. L. Garrison, (1958d), "Alternate Explanations of Urban Rank Size Relationships," *Annals* of the Association of American Geographers **48**, 83–91.

Berry, B. J. L. (1960), "An Inductive Approach to the Regionalization of Economic Development," in Norton Ginsburg, ed., *Essays on Geography and Economic Development,* Chicago: The University of Chicago, Department of Geography, Research Paper No. 62, pp. 78–107.

Berry, B. J. L. and A. Pred (1961), *Central Place Studies,* Bibliography Series 1, Philadelphia: Regional Science Institute.

Berry, B. J. L. (1961), "City Size Distributions and Economic Development," *Economic Development and Cultural Change* **9**, 573–88.

Berry, B. J. L. and H. G. Barnum (1962), "Aggregate Relations and Elemental Components of Central Place Systems," *Journal of Regional Science* **4**, 35–68.

Berry, B. J. L., H. G. Barnum, and R. J. Tennant (1962), "Retail Location and Consumer Behavior," *Papers and Proceedings*, Regional Science Association **9**, 65–106.

Berry, B. J. L. and H. M. Mayer (1962), *Comparative Studies of Central Place Systems*, Final Report NONR 2121-18 and NR 389-126, Geography Branch, U. S. Office of Naval Research.

Berry, B. J. L. (1963), "Commercial Structure and Commercial Blight," *University of Chicago, Department of Geography Research Paper*, 85.

Berry, B. J. L., J. W. Simmons, and R. J. Tennant (1963), "Urban Population Densities: Structure and Change," *Geographical Review* **53**, 389–405.

Berry, B. J. L. (1964a), "Approaches to Regional Analysis: A Synthesis," *Annals* of the Association of American Geographers **54**, 2–12.

Berry, B. J. L. (1964b), "Cities as Systems within Systems of Cities," *Papers and Proceedings*, Regional Science Association **13**, 147–63.

Berry, B. J. L. and A. Pred (1965), *Central Place Studies: A Bibliography of Theory and Applications,* Philadelphia: Regional Science Research Institute.

Berry, B. J. L. (1965), "Identification of Declining Regions: An Empirical Study of the Dimensions of Rural Poverty," R. S. Thoman and W. D. Wood, eds., *Areas of Economic Stress in Canada*, Kingston, Ontario: Queen's University Press, pp. 22–66.

Berry, B. J. L., et al. (1966), "Essays on Commodity Flows and the Spatial Structure of the Indian Economy," *Research Papers* **111**, Department of Geography, University of Chicago.

Berry, B. J. L. (1967), *Geography of Market Centers and Retail Distribution,* Englewood Cliffs, N. J.: Prentice-Hall.

Berry, B. J. L. and D. F. Marble, eds. (1967), *Spatial Analysis: A Reader in Statistical Geography,* Englewood Cliffs, N. J.: Prentice-Hall.

Berry, B. J. L. (1968a), "A Summary: Spatial Organization and Levels of Welfare: Degree of Metropolitan Market Participation as a Variable in Economic Development," *Economic Development Administration Review,* June, pp. 1–6.

Berry, B. J. L. (1968b), "A Synthesis of Formal and Functional Regions Using a General Field Theory of Spatial Behavior," in Berry and Marble (1968), pp. 419–28.

Berry, B. J. L. (1968c), *Metropolitan Area Definition: A Re-evaluation of Concept and Statistical Practice,* Washington, D. C.: Bureau of the Census Working Paper, No. 28.

Berry, B. J. L. and E. Neils (1969), "Location, Size, and Shape of Cities as Influenced by Environmental Factors," in H. S. Perloff, ed., *The Quality of the Urban Environment,* Baltimore: Resources for the Future, pp. 257–302.

Berry, B. J. L. (1969), "Relationships between Regional Economic Development and the Urban System—The Case of Chile," *Tijdschrift voor Economische en Sociale Geografie* **60**, 283–307.

Berry, B. J. L. (1972), "Hierarchical Diffusion: The Basis of Developmental Filtering and Spread in a System of Growth Centers," in N. M. Hansen, ed., *Growth Centers in Regional Economic Development,* New York: Free Press, pp. 108–38.

Berry, B. J. L. (1973), *The Human Consequences of Urbanization—Divergent Paths in the Urban Experience of the Twentieth Century,* London: The Macmillan Press, Ltd.

Bertalanffy, L. von (1951), "An Outline of General System Theory," *British Journal of the Philosophy of Science* **1**, 134–65.

Bertalanffy, L. von (1963), "General Systems: A New Approach to the Unity of Sciences," *Human Biology* **53**, 429–40.

Bertalanffy, L. von (1968), *General System Theory,* New York: Braziller.

Beveridge, W. (1945), *Full Employment in a Free Society*, New York: W. W. Norton.

Blaikie, P. M. (1971), "Spatial Organization of Agriculture in Some North Indian Villages, Part I," *Transactions*, Institute of British Geographers **53**, 15–30.

Blair, J. M. (1972), *Economic Concentration: Structure, Behavior, and Public Policy,* New York: Harcourt Brace Jovanovich.

Blaug, M. (1968), *Economic Theory in Retrospect*, Homewood, Ill.: Richard D. Irwin.

Bloom, C. C. (1955), *State and Local Tax Differentials,* Iowa City: Bureau of Business Research, University of Iowa.

Blumenfeld, H. (1955), "The Economic Base of the Metropolis," *Journal of the American Institute of Planners* **21**, 114–232.

Board of Trade (1968), *The Movement of Manufacturing Industry in the United Kingdom,* London: H. M. S. O.

Bogue, D. J. (1949), *The Structure of the Metropolitan Community,* Ann Arbor: University of Michigan Press.

Borchert, J. R. (1963), "The Urbanization of the Upper Midwest 1930-1960," *Upper*

Midwest Economic Study, Urban Report No. 2, Minneapolis, Minn.: University of Minnesota.

Borchert, J. R. (1967), "American Metropolitan Evolution," *Geographical Review* **57**, 301–32.

Borts, G. H. (1960), "The Equalization of Returns and Regional Economic Growth," *American Economic Review* **50**, 319–47.

Borts, G. H. and J. L. Stein (1964), *Economic Growth in a Free Market,* New York: Columbia University Press.

Bos, H. C. (1965), *Spatial Dispersion of Economic Activity,* Rotterdam: University Press.

Boudeville, J. R. (1966), *Problems of Regional Economic Planning,* Edinburgh: Edinburgh University Press.

Boulding, K. E. (1970), "Fun and Games with the Gross National Product—The Role of Misleading Indicators in Social Policy," in Harold W. Helfrich, ed., *The Environmental Crisis,* New Haven: Yale University Press, pp. 157–70.

Boulding, K. E. (1953), "Toward a General Theory of Growth," *Canadian Journal of Economics and Political Science* **19**, 326–40.

Boulding, K. E. (1956), "General Systems Theory—The Skeleton of Science," *Management Science* **2**, 197–208.

Böventer, E. von (1961), "The Relationship Between Transportation Costs and Location Rent in Transportation Problems," *Journal of Regional Science* **3**, 27–40.

Böventer, E. von (1962), *Theorie des räumlichen Gleichgewichts,* Tübingen: Mohr (Siebeck).

Böventer, E. von (1963), "Towards a United Theory of Spatial Economic Structure," *Papers and Proceedings*, Regional Science Association **10**, 163–87.

Bowen, H. R. (1955), *The Business Enterprise as a Subject for Research,* New York: Social Science Research Council Pamphlet, 11.

Bramhall, D. F. (1961), "Projecting Regional Accounts and Industrial Location: Reflections on Policy Applications," *Papers,* Regional Science Association **7**, 89–118.

Bramhall, D. F. (1969), "An Introduction to Spatial Equilibrium," in Karaska and Bramhall (1969), pp. 467–76.

Bridges, B. (1965), "State and Local Inducements for Industry," *National Tax Journal* **18**, 1–14 and 175–92.

Britton, D. K. and K. Ingersent (1964), "Trends in Concentration in British Agriculture," *Journal of Agricultural Economics* **21**, 26–52.

Britton, J. N. H. (1969), "A Geographical Approach to the Examination of Industrial Linkages," *Canadian Geographer* **13**, 185–98.

Britton, J. N. H. (1974), "Environmental Adaptation of Industrial Plants: Service Linkages, Locational Environment, and Organization," in F. E. I. Hamilton, ed., *Spatial Perspectives on Industrial Organization and Decision Making,* London: Wiley, pp. 363–90.

Bromley, R. J. (1971), "Markets in the Developing Countries: A Review," *Geography* **56**, 124–32.

Brookfield, H. (1975), *Interdependent Development,* Pittsburgh: University of Pittsburgh Press.

Brown, L. A. (1968a), "Diffusion Dynamics: A Review and Revision of the Quantitative Theory of the Spatial Diffusion of Innovation," *Lund Studies in Geography, Series B*, 29.

Brown, L. A. (1968b), *Diffusion Processes and Location: A Conceptual Framework and Bibliography,* Philadelphia Regional Science Research Institute.

Brown, L. A. and K. R. Cox (1971), "Empirical Regularities in the Diffusion of Innovation," *Annals* of the Association of American Geographers **61**, 551–59.

Brown, R. (1948), *Historical Geography of the United States,* New York: Harcourt Brace Jovanovich.

Brown, R. (1963), *Explanations in Social Science,* Chicago: Aldine.

Brush, J. E. (1953), "The Hierarchy of Central Places in Southwestern Wisconsin," *Geographical Review* **43**, 380–402.

Brush, J. E. and H. E. Bracey (1955), "Rural Service Centers in Southwestern Wisconsin and Southwestern England," *Geographical Review* **45**, 559–69.

Buckley, W., ed. (1968), *Modern Systems Research for the Behavioral Scientist,* Chicago: Aldine.

Bunge, W. (1966), "Theoretical Geography," *Lund Studies in Geography*, 2d ed., *Series C*, No. 1.

Burstall, R. M., R. A. Leaver, and J. E. Sussams (1962), "Evaluation of Transport Costs for Alternative Factory Sites—A Case Study," *Operational Research Quarterly* **13**, 345–54.

Burton, I. (1963), "The Quantitative Revolution and Theoretical Geography," *Canadian Geographer* **7**, 151–62.

Cameron, G. C. and B. D. Clark (1966), *Industrial Movement and the Regional Problem,* Glasgow: Oliver and Boyd.

Cameron, G. C. (1968), "The Regional Problem in the United States—Some Reflections on a Viable Federal Strategy," *Regional Studies* **2**, 207–20.

Campbell, A. K. (1958), "Taxes and Industrial Location in the New York Metropolitan Region," *National Tax Journal* **11**, 195–218.

Cao-Pinna, V. (1961), "Problems of Establishing and Using Regional Input-Output Accounting," in Isard and Cumberland (1961), pp. 305–38.

Carrothers, G. A. P. (1956), "An Historical Review of the Gravity and Potential Concepts of Human Interaction," *Journal of the American Institute of Planners* **22**, 94–102.

Carruthers, W. I. (1957), "The Classification of Service Centers in England and Wales—An Analysis of Public Road Transport Services," *Geographical Journal* **122**, 371–85.

Carruthers, W. I. (1967), "Major Shopping Centers in England and Wales, 1961," *Regional Studies* **1**, 65–81.

Carter, H. (1976), *The Study of Urban Geography,* 2d ed., London: Edward Arnold.

Casetti, E. (1966), "Optimal Location of Steel Mills Serving the Quebec and Southern Ontario Steel Market," *Canadian Geographer* **10**, 27–39.

Chamberlain, E. H. (1936), *The Theory of Monopolistic Competition,* Cambridge: Harvard University Press.

Chandler, A. D., Jr. and F. Redlich (1961), "Recent Developments in American Business Administration and Their Conceptualization," *Business History Review* **35**, 1–27.

Chandler, A. D., Jr. (1962), *Strategy and Structure: Chapters in the History of the Industrial Enterprise,* Cambridge: MIT Press.

Chandler, A. D., Jr., ed. (1965), *The Railroads: The Nation's First Big Business,* New York: Harcourt Brace Jovanovich.

Chapman, J. E. and W. H. Wells (1958), *Factors in Industrial Development in Atlanta,* Bureau of Business and Economic Research, College of Business Administration, Georgia State University.

Chenery, H. B. and P. G. Clark (1959), *Interindustry Economics,* New York: Wiley.

Chenery, H. B. (1962), "Development Policies for Southern Italy," *Quarterly Journal of Economics* **76**, 515–47.

Chicago and Eastern Illinois Railroad (1953), *Industrial Potentialities of Southern Illinois,* Chicago.

Chinitz, B. and R. Vernon (1960), "Changing Forces in Industrial Location," *Harvard Business Review* **38**, 126–36.

Chinitz, B. (1960), *Freight and the Metropolis,* Cambridge: Harvard University Press.

Chinitz, B. (1961), "Contrasts in Agglomeration: New York and Pittsburgh," *American Economic Review,* Proceedings **51**, 279–89.

Chisholm, M. (1962), *Rural Settlement and Land Use,* London: Hutchinson.

Chisholm, M. (1963), "Tendencies in Agricultural Specialization and Regional Concentration of Industry," *Papers and Proceedings,* Regional Science Association **10**, 157–62.

Chisholm, M. (1966), *Geography and Economics,* London: Bell.

Chisholm, M. (1967), "General Systems Theory and Geography," *Transactions* of the Institute of British Geographers **42**, 45–52.

Chisholm, M. (1971), "In Search of a Basis for Location Theory: Micro economics or Welfare Economics," in C. Board, et al., eds., *Progress in Geography* **3**, London: Edward Arnold, pp. 111–33.

Chorley, R. J. (1962), "Geomorphology and General Systems Theory," *U. S. Geological Survey, Professional Paper* **500B**.

Chorley, R. J. (1964), "Geography and Analogue Theory," *Annals* of the Association of American Geographers **55**, 351–59.

Chorley, R. J. and P. Haggett, eds. (1966), *Frontiers in Geographical Teaching,* London: Methuen.

Chorley, R. J. and P. Haggett (1967), *Models in Geography,* London: Methuen.

Christaller, W. (1966), *Central Places in Southern Germany,* trans. C. W. Baskin, Englewood Cliffs, N. J.: Prentice-Hall.

Clairmonte, F. (1960), *Economic Liberalism and Underdevelopment: Studies in the Disintegration of an Idea,* Bombay: Asia Publishing House.

Clark, C. (1940), *The Conditions of Economic Progress,* London: Macmillan.

Clark, C. (1951), "Urban Population Densities," *Journal of the Royal Statistical Society, Series A* **114**, 490–96.

Clark, C. (1967), *Population Growth and Land Use,* London: Macmillan.

Clark, P. J. and F. C. Evans (1954), "Distance to Nearest Neighbor as a Measure of Spatial Relationships in Population," *Ecology* **35**, 445–53.

Cleef, E. van (1949), "Maps for Appraisals," *The Appraisal Journal* **17**, 219–31.

Cliff, A. D. (1968), "The Neighborhood Effect in the Diffusion of Innovations," *Transactions* of the Institute of British Geographers **44**, 75–84.

Cliffe, R. A. (1961), "A Reconnaissance of National Transportation," in National Academy of Science, *Transportation Design Considerations,* Washington, D. C.

Cohn, E. J. (1954), *Industry in the Pacific Northwest and the Location Theory,* New York: King's Crown Press.

Cole, J. P. and C. A. M. King (1968), *Quantitative Geography*, London: Wiley.

Committee of New England, National Planning Association (1954), *Freight Rates and New England's Competitive Position,* Report No. 12, Boston.

Common Carrier Conference of Domestic Water Carriers (1964), *Freight Rate Discrimination in the United States: A Catalog of Typical Current Rate Comparisons,* Chicago.

Conkling, E. C. (1962), *A Geographical Analysis of Diversification in South Wales, Studies in Geography* **7**, Evanston, Ill.: Northwestern University.

Conkling, E. C. (1963), "South Wales: A Case Study of Industrial Diversification," *Economic Geography* **39**, 258–72.

Conkling, E. C. (1964), "The Measurement of Diversification," G. Manners, ed., *South Wales in the Sixties,* London: Pergamon Press, pp. 161–83.

Conkling, E. C. and M. Yeates (1976), *Man's Economic Environment,* New York: McGraw-Hill.

Cooper, L. (1963), "Location—Allocation Problems," *Operational Research* **11**, 331–43.

Cooper, L. (1964), "Heuristic Methods for Location—Allocation Problems," *Society for Industrial and Applied Mathematics Review* **6**, 37–52.

Cooper, L. (1967), "Solutions of Generalized Locational Equilibrium Models," *Journal of Regional Science* **7**, 1–8.

Cooper, L. (1968), "An Extension of the Generalized Weber Problem," *Journal of Regional Science* **8**, 181–97.

Cootner, P. H. (1963), "The Role of the Railroads in United States Economic Growth," *Journal of Economic History* **23**, 477–521.

Cotterill, C. H. (1950), *Industrial Plant Location: Its Application to Zinc Smelting,* St. Louis: American Zinc, Lead, and Smelting Co.

Cox, K. R. (1965), "The Application of Linear Programming to Geographic Problems," *Tijdschrift voor Economische en Sociale Geografie* **56**, 228–36.

Craig, P. G. (1957), "Location Factors in the Development of Steel Centers," *Papers and Proceedings*, Regional Science Association **3**, 249–65.

Crowe, P. R. (1938), "On Progress in Geography," *Scottish Geographical Magazine* **54**, 1–19.

Crum, R. J. (1967), "Simulated Interregional Models of the Livestock-Meat Economy," *Agricultural Economic Reports* **117**, Economic Research Service, U. S. Department of Agriculture.

Currie, A. W. (1965), "Freight Rates and Regionalism," in J. J. Deutsch et al., eds., *The Canadian Economy: Selected Readings,* Toronto: Macmillan.

Curry, L. (1964), "The Random Spatial Economy: An Explanation in Settlement Theory," *Annals* of the Association of American Geographers **54**, 138–46.

Curry, L. (1966), "Chance and Landscape," in J. W. House, ed., *Northern Geographical Essays,* Newcastle: Oriel Press, pp. 40–55.

Curry, L. (1967), "Quantitative Geography," *Canadian Geographer* **11**, 265–79.

Cyert, R. M. and J. G. March (1963), *A Behavioral Theory of the Firm*, Englewood Cliffs, N. J.: Prentice-Hall.

Czamanski, S. (1964), "A Model of Urban Growth," *Papers*, Regional Science Association **13**, 177–200.

Czamanski, S. (1965), "Industrial Location and Urban Growth," *Town Planning Review* **36**, 165–80.

Dacey, M. F. (1962), "Analysis of Central Place and Point Patterns by a Nearest Neighbor Method," *Lund Studies in Geography, Series B, Human Geography*, 24.

Daggett, S. and J. P. Carter (1947), *The Structure of Transcontinental Railroad Rates,* Berkeley: University of California.

Daggett, S. (1955), *Principles of Inland Transportation,* New York: Harper & Row.

Daggett, S. (1968), "The System of Alfred Weber," in R. H. T. Smith, E. J. Taafe, and L. J. King, eds., *Readings in Economic Geography,* Skokie, Illinois: Rand McNally, pp. 58–64.

Daly, M. T. (1972), *Techniques and Concepts in Geography,* Melbourne: Nelson, Chapter 4.

Danielsson, A. (1964), "The Locational Decision from the Point of View of the Individual Company," *Ekonomisk Tidskrift* **66**, 47–87.

Darwent, D. F. (1969), "Growth Poles and Growth Centers in Regional Planning—A Review," *Environment and Planning* **1**, 5–31.

Davies, W. K. D. (1967), "Centrality and the Central Place Hierarchy," *Urban Studies* **4**, 61–79.

Davis, L. (1966), "The Capital Markets and Industrial Concentration," *Economic History Review* **19**, 255–72.

de Souza, A. R. and P. W. Porter (1974), *The Underdevelopment and Modernization of the Third World*, Washington, D.C.: Association of American Geographers Commission on College Geography, Resource Paper No. 28.

Devletogou, N. E. (1965), "A Dissenting View of Duopoly and Spatial Competition," *Economica* **32**, 146–60.

Dicken, P. (1971), "Some Aspects of the Decision-Making Behavior of Business Organizations," *Economic Geography* **47**, 426–37.

Dickinson, R. E. (1964), *City and Region*, London: Routledge and Kegan Paul.

Dodd, S. C. (1950), "The Interactance Hypothesis," *American Sociological Review* **15**, 245–56.

Dodd, S. C. (1953), "Testing Message Diffusion in Controlled Experiments: Charting the Distance and Time Factors—The Interactance Hypothesis," *American Sociological Review* **18**, 410–16.

Dodd, S. C. (1955), "Diffusion is Predictable: Testing Probability Models for Laws of Interaction," *American Sociological Review* **20**, 292–401

Dodge, F. W. Company (1969), *Dow Building Cost Calculator and Valuation Guide,* New York: McGraw-Hill.

Dorfman, R., P. A. Samuelson and R. M. Solow (1958), *Linear Programming and Economic Analysis,* New York: McGraw-Hill.

Downs, R. M. and D. Stea, eds. (1973), *Image and Environment: Cognitive Mapping and Spatial Behavior,* Chicago: Aldine.

Doxiadis, C. (1969), "The Prospect of an International Megalopolis," in M. Wade, ed., *The International Megalopolis,* Windsor, Ontario: University of Windsor Press, pp. 3–32.

Drewett, R., J. Goddard and N. Spence (1976), *British Cities: Urban Population and Employment Trends, 1951–1971,* London: Department of the Environment.

Due, J. F. (1961), "Studies of State-Local Tax Influences on Location of Industry," *National Tax Journal* **14**, 163–73.

Duncan, O. D., et al. (1960), *Metropolis and Region,* Baltimore: Johns Hopkins Press.

Duncan, O. D., R. P. Cuzzort and B. Duncan (1961), *Statistical Geography: Problems of Analysing Areal Data,* New York: The Free Press of Glencoe.

Dunn, E. S. (1954), *The Location of Agricultural Production,* Gainesville: University of Florida Press.

Dunn, E. S. (1956), "The Market Potential Concept and the Analysis of Location," *Papers and Proceedings*, Regional Science Association **2**, 183–94.

Dunning, J., ed. (1971), *The Multinational Enterprise,* London: George Allen & Unwin.

Durand, L. (1964), "The Major Milksheds of the Northeastern Quarter of the United States," *Economic Geography* **40**, 9–33.

Duskin, G. L. and R. L. Moomaw (1967), *Economic Development Centers: A Review,* Washington: Office of Economic Research Staff Paper, Economic Development Administration, U. S. Department of Commerce.

Easterlin, R. A. (1960), "Interregional Differences in Per Capita Income, Population, and Total Income, 1840-1950," in National Bureau of Economic Research, Conference on Research in Income and Wealth, *Trends in the American Economy in the Nineteenth Century,* Princeton, pp. 73–140.

Economic Commission for Europe (1967), *Criteria for Location of Industrial Plants,* New York: United Nations.

Economic Development Administration (1967), *Regional Economic Development in the United States,* Parts 1, 2, and 3, Washington, D. C.: U. S. Department of Commerce.

Edwards, R. S. and H. Townsend, (1958), *Business Enterprise,* London: Macmillan.

Eighmy, T. H. (1972), "Rural Periodic Markets and the Extension of an Urban System: A Western Nigeria Example," *Economic Geography* **48**, 299–315.

Eliot Hurst, M. E. (1972), *A Geography of Economic Behavior,* North Scituate, Mass.: Duxbury.

Eliot Hurst, M. E., ed. (1974), *Transportation Geography: Comments and Readings*, New York: McGraw-Hill.

Ellis, G. H. (1949), "Why New Manufacturing Establishments Located in New England, Aug. 1945-June 1948," *Federal Reserve Bank of Boston, Monthly Review* **31**, 1–12.

Emery, F. E. and O. A. Oeser (1958), *Information Decision and Action: A Study of the Psychological Determinants of Changes in Farming Techniques,* Melbourne: Melbourne University Press.

Enke, S. (1951), "Equilibrium Among Spatially Separate Markets—Solution by Electric Analogue," *Econometrica* **19**, 40–47.

Estall, R. C. (1972), *A Modern Geography of the United States*, London: Pelican.

Estall, R. C. and R. O. Buchanan (1973), *Industrial Activity and Economic Geography*, 3d ed., London: Hutchinson.

European Free Trade Association (1965), *Regional Development Policies in EFTA*, Geneva.

Ezekiel, M. and K. A. Fox (1959), *Methods of Correlation and Regression Analysis*, 3rd ed., New York: Wiley.

Fantus Company (1962), *Cost Comparison Study*, Manitoba Department of Industry and Commerce, Winnipeg.

Fair, M. L. and E. W. Williams (1959), *Economics of Transportation*, New York: Harper.

Fay, C. R. (1950), *Great Britain: From Adam Smith to the Present Day*, 5th ed., London: Longmans Green & Co.

Ferguson, C. E. (1960), "Relationship of Business Size to Stability, An Empirical Approach," *Journal of Industrial Economics* **9**, 43–62.

Fetter, F. A. (1924), "The Economic Law of Market Areas," *Quarterly Journal of Economics* **38**, 520–23.

Firey, W. (1960), *Man, Mind, and Land: A Theory of Resource Use*, New York: Free Press.

Fisher, J. C., ed. (1966), *City and Regional Planning in Poland*, Ithaca, New York: Cornell University Press.

Fleming, D. K. and G. Krumme (1968), "The Royal-Hoesch Union: Case Analysis of Adjustment Patterns in the European Steel Industry," *Tijdschrift voor Economische en Sociale Geografie* **59**, 177–99.

Florence, P. Sargant (1933), *The Logic of Industrial Organization*, London: Routledge & Kegan Paul.

Florence, P. S., W. G. Fritz and R. C. Gilles (1943), "Measures of Industrial Distribution," *Industrial Location and National Resources*, Washington, D. C.: U. S. National Resources Planning Board, pp. 105–24.

Florence, P. S. (1948), *Investment Location and Size of Plant*, London: National Institute of Economic and Social Research.

Florence, P. S. (1962), *Postwar Investment, Location, and Size of Plant*, London: National Institute of Economic and Social Research.

Floyd, J. S. (1952), *Effects of Taxation on Industrial Location*, Chapel Hill: University of North Carolina Press.

Foley, D. L. (1956), "Factors in the Location of Administrative Offices, with Particular Reference to the San Francisco Bay Area," *Papers and Proceedings*, Regional Science Association **2**, 318–26.

Forrester, J. W. (1968), *Principles of Systems*, Cambridge, Mass.: Wright-Allen Press.

Found, W. C. (1971), *A Theoretical Approach to Rural Land Use Patterns*, London: Edward Arnold.

Foust, J. Brady (1975), "Ubiquitous Manufacturing," *Annals* of the Association of American Geographers **65**, 13–17.

Frank, A. G. (1967), "Sociology of Development and Underdevelopment of Sociology," *Catalyst* **3**, Buffalo, N. Y.: State University of New York at Buffalo, pp. 20–73.

Frank, A. G. (1969), *Capitalism and Underdevelopment in Latin America*, New York: Monthly Review Press.

Frank, A. G. (1970), *Latin America: Underdevelopment or Revolution*, New York: Monthly Review Press.

Freeman, J. W. and H. B. Rodgers (1966), *Lancashire, Cheshire and the Isle of Man*, London: Nelson.

Friedmann, J. and W. Alonso (1964), *Regional Development and Planning: A Reader*,

Cambridge, Mass.: MIT Press.

Friedmann, J. and J. Miller (1965), "The Urban Field," *Journal of the American Institute of Planners* **31**, 312–20.

Friedmann, J. (1966), *Regional Development Policy: A Case Study of Venezuela,* Cambridge, Mass.: MIT Press.

Friedmann, J. (1967), "A Conceptual Model for the Analysis of Planning Behavior," *Administrative Science Quarterly* **12**, 225–52.

Friedmann, J. (1969), *A General Theory of Polarized Development,* Los Angeles: University of California School of Architecture and Urban Planning.

Friedmann, J. et al. (1970), *Urbanization and National Development: A Comparative Analysis,* Los Angeles: University of California School of Architecture and Planning.

Friedmann, J. (1972), "A General Theory of Polarized Development," in N. M. Hansen, ed., *Growth Centers in Regional Economic Development,* New York: Free Press, pp. 82–107.

Friedmann, J. (1973), *Urbanization, Planning, and National Development,* Beverly Hills, California: Sage.

Fuchs, V. R. (1959), "Changes in the Location of U. S. Manufacturing Since 1929," *Journal of Regional Science* **1**, 1–18.

Fuchs, V. R. (1962a), *Changes in the Location of Manufacturing in the United States Since 1929,* New Haven, Conn.: Yale University Press.

Fuchs, V. R. (1962b), "The Determinants of the Redistribution of Manufacturing in the United States Since 1929," *Review of Economics and Statistics* **44**, 167–77.

Fuchs, V. R. (1962c), "Statistical Explanations of the Relative Shift of Manufacturing Among Regions of the United States," *Papers*, Regional Science Association **8**, 105–26.

Fuchs, V. R. (1967), *Differentials in Hourly Earnings by Region and City Size, 1959,* New York: Columbia University Press.

Fulton, M. (1955), "Plant Location—1965," *Harvard Business Review* **33**, 40–50.

Fulton, M. and L. C. Hoch (1959), "Transportation Factors Affecting Location Decisions," *Economic Geography* **35**, 51–59.

Fulton, M. (1960), "Where to Locate Your Plant," *American Machinist/Metalworking Manufacturing,* December 12, 1960, pp. 121–28.

Galbraith, J. K. (1966), *The New Industrial State,* Boston: Houghton-Mifflin.

Galbraith, J. K. (1974), *Economics and the Public Purpose,* Boston: Houghton-Mifflin.

Gambini, R., D. Huff and G. F. Jenks (1968), "Geometric Properties of Market Areas," *Papers*, Regional Science Association **20**, 89–92.

Garner, B. J. (1966), "The Internal Structure of Retail Nucleations," *Northwestern University, Department of Geography, Research Paper* **12**.

Garner, B. J. (1967), "Models of Urban Geography and Settlement Location," in R. J. Chorley and P. Haggett, eds., *Models in Geography,* London: Methuen, pp. 303–60.

Garrison, W. L. and D. F. Marble (1957), "The Spatial Structure of Agricultural Activities," *Annals* of the Association of American Goegraphers **47**, 137–44.

Garrison, W. L. (1959-1960), "Spatial Structure of the Economy," *Annals* of the Association of American Geographers **49**, 232–39; **49**, 471–82; **50**, 357–73.

Garrison, W. L. (1960), "Connectivity of the Inter-State Highway System," *Papers and Proceedings*, Regional Science Association **6**, 121–37.

Garrison, W. L. and D. F. Marble, eds. (1967), *Quantitative Geography, Part I, Economic and Cultural Topics,* Studies in Geography, 13, Evanston, Ill.: Northwestern University.

Gasson, R. (1966), "The Changing Location of Intensive Crops in England and Wales," *Geography* **51**, 16–28.

Getis, A. (1963), "The Determination of the Location of Retail Activities With the Use of a Map Transformation," *Economic Geography* **39**, 14–22.

Ghosh, A. (1965), *Efficiency in Location and Inter-Regional Flows: The Indian Cement Industry During the Five Year Plans 1950-1959,* Amsterdam: North-Holland Publishing Company.

Gibrat, R. (1927), *Les Inégalites Économiques,* Paris: Sirey.

Gilmour, J. M. (1974), "External Economies of Scale, Inter-Industrial Linkages and Decision Making in Manufacturing," in F. E. I. Hamilton, ed., *Spatial Perspectives on Industrial Organization and Decision Making,* London: Wiley, pp. 363–93.

Gitlow, A. L. (1954), "Wages and the Allocation of Employment," *Southern Economic Journal* **21**, 62–83.

Goddard, J. B. (1975a), *Office Location in Urban and Regional Development,* London: Oxford University Press.

Goddard, J. B. (1975b), "Organizational Information Flows and the Urban System," *Economie Appliquée* **38**, 125–64.

Goldman, T. A. (1958), "Efficient Transportation and Industrial Location," *Papers*, Regional Science Association **4**, 91–106.

Golledge, R. G., G. Rushton and W. A. V. Clark (1966), "Some Spatial Characteristics of Iowa's Dispersed Farm Population and Their Implications for the Grouping of Central Place Functions," *Economic Geography* **42**, 261–72.

Golledge, R. G. (1967), "Conceptualizing the Market Decision Process," *Journal of Regional Science* **7**, 2S, 239–58.

Golledge, R. G. and L. A. Brown (1967), "Search, Learning, and the Market Decision Process," *Geografiska Annaler* **49B**, 116–24.

Golledge, R. G. and D. Amedeo (1968), "On Laws in Geography," *Annals* of the Association of American Geographers **58**, 760–74.

Gottmann, J. (1961), *Megalopolis,* Cambridge, Mass.: MIT Press.

Gould, P. R. (1963), "Man Against His Environment: A Game Theoretic Framework," *Annals* of the American Geographers **53**, 290–97.

Gould, P. R. (1966), "On Mental Maps," *Michigan Inter-University Community of Mathematical Geographers,* Discussion, Paper 9.

Gould, P. R. (1967), "On the Geographic Interpretation of Eigenvalues," *Transactions of the Institute of British Geographers* **42**, 53–86.

Gould, P. R. and R. R. White (1968), "The Mental Maps of British School Leavers," *Regional Studies* **2**, 161–82.

Gould, P. R. (1969), "Spatial Diffusion," *Association of American Geographers, Commission on College Geography Resource Paper*, 4.

Gould, P. R. and R. R. White (1974), *Mental Maps,* Harmondsworth: Penguin.

Green, A. G. (1969), "Regional Inequality, Structural Change, and Economic Growth in Canada—1890-1956," *Economic Development and Cultural Change* **17**, 567–83.

Greenhut, M. L. (1951), "Observations of Motives to Industrial Location," *Southern Economic Journal* **18**, 225–28.

Greenhut, M. L. (1952a), "Integrating the Leading Theories of Plant Location," *Southern Economic Journal* **18**, 526–38.

Greenhut, M. L. (1952b), "Size and Shape of the Market Area of a Firm," *Southern Economic Journal* **19**, 37–50.

Greenhut, M. L. (1955), "A General Theory of Plant Location," *Metroeconomia* **7**, 59–72.

Greenhut, M. L. (1956), *Plant Location in Theory and Practise,* Chapel Hill: University of North Carolina Press.

Greenhut, M. L. (1957), "Games, Capitalism, and General Economic Theory," *The Manchester School of Economic and Social Studies* **25**, 61–88.

Greenhut, M. L. (1959), "An Empirical Model and a Survey: New Plant Location in

Forida,'' *Review of Economics and Statistics* **61**, 433–48.

Greenhut, M. L. (1959), ''Space and Economic Theory,'' *Papers*, Regional Science Association **5**, 267–80.

Greenhut, M. L. (1960), ''Size of Markets vs Transport Costs in Industrial Location Surveys and Theory,'' *Journal of Industrial Economics* **8**, 172–84.

Greenhut, M. L. (1963), *Microeconomics and the Space Economy*, Chicago; Scott Foresman.

Greenhut, M. L. (1964), ''When is the Demand Factor of Location Important?'' *Land Economics* **40**, 175–84.

Greenhut, M. L. (1967), ''Interregional Programming and the Demand Factor of Location,'' *Journal of Regional Science* **7**, 151–60.

Gregory, S. (1963), *Statistical Methods and the Geographer*, London: Longmans.

Griliches, Z. (1957), ''Hybrid Corn: An Exploration in the Economics of Technological Change,'' *Econometrica* **25**, 501–22.

Grotewold, A. (1959), ''Von Thünen in Retrospect,'' *Economic Geography* **35**, 346–55.

Groves, P. A. (1971), ''Towards a Typology of Intrametropolitan Manufacturing,'' *University of Hull, Department of Geography, Occasional Papers*, No. 16.

Haber, W., E. McKean and H. Taylor (1959), *The Michigan Economy: Its Potentials and Problems*, Kalamazoo, Mich.: W. E. Upjohn Institute for Employment Research.

Hägerstrand, T. (1952), ''The Propagation of Innovation Waves,'' *Lund Studies in Geography, Series B*, No. 4.

Hägerstrand, T. (1957), ''Migration and Area: Survey of a Sample of Swedish Migration Fields,'' in D. Hannerberg, T. Hägerstrand, and B. Odeving, eds., *Migration in Sweden: A Symposium, Lund Studies in Geography, Series B*, 13, 27–158.

Hägerstrand, T. (1960), ''Aspects of the Spatial Structure of Social Communications and the Diffusion of Information,'' *Papers and Proceedings*, Regional Science Association **16**, 27–42.

Hägerstrand, T. (1965a), ''Quantitative Techniques for Analysis of the Spread of Information and Technology,'' in *Education and Economic Development*, C. A. Anderson and M. J. Bowman, eds., Chicago: Aldine.

Hägerstrand, T. (1965b), ''A Monte Carlo Approach to Diffusion,'' *European Journal of Sociology*, **6**, 43–76.

Hägerstrand, T. (1967a), *Innovation Diffusion as a Spatial Process* (trans. and postscript by A. Pred), Chicago: University of Chicago Press.

Hägerstrand, T. (1967b), ''On Monte Carlo Simulation of Diffusion,'' in W. L. Garrison and D. F. Marble, eds., *Quantitative Geography, Part I, Economic and Cultural Topics, Northwestern University Studies in Geography* **13**, 1–32.

Haggett, P. (1965), *Locational Analysis in Human Geography*, London: Edward Arnold.

Haggett, P. (1966), ''Changing Concepts in Economic Geography,'' in R. J. Chorley and P. Haggett, eds., *Frontiers in Geographical Teaching*, London: Methuen, pp. 101–17.

Haggett, P. and R. J. Chorley (1967), ''Models, Paradigms, and the New Geography,'' in *Models in Geography*, London: Methuen, pp. 19–41.

Haggett, P. and R. J. Chorley (1969), *Network Analysis in Geography*, London: Edward Arnold.

Haggett, P. (1975), *Geography: A Modern Synthesis*, 2d ed., New York: Harper & Row.

Hagood, M. J. and D. Price (1952), *Statistics for Sociologists*, New York: Holt.

Hague, D. C. and P. K. Newman (1952), *Costs in Alternative Locations: The Clothing Industry, Occasional Papers*, 15, National Institute of Economic and Social Research, Cambridge: Cambridge University Press.

Hague, D. C. and J. H. Dunning (1954), ''Costs in Alternative Locations: The Radio Industry,'' *Review of Economic Studies* **22**, 203–13.

Haig, R. M. (1926), ''Toward an Understanding of the Metropolis,'' *Quarterly Journal of*

Economics **40**, 421–33.

Hale, C. W. (1967), "The Mechanism of the Spread Effect in Regional Development," *Land Economics* **43**, 434–45.

Hall, A. D. and R. E. Fagen (1956), "Definition of System," *General Systems* **1**, 18–28.

Hall, M., ed. (1959), *Made in New York: Case Studies in Metropolitan Manufacturing,* Cambridge, Mass.: Harvard University Press.

Hall, P. (1962), *The Industries of London,* London: Hutchinson.

Hall, P. (1966a), *The World Cities,* London: Weidenfeld & Nicolson.

Hall, P., ed. (1966b), *Von Thünen's Isolated State,* London: Pergamon.

Hall, P. (1966c), "Britain's Uneven Shrinkage," *New Society,* April 1966, pp. 18–19.

Hall, P., H. Gracey, R. Drewett, and R. Thomas (1973), *The Containment of Urban England, Volume I: Urban and Metropolitan Growth Processes,* London: George Allen & Unwin.

Hamilton, F. E. I. (1967), "Models of Industrial Location," in R. J. Chorley and P. Haggett, eds., *Models in Geography,* London: Methuen, pp. 361–424.

Hamilton, F. E. I. (1969), *Regional Economic Analysis in Britain and the Commonwealth,* London: Weidenfeld & Nicolson.

Hamilton, F. E. I. (1970a), "Changes in the Industrial Geography of East Europe Since 1940," *Tijdschrift voor Economische en Sociale Geographie.*

Hamilton, F. E. I. (1970b), "Planning the Location of Industry in East Europe," *Economics of Planning* **6**, No. 2, 3–7.

Hamilton, F. E. I. (1971), "Locating Industry in East Europe: An Approach to Spatial Decision-Making in Planned Economies," *Transactions and Papers,* Institute of British Geographers **52**.

Hamilton, F. E. I. (1974), "A View of Spatial Behavior, Industrial Organizations, and Decision-Making," in *Spatial Perspectives on Industrial Organization and Decision-Making,* London: John Wiley, pp. 3–43.

Hannerberg, D., T. Hägerstrand and B. Odeving, eds. (1957), "Migration in Sweden: A Symposium," *Lund Studies in Geography, Series B,* 13.

Hansen, N. M. (1967a), "Human Resources and Regional Development: Some Lessons From French Experience," *Southern Economic Journal* **34**, 123–32.

Hansen, N. M. (1967b), "Toward a New Approach in Regional Economic Policy," *Land Economics* **43**, 377–83.

Hansen, N. M. (1968a), "Public Policy and Regional Development," *Quarterly Review of Economics and Business* **8**, 51–60.

Hansen, N. M. (1968b), "Growth Centers and Regional Development: Some Preliminary Considerations," *Discussion Papers*, 5, Lexington: Program on the Role of Growth Centers in Regional Economic Development, University of Kentucky.

Hansen, N. M. (1968c), *French Regional Planning,* Bloomington, Ind.: Indiana University Press.

Hansen, N. M. (1968d), "Regional Development and the Rural Poor," *Journal of Human Resources* **4**, 205–14.

Hansen, N. M. (1969a), "Growth Center Policy in the United States," *Discussion Papers,* 14, Lexington: Program on the Role of Growth Centers in Regional Economic Development, University of Kentucky.

Hansen, N. M. (1969b), "French Regional Planning Experience," *Journal of the American Institute of Planners* **35**, 362–68.

Hansen, W. L. and C. M. Tiebout (1963), "An Intersectoral Flows Analysis of the California Economy," *Review of Economics and Statistics* **45**, 409–18.

Harris, C. D. (1943), "Functional Classification of Cities in the United States," *Geographical Review* **33**, 86–99.

Harris, C. D. and E. L. Ullman (1945), ''The Nature of Cities,'' *Annals* of the American Academy of Political and Social Science **242**, 7–17.

Harris, C. D. (1954), ''The Market as a Factor in the Localization of Industry in the U. S.,'' *Annals* of the Association of American Geographers **44**, 315–48.

Hartshorne, R. (1926), ''The Economic Geography of Plant Location,'' *Annals of Real Estate Practice* **7**, 40–76.

Hartshorne, R. (1927), ''Location as a Factor in Geography,'' *Annals* of the Association of American Geographers **17**, 92–99.

Hartshorne, R. (1939), *The Nature of Geography,* Washington, D. C.: Association of American Geographers.

Hartshorne, R. (1959), *Perspective on the Nature of Geography,* Skokie, Ill.: Rand McNally.

Harvey, D. (1963), ''Locational Change in the Kentish Hop Industry and the Analysis of Land Use Patterns,'' *Transactions* of the Institute of British Geographers **33**, 123–44.

Harvey, D. (1966), ''Theoretical Concepts and the Analysis of Agricultural Land Use Patterns in Geography,'' *Annals* of the Association of American Geographers **56**, 361–74.

Harvey, D. (1967a), ''Models of the Evolution of Spatial Patterns in Human Geography,'' in R. J. Chorley and P. Haggett, eds., *Models in Geography,* London: Methuen, pp. 549–608.

Harvey, D. (1967b), ''The Problem of Theory Construction in Geography,'' *Journal of Regional Science* **7**, 211–16.

Harvey, D. (1969a), ''Conceptual and Measurement Problems in the Cognitive Behavioral Approach to Location Theory,'' in K. R. Cox and R. G. Golledge, eds., *Behavioral Problems in Geography: A Symposium, Northwestern University Studies in Geography* **17**, 35–67.

Harvey, D. W. (1969b), *Explanation in Geography,* London: Edward Arnold.

Harvey, D. (1972), *Society, the City, and the Space-Economy of Urbanism,* Washington, D. C.: Association of American Geographers, Commission on College Geography, Resource Paper No. 18

Harvey, D. (1975), ''The Geography of Capitalist Accumulation: A Reconstruction of the Marxian Theory,'' *Antipode* **7**, 9–21.

Havlicek, J., R. L. Rizek and G. C. Judge (1965), *Spatial Structure of the Livestock Economy: II. Spatial Analyses of the Flow of Slaughter Livestock in 1955 and 1960*, Brookings, South Dakota: North Central Regional Research Bulletins, 159, Agricultural Experiment Station, South Dakota State University.

Hawley, A. H. (1955), ''Land Value Patterns in Okayama, Japan, 1940 and 1952,'' *The American Journal of Sociology* **60**, 487–92.

Hay, A. and R. H. T. Smith (1966), ''Preliminary Estimates of Nigeria's Interregional Trade and Associated Money Flows,'' *Nigerian Journal of Economic and Social Studies* **8**, 9–35.

Hay, A. M. (1971), ''Notes on the Economic Basis for Periodic Marketing in Developing Countries,'' *Geographical Analysis* **3**, 393–401.

Hay, A. M. (1973), *Transport for the Space Economy: A Geographical Study,* London: Macmillan.

Hayter, R. (1976), ''Corporate Strategies and Industrial Change in the Canadian Forest Product Industries,'' *Geographical Review* **66**, 209–28.

Hecock, R. D. and J. F. Rooney (1968), ''Towards a Geography of Consumption,'' *Professional Geographer* **20**, 392–95.

Heilbroner, R. L. (1972), *The Economic Problem,* 3d ed., Englewood Cliffs, N. J.: Prentice-Hall.

Helvig, M. (1964), *''Chicago's External Truck Movements,'' University of Chicago, De-*

partment of Geography Research Paper **90**.

Henderson, J. M. (1958), *The Efficiency of the Coal Industry: An Application of Linear Programming,* Cambridge, Mass.: Harvard University Press.

H M S O (1973), *Regional Development Incentives, Report, Session 1973–74*, London: House of Commons Expenditure Committee (Trade and Industry Sub-Committee), 665107.

Hermansen, T. (1972), "Development Poles and Related Theories," in N. M. Hansen, ed., *Growth Centers in Regional Economic Development,* New York: Free Press, pp. 160–203.

Hicks, J. R. (1959), *Essays in World Economics,* Oxford: Oxford University Press.

Hidore, J. J. (1963), "The Relations Between Cash Grain Farming and Land Forms," *Economic Geography* **39**, 84–89.

Highsmith, R. M. and R. M. Northam (1968), *World Economic Activity: A Geographic Analysis,* New York: Harcourt, Brace, and World.

Hill, L. E. (1964), "Rates of Return on Municipal Subsidies to Industry: Comment," *Southern Economic Journal* **30**, 358–59.

Hill, P. and R. H. T. Smith (1972), "The Spatial and Temporal Synchronization of Periodic Markets: Evidence From Four Emirates in Northern Nigeria," *Economic Geography* **48**, 345–55.

Hirsch, S. (1967), *Industrial Location and International Competitiveness,* Oxford: Clarendon Press.

Hirsch, W. Z. (1959), "Interindustry Relations of a Metropolitan Area," *Review of Economics and Statistics* **41**, 360–69.

Hirsch, W. Z. (1961), "Regional Fiscal Development and Local Industrial Development, *Papers and Proceedings*, Regional Science Association **7**, 119–30.

Hirsch, W. Z., ed. (1966), *Regional Accounts for Policy Decisions,* Baltimore: Johns Hopkins Press.

Hirschman, A. O. (1958), *The Strategy of Economic Development,* New Haven, Conn.: Yale University Press.

Hodge, G. (1966), "Urban Systems and Regional Policy," *Canadian Public Administration* **9**, 181–93.

Hodge, G. (1968), "Urban Structure and Regional Development," *Papers and Proceedings,* Regional Science Association **21**, 101–24.

Holt, R. A. (1964), *The Changing Industrial Geography of the Cotton Areas of Lancashire: A Study of Mill Conversion and Employment Structure,* unpublished MA Thesis, University of Manchester.

Hoover, E. M. (1936), "The Measurement of Industrial Localization," *Review of Economics and Statistics* **18**, 162–71.

Hoover, E. M. (1937), *Location Theory and the Shoe and Leather Industries,* Cambridge, Mass.: Harvard University Press.

Hoover, E. M. (1948), *The Location of Economic Activity,* New York: McGraw-Hill.

Hoover, E. M. and R. Vernon (1959), *Anatomy of a Metropolis,* Cambridge, Mass.: Harvard University Press.

Hoover, E. M. (1964), "Spatial Economics: The Partial Equilibrium Approach," *University of Pittsburgh Center for Regional Economic Studies, Occasional Paper,* 2.

Hoover, E. M. (1966), *Computerized Location Models for Assessing of Indirect Impacts of Water Resource Projects,* Institute for Urban and Regional Studies, St. Louis: Washington University.

Hoover, E. M. (1967a), "Some Programmed Models of Industry Location," *Land Economics* **43**, 303–11.

Hoover, E. M. (1967b), "Some Old and New Issues in Regional Development," Economic

Development Administration, U. S. Department of Commerce, *Regional Economic Development in the United States,* Part 1, 4, pp. 19–40.

Horvath, R. J. (1969), ''Von Thünen's Isolated State and the Area Around Addis Ababa, Ethiopia,'' *Annals* of the Association of American Geographers **59**, 308–23.

Hotelling, H. (1929), ''Stability in Competition,'' *Economic Journal* **39**, 41–57.

House, J. W. (1969), *Industrial Britain: The North East*, Devon, England: David & Charles, Newton Abbot.

Huff, D. L. (1960), ''A Topographical Model of Consumer Space Preferences,'' *Papers and Proceedings*, Regional Science Association **6**, 159–73.

Hunker, H. L. (1958), ''Industrial Evolution of Columbus, Ohio,'' *Bureau of Business Research Monograph,* 93, Ohio State University.

Hunker, H. and A. J. Wright (1963), *Factors of Industrial Location in Ohio*, Columbus: The Ohio State University Press.

Huntsberger, D. V. (1961), *Elements of Statistical Inference,* Boston: Allyn and Bacon.

Hurd, R. M. (1924), *Principles of City Land Values,* New York: The Record and Guide.

Huxley, J. S. (1932), *Problems of Relative Growth,* London: Methuen.

Hymer, S. (1972), ''The Multinational Corporation and the Law of Uneven Development,'' in J. N. Bhagwati, ed., *Economics and World Order,* London: Macmillan, pp. 113–40.

Hyson, C. D. and W. P. Hyson (1950), ''The Economic Law of Market Areas,'' *Quarterly Journal of Economics* **64**, 319–27.

Innis, H. A. and A. R. M. Lower (1936), *Settlement and the Forest and Mining Frontier,* Toronto: Macmillan.

Institute of Economic Affairs (1973), *Mergers, Takeovers, and the Structure of Industry,* London: Institute of Economic Affairs.

Isard, W. (1948), ''Some Locational Factors in the Iron and Steel Industry Since the Early 19th Century,'' *Journal of Political Economy* **56,** 203–17.

Isard, W. and W. H. Capron (1949), ''The Future Locational Pattern of Iron and Steel Production in the United States,'' *Journal of Political Economy* **57**, 118–33.

Isard, W. (1949), ''The General Theory of Location and Space Economy,'' *Quarterly Journal of Economics* **63**, 476–506.

Isard, W. and V. Whitney (1950), ''Atomic Power and the Location of Industry,'' *Harvard Business Review* **28**, 45–54.

Isard, W. and J. H. Cumberland (1950), ''New England as a Possible Location for an Integrated Iron and Steel Works,'' *Economic Geography* **26**, 245–59.

Isard, W. (1951), ''Distance Inputs and the Space-Economy,'' *Quarterly Journal of Economics* **65**, 181–98.

Isard, W. (1952), ''A General Location Principle of an Optimum Space Economy,'' *Econometrica* **20**, 406–30.

Isard, W. and R. E. Kuenne (1953), ''The Impact of Steel on the Greater New York-Philadelphia Industrial Region,'' *Review of Economics and Statistics* **35**, 289–301.

Isard, W. and R. Kevesh (1954), ''Economic Structure Interrelations of Metropolitan Regions,'' *American Journal of Sociology* **60**, 152–62.

Isard, W. and E. W. Schooler (1955), *Location Factors in the Petrochemical Industry,* Washington, D. C.: Office of Technical Services, Area Development Division, U. S. Department of Commerce.

Isard, W. (1956), *Location and Space Economy,* Cambridge: MIT Press.

Isard, W. (1957), ''General Interregional Equilibrium,'' *Papers,* Regional Science Association **3**, 35–60.

Isard, W. (1958), ''Interregional Linear Programming: An Elementary Presentation and a General Model,'' *Journal of Regional Science* **1**, 1–59.

Isard, W. and E. W. Schooler (1959), ''Industrial Complex Analysis, Agglomeration

Economies, and Regional Development,'' *Journal of Regional Science* **1**, 19–33.

Isard, W., E. W. Schooler and T. Vietorisz (1959), *Industrial Complex Analysis and Regional Development*, Cambridge: MIT Press.

Isard, W. (1960), *Methods of Regional Analysis*, Cambridge: MIT Press.

Isard, W. and J. H. Cumberland, eds. (1961), *Regional Economic Planning: Techniques of Analysis for Less Developed Areas*, Paris: Organization for European Economic Cooperation.

Isard, W. and T. A. Reiner (1962), ''Aspects of Decision-Making Theory and Regional Science,'' *Papers and Proceedings*, Regional Science Association **9**, 25–34.

Isard, W. and T. H Tung (1964), ''Some Concepts for the Analysis of Spatial Organization,'' *Papers and Proceedings*, Regional Science Association **11**, 17–40, and **12**, 1–25.

Isard, W. (1967), ''Game Theory, Location Theory, and Industrial Agglomeration,'' *Papers and Proceedings*, Regional Science Association **18**, 1–11.

Isard, W. and T. E. Smith (1967), ''Location Games: With Applications to Classic Location Problems,'' *Papers*, Regional Science Association **19**, 45–80.

Isard, W., T. W. Langford and E. Romanoff (1967), *Preliminary Input-Output Tables for the Philadelphia Region*, Philadelphia: Regional Science Research Institute.

Isard, W. and T. E. Smith (1968), ''Coalition Locational Games: Paper 3,'' *Papers*, Regional Science Association **20**, 95–107.

Isard, W. (1969), *General Theory: Social, Political, Economic, and Regional*, Cambridge: MIT Press.

Janelle, D. G. (1968), ''Central Place Development in a Time-Space Framework,'' *Professional Geographer* **20**, 5–10.

Janelle, D. G. (1969), ''Spatial Reorganization: A Model and a Concept,'' *Annals* of the Association of American Geographers **59**, 348–64.

Johnson, E. A. J. (1970), *The Organization of Space in Developing Countries*, Cambridge: Harvard University Press.

Johnson, B. L. C. (1958), ''The Distribution of Factory Population in the West Midlands Conurbation,'' *Transactions and Papers*, Institute of British Geographers **25**, 209–23.

Johnson, P. S. (1975), *The Economics of Invention and Innovation*, London: Martin Robertson.

Johnson, R. E. (1958), ''Application of Linear Programming to Plant Location Decisions,'' *Engineering Economist* **4**, 1–16.

Johnston, R. J. (1966), ''Central Places and the Settlement Pattern,'' *Annals* of the Association of American Geographers **56**, 541–49.

Judge, G. C., J. Havlicek and R. L. Rizek (1964), *Spatial Structure of the Livestock Economy: I. Spatial Analyses of the Meat Marketing Sector in 1955 and 1960*, Brookings, South Dakota: North Central Regional Research Bulletins **157**, Agricultural Experiment Station, South Dakota State University.

Kahn, H. and A. J. Wiener (1967), *The Year 2000*, New York: Macmillan.

Kansky, K. J. (1963), ''Structure of Transportation Networks,'' *University of Chicago, Department of Geography Research Paper*, 84.

Kaplan, A. (1964), *The Conduct of Inquiry*, San Francisco: Chandler.

Kaplan, A. D. H. (1948), *Small Business: Its Place and Problems*, New York: McGraw-Hill.

Karaska, G. J. (1966), ''Interindustry Relations in the Philadelphia Economy,'' *East Lakes Geographer* **2**, 80–96.

Karaska, G. J. (1968), ''Variations of Input-Output Coefficients for Different Levels of Aggregation,'' *Journal of Regional Science* **8**, 215–27.

Karaska, G. J. and D. F. Bramhall (1969), *Locational Analysis for Manufacturing: A Selection of Readings*, Cambridge, Mass.: MIT Press.

Katona, G. and J. N. Morgan (1950), *Industrial Mobility in Michigan,* University Survey Research Center, Institute for Social Research, University of Michigan.

Katona, G. and J. Morgan (1952), "The Quantitative Study of Factors Determining Business Decisions," *Quarterly Journal of Economics* **66**, 67–90.

Katz, D. and R. L. Kahn (1966), *The Social Psychology of Organizations,* New York: Wiley.

Katzman, M. T. (1974), "The Von Thünen Paradigm, the Industrial Urban Hypothesis, and the Spatial Structure of Agriculture," *American Journal of Agricultural Economics* **56**, 683–97.

Keeble, D. E. (1968), "Industrial Decentralization and the Metropolis: The N. W. London Case," *Transactions* of the Institute of British Geographers **44**, 1–54.

Kennelly, R. A. (1954–55), "The Location of the Mexican Steel Industry," *Revista Geografica* **15**, 109–29, **16**, 60–77.

Kerr, D. and J. Spelt (1960), "Some Aspects of Industrial Location in Southern Ontario," *Canadian Geographer* **15**, 12–25.

Keynes, J. M. (1936), *The General Theory of Employment, Interest, and Money,* New York: Harcourt, Brace.

King, L. J. (1961), "A Multivariate Analysis of the Spacing of Urban Settlements in the United States," *Annals* of the Association of American Geographers **51**, 222–33.

King, L. J. (1962), "A Quantitative Expression of the Pattern of Urban Settlements in Selected Areas of the United States," *Tijdschrift voor Economische en Sociale Geografie* **53**, 1–7.

King, L. J. (1966), "Approaches to Locational Analysis: An Overview," *East Lakes Geographer* **2**, 1–16.

King, L. J. (1969), *Statistical Analysis in Geography,* Englewood Cliffs, N. J.: Prentice-Hall.

King, L. J. (1976), "Alternatives to a Positive Economic Geography," *Annals* of the Association of American Geographers **66**, 293–308.

Kirk, W. (1963), "Problems of Geography," *Geography* **48**, 357–71.

Knos, D. W. (1962), *Distribution of Land Values in Topeka, Kansas,* Lawrence: University of Kansas Press.

Koch, A. R. and M. M. Snodgrass (1959), "Linear Programming Applied to Location and Product Flow Determination in the Tomato Processing Industry," *Papers,* Regional Science Association **5**, 151–64.

Kolars, J. F. and J. D. Nystuen, (1974a), *Geography: The Study of Location, Culture, and Environment,* New York: McGraw-Hill.

Kolars, J. F. and J. D. Nystuen, (1974b), *Human Geography, Spatial Design in World Society,* New York: McGraw-Hill.

Koopmans, T. C. and M. Beckmann (1957), "Assignment Problems and the Location of Economic Activity," *Econometrica* **25**, 53–76.

Krumme, G. (1969a), "Notes on Locational Adjustment Patterns in Industrial Geography," *Geografiska Annaler* **51B**, 15–20.

Krumme, G. (1969b), "Toward a Geography of Enterprise," *Economic Geography* **43**, 30–40.

Krumme, G. (1970), "The Inter-Regional Corporation and the Region," *Tijdschrift voor Economische en Sociale Geografie* **61**, 318–33.

Krutilla, J. V. (1955), "Locational Factors Influencing Recent Aluminum Expansion," *Southern Economic Journal* **21**, 273–88.

Kuenne, R. E. (1968), "Approximate Solution to a Dynamic Combinatorial Problem in Space," *Journal of Regional Science* **8**, 165–80.

Kuhn, H. W. and R. E. Kuenne (1962), "An Efficient Algorithm for the Numerical Solution of the Generalized Weber Problem in Space Economics,'' *Journal of Regional Science* **4**, 21–33.

Kuznets, S. (1961), *Capital in the American Economy: Its Formation and Financing,* National Bureau of Economic Research: Princeton University Press.

Lampard, E. (1955), ''The History of Cities in the Economically Advanced Areas,'' *Economic Development and Cultural Change,* **3,** 81–136.

Lasuen, J. R. (1969), ''On Growth Poles,'' *Urban Studies* **6**, 137–61.

Launhardt, W. (1882), ''Die Bestimmung des Zweckmässigsten Standorts einer Gewerblichen Anlage,'' *Zeitschrift des Vereins Deutscher Ingenieure* **26**, 106–15.

Launhardt, W. (1885), *Mathematische Bergründung der Volkwirtschaftslehre,* Leipzig.

Lean, W. (1969), *Economics of Land Use Planning: Urban and Regional,* London: The Estates Gazette.

Lefeber, L. (1958), *Allocation in Space,* Amsterdam: North-Holland Publishing Co.

Lefeber, L. (1966), *Location and Regional Planning,* Training Seminar Series 7, Center of Planning and Economic Research, Athens, Greece.

Leibenstein, H. (1954), *Economic Backwardness and Economic Growth,* New York: Wiley.

Leontief, W. W. (1951), ''Input-Output Economics,'' *Scientific American* **185**, 15–21.

Leontief, W. W., et al. (1953), *Studies in the Structure of the American Economy,* Oxford: Oxford University Press.

Leontief, W. W. (1963), ''The Structure of Development,'' *Scientific American* **209**, 146–66.

Leontief, W. W. (1965), ''The Structure of the U. S. Economy,'' *Scientific American* **212**, 25–35.

Lerner, A. P. and H. W. Singer (1937), ''Some Notes on Duopoly and Spatial Competition,'' *Journal of Political Economy* **45**, 145–86.

Lewis, P. W. (1969), ''A Numerical Approach to the Location of Industry,'' *University of Hull, Department of Geography, Occasional Papers,* 13.

Lewis, W. A. (1955), *The Theory of Economic Growth,* London: Allen & Unwin.

Lewthwaite, G. R. (1964), ''Wisconsin Cheese and Farm Type: A Locational Hypothesis,'' *Economic Geography* **40**, 95–112.

Lichtenberg, R. M. (1960), *One Tenth of a Nation,* Cambridge: Harvard University Press.

Lindberg, O. (1953), ''An Economic-Geographic Study of the Swedish Paper Industry,'' *Geografiska Annaler* **35**, 28–40.

Lindsay, R. (1956), ''Regional Advantage in Oil Refining,'' *Papers,* Regional Science Association **2**, 304–17.

Lionberger, H. F. (1960), *Adoption of New Ideas and Practices,* Ames: Iowa State University Press.

Lipsey, R. G. and P. O. Steiner (1975), *Economics,* 4th ed., New York: Harper & Row.

Liu, B. (1969), *Employment Multipliers and Employment Projections: An Economic Base Study for the St. Louis Region,* St. Louis Regional Industrial Development Corporation.

Lloyd, P. E. (1965a), ''A Method for Conducting Rapid Reconnaissance Surveys of Manufacturing in Australian Cities,'' *Australian Geographical Studies* **3**, 31–38.

Lloyd, P. E. (1965b), ''Industrial Changes in the Merseyside Development Area 1949–1959,'' *Town Planning Review* **35**, 285–98.

Lloyd, P. E. and P. Dicken (1968), ''The Data Bank in Regional Studies of Industry,'' *Town Planning Review* **38**, 304–16.

Locklin, D. P. (1960), *The Economics of Transportation,* Homewood, Ill.: Irwin.

Logan, M. I. (1966), ''Locational Behavior of Manufacturing Firms in Urban Areas,'' *Annals* of the Association of American Geographers **56**, 451–66.

Lösch, A. (1938), ''The Nature of Economic Regions,'' *Southern Economic Journal* **5**, 71–78.

Lösch, A. (1954), *The Economics of Location,* New Haven: Yale University Press.

Lowe, J. and Moryadas (1975), *The Geography of Movement*, Boston: Houghton-Mifflin.

Lowry, I. S. (1965), "A Short Course in Model Design," *Journal of the American Institute of Planners* **31**, 158–65.

Lukerman, F. and P. W. Porter (1960), "Gravity and Potential Models in Economic Geography," *Annals* of the Association of American Geographers **50**, 493–504.

Lukerman, F. (1966), "Empirical Expressions of Nodality and Hierarchy in a Circulation Manifold," *East Lakes Geographer* **2**, 17–44.

Luttrell, W. F. (1952), *The Cost of Industrial Movement, Occasional Papers,* No. 14, National Institute of Economic and Social Research, Cambridge: Cambridge University Press.

Luttrell, W. F. (1962), *Factory Location and Industrial Movement,* London: National Institute of Economic and Social Research.

Lutz, V. (1962), *Italy: A Study in Economic Development,* Oxford: Oxford University Press.

Lynch, K. (1960), *The Image of the City,* Cambridge, Mass.: MIT Press.

McCarty, H. H. and J. B. Lindberg (1966), *A Preface to Economic Geography,* Englewood Cliffs, N. J.: Prentice-Hall.

McCarty, H. H. (1940), *The Geographical Basis of American Economic Life,* New York: Harper.

McCarty, H. H. (1954), "An Approach to a Theory of Economic Geography," *Economic Geography* **30**, 95–101.

McCarty, H. H., J. C. Hook and D. S. Knos (1956), *The Measurement of Association in Industrial Geography,* Iowa City: Department of Geography, University of Iowa.

McCarty, H. H. (1959), "Towards a More General Economic Geography," *Economic Geography* **33**, 283–89.

McCrone, G. (1969), *Regional Policy in Britain,* London: Allen & Unwin.

McDaniel, R. and M. E. Eliot Hurst (1968), *A Systems Analytic Approach to Economic Geography,* Association of American Geographers, Commission on College Geography, Publication 8.

Machlup, F. (1949), *The Basing Point System,* Homewood, Ill.: Irwin.

Mackay, J. R. (1958), "The Interactance Hypothesis and Boundaries in Canada," *Canadian Geographer* **11**, 1–8.

McKim, W. (1972), "The Periodic Market System in Northeastern Ghana," *Economic Geography* **48**, 333–44.

McNee, R. B. (1958), "Functional Geography of the Firm, With an Illustrated Case Study From the Petroleum Industry," *Economic Geography* **34**, 321–27.

McNee, R. B. (1959), "The Changing Relationships of Economics and Economic Geography," *Economic Geography* **35**, 189–98.

McNee, R. B. (1960), "Towards a More Humanistic Economic Geography: The Geography of Enterprise," *Tijdschrift voor Economische en Sociale Geografie* **51**, 201–5.

McNee, R. B. (1963), "The Spatial Evolution of the Sun Oil Company," *Annals* of the Association of American Geographers **53**, 609.

Madden, C. H. (1956), "Some Indicators of Stability in the Growth of Cities in the United States," *Economic Development and Cultural Change* **4**, 236–52.

Magdoff, H. (1969), *The Age of Imperialism*, New York: Monthly Review Press.

Malinowski, Z. S. and W. N. Kinnard (1961), *Personal Factors Influencing Small Manufacturing Plant Locations,* University of Connecticut, for the Small Business Administration.

Management and Economic Research Incorporated (1967), *Industrial Location as a Factor in Regional Economic Development,* Washington, D. C.: Economic Development Administration, U. S. Department of Commerce.

Manners, G. (1964), *The Geography of Energy,* Chicago: Aldine.

Mansfield, E. (1968a), *The Economics of Technological Change*. New York: Norton.

Mansfield, E. (1968b), *Industrial Research and Technological Innovation,* New York: Norton.

Maranzana, F. E. (1964), "On the Location of Supply Points to Minimize Transport Costs," *Operational Research Quarterly* 15, 261–70.

Marble, D. F. and J. D. Nystuen (1963), "An Approach to the Direct Measurement of Community Mean Information Fields," *Papers and Proceedings,* Regional Science Association **11**, 99–109.

March, J. G. and H. A. Simon (1958), *Organlzations,* New York: Wiley.

Marcus, M. (1965), "Agglomeration Economies: A Suggested Approach," *Land Economics* **41**, 279–84.

Marshall, A. (1920), *Principles of Economics,* 8th ed., London: Macmillan.

Marshall, J. U. (1969), "The Location of Service Towns," *University of Toronto, Department of Geography, Research Paper,* 3.

Martellaro, J. A. (1965), *Economic Development in Southern Italy,* Washington, D.C.: Catholic University of America Press.

Martin, J. E. (1966), *Greater London: An Industrial Geography,* Chicago: University of Chicago Press.

Maruyama, M. (1963), "The Second Cybernetics: Deviation Amplifying Mutual Causal Processes," *American Scientist* **51**, 164–79.

Marx, K. (1918), *Capital: A Critique of Political Economy,* London: William Gliesher.

Massey, D. B. (1968), "Problems of Location: Linear Programming," *Working Papers*. 14, London: Center for Environmental Studies.

Mattingly, P. F. (1972), "Intensity of Agricultural Land Use Near Cities: A Case Study," *Professional Geographer* **24**, 7–10.

Maxfield, D. W. (1969), "An Interpretation of the Primal and the Dual Solutions of Linear Programming," *Professional Geographer* **21**, 255–63.

Maxwell, J. W. (1965), "The Functional Structure of Canadian Cities," *Geographical Bulletin* **7**, 79–104.

Mayhew, A. (1969), "Regional Planning and the Development Areas in West Germany," *Regional Studies* **3**, 73–139.

Meehan, E. J. (1968), *Explanation in Social Science: A System Paradigm,* Homewood, Ill.: The Dorsey Press.

Meier, R. L. (1962), *A Communications Theory of Urban Growth,* Cambridge, Mass.: MIT Press.

Meinig, D. W. (1962), "A Comparative Historical Geography of Two Railnets: Columbia Basin and South Australia," *Annals* of the Association of American Geographers **52**, 394–413.

Melamid, A. (1962), "Geography of the World Petroleum Price Structure," *Economic Geography* **38**, 283–98.

Mennes, J. B. M., J. Tinbergen and J. G. Waardenburg (1969), *The Element of Space in Development Planning,* Amsterdam: North-Holland Publishing Co.

Miehle, W. (1958), "Link-Length Minimization in Networks," *Operations Reaearch* **6**, 232–43.

Miernyk, W. H. (1965), *The Elements of Input-Output Analysis,* New York: Random House.

Miles, C. (1968), "Lancashire Textiles: A Case Study of Industrial Change," *Occasional Papers,* No. 23, National Institute of Economic and Social Research, Cambridge: Cambridge University Press.

Miller, J. G. (1955), "Toward a General Theory for the Behavioral Sciences," *American Psychologist* **10**, 513–31.

Miller, R. E. (1963), *Domestic Airline Efficiency: An Application of Linear Programming,* Cambridge, Mass.: MIT Press.

Mills, E. S. and M. R. Lav (1964), ''A Model of Market Areas With Free Entry,'' *Journal of Political Economy* **72**, 278–88.

Mishan, E. J. (1969), *The Costs of Economic Growth,* Harmondsworth, England: Penguin.

Moroney, J. R. and J. M. Walker (1966), ''A Regional Test of the Heckscher-Ohlin Hypothesis,'' *Journal of Political Economy* **74**, 573–86.

Moroney, J. R. (1972), *The Structure of Production in American Manufacturing,* Chapel Hill: University of North Carolina Press.

Morrill, R. L. (1963a), ''The Distribution of Migration Distances,'' *Papers and Proceedings,* Regional Science Association **11**, 75–84.

Morrill, R. L. (1963b), ''The Development and Spatial Distribution of Towns in Sweden,'' *Annals* of the Association of American Geographers **53**, 1–14.

Morrill, R. L. (1965), ''Migration and the Spread and Growth of Urban Settlement,'' *Lund Studies in Geography, Series B,* 26.

Morrill, R. L. and F. R. Pitts (1967), ''Marriage, Migration, and Mean Information Field,'' *Annals* of the Association of American Geographers **57**, 401–22.

Morrill, R. L. (1968), ''Waves of Spatial Diffusion,'' *Journal of Regional Science* **8**, 1–18.

Morrill, R. L. (1970), *The Spatial Organization of Society,* Belmont, Cal.: Wadsworth.

Moser, C. A. and W. Scott (1961), *British Towns: A Statistical Study of Their Social and Economic Differences,* London: Oliver & Boyd.

Moses, L. N. (1958), ''Location and the Theory of Production,'' *Quarterly Journal of Economics* **72**, 259–72.

Moses, L. N. (1960), ''A General Equilibrium Model of Production, Interregional Trade, and Location of Industry,'' *Review of Economics and Statistics* **42**, 373–99.

Mountjoy, A. B. (1963), *Industrialization and Under-Developed Countries,* London: Hutchinson.

Mueller, E. A., A. Wilken and M. Wood (1961), *Location Decisions and Industry Mobility in Michigan*, Ann Arbor: Institute for Social Research, University of Michigan.

Mueller, E. and J. N. Morgan (1962), ''Location Decisions of Manufacturers,'' *American Economic Review,* Papers and Proceedings **502**, 204–17.

Muller, P. O. (1973), ''Trend Surfaces of American Agricultural Patterns: A Macro-Thünian Analysis,'' *Economic Geography* **49**, 228–42.

Mumford, L. (1934), *Technics and Civilization*, New York: Harcourt, Brace & World.

Muncy, D. A. (1954), ''Land for Industry—A Neglected Problem,'' *Harvard Business Review* **32**, 51–63.

Murata, K. (1959), ''A Viewpoint on Economic Geography From Location Theory,'' *Proceedings of the IGU Regional Conference in Japan 1957,* pp. 434–39.

Murdie, R. A. (1965), ''Cultural Differences in Consumer Travel,'' *Economic Geography* **41**, 211–33.

Murphey, R. E. and H. Spittal (1945), ''Movements in the Center of Coal Mining in the Appalachian Plateaus,'' *Geographical Review* **35**, 624–33.

Murphey, R. E. (1966), *The American City,* New York: McGraw-Hill.

Myint, H. (1964), *The Economics of the Developing Countries,* London: Hutchinson.

Myrdal, G. M. (1957a), *Economic Theory and Underdeveloped Regions,* London: Duckworth.

Myrdal, G. (1957b), *Rich Lands and Poor,* New York: Harper & Row.

National Building Agency (1968), *Land Costs and Housing Development,* London.

National Bureau of Economic Research (1962), *The Rate and Direction of Inventive Activity: Economic and Social Factors,* Princeton, N. J.: Princeton University Press.

Neft, D. S. (1966), ''Statistical Analysis for Areal Distributions,'' *Monograph Series* **2**,

Philadelphia: Regional Science Research Institute.

Nelson, H. J. (1955), "A Service Classification of American Cities," *Economic Geography* **31**, 189–210.

Nelson, R. L. (1963), *Concentration in the Manufacturing Industries of the United States: A Mid-Century Report,* New Haven, Conn.: Yale University Press.

Neuhoff, M. C. (1953), *Techniques of Plant Location,* Washington, D. C.: U. S. G. P. O.

Newcombe, V. Z. (1969), "Creating an Industrial Development Pole in Southern Italy," *Journal of the Town Planning Institute* **55**, 157–61.

Nichols, V. (1969), "Growth Poles: An Evaluation of Their Propulsive Effect," *Environment and Planning* **1**, 193–208.

Niedercorn, J. H. and E. F. R. Hearle (1964), "Recent Land Use Trends in 48 Large American Cities," *Land Economics* **40**, 105–10.

Nordbeck, S. (1971), "Urban Allometric Growth," *Geografiska Annaler* **53B**, 54–67.

North, D. C. (1955), "Location Theory and Regional Economic Growth," *Journal of Political Economy* **63**, 243–58.

North, D. C. (1956), "The Spatial and Interregional Framework of the U. S. Economy," *Papers and Proceedings,* Regional Science Association **2**, 201–9.

Nourse, H. O. (1967), *The Electronics Industry and Economic Growth in Illinois,* Department of Business and Economic Development, State of Illinois.

Nourse, H. O. (1968), *Regional Economics,* New York: McGraw-Hill.

Noyes Development Corporation (1965), *Investment and Plant Location in Canada 1965,* Plant Location Study No. 3, New York.

Nystuen, J. D. (1963), "Identification of Some Fundamental Concepts," *Papers* of the Michigan Academy of Science, Arts, and Letters **48**, 333–84.

Okun, B. and R. W. Richardson (1961), "Regional Income Inequality and Internal Population Migration," *Economic Development and Cultural Change* **9**, 128–43.

Olsson, G. and A. Persson (1964), "The Spacing of Central Places in Sweden," *Papers and Proceedings,* Regional Science Association **12**, 87–93.

Olsson, G. (1965a), "Distance and Human Interaction: A Migration Study," *Geografiska Annaler* **47B**, 3–43.

Olsson, G. (1965b), *Distance and Human Interaction: A Review and Bibliography,* Philadelphia: Regional Science Research Institute.

Olsson, G. (1967), "Central Place Systems, Spatial Interaction, and Stochastic Processes," *Papers and Proceedings,* Regional Science Association **18**, 13–46.

Ontario Economic Council (1967), *Why, Where, and How and Would They Do It Again?* Toronto.

Orr, S. C. and J. B. Cullingworth (1969), *Urban and Regional Studies,* London: Allen & Unwin.

Palander, T. (1935), *Beitrage zur Standortstheorie,* Uppsala: Almqvist & Wiksells Boktryckeri.

Parker, J. E. S. (1974), *The Economics of Innovation: The National and Multinational Enterprise in Technological Change,* London: Longmans.

Parr, J. B. (1965a), "Specialization, Diversification, and Regional Development," *Professional Geographer* **6**, 21–25.

Parr, J. B. (1965b), *The Nature and Function of Growth Poles in Economic Development,* Seattle: University of Washington. (Mimeographed)

Parr, J. (1966), "Out Migration and the Depressed Area Problem," *Land Economics* **42**, 149–59.

Parr, J. (1969), "City Hierarchies and the Distribution of City Size: A Reconsideration of Beckmann's Contribution," *Journal of Regional Science* **9**, 239–53.

Patel, S. J. (1964), ''The Economic Distance Between Nations: Its Origin, Measurement, and Outlook,'' *The Economic Journal* **74**, 119–31.

Pedersen, P. O. (1970), ''Innovation Diffusion Within and Between National Urban Systems,'' *Geographical Analysis* **2**, 203–54.

Peet, J. R. (1969), ''The Spatial Expansion of Commercial Agriculture in the Nineteenth Century,'' *Economic Geography* **45**, 283–301.

Pennsylvania Economic League (1960), *Comparative Tax, Water, and Sewer Costs for Philadelphia and 81 Other Municipalities in Pennsylvania, New Jersey, Delaware, and Maryland,* Philadelphia.

Penrose, E. (1959), *The Theory of the Growth of the Firm,* Oxford: Basil Blackwell.

PEP (1962), *Regional Development in the European Economic Community,* London: Allen & Unwin.

Perloff, H. S., E. S. Dunn, E. E. Lampard, and R. F. Muth (1960), *Regions, Resources, and Economic Growth,* Baltimore: Johns Hopkins Press.

Perloff, H. S. (1963), ''How a Region Grows: Area Development in the U. S. Economy,'' *Supplement Paper* **17**, New York: Committee for Economic Development.

Perloff, H. S. and L. Wingo, Jr., eds. (1968), *Issues in Urban Economics,* Baltimore: Johns Hopkins Press.

Perroux, F. (1950), ''Economic Space: Theory and Application,'' *Quarterly Journal of Economics* **64**, 89–104.

Pfouts, R. W. (1960), *The Techniques of Urban Economic Analysis,* New York: Chandler Davis.

Phillips, A. (1956), ''Concentration, Scale, and Technological Change in Selected Manufacturing Industries, 1899-1939,'' *Journal of Industrial Economics* **4**, 179–93.

Ponsard, C. (1955), ''Economie et Espace: Essai d'Integration du Facteurs Spatial dans l'Analyse Economique, *Observation Economique* **8**, Paris: Ecole Practique des Haute Etudes.

Ponsard, C. (1958), ''Histoire des Théories Economique Spatiales,'' *Etudes et Memoires* **41**, Paris: Centre d'Etudes Economique.

Poulantzas, N. (1975), *Classes in Contemporary Capitalism*, London: New Left Books.

Pounds, N. J. G. (1960), ''The Industrial Geography of Modern Poland,'' *Economic Geography* **36**, 231–53.

Pratten, C. and R. M. Dean (1956), *The Economics of Large-Scale Production in British Industry,* Cambridge: Cambridge University Press.

Pratten, C. F. (1971), *Economies of Scale in Manufacturing Industry,* Cambridge: Cambridge University Press.

Pred, A. R. (1964), ''The Intra-Metropolitan Location of Manufacturing,'' *Annals* of the Association of American Geographers **54**, 165–80.

Pred, A. R. (1965a), ''Industrialization, Initial Advantage, and American Metropolitan Growth,'' *Geographical Review* **55**, 158–85.

Pred, A. R. (1965b), ''The Concentration of High-Value-Added Manufacturing,'' *Economic Geography* **41**, 108–32.

Pred, A. (1966a), ''Some Locational Relationships Between Industrial Inventions, Industrial Innovations, and Urban Growth,'' *East Lakes Geographer* **2**, 45–70.

Pred, A. R. (1966b), *The Spatial Dynamics of U. S. Urban-Industrial Growth, 1800–1914,* Cambridge, Mass.: MIT Press.

Pred, A. R. (1967a), ''Behavior and Location, Part I,'' *Lund Studies in Geography, Series B,* 27.

Pred, A. R. (1967b), ''Behavior and Location, Part 2,'' *Lund Studies in Geography, Series B,* 29.

Pred, A. R. (1971), ''Large-City Interdependence and the Pre-Electronic Diffusion of Innovations in the U. S.,'' *Geographical Analysis* **3**, 165–81.

Pred, A. R. (1974), ''Major Job-Providing Organizations and Systems of Cities,'' Association of American Geographers, Commission on College Geography, *Resource Paper No. 27*.

Predöhl, A. (1928), ''The Theory of Location in Its Relation to General Economics,'' *Journal of Political Economy* **36**, 371–90.

Rawstron, E. M. (1951), ''The Distribution of Steam-Driven Power Stations in Great Britain,'' *Geography* **36**, 249–62.

Rawstron, E. M. (1954), ''Power Production and the River Trent,'' *East Midland Geographer* **2**, 23–30.

Rawstron, E. M. (1958), ''Some Aspects of the Location of Hosiery and Lace Manufacture in Great Britain,'' *East Midland Geographer* **9**, 16–28.

Rawstron, E. M. (1966), ''Electric Power Generation,''K. C. Edwards, ed., *Nottingham and Its Region*, prepared for the meeting of the British Association for the Advancement of Science, Nottingham, pp. 310–14.

Rawstron, E. M. (1970), ''Where x, then abc: Some Thoughts Upon a Comprehensive Theory of the Geography of Production,'' R. H. Osborne, F. A. Barnes, and J. C. Doornkamp, eds., *Geographical Essays in Honour of K. C. Edwards,* Department of Geography, University of Nottingham, pp. 242–47.

Ray, D. M. (1967), ''Cultural Differences in Consumer Travel Behavior in Eastern Ontario,'' *Canadian Geographer* **11**, 143–56.

Ray, D. M., P. Y. Villeneuve and R. A. Roberge (1974), ''Functional Prerequisites, Spatial Diffusion, and Allometric Growth,'' *Economic Geography* **50**, 341–51.

Ray, M. (1965), ''Market Potential and Economic Shadow: A Quantitative Analysis of Industrial Location in Southern Ontario,'' *Research Papers,* 101, Department of Geography, University of Chicago.

Rees, J. (1972), ''The Industrial Corporation and Location Decision Analysis,'' *Area 4,* pp. 199–205.

Reifler, R. M. (1957), ''Estimating Wage Rates in Different Areas—A Plant Location Technique,'' *Industrial Development,* September 1957, pp. 5–9.

Renner, G. T. (1947), ''Geography of Industrial Localization,'' *Economic Geography* **23**, 167–89.

Renner, G. T. (1950), ''Some Principles and Laws of Economic Geography,'' *Journal of Geography* **49**, 14–22.

Reynolds, D. R. and M. L. McNulty (1968), ''On the Analysis of Political Boundaries, A Perceptual Approach,'' *East Lakes Geographer* **4**, 21–38.

Richardson, H. W. (1969a), *Elements of Regional Economics,* London: Penguin.

Richardson, H. W. (1969b), *Regional Economics,* London: Weidenfeld & Nicolson.

Richardson, H. W. (1973), *Regional Growth Theory,* London: Macmillan.

Richter, C. E. (1969), ''The Impact of Industrial Linkages on Geographic Association,'' *Journal of Regional Science* **9**, 19–28.

Rizek, R. L., G. C. Judge and J. Havlicek (1965), ''Spatial Structure of the Livestock Economy: III, Joint Spatial Analyses of Regional Slaughter and the Flows and Pricing of Livestock and Meat,'' *North Central Regional Research Bulletins*, 163, Brookings, South Dakota: Agricultural Experiment Station, South Dakota State University.

Robertson, C. W. (1956), ''The Löschian Landscape: A Review,'' *Scottish Geographical Magazine* **72**, 81–84.

Robinson, A. H. (1966), ''The Necessity of Weighting in Correlation of Areal Data,'' *Annals* of the Association of American Geographers **46**, 233–36.

Robinson, E. A. G. (1958), *The Structure of Competitive Industry,* Cambridge: Cambridge University Press.

Robinson, E. A. G. (1967), *Location Theory, Regional Economics, and Backward Areas,* papers presented to the International Economic Association, Conference on Backward Areas in Developed Countries, Varenna, Italy, 1967, London: Macmillan.

Robinson, J. (1934), *The Economics of Imperfect Competition,* London: Macmillan.

Robinson, J. (1951), "Introduction" in R. Luxemburg, *The Accumulation of Capital,* New Haven; Yale University Press.

Rodgers, A. L. (1952), "Industrial Inertia: A Major Factor in the Location of the Steel Industry in the U. S.," *Geographical Review* **42**, 56–66.

Rodgers, A. (1957), "Some Aspects of Industrial Diversification in the United States," *Economic Geography* **33**, 16–30.

Rodgers, A. (1970), "Migration and Industrial Development: The Southern Italian Experience," *Economic Geography* **46**, 111–35.

Rodgers, H. B. (1962), "The Changing Geography of the Lancashire Cotton Industry," *Economic Geography* **38**, 299–314.

Roepke, H. G. (1959), "Changes in Corn Production on the Northern Margin of the Corn Belt," *Agricultural History* **33**, 126–32.

Roepke, H. G. ed. (1967), *Readings in Economic Geography,* New York: Wiley.

Rostow, W. W. (1960), *The Stages of Economic Growth: A Non-Communist Manifesto,* Cambridge, England: Cambridge University.

Rushton, G. (1969), "Analysis of Spatial Behavior by Revealed Space Preference," *Annals* of the Association of American Geographers **59**, 391–400.

Russell, J. (1959), "Geography of Industrial Costs," *Industrial Development* **128**, November 1969, 6–10.

Sampson, R. (1961), *Railroad Shipments and Rates From the Pacific Northwest,* Eugene: University of Oregon, Bureau of Business Research.

Sampson, R. J. and M. T. Farris (1966), *Domestic Transportation: Practise, Theory, and Policy,* Boston: Houghton Mifflin.

Samuelson, P. (1964), *Economics: An Introductory Analysis*, 6th ed., New York: McGraw-Hill.

Schlebecker, J. T. (1960), "The World Metropolis and the History of American Agriculture," *Journal of Economic History* **20**, 187–208.

Schumacher, E. F. (1973), *Small is Beautiful,* London: Blond & Briggs, Ltd.

Schumpeter, J. A. (1939), *Business Cycles: A Theoretical Historical and Statistical Analysis of the Capitalist Process,* New York: McGraw-Hill.

Scitovsky, T. (1954), "Two Concepts of External Economies," *Journal of Political Economy* **62**, No. 2, 143–51.

Scott, E. P. (1970), "The Spatial Structure of Rural Northern Nigeria: Farmers, Periodic Markets, and Villages," *Economic Geography* **48**, 316–32.

Seers, D. (1972), "What Are We Trying to Measure?" *The Journal of Development Studies,* B, pp. 21–36.

Segal, M. (1960), *Wages in the Metropolis,* Cambridge, Mass.: Harvard University Press.

Seidman, J. (1942), *The Needle Trades,* New York: Oxford University Press.

Serck-Hanssen, J. (1963), "A Programming Model for a Fishing Region in Northern Norway," *Papers,* Regional Science Association **12**, 107–18.

Seyfried, W. R. (1963), "The Centrality of Urban Land Values," *Land Economics* **39**, 275–85.

Shakashita, N. (1968), "Production Function, Demand Function, and Location Theory of the Firm," *Papers,* Regional Science Association **20**, 109–22.

Shubik, M., ed. (1964), *Game Theory and Related Approaches to Social Behavior,* New York: Wiley.

Siebert, H. (1969), *Regional Economic Growth: Theory and Policy,* Scranton, Pa.: International Textbook.

Siegel, S. (1956), *Nonparametric Statistics for the Behavioral Sciences,* New York:

McGraw-Hill.

Simon, H. A. (1952), ''A Behavioral Model of Rational Choice,'' *Quarterly Journal of Economics* **69**, 99–118.

Simon, H. A. (1955), ''On a Class of Skew Distribution Functions,'' *Biometrika* **42**, 425–40.

Simon, H. A. (1959), ''Theories of Decision-Making in Economics and Behavioral Sciences,'' *American Economic Review* **49**, 253–83.

Simon, H. A. (1960), *The New Science of Management Decision*, New York: Harper & Row.

Sinclair, R. (1967), ''Von Thünen and Urban Sprawl,'' *Annals* of the Association of American Geographers **57**, 72–87.

Skinner, G. W. (1964), ''Marketing and Social Structure in Rural China,'' *Journal of Asian Studies* **24**, 3–43.

Slater, L. J. (1967), ''Fortran Programs for Economists,'' *Occasional Papers,* 13, Department of Applied Economics, University of Cambridge.

Smailes, P. (1969), ''Some Aspects of the South Australian Urban System,'' *Australian Geographer* **11**, 29–51.

Smith, Adam (1950), *Wealth of Nations,* 6th ed., London: Methuen.

Smith, D. L. (1966), ''Market Gardening on Adelaide's Urban Fringe,'' *Economic Geography* **42**, 19–36.

Smith, D. M. (1962), ''The Cotton Industry in the East Midlands,'' *Geography* **37**, 256–69.

Smith, D. M. (1963), ''The British Hosiery Industry at the Middle of the Nineteenth Century: An Historical Study in Economic Geography,'' *Transactions and Papers,* Institute of British Geographers **32**, 125–42.

Smith, D. M. (1964), ''Birmingham's Gun Quarter and Its Workshops,'' *Journal of Industrial Archaeology* **1**, 106–19.

Smith, D. M. (1965), *The Industrial Archaeology of the East Midlands,* Devon, England: David & Charles, Newton Abbott.

Smith, D. M. (1966), ''A Theoretical Framework for Geographical Studies of Industrial Location,'' *Economic Geography* **42**, 95–113.

Smith, D. M. (1968), ''Identifying the 'Grey' Areas—A Multivariate Approach,'' *Regional Studies* **2**, 183–93.

Smith, D. M. (1969a), *Industrial Britain: The North West,* Devon, England: David & Charles, Newton Abbott.

Smith, D. M. (1969b), ''Industrial Location and Regional Development: Some Recent Trends in North West England,'' *Environment and Planning* **1**, 173–91.

Smith, D. M. (1970), ''On Throwing Weber Out With the Bathwater: A Note on Industrial Location and Linkage,'' *Area,* 1970, **1**, 15–18.

Smith, D. M. and T. H. Lee (1970), ''A Programmed Model for Industrial Location Analysis'' *Discussion Papers,* 1, Carbondale, Ill.: Department of Geography, Southern Illinois University.

Smith, D. M. (1971), *Industrial Location,* New York: Wiley.

Smith, D. M. (1974), ''Who Gets What Where and How: A Welfare Focus for Human Geography,'' *Geography* **59**, 289–97.

Smith, P. J. (1962), ''Calgary: A Study in Urban Pattern,'' *Economic Geography* **38**, 315–29.

Smith, R. D. P. (1968), ''The Changing Urban Hierarchy,'' *Regional Studies* **2**, 1–19.

Smith, R. H. T. (1964), ''Toward a Measure of Complementarity,'' *Economic Geography* **40**, 1–8.

Smith, R. H. T. (1965a), ''Method and Purpose in Functional Town Classification,'' *Annals* of the Association of American Geographers **55**, 539–48.

Smith, R. H. T. (1965b), "The Functions of Australian Towns," *Tijdschrift voor Economische en Sociale Geografie* **53**, 81–92.

Smith, R. H. T., E. J. Taaffe and L. J. King, eds. (1967), *Readings in Economic Geography*, Skokie, Ill.: Rand McNally.

Smith, W. (1952a), *An Economic Geography of Great Britain*, 2d ed., London: Methuen.

Smith, W. (1952b), *Geography and the Location of Industry*, Inaugural Lecture, University of Liverpool.

Smith, W. (1955), "The Location of Industry," *Transactions* of the Institute of British Geographers **21**, 1–18.

Smith, W. (1968), *An Historical Introduction to the Economic Geography of Great Britain,* London: G. Bell & Sons.

Smithies, A. F. (1941), "Optimum Location in Spatial Competition," *Journal of Political Economy* **49**, 423–39.

Söderman, S. (1975), *Industrial Location Planning,* Stockholm: Almquist & Wiksell Intl. (Halsted Press).

Spence, N. A. (1968), "A Multifactor Uniform Regionalization of British Counties on the Basis of Employment Data for 1961," *Regional Studies* **2**, 87–104.

Spiegelman, R. G. (1964), "A Method for Determining the Location Characteristics of Footloose Industries: A Case Study of the Precision Instrument Industry," *Land Economics* **40**, 79–86.

Spiegelman, R. G. (1966), "Analysis of Urban Agglomeration," *U. S. Department of Agriculture, Economic Report No. 96.*

Spiegelman, R. G. (1968), "A Study of Industry Location Using Multiple Regression Techniques," *Agricultural Economic Reports, No. 140,* Economic Research Service, U. S. Department of Agriculture.

Stafford, H. A. (1960), "Factors in the Location of the Paperboard Container Industry," *Economic Geography* **36**, 260–66.

Stafford, H. A. (1963), "The Functional Basis of Small Towns," *Economic Geography* **39**, 165–75.

Stafford, H. A. (1966), "Population as a Determinant of Industrial Type," *East Lakes Geographer* **2**, 71–79.

Stafford, H. A. (1969), "An Industrial Location Decision Model," *Proceedings,* Association of American Geographers **1**, 141–45.

Steed, G. P. F. (1968), "Commodity Flows and Interindustry Linkages of Northern Ireland's Manufacturing Industries," *Tijdschrift voor Economische en Sociale Geografie,* September/October 1968, pp. 245–59.

Steed, G. P. F. (1971a), "Changing Processes of Corporate Environment Relations," *Area* **3**, 207–11.

Steed, G. P. F. (1971b), "Forms of Corporate Environmental Adaptation," *Tijdschrift voor Economische en Sociale Geografie* **62**, 90–94.

Steed, G. P. F. (1971c), "Locational Implications of Corporate Organization of Industry," *Canadian Geographer* **15**, 54–57.

Steed, G. P. F. (1971d), "Plant Adaptation, Firm Environments, and Location Analysis," *Professional Geographer* **23**, 324–28.

Stefaniak, N. J. (1963), "A Refinement of Haig's Theory," *Land Economics* **4**, 428–33.

Stevens, B. H. (1958), "An Interregional Linear Programming Model," *Journal of Regional Science* **1**, 60–98.

Stevens, B. H. and R. E. Coughlin (1959), "A Note on Inter-Areal Linear Programming for a Metropolitan Region," *Journal of Regional Science* **1**, 75–83.

Stevens, B. H. (1961a), "An Application of Game Theory to a Problem in Location

Strategy,'' *Papers and Proceedings,* Regional Science Association **7**, 143–57.

Stevens, B. H. (1961b), ''Linear Programming and Location Rent,'' *Journal of Regional Science* **3**, 15–26.

Stevens, B. H. and C. A. Brackett (1967), *Industrial Location: A Review and Annotated Bibliography of Theoretical, Empirical, and Case Studies,* Bibliography Series 3, Philadelphia: Regional Science Research Institute.

Stevens, B. H. (1968), ''Location Theory and Programming Models: The Von Thünen Case,'' *Papers and Proceedings,* Regional Science Association **11**, 19–34.

Stewart, C. T., Jr. (1958), ''The Size and Spacing of Cities,'' *Geographical Review* **48**, 222–45.

Stewart, J. Q. (1942), ''A Measure of the Influence of Population at a Distance,'' *Sociometry* **5**, 63–71.

Stewart, J. Q. (1947), ''Empirical Mathematical Rules Governing the Distribution and Equilibrium of Population,'' *Geographical Review* **37**, 461–85.

Stewart, J. Q. (1948), ''Demographic Gravitation—Evidence and Applications,'' *Sociometry* **11**, 31–58.

Stewart, J. Q. and W. Warntz (1958a), ''Physics of Population Distribution,'' *Journal of Regional Science* **1**, 99–123.

Stewart, J. Q. and W. Warntz (1958b), ''Macrogeography and Social Science,'' *Geographical Review* **48**, 167–84.

Stillwell, F. J. B. (1969), ''Regional Growth and Structural Adaptation,'' *Urban Studies* **6**, 162–78.

Stocking, G. W. (1954), *Basing Point Pricing and Regional Development,* Chapel Hill: University of North Carolina Press.

Stolper, W. (1955), ''Spatial Order and the Economic Growth of Cities,'' *Economic Development and Cultural Change* **3**, 137–46.

Stolper, W. F. (1958), ''Economic Development, Taxation, and Industrial Location in Michigan,'' *Michigan Tax Study Staff Papers.*

Stouffer, S. A. (1940), ''Intervening Opportunities: A Theory Relating Mobility and Distance,'' *American Sociological Review* **5**, 845–67.

Strasma, J. D. (1959), ''Taxation of Industry,'' *Federal Reserve Bank of Boston, New England Business Review,* February, pp. 1–4; March, pp. 1–4.

Striet, M. E. (1969), ''Spatial Associations and Economic Linkages Between Industries,'' *Journal of Regional Science* **9**, 177–88.

Szentes, T. (1971), *The Political Economy of Underdevelopment,* Budapest: Akadémiai Kiadó.

Taaffe, E. J., R. L. Morrill and P. R. Gould (1963), ''Transport Expansion in Underdeveloped Countries: A Comparative Analysis,'' *Geographical Review* **53**, 503–29.

Taaffe, E. J., ed. (1970), *Geography*, Englewood Cliffs, N. J.: Prentice-Hall.

Taaffe, E. J. and H. Gauthier (1973), *Geography of Transportation*, Englewood Cliffs, N. J.: Prentice-Hall.

Tarrant, J. (1973), ''Comments on the Lösch Central Place System,'' *Geographical Analysis* **5**, 113–21.

Tattersall, J. N. (1962), ''Exports and Economic Growth: The Pacific Northwest, 1880–1960,'' *Papers and Proceedings*, Regional Science Association **9**, 215–34.

Taylor, M. J. (1969), ''Industrial Linkage, Seed-Bed Growth, and the Location of Firms,'' *University College London, Department of Geography, Occasional Paper No. 3.*

Taylor, M. J. (1970), ''Location Decisions of Small Firms,'' *Area* **2**, 51–54.

Teitz, M. B. (1968), ''Locational Strategies for Competitive Systems,'' *Journal of Regional Science* **8**, 135–48.

Teitz, M. B. (1968), ''Towards a Theory of Public Facility Location,'' *Papers and Proceedings,* Regional Science Association **21**, 35–51.

Thoman, R. S. and P. Corbin (1974), *The Geography of Economic Activity,* 2nd ed., New York: McGraw-Hill.

Thomas, E. N. (1961), "Towards an Expanded Central Place Model," *Geographical Review* **51**, 400–411.

Thomas, E. N. (1962), "The Stability of Distance—Population Size Relationships for Iowa Town From 1900–1950," *Lund Studies in Geography, Series B,* 24.

Thomas, E. N. and D. L. Anderson (1965), "Additional Comments on Weighting Values in Correlation Analysis of Areal Data," *Annals* of the Association of American Geographers **5**, 492–505.

Thomas, R. W. (1975), "Some Functional Characteristics of British City Central Areas: An Application of Allometric Principles," *Regional Studies* **9**, 369–78.

Thompson, J. H. (1955), "A New Method for Measuring Manufacturing," *Annals* of the Association of American Geographers **45**, 416–36.

Thompson, J. H. (1961), *Methods of Plant Site Selection Available to Small Manufacturing Firms,* Morgantown: West Virginia University Press.

Thompson, J. H., S. C. Surfrin, P. R. Gould and M. A. Buck (1962), "Towards a Geography of Economic Health: The Case of New York State," *Annals* of the Association of American Geographers **52**, 1–20.

Thompson, J. H. (1966), "Some Theoretical Considerations for Manufacturing Geography," *Economic Geography* **42**, 356–65.

Thompson, W. R. (1957a), "The Coefficient of Localization: An Appraisal," *Southern Economic Journal* **23**, 320–25.

Thompson, W. R. (1957b), "Importance of State and Local Taxes in Industrial Costs," *National Tax Association Proceedings,* pp. 185–90.

Thompson, W. R. and J. M. Mattila (1959), *An Econometric Model of Postwar State Industrial Development*, Detroit: Wayne State University.

Thompson, W. R. (1965), *A Preface to Urban Economics,* Baltimore: Johns Hopkins Press.

Thorngren, B. (1970), "How Do Contact Systems Affect Regional Development?" *Environment and Planning* **2**, 409–27.

Tiebout, C. M. (1956), "Exports and Regional Economic Growth," *Journal of Political Economy* **64**, 160–69.

Tiebout, C. M. (1957), "Location Theory, Empirical Evidence, and Economic Evolution," *Papers and Proceedings,* Regional Science Association **3**, 74–86.

Tiebout, C. M. (1962), *The Community Economic Base Study,* New York: Committee for Economic Development.

Tinbergen, J. (1961), "The Spatial Dispersion of Production: A Hypothesis," *Schweizerische Zeitschrift für Volkswirtschaft und Statistic* **97**, 1–15.

Tinbergen, J. (1964), "Sur Une Modele de la Dispersion Géographique de l'Activité Economique," *Revue d'Economie Politique* **74**, 30–44.

Tobler, W. R. (1963), "Geographic Area and Map Projections," *Geographical Review* **53**, 59–78.

Törnqvist, G. (1962), "Transport Costs as a Location Factor for Manufacturing Industry," *Lund Studies in Geography, Series B,* 23.

Törnqvist, G. (1968), "Flows of Information and the Location of Economic Activities," *Lund Studies in Geography, Series B,* 30.

Törnqvist, G. (1970), "Contact Systems and Regional Development," *Lund Studies in Geography, Series B,* 35.

Toulmin, S. (1953), *The Philosophy of Science—An Introduction,* New York: Harper & Row.

Townroe, P. M. (1968), "Industrial Location and Regional Economic Policy: A Selected Bibliography," *Occasional Papers,* 2, Centre for Urban and Regional Studies, University of Birmingham.

Townroe, P. M. (1969), "Locational Choice and the Individual Firm," *Regional Studies* **3**, 15–24.

Townroe, P. M. (1971), "Industrial Location Decisions," *Occasional Paper,* 15, Centre for Urban and Regional Studies, University of Birmingham.

Townroe, P. M. (1972), "Some Behavioral Considerations in the Industrial Location Decision," *Regional Studies* **6**, 261–72.

Toyne, P. (1974), *Organization, Location, and Behavior,* New York: Wiley.

Tulpule, A. H. (1969), "Dispersion of Industrial Employment in the Greater London Area," *Regional Studies* **3**, 25–40.

Ullman, E. L. (1940–1941), "A Theory of Location for Cities," *American Journal of Sociology* **46**, 853–64.

Ullman, E. L. (1954), "Amenities as a Factor in Regional Growth," *Geographical Review* **44**, 119–32.

Ullman, E. L. (1957), *American Commodity Flow,* Seattle: University of Washington Press.

Ullman, E. L. (1958), "Regional Development and the Geography of Concentration," *Papers and Proceedings,* Regional Science Association **4**, 179–98.

Ullman, E. L. and M. F. Dacey (1962), "The Minimum Requirements Approach to the Urban Economic Base," *Lund Studies in Geography, Series B*, 24.

Ullman, E. L. (1962), "The Nature of Cities Reconsidered," *Papers and Proceedings,* Regional Science Association **9**, 7–24.

United Nations (1963), *A Study of Industrial Growth,* New York: Department of Economic and Social Affairs, United Nations.

U. S. Bureau of the Census (1968), "Metropolitan Area Definitions: A Re-Evaluation of Concept and Statistical Practice," *Working Papers,* 28, Washington: U. S. Department of Commerce.

U. S. Federal Trade Commission (1969), *Economic Report on Corporate Mergers,* Washington, D. C.

U. S. National Science Foundation (1963), *Research and Development in Industry,* Washington, D. C.

Unwin, D. J. (1976), "An Introduction to Trend Surface Analysis," *Concepts and Techniques in Modern Geography,* 5, University of Newcastle-Upon-Tyne.

Vajda, S. (1960), *Introduction to Linear Programming and the Theory of Games,* New York: Barnes & Noble.

Vajda, S. (1961), *The Theory of Games and Linear Programming,* New York: Wiley.

Valavanis, S. (1955), "Lösch on Location: A Review Article," *American Economic Review* **45**, 637–44.

Vance, J. E., Jr. (1970), *The Merchant's World: The Geography of Wholesaling,* Englewood Cliffs, N. J.: Prentice-Hall.

Van Valkenberg, S. and C. C. Held (1952), *Europe,* New York: Wiley.

Vergin, R. C. and J. D. Rogers (1967), "An Algorithm and Computational Procedure for Locative Economic Facilities," *Management Science* **13**, 240–54.

Viner, J. (1937), *Studies in the Theory of International Trade,* London: Harper.

Vining, R. (1955), "A Description of Certain Spatial Aspects of an Economic System," *Economic Development and Cultural Change* **3**, 147–95.

Vyver, F. T. de (1951), "Labor Factors in the Industrial Development of the South," *Southern Economic Journal* **18**, 189–205.

Walker, H. M. and J. Lev (1953), *Statistical Inference,* New York: Holt, Rinehart, & Winston.

Ward, R. J., ed. (1967), *The Challenge of Development: Theory and Practice,* Chicago: Aldine.

Warntz, W. (1957), "Contributions Towards a Macro-Economic Geography: A Review," *Geographical Review* **47**, 420–42.

Warntz, W. (1959), *Toward A Geography of Price,* Philadelphia: University of Pennsylvania Press.

Warntz, W. (1961), "Transatlantic Flights and Pressure Patterns," *Geographical Review* **51**, 187–212.

Warntz, W. (1965), *Macrogeography and Income Fronts,* Philadelphia: Regional Science Research Institute.

Warntz, W. (1967), "Global Science and the Tyranny of Space," *Papers and Proceedings,* Regional Science Association **19**, 7–19.

Warren, K. (1973), *American Steel Industry, 1850–1970: A Geographical Interpretation,* Oxford: Clarendon Press.

Watkins, M. H. (1963), "A Staple Theory of Economic Growth," *Canadian Journal of Economics and Political Science* **29**, Part 2, 141–58.

Watts, H. D. (1970), "The Location of Aluminum Reduction Plants in the U. K.," *Tijdschrift voor Economische en Sociale Geografie* **61**, 148–59.

Watts, H. D. (1971), "The Location of the Beet Sugar Industry in England and Wales, 1912–1936," *Transactions* of the Institute of British Geographers **53**, 95–116.

Watts, H. D. (1974), "Spatial Rationalization in Multi-Plant Enterprises," *Geoforum* **17**, 69–76.

Weber, A. (1909), *Theory of the Location of Industries,* Chicago: University of Chicago Press.

Webber, M. J. (1972), *The Impact of Uncertainty on Location,* Cambridge: MIT Press.

Werner, C. (1968), "The Law of Refraction in Transportation Geography: Its Multi-Variate Extensions," *Canadian Geographer* **12**, 28–40.

Whitman, E. S. and W. J. Schmidt (1966), *Plant Relocation*, New York: American Management Association.

Williams, J. D. (1966), *The Compleat Strategyst,* New York: McGraw-Hill.

Williams, W. V. (1967), "A Measure of the Impact of State and Local Taxes on Industrial Location," *Journal of Regional Science* **7**, 49–59.

Williamson, J. C. (1965), "Regional Inequality and the Process of National Development: A Description of Patterns," *Economic Development and Cultural Change* **13**, Part II.

Wilson, T., ed. (1965), *Papers on Regional Development,* Oxford: Blackwell.

Winsborough, H. H. (1959), "Variations in Industrial Composition with City Size," *Papers and Proceedings,* Regional Science Association **5**, 121–31.

Wise, M. J. (1949), "On the Evolution of the Jewellery and Gun Quarters in Birmingham," *Transactions* of the Institute of British Geographers **15**, 57–72.

Woldenberg, M. J. (1968), "Energy Flow and Spatial Order: Mixed Hierarchies of Central Places," *Geographical Review* **58**, 552–74.

Woldenberg, M. J. and B. J. L. Berry (1968), "Rivers and Central Places: Analogous Systems?" *Journal of Regional Science* **7**, 129–39.

Wolfe, R. I. (1962), "Transportation and Politics: The Example of Canada," *Annals* of the Association of American Geographers **52**, 176–90.

Wolpert, J. (1964), "The Decision Process in Spatial Context," *Annals* of the Association of American Geographers **54**, 537–58.

Wolpert, J. (1965), "Behavioral Aspects of the Decision to Migrate," *Papers and Proceedings,* Regional Science Association **15**, 159–72.

Wolpert, J. (1966), "Migration as an Adjustment to Environmental Stress," *Journal of Social Issues* **22**, 92–102.

Wonnacott, R. J. (1963), "Manufacturing Costs and the Comparative Advantage of United

States Regions,'' *Study Papers,* 9, Minneapolis: Upper Midwest Economic Study, University of Minnesota.

Wonnacott, R. J. (1964), ''Wage Levels and Employment Structure in United States Regions,'' *Journal of Political Economy* **72**, 414–19.

Wood, P. A. (1969), ''Industrial Location and Linkage,'' *Area* **2**, 32–39.

Yaseen, L. C. (1956), *Plant Location,* New York: American Research Council.

Yeates, M. H. (1965), ''Some Factors Affecting the Spatial Distribution of Chicago Land Values,'' *Economic Geography* **41**, 55–70.

Yeates, M. H. (1966), *Delimination of Development Regions in Canada,* Ottawa: Area Development Agency Report, Department of Industry.

Yeates, M. H. (1968), *An Introduction to Quantitative Analysis in Economic Geography,* New York: McGraw-Hill.

Yeates, M. H. and P. E. Lloyd (1970), *Impact of Industrial Incentives: Southern Georgian Bay Region,* Ontario, Ottawa: Queen's Printer.

Yeates, M. H. (1974), *An Introduction to Quantitative Analysis in Human Geography,* New York: McGraw-Hill.

Yeates, M. H. and B. J. Garner (1976), *The North American City,* 2d ed., New York: Harper & Row.

Zeeman, E. C. (1976), ''Catastrophe Theory,'' *Scientific American* **234**, No. 4, 65–83.

Zelinsky, W. (1958), ''A Method for Measuring Changes in the Distribution of Manufacturing Activity in the United States, 1939–1947'' *Economic Geography* **34**, 95–126.

Zimmerman, E. W. (1951), *World Resources and Industry,* New York: Harper & Row.

Zipf, G. K. (1946), ''The P_1P_2/D Hypothesis and Intercity Movement of Persons,'' *American Sociological Review* **11**, 677–86.

Zipf, G. K. (1949), *Human Behavior and the Principle of Least Effort,* Reading, Mass.: Addison-Wesley.

Index of Names

Subject Index